Alcott, Louisa May,
1832-1888.

Moods.

$13.00

DATE			

MOODS

AMERICAN WOMEN WRITERS SERIES

Joanne Dobson, Judith Fetterley, and Elaine Showalter, series editors

ALTERNATIVE ALCOTT
Louisa May Alcott
Elaine Showalter, editor

MOODS
Louisa May Alcott
Sarah Elbert, editor

STORIES FROM THE COUNTRY OF
LOST BORDERS
Mary Austin
Marjorie Pryse, editor

CLOVERNOOK SKETCHES AND
OTHER STORIES
Alice Cary
Judith Fetterley, editor

HOBOMOK AND OTHER WRITINGS
ON INDIANS
Lydia Maria Child
Carolyn L. Karcher, editor

"HOW CELIA CHANGED HER MIND"
AND SELECTED STORIES
Rose Terry Cooke
Elizabeth Ammons, editor

THE LAMPLIGHTER
Maria Susanna Cummins
Nina Baym, editor

RUTH HALL AND OTHER
WRITINGS
Fanny Fern
Joyce Warren, editor

*A NEW HOME, WHO'LL
FOLLOW?*
Caroline M. Kirkland
Sandra A. Zagarell, editor

QUICKSAND AND *PASSING*
Nella Larsen
Deborah E. McDowell, editor

OLDTOWN FOLKS
Harriet Beecher Stowe
Dorothy Berkson, editor

HOPE LESLIE
Catharine Maria Sedgwick
Mary Kelley, editor

THE HIDDEN HAND
E.D.E.N. Southworth
Joanne Dobson, editor

"THE AMBER GODS" AND
OTHER STORIES
Harriet Prescott Spofford
Alfred Bendixen, editor

WOMEN ARTISTS, WOMEN
EXILES: "Miss Grief" and
Other Stories
Constance Fenimore Woolson
Joan Myers Weimer, editor

MOODS

LOUISA MAY ALCOTT

Edited and with an Introduction by

SARAH ELBERT

RUTGERS UNIVERSITY PRESS

New Brunswick and London

Library of Congress Cataloging-in-Publication Data
Alcott, Louisa May, 1832–1888.
Moods / Louisa May Alcott ; edited and with an introduction by Sarah Elbert.
p.   cm.
Includes bibliographical references.
ISBN 0-8135-1669-2 (cloth)—ISBN 0-8135-1670-6 (pbk.)
I. Elbert, Sarah.   II. Title.
PS1017.M6   1991
813′.4—dc20
90-48069
CIP

British Cataloging-in-Publication information available

Copyright © 1991 by Rutgers University Press
Manufactured in the United States of America

To Madeleine B. Stern and
Leona Rostenberg

CONTENTS

ACKNOWLEDGMENTS

I AM GRATEFUL for the years of advice, generously shared wisdom, and encouragement of Madeleine B. Stern and Leona Rostenberg. Thanks to their work, and also the scholarship of Joel Myerson and Daniel Shealy, Louisa May Alcott's hidden voices have been revealed. Marcia Moss, curator at Concord Free Public Library, is a friend in need; the staff at Houghton Library, Harvard University, provided expertise and precious copies of the two nineteenth-century editions of *Moods*. Linda Ganley's professional services are "Just Your Type." The unfailing hope, faith, and charity of Leslie Mitchner complements her editorial discernment. Joanne Dobson clarified prose, organization, and some factual details. Jane Dieckmann is a first-rate textual critic and editor. Students in SUNY Binghamton's graduate seminar, American History through Literature, provided stimulating critiques, and the willingness to experiment as historians with studies of nineteenth-century fiction. Patricia West, Holly Blake, Jennifer Scanlon, Amal Muhammad, Rochella Thorpe, Janet Coffman, Mary Petrusewicz, Amy Butler, and Rikke Andersen, among many others, particularly helped in hearing the "doubled voice." Dick and Jane Dalfiume have blessed me with friendship and support. My special thanks to Barbara Scott and also to Carole McCarthy because she looked forward to reading *Moods*. George Cotkin and Thomas W. Africa are thanked for their understanding. Alison Lurie, Alice Kessler-Harris, Sue Armitage, and Corky Bush demonstrate that woman, unlike man, need not choose between "perfection of the life, or of the work" (W. B. Yeats, 1932).

——"Moods." Genius burned so fiercely that for four weeks I wrote all day and planned nearly all night, being quite possessed by my work. I was perfectly happy, and seemed to have no wants. Finished my book, or a rough draught of it, and put it away to settle. Mr. Emerson offered to read it when Mother told him it was "moods" and had one of his sayings for motto. Daresay nothing will ever come of it; but it *had* to be done, and I'm the richer for a new experience.[1]

THREE MONTHS shy of her twenty-eighth birthday, Louisa May Alcott celebrated the "rough draught" of her first adult novel. After ten years of writing, teaching, and sewing for a living, she had published enough in 1860 to support her family and could "look more hopefully into the future," she said, "while my paper boats sailed gaily over the Atlantic" (*Journals,* Apr. 1860). This delicate pun made light of what she knew was a "great thing," her publication of two stories in the prestigious *Atlantic Monthly Magazine.* Fifty dollars for each *Atlantic* story was a token sum for a family dependent upon the author as their sole breadwinner. Born into New England's romantic reform movement, Louisa May Alcott tested the limits of romantic individualism in both her life and fiction. Her parents, proud son and daughter of the American Revolution, were desperately poor, and in 1842 her father, Bronson Alcott, founded Fruitlands, a short-lived communal farm, in an attempt to combine spiritual perfectionism and agrarian self-reliance. The result was a domestic disaster; spiritual perfectionism required a spartan diet of cottage bread, squash, apples, and potatoes, washed down by mugs of water. The only beasts of burden, as Louisa's mother put it, were the girls and women who did most of the household's work, gathering a meager harvest in the fields while the men were busily engaged in philosophic conversations. Fruitlands failed but the Alcotts miraculously survived as a family, largely because Abigail May Alcott subsequently rallied herself and her two eldest daughters, Anna and Louisa, to become breadwinners as well as breadmakers for the entire family.

The Alcotts never ceased encouraging one another's efforts in self-expression and self-reliance. Eventually, in 1868, Louisa May Alcott's *Little Women* immortalized her family, "for though we do have to work, we make fun for ourselves, and are a pretty jolly set, as Jo would say" (ch. 1, "Playing Pilgrims"). *Little Women* also revealed the history of *Moods* in chapter 27, "Literary Lessons".

Jo March, like Louisa May Alcott herself, sewed, cleaned, worked as a teacher, governess, companion; and both the author and her most famous heroine wrote romances, sensational stories, and a beloved first novel, *Moods*. Paying attention to clues the author herself planted in *Little Women,* readers of this edition of *Moods* will understand that, as Jo said, "she could laugh at her poor little book, yet believe in it still, and feel herself the wiser and stronger for the buffeting she had received. . . . And I've got the joke on my side, after all; for the parts that were taken straight out of real life are denounced as impossible and absurd and the scenes that I made up out of my own silly head are pronounced 'charmingly natural, tender, and true.' So I'll comfort myself with that; and, when I'm ready, I'll up again and take another" (ch. 17).

Alcott eventually published two versions of her novel *Moods,* one in 1864 and the other in 1882, with eighteen years of work and success between the two editions. The book she began drafting in 1860 looked backwards toward her own girlhood when she was "a wilfull, moody girl" as she half-jokingly called herself (*Journals,* May 1850). Over the next four years the frank, touchingly hopeful references to writing the first version of *Moods,* which Alcott never erased from her *Journals,* are interspersed with terse, businesslike references to the profitable tales she swiftly wrote and easily published under pseudonyms during the same period.

The *Journals* of Louisa May Alcott in the late 1850s and 1860s reflect the range of her talent and ambition, and offer substantial evidence as well that writing for a living meant strategically producing for a diversified literary marketplace. During double working days when plots "simmered" in her head while hands sewed and scrubbed, she became a professional writer. Skill gradually matched talented determination as she penned sensational melodramas, domestic romances, antislavery thrillers, children's stories, poems, and a serious novel.

Traditionally Alcott has been considered a children's writer. In 1943, however, Leona Rostenberg discovered that the author of domestic classics (the *Little Women* series) had also written, under pseudonyms, numerous sensational tales similar to those stories written by Jo March. A quiet revaluation of Alcott began, and gathered popular momentum in 1975 and 1976 when Madeleine B. Stern, Rostenberg's colleague, reprinted and introduced nine of Alcott's major sensational tales (*Behind a Mask* and *Plots and Counterplots*). Consequently modern scholars have identified a correspondence between Louisa May Alcott's canny separation of her literary markets and the nineteenth-century concept of "separate spheres" which divided home from workplace, sharpened the social boundaries separating genteel ladies from working women, and gradually turned childhood and youth in all classes into a protected stage of life. As Americans gradually shaped their new culture, the romantic ideal of courtship and love collided with an older code of prescribed marital roles for husbands and wives. In the nineteenth century, men and women married for love; the performance of marital roles, however, was dictated by duty. Louisa May Alcott's fiction, beginning with *Moods*, (1864), was to deal with the troubled marriages that often resulted from this century-long contradiction. Romantic love led young men and women to appreciate one another's individuality. Marriage, on the other hand, subsumed true selves to unequal, prescribed social roles.

Alcott's sensation tales reveal an imagination that strays far from the expectations of middle-class domesticity. They are lavishly strewn with Gothic horrors, ranging from scheming women and confidence men to opium addiction, madness, and murder. Surprising many readers who had grown up with *Little Women,* the new interpretations generated by the discovery of these tales strongly suggested that the famously toasty childhood described in *Little Women* was, in reality, more like a miserable melodrama with no rescue at the end. Knowing that Alcott based her most famous novel loosely on the facts of her financially impoverished but culturally rich childhood in Concord, Massachusetts, with her three sisters, Anna, Elizabeth, and May, her passionate and work-worn mother, Abba May Alcott, and her ambitious, self-educated father, the transcendentalist educator Bronson Alcott, readers have traditionally assumed that Jo

Introduction

March's emotional life is a complete and faithful representation of Alcott's own youthful experiences. Martha Saxton's *Louisa May* conflated the sensational heroines with their creator, contending that Alcott was not her own Jo March, the young girl author with a tomboy's spirit, but was rather "depressed and sullen," "a woman divided between the impulsive, outgoing, opinionated, large-spirited woman she was meant to be and the withdrawn, hostile introvert who kept that vital woman locked up," (7). A lively debate has since ensued among scholars with "revisionists" on both sides. The darker side of Alcott's life and works is brilliantly emphasized by Judith Fetterley in several articles elucidating "Alcott's inner civil war." Fetterley urges readers to consider Jo March's writing career and its relation to her romance with Professor Bhaer in *Little Women*. As a writer of "penny dreadfuls" the young Jo March is urged to give up such unseemly use of her talents by Professor Bhaer. And, although she continues to write, she does burn her sensation stories and subsequently marries the good German professor, ultimately combining "healthy" domesticity with "healthy" domestic fiction.

While the fictional Jo March ultimately marries, has three children, and limits herself to writing "domestic pap," however, Louisa May Alcott, herself "a working woman all her life," goes far beyond the cozy domesticity of the *Little Women* series to write *Work, Diana and Persis, A Modern Mephistopheles,* and most important, to revise and republish *Moods.* The doctrine of separate spheres was too limited to contain the complexity of Alcott's demand for human rights, part of the larger struggle she identified with in signing her letters, "Yours for Reform, LMA." At one and the same time, she cherished the traditional role of woman and regarded woman's rights as central to the larger cause. *Moods,* in particular, revealed the contradictions between romantic love with its validation of companionate marriage and the nineteenth-century reality of troubled marriages burdened by female dependency and prescribed spousal role obligations. Love and duty romantically conflicted in the first edition of *Moods,* and Alcott's heroine struggled unsuccessfully to subsume love to duty. A young author, Louisa May Alcott, innocently laid bare a common, but private, household grief. Her indiscretion troubled, even angered, critics, and certainly *Moods* violated her publisher's instincts for popular literature. A. K. Loring, well known as a juvenile publisher, had a notably successful association with Horatio Alger, Jr., whose books reflected Loring's own credo that stories of action, carrying moral lessons, were bound to sell. Loring wrote to Louisa May Alcott:

I judge a book by the impression it makes and leaves in my mind, by the *feelings* solely as I am no scholar.—A story that touches and moves me, I can make others read and believe in.—What I like is conciseness in introducing the characters, getting them upon the stage and into action as quickly as possible.—Then I like a story of constant action, bustle and motion,—Conversations and descriptive scenes are delightful reading when well drawn but are too often skipped by the reader who is anxious to see what they do next, and it's folly to write what will be skipped in reading. . . . I like a story that starts to teach some lesson of life (and) goes steadily on increasing in interest till it culminates with the closing chapter leaving you spell bound, enchanted and exhausted with the intensity with which it is written, the lesson forcibly told, and a yearning desire to turn right back to the beginning and enjoy it over again . . .[2]

Capitalizing on the success of *Little Women,* Loring issued a second edition of *Moods* in 1871, without the author's consent. Then, in 1881, Loring went bankrupt, and he transferred the copyright of *Moods* to Louisa May Alcott for the sum of one dollar. Thus she was able to revise her first, cherished novel, and she published the revised *Moods* in 1882 with Roberts Brothers.

Between the first published *Moods* (1864) and the 1882 revised edition was Alcott's own psycho-sexual maturation, and there were both losses and additions to the Alcott family, their circle of old friends, and Louisa Alcott's own, increasingly sophisticated coterie of women writers, artists, and reformers of both sexes. Historical forces in the eighteen-year period resonated in Alcott's life and works as well: the Civil War and the Reconstruction period ushered in a modern nation-state and the provincial, closely knit Concord village became a streetcar suburb of Boston.

The satisfaction of understanding Alcott's development as a major writer awaits the reader of the first *Moods,* which has been unavailable since the mid-nineteenth century. The revised *Moods* (1882) is a tidier, more formulaic work, but it is the first version, presented in this volume, which moves readers deeply, presaging all the themes and characters that were to make *Little Women* and its sequels classics of American fiction. This version of *Moods* (1864) presents the stormy transformation of society, the construction of modern values, and a new relationship between the sexes. And, by endowing a respectable, hearthside heroine, Sylvia Yule, with the passions usually reserved to fallen women, Alcott struck a major blow for domestic realism. Although Alcott removed two characters from the second version of the novel, this change does not alter her original themes. Sure-handed and thoroughly focused in her cuts and rewrites, Alcott removed many Gothic touches, as both out-of-date and distracting. She centered the action of the later novel on Sylvia's progress to confident womanhood. By 1882, having established the importance of female adolescence to readers of *Little Women,* she could count on their empathy for Sylvia's "moods." She could, moreover, lead her readers confidently toward a new, happy ending. But it is in the early, romantic version of *Moods* that Louisa May Alcott first steps out from behind a mask and presents little women, true women, and scheming, fallen women—all in one novel under her own name. The writing of *Moods,* the long series of disappointments before it was finally published, and the revealing mixed reviews all shaped her choices in life and work.

The determination to be a professional writer explains the enormous range of Alcott's works as well as the surprising stylistic similarities in her sensation stories, domestic fiction, and antislavery romances. *Moods,* with the Gothic sensuality of its first version, is notably linked with the sensation stories and antislavery tales written in the same period. And, since the central theme of *Moods* and its heroine Sylvia's adventures also prefigure Jo's struggles with herself and her world in *Little Women, Moods* is an important bridge between Gothic and domestic realism. The literary reception of the first *Moods,* as we shall see, alternately praised its "transcendental" motifs, and denied the author's right to draw any profound meaning out of a girl's entrance into young womanhood. Alcott, as a young writer, dared to combine domestic fiction, sensation tale, and "serious" philosophic literature in the same volume. Her heroine, seventeen-year-old Sylvia Yule, takes the path less traveled in the mid-nineteenth century; she tries for adventure, friendship, and experience in the larger world. Finding this direct Emersonian path to individuality denied to her as a young woman, lonely and "moody," she marries Geoffrey Moor on the rebound. Her choice becomes a tragedy when, recognizing her mistake, she frankly acknowledges to her husband that her true love is his best friend, Adam Warwick. It seems almost certain that Alcott's publisher, A. K. Loring, in 1864, insisted that a heroine who dared even consider divorce and remarriage under these circumstances must pay with her life.

Conventional fiction in the nineteenth century reflected the commonplace belief in a married woman's exclusive dedication to family life and service to her loved ones. Alcott, in *Moods,* raised a personal and a

Introduction

social question: how could a woman marry and still develop her own unique gifts? As she herself sat writing *Moods* in 1861, Louisa May, so frequently the Alcotts' maid of all work, as well as principal breadwinner, knew that, for once, the entire household centered around her own acknowledged try for glory.

—Another turn at "Moods," which I remodelled. From the 2d to the 25th I sat writing, with a run at dusk; could not sleep, and for three days was so full of it I could not stop to get up. Mother made me a green silk cap with a red bow, to match the old green and red party wrap, which I wore as a "glory cloak." Thus arrayed I sat in groves of manuscripts, "living for immortality," as May said. Mother wandered in and out with cordial cups of tea, worried because I couldn't eat. Father thought it fine, and brought his reddest apples and hardest cider for my Pegasus to feed upon. All sorts of fun was going on; but I didn't care if the world returned to chaos if I and my inkstand only "lit" in the same place.

It was very pleasant and queer while it lasted; but after three weeks of it I found that my mind was too rampant for my body, as my head was dizzy, legs shaky, and no sleep would come. So I dropped the pen, and took long walks, cold baths, and had Nan up to frolic with me. Read all I had done to my family; and Father said: "Emerson must see this, Where did you get your metaphysics?" Mother pronounced it wonderful, and Anna laughed and cried, as she always does, over my works, saying, "My dear, I'm proud of you."

So I had a good time, even if it never comes to anything; for it was worth something to have my three dearest sit up till midnight listening with wide-open eyes to Lu's first novel. (*Journals,* Feb. 1861)

The war came and then a long hard year when selling stories did not provide enough income and school teaching, boarding round, and sewing came back to haunt the author. Anonymous tales, however, did pay, and as she sewed "blue flannel jackets" and baby clothes for her sister Anna's prospective child, she admitted that "I reel off my thrilling tales and mess up my work in a queer but interesting way." She may well have been referring to "Pauline's Passion and Punishment," a predecessor to *Moods*. In 1862 the thrilling tale went off to *Frank Leslie's Illustrated Newspaper,* and Louisa May Alcott, at thirty years old, subsequently went to war.

In December she was off to Georgetown's Union Hotel Hospital to

Introduction

nurse soldiers wounded in battle; her letters home eventually became *Hospital Sketches* (1863), narrated by a Dickensian heroine, Nurse Tribulation Periwinkle. Scarcely a month later Louisa Alcott was a victim of typhoid fever. She was invalided home to Concord; for three weeks her life was endangered as the fever raged. Once the fever had broken, Alcott saw herself in the mirror, the lovely chestnut hair cut off, and her image, "queer, thin-faced, big-eyed" (*Journals,* Jan. 1863). She had terrifying nightmares, recorded in her *Journals,* and they reflected, as did the themes of her Civil War fiction, the pressing personal issues and the innate understanding of female psycho-sexual issues to be found in *Moods:*

> As I shall forget the strange fancies that haunted me I shall amuse myself with recording some of them. The most vivid & enduring was a conviction that I had married a stout, handsome Spaniard dressed in black velvet with very soft hands & a voice that was continually saying, "Lie still, my dear." This was mother, I suspect, but with all the comfort I often found in her presence there was blended an awful fear of the Spanish spouse who was always coming after me, appearing out of closets, in at windows, or threatening me dreadfully all night long. I appealed to the Pope & really got up & made a touching plea in something meant for Latin they tell me. Once I went to heaven & found it a twilight place with people darting thro the air in a queer way. All very busy & dismal & ordinary. Miss Dix, W. H. Channi[n]g & other people were there but I thought it dark & "slow" & wished I hadn't come. A mob at Baltimore breaking down the door to get me; being hung for a witch, burned, stoned & otherwise maltreated were some of my fancies. Also being tempted to join Dr. W. & two of the nurses in worshipping the Devil. Also tending millions of sick men who never died or got well. (Jan. 1863)

Current studies of Alcott's life and works understand her nightmares as sexually suggestive, anxious indicators of what Elaine Showalter identifies as Alcott's "mingled desires toward men and women, black and white, and her confusion of sexual and racial boundaries." In opposition to her diabolic sexual fancy, Alcott also envisioned an aseptic celestial city. Her inner conflict, as usual, expressed itself in historically specific images: a heaven based solely on intellect, self-control, and deferred gratification was dull. Sensual, passionate pleasures were dangerous, possibly enslaving, but certainly exciting. Bronson Alcott insisted that merely being good was insufficient; his daughters must also love to be good. Louisa Alcott's dreams reveal her sexual energy, however, and her fear that marriage was an alluring form of slavery.

Modern psychoanalytic interpretations of Alcott's nightmares are plausible enough, and critics agree upon the important relationship between Alcott's dreams recorded during her convalescence and the fiction she wrote in that decade. Nevertheless, some current interpretations assume that the forms of psycho-sexual phenomena are transhistorical (or universal); Alcott's fantasies, both her nightmares and her fictions, were, however, culturally specific and related to the social construction of femininity. *Moods* treats the woman problem in a strikingly new way, seriously linking sexual passion without sexual equality to slavery; the novel's images mirror the slavery spectres raised by Alcott herself and by friends, Theodore Parker, Frank Sanborn, and Moncure Conway. Similar lurid images were also evoked in essays and petitions drafted by Henry David Thoreau and William Lloyd Garrison, among others.

Each alternative experienced in Alcott's nightmares is presented in the person of a specific female character in *Moods*. Alcott herself is alternately threatened, appealing, and touching in the words of her *Journals* as she presents her nightmares' evidence of desire and her depressing social alternatives. She can love to be good (sexless) and go to a dismal heaven, or she can affirm desire, and risk being hung, burned, and stoned as a witch. Finally, she can mask her adult sexuality in an acceptable maternal role, "tending millions of sick men who never died or got well." Dorothy Dix, who recruited Civil War nurses, was careful to hire only married women or mature, "sensible" spinsters. Louisa May Alcott was certainly not married, nor it would seem, was she as "sensible" as appearances might have suggested. As Civil War volunteers, women were extending their household sphere into the public domain, yet their role was not unambiguously maternal; both romance and passion lurked in the darkened night wards when women were the nurturing, tender confidantes of strange men and men were helpless and vulnerable.

Louisa Alcott's "fancies" might have remained in the realm of private dreams and nightmares, confided only to her *Journals*. *Moods*, however, evidences her conscious public acknowledgment of sexuality as part of the woman problem. Nina Baym cogently remarks that woman writers of nineteenth-century domestic fiction reacted against the earlier novels of seduction in the Richardsonian tradition. Woman's fiction generally portrayed heroines struggling to become full persons, not just the inevitable victims of sexual prey. Women writers sought to counter their disadvantage compared to men by creating heroines who transcended physical sexuality rather than integrating it into their adult personalities. Baym views *Little Women* as the end of the genre she defines as "woman's fiction," forcefully arguing that it signals the compromise or simplification of a long-standing feminine narrative tradition, in order to direct Alcott's message at children. This redirection does present a loving family but at the cost of woman's lonely, heroic self-transcendence.

Moods is not treated in Baym's path-breaking study. Repossessing "decent" women's sexual passion and presenting a heroine who struggles to integrate it into her adult self, Alcott broke through the antebellum convention of women's fiction. Certainly the second edition, revised eighteen years after the first version, comes close to compromising by pretending that the novel was directed at eighteen-year-old young women who "alone among my readers have divined the real purpose of the book in spite of its many faults, and have thanked me for it" (Preface, 1882). This, of course, is hindsight; *Moods* was written for adults, hoping to make them aware of the "moody" adolescent stage of young women. Girls needed recognition and breathing space to become true women. Alcott did not deny her identification with Sylvia's dilemma, however, and she added that "the observation and experience of the woman have confirmed much that the instinct and imagination of the girl [Sylvia] felt and tried to describe. . . ."

In the long nights and days she spent recovering from her fever, Alcott started on her path to becoming very much a part of what Jane Tompkins calls the "other American Renaissance," the ambitious and often fascinating body of mid-century American writing by women; her convalescence served as an incubation period for her stories. Following her established pattern, the author practiced her themes in storytelling and family theatricals before she swiftly, skillfully wrote them out for a living. "The old fancies still lingered, seeming so real I believed in them and deluded mother and May with the most absurd stories, so soberly told that they thought them true," she wrote, as she received the ten dollars due her for six weeks of war service (*Journals*, Feb. 1863). The ill effects of the calomel prescribed during her illness (an insidious form of mercury poisoning) would slowly weaken her nervous system and drain her prized energy for the rest of her life.

Introduction

Alcott's convalescence was cheered also by the birth of Anna's son, and the "happy aunt" had time and a renewed need for income to spur the "arrangement" of her war letters into several "Hospital Sketches." Moncure Conway and Frank Sanborn, co-editors, virtually guaranteed publication in the *Boston Commonwealth*. The sketches were noticed, admired, commended by Henry James, Sr., and solicited by both Redpath and Roberts Brothers for a book. Alcott chose Redpath and plunged immediately into another drafting of *Moods*, feeling, as she said, encouraged by the commendation bestowed on *Hospital Sketches*.

In November 1863 *Moods* went to Redpath, and Alcott hurried right on with a children's Christmas tale for Redpath, and another Civil War tale for the *Atlantic*. Customarily Louisa Alcott went over her accounts on New Year's Day; in 1864 she discovered that she had earned nearly six hundred dollars by writing alone. She therefore allowed herself a sustained note of optimism when Redpath "came flying up to get *Moods*, promising to have it out by May." Alas, the very next day printers found that the story was too long for one volume and two volumes would not be profitable. Unwilling to cut it in half, she took her literary child home and tried to finish a shorter book in a month. The Alcott household, however, required Louisa's housekeeping services and so the writer grubbed away as maid of all work. Self-pityingly she noted that May received flowers and free art lessons from a family friend. "Wish I could do the same, but suppose as I never do that it is best for me to work and wait and do all for myself," wrote "Moody Minerva" (*Journals*, Jan. 1864). She was reading all the time: Scott, Dickens, Goethe, Tennyson, and especially *Bleak House* in which the term "little woman" appears again and again to signal the moody period at the close of a girl's childhood and the beginning of her young womanhood.

And then, finally, in September, Mrs. Caroline Dall, a literary friend if ever there was one, came to visit the Alcotts and took *Moods* home to read. She was a notable intellectual in her own right and the friend of Margaret Fuller and the whole Boston Radical Club, whose faithful recording secretary she often was. Mrs. Dall said what Alcott must have dreamed a friendly critic would say: "No American author had showed so much promise; that the plan was admirable, the execution unequal but often magnificent . . . the book must be got out" (*Journals*, Sept. 1864). Dall then sent *Moods* to Loring who liked it but, like all the others, wanted it shortened.

Scarcely a month later, while writing several chapters of *Work*, Alcott was inspired one night to shorten and arrange *Moods*. As she put it, "the whole plan laid itself smoothly out before me," and she "began to write it all over again."

> The fit was on strong & for a fortnight I hardly ate, slept or stirred but wrote, wrote like a thinking machine in full operation. When it was all rewritten, without copying, I found it much improved though I'd taken out ten chapters & sacrificed many of my favorite things, but being resolved to make it simple, strong & short I let every thing else go & hoped the book would be better for it.
>
> Sent it to Loring & a week after as I sat hammering away at the parlor carpet, dusty, dismal & tired a letter came from Loring praising the story more enthusiastically than ever, thanking me for the improvements, & proposing to bring out the book at once. Of course we all had a rapture & I finished my work "double quick" regardless of weariness, toothache or blue devils.
>
> Next day I went to Boston & saw Loring. A brisk, business-like man who *seemed* in earnest & said many complimentary things about Hospital Sketches & its author. It was agreed to bring out the book immediately & Mrs. Dall offered to read the proof with me, Loring to give me ten cents copyright on all copies sold, I forfeiting the copyright on such as are given to newspapers. Settlements to be made once in three months from the time of its publication.
>
> Was glad to have the old thing under way again but didn't quite believe it would ever come out after so many delays & disappointments. (*Journals*, Oct. 1864)

On Christmas Eve 1864 the author received ten free copies from Loring and the first *Moods* went to her mother for a sixty-fourth birthday gift. The accompanying note said that she was "happy, very happy." "Now if it makes a little money and opens the way for more, I shall be satisfied, and you in some measure repaid for all the sympathy, help, and love that have done so much for me in these hard years. I hope Success will sweeten me and make me what I long to become more than a great writer—a good daughter" (*Journals*, Oct. 1864).

In acknowledging "these hard years" spent redrafting *Moods* as she simultaneously wrote for a living, Alcott also admitted that adversity did not "sweeten" a writer's temper. She was angry and determined to be a great writer, even though the words were carefully tucked between a longing for sweet success and a deep appreciation for her mother's faith.

Introduction

Predecessors to Moods

THE PREDECESSORS to *Moods*—pseudonymous sensation tales and acknowledged antislavery stories—took up the burden of proving that the "most important choice" of a woman's life in nineteenth-century America involved the problem of inequality in its most intimate sense. Unlike *Moods* these powerful thrillers laid no claim to literary art. They sharpened Alcott's writing skills, however, and, more important, they boldly began her reclamation of woman's passion: for both good and evil.

In all the sensation tales and antislavery stories preceding the publication of *Moods* in 1864, unbridled sensuality and principled struggles for equality vie in each heroine for pride of place. The social relations of each woman's life delicately predict whether she will be governed by her higher or lower passions. Small acts of kindness performed by faithful friends can compensate for a lost family or a contentious home, providing the encouragement necessary to a woman pilgrim's progress. Undeniably Alcott's stories acknowledge that it is a man's world and woman must fight for a place in it. Losing her struggle, she must live alone or die uttering the battle cry of freedom.

In the sensation tales women clearly suffer from inequities implicit in their prescribed gender roles. In December 1862, as she was nursing at the Union Hotel Hospital, Alcott received a letter announcing that "Pauline's Passion and Punishment" won Frank Leslie's prize of one hundred dollars. This story, featuring a Cuban heroine-villainess, has for its opening scene a sunset lit room, virtually the same setting as the first chapter in *Moods*. In the anonymous sensation tale, passionate, willful Pauline Valery Laroche appears in a black lace scarf, worn "over her blond hair as Spanish women wear their veils." Betrayed by Redmond, her true love, Pauline conceives a passion for revenge so boundless that it propels two innocent people over a cliff to their deaths. Manuel Laroche and poor "spaniel like" Babie, Redmond's wife, go down clinging to one another. The guilty lovers, Pauline and Redmond, remain alive, standing at the edge of the cliff; they are punished by surviving together, yet forever separated by guilt. Louisa May Alcott, as "Anonymous," says "beware of your wish—you may get it."

"A Whisper in the Dark" and "A Pair of Eyes" at cursory readings seem to be the purest examples of anonymous Gothic melodrama; but within the context of Alcott's life and work in this period, they focus tellingly on the dilemma of seventeen-year-old women, just at the end of childhood, passionately hungry for life and virtually without direct experience of it. This is the stage in a female life Alcott deals with in *Moods* and later makes famous in *Little Women*. Orphaned girls at childhood's end transform themselves, sometimes with the help of surrogate kin, in the narrative tradition of antebellum women's fiction until *Little Women* (1868) democratically transforms fictional family life and makes it a way station to self-reliant young womanhood. "Whisper" tentatively begins this new literary tradition and *Moods* expansively connects a plea for reforming marital roles with a demand for the recognition of female adolescence as an important trying-out period.

In "Whisper" and "A Pair of Eyes" the young women are refined, handsome creatures, possessing fortunes but still unable to lead independent lives. Sibyl's uncle, in "Whisper," wants to marry her and gain control of the fortune. A seemingly motherless child, she still bravely refuses him, and is locked up in a house of horrors. Her lost mother, mad and imprisoned on a floor above her, whispers and secretly writes notes urging the girl to leave before she too is driven to madness. Sibyl escapes and is finally rescued by her handsome young cousin. She recoups her fortune, marries the cousin, and lives almost happily ever after; she cannot ever forget her mother's ghost, whispering to her in the dark.

Sibyl's claim to possession of herself and her property is reflective of the emergence of slavery as a white American woman's issue, and the identification of the white woman with Afro-American bondage is crucial to understanding *Moods,* although neither the peculiar institution nor the Civil War appear in the novel. Many nineteenth-century readers and writers understood slavery in evangelical terms as sin, and they saw the free family as a loving bulwark against sin. Liberal religious women, such as Alcott herself, were concerned with slavery as a denial of natural rights and consequently as a major impediment to voluntarism and republican progress. Such women therefore connected women's rights to abolition as part of the struggle for universal democracy.

In "My Contraband," the hero, a "fine mulatto" named Robert, has a ghastly wound that lays open one-half of his face, leaving the other, notably handsome side, intact. This sabre cut creates a visible boundary that mirrors his psychic wound as a "contraband"; he is neither slave nor free, neither black nor white. Robert is his dead master's son and half brother to Mas'r Ned who, having sold his own brother off, rapes Robert's wife, Lucy, driving her to suicide. The entire story is narrated by Faith Dane, an abolitionist spinster whose stern task involves reluctantly nursing the

Introduction

wounded rebel Ned, while also giving Robert the respect and help he deserves. Gratefully, Robert takes Faith's last name as his own. Although only a tantalizing hint of miscegenation wafts across the staid *Atlantic*'s pages, Faith is with Robert Dane as he dies. In this story the sexual volatility of race mixing is confined within the peculiar institution of slavery. Faith's passion is focused on Robert's legitimate desire for revenge, and she links it to retribution for the sisterhood of women. It is an acceptable "passion and punishment," one in which a self-respecting woman finds revenge for her entire sex through nurturing and inspiring an outcast man.

"My Contraband" is not the boldest of Alcott's abolitionist stories of this period, but it is the closest to *Moods* in several ways, most notably in featuring Faith Dane as nurse and abolitionist. Faith Dane also appears in *Moods* as the heroine's surrogate mother and closest friend.

Alcott wrote her most radical antislavery story, "An Hour," for the *Atlantic,* noting that she was fairly sure they would not take it. She was right, but the *Boston Commonwealth* published it serially and Alcott had the satisfaction of seeing in print her creation, a mulatto heroine who loved her young master and plotted a slave revolt. Millie, in "An Hour," joined her fellow conspirators as her master-lover frantically tried to free the slaves before they freed themselves and the drums of the Grand Army resounded in the neighborhood.

In a fit of disappointment when *Moods* was rejected once again as too lengthy, Louisa Alcott declared that she would never touch it again and wrote a "blood and thunder story or novelette of several hundred pages to relieve my feelings and called it 'V.V.'!" Alcott's seventeen-year-old blond heroine wears a bracelet to conceal the slave brand upon her arm. Jealously guarded and trained as a dancer-courtesan by her male cousin, a professional dancer and confidence man, Virginie Varens marries the aristocratic young man she is supposed to con, sees him killed on their wedding night by her cousin, and goes on to fortune, murder, and eventual suicide by poison rather than facing imprisonment for life in a gloomy castle. Virginie is the most physically gorgeous and daring of all Alcott's sensational heroines and, despite her outcast, orphan status at the beginning of the novelette, no reader can truly call her a victim. She is mistress of a hundred disguises and she attracts suitors in a manner calculated to soothe the most rejected author. Virginie has one important link to *Moods* in portraying a passionate woman who is also capable of true love for both man and child. Virginie, outcast and fallen as she is, wants to restore herself and the child of her ill-fated, brief marriage to a respectable family. And, almost as a foreshadowing of the final draft of *Moods,* Virginie finally chooses death and a new integrity over life imprisonment.

Voluntary slavery is what concerns Alcott in *Moods,* both man's choice to be a master and woman's "choice" to be a slave. An English governess, the orphaned Jane Eyre, calls her employer-lover "Master" in one of Alcott's favorite novels. No freeborn American heroine would do so. Yet the temptation to seek such a husband-master, and to willingly enslave oneself to romantic love, to sexual passion, or to the "ceaseless craving for affection" in the absence of equality between the sexes is what occupies Alcott in *Moods.*

Reading Moods

AS READERS steeped in the tradition of modernist individualism, we are the audience *Moods* deserves. Romantic courtships and sexual passion lead to the discovery and sharing of true selves, and then, tragically, sex-role divisions within marriage threaten the selfhood bravely revealed within the circle of love. The narrative voice of *Moods* sends a delighted shiver through us; through the membrane of Alcott's own time it echoes *Jane Eyre, The Scarlet Letter,* and Dickens's *Bleak House.* When we read it as a modern work, the twisted adventure of three lovers in search of their principled true selves seems familiar. All of them—Adam Warwick, Geoffrey Moor, and Sylvia Yule—have distinct characteristics that color their perceptions of one another, and their relationships to the natural world. In true Dickensian fashion even their personal possessions are endowed with the owners' unique attributes. Glimpsed at first as ideal types (ingenue, hero, poet), Sylvia, Adam, and Geoffrey gradually become real people to one another and, simultaneously, to the reader as well. Their struggle for integrity is troubled by the uneasy fit between self and social role, an early modern problem. And there is an even more striking modernity in *Moods:* the unfolding of deep psychological confusion in each of the principal characters.

To be sure, Alcott's treatment of this process is uneven, even clumsy at times, but the confusion about what we would call the ideal self, the despised/imperfect self, and the true self makes *Moods* an important work. The idealized self, Alcott argues, is a dangerously romantic internalization of prescribed social roles, it merely reflects our concern for what others think of us, and it can lead, contradictorily, to either cowardly conformity or reckless nonconformity. The true self is not grandiose at all in Alcott's view; it acknowledges desires that may be immoral (despised/imperfect), and it develops a capacity for responsible moral choice. *Moods* insists that while this true self is subjective and internal, it is reflected and strengthened in the eyes of family and close friends. Above all the period of courtship provides a potential mirroring of true selves for young men and women in Alcott's first novel and in its more famous successor, *Little Women*. Sylvia Yule, lacking a mother's selfless mirroring in *Moods,* is particularly vulnerable in seeking to know herself and others. She innocently reveals her yearnings to male suitors who see her only as a desirable object, an admiring mirror of their own idealized selves. Sylvia mistakenly chooses conformity to her proper female role (wife) and then considers radical nonconformity (divorce) before reconciling passion and principles through a painful, internal struggle.

Not everyone in the novel seeks to reconcile desire and principles within a marital role. Sylvia's father has mortgaged his soul in marrying for money and then burying himself in commerce. His two older children, Mark (Max in *Moods,* 1882) and Prue are shallow and prosaic respectively. Faith Dane also is not in search of her true self. In "My Contraband" she finds herself through a dedication to abolitionist principles, and in *Moods* she is presumably a mature veteran of that struggle, embracing woman's rights with as much courage and strength as she exhibited during the Civil War. In order to follow the moral choices dictated by her true self Faith Dane remains a spinster, and that fact helps us to understand the second important theme of the novel: individual differences are greater than the social or biological differences between the male sex and the female sex. Sylvia and her sister have entirely different temperaments and principles despite their both being women and members of the same family. While "manliness" is socially defined as an inherent biological quality, Faith Dane and Sylvia discuss the incomplete humanity of both Warwick and Moor. Each man seeks to dominate; Warwick is guilty of active, forthright domination in his relationships, and Moor passively manipulates his friends. Moore and Warwick are as dissimilar in their masculinity as Sylvia and Prue are in their femininity. Indeed Sylvia recognizes a great similarity between the bravery of Warwick and Faith Dane.

In *Moods,* romantic tangles are clearly sexual politics and they demonstrate that the Victorian crisis of masculinity collided with the ideal of romantic courtship and companionate marriage. The uneasy fit between self and social role continues to be sexually specific in Alcott's third theme: the problem of identifying one's true self involves figuring out how much of one's talent and temperament is inherited and how much is the result of socialization. Readers of either edition of *Moods* learn the temperamental inheritance of each character in a chapter entitled "Dull but Necessary," and the inherited temperament of each character is then shaped for good or ill by domestic nurturance or the lack thereof and by larger social forces. Warwick's domineering tendencies are made gentle by the memory of a loving mother, and Sylvia's moodiness and passionate impulses result from her parents' unhappy, stormy marriage. The lack of warm domestic ties leads Warwick to seek marriage when his temperament would be better suited to bachelorhood. Sylvia's temperament might have been amelio-rated by good mothering or by a suitable period of female adolescence, during which time she could have experimented in the real world without danger from male companions. *Moods* sought to change both nature and nurture. Making marriage a choice and not a compulsory duty would facilitate the union of true selves and that would, in turn, improve one's inherited qualities. Creating dignified, well-compensated work for men and women would eliminate marrying for a living and facilitate egalitarian relationships within or without marriage. A first novel, written by the daughter of Concord's transcendentalist circle, aimed at nothing less than depicting this complex dilemma.

Looking backward to Gothic tales and sensation stories, we see that the double triangle in *Moods,* as the novel's romantic vehicle, is not terribly important in itself. Ottila captures Adam, and Adam falls in love with Sylvia. Sylvia falls in love with Adam but thinks that he really loves Ottila. Moor loves Sylvia and gets her on the rebound. Adam drops Ottila and comes back for Sylvia; Sylvia almost drops Moor for Adam. And so it goes. The reader, unlike the lovers, always knows the truth about these mis-alliances, and the question of whether or not the characters can learn the truth about themselves is part of the suspense Alcott creates. In the second edition of *Moods* Alcott erases Ottila so easily that the modern reader's suspicion of the romantic liaison as a mere device is confirmed. We may feel a slight loss at the absence of this tropical creature but our loss is retrospective.

Louisa May Alcott's *Journals* reveal her fascination with *Jane Eyre.* Henry James, when reviewing *Moods* in 1864, disparagingly likened Adam Warwick to Rochester in the Brontë novel. James failed to appreciate that

Warwick in *Moods,* while indeed a Rochester-like hero, withdraws from a mistaken passion for the creole beauty Ottila and then, although he falls in love with his Jane (in the person of Sylvia Yule), he loses her through his own false pride. Alcott's fascination with *Jane Eyre* lies in the conflict between a young woman's passionate hero worship and the fact of her social inequality. She is victimized not only by her poverty and orphanhood but also by her gender. Brontë's attempted solution to this problem is the Gothic portrayal of fire, Bertha's death, and the maiming of Rochester. Blinded and crippled in the fire, Rochester loses much of his mastery while Jane discovers her own self-reliance; they are more nearly equals when Rochester acknowledges his dependence on Jane.

Working on "Success" (*Work*) at the same time she drafted and redrafted *Moods,* Alcott had the heroine of *Work,* Christie Devon, roundly denounce the Jane-Rochester match as an "unequal bargain." Alcott takes up the problem of romantic love and gender inequality in an attempt to resolve the conflict in *Jane Eyre.* Written nearly twenty years before *Moods,* Brontë's novel inspired a convention in which Byronic hero and heroine flee from society to a natural paradise of their own. Jane Eyre has an alternative suitor, St. John Rivers, who offers her a life of mutual sacrifice and high purpose. He is described as Mr. Greatheart, the boatman in *The Pilgrim's Progress,* a helpful guide on Jane's pilgrimage. Similarly, Sylvia Yule takes refuge from Warwick's betrayal with Geoffrey Moor, and his name echoes Moor House, the home of St. John Rivers and his sisters, Diana and Mary.

Sylvia Yule refers to Moor as the Master of his neighboring manse, recalling Jane Eyre's habit of referring to Mr. Rochester as Master. Fearing his "pious tyranny," Sylvia refuses to pay a neighborly call on the "Saint" when he returns home from nursing his dying sister. And so, Moor, in the second chapter, discovers Sylvia first through the evidence of her homemade window seat, "looking very much like a newly deserted nest." Having flown the nest, she is outside digging in the garden where Moor mistakes her for a gardener's lad. Sylvia's window seat is yet another reminder of Jane Eyre who takes refuge in a crimson window seat, hiding from the awful Reed family who torment her because, like Sylvia, she is not a "contented, happy little child."

Nevertheless, Alcott's virtual invention of the American Girl is temporally and geographically specific. Sylvia is not Jane Eyre. This heroine cannot choose to leave her well-meaning but dismal family, and they in turn cannot give her the wholehearted permission she needs to experience the world directly. In later life Alcott was to refer to "dear old Concord," and to Emerson specifically, as loved ones who must not be shocked by public acknowledgment of her passion tales. And, of course, Alcott's single life did not free her from enormous domestic responsibilities.

Houses and their masters play an important role in *Moods* and Alcott draws them from her own life. Moor's house is the "olde Manse," Hawthorne's house in Concord, and Sylvia's charming habit of borrowing her neighbor's books unmistakably mirrors Louisa's easy access to Emerson's library next door to the Alcott's modest house. It is precisely in Alcott's youth and young womanhood that the American family home becomes a sacred icon, the locus of republican virtue, and a refuge from materialist strivings. But the family home was also woman's prison until, paradoxically, separate spheres that removed man from productive work in his own or his master's house made a middle-class woman's home her castle. *Moods,* in the first edition, is a testimony to that process. The reader does well to note that, of the women in this novel, only Faith Dane has a cottage of her own, and she makes it a refuge for the homeless of her own sex. Moor and Sylvia's father have houses; her sister Prue marries a widower with nine children and goes to his house as a stepmother and housekeeper, announcing that she is determined to love the Reverend Gamaliel Bliss and she indeed learns to do so.

Moods presents an American Rochester modeled on Henry David Thoreau, in the character of Adam Warwick. He is a very tempting mate to Sylvia. Warwick has no house to keep but rather claims the world at large and nature in particular as his domain. Moreover, he offers to share nature with Sylvia and to teach her its secrets. Somewhat like Rochester, he does have a sexual secret as well in the first *Moods;* he is betrothed to Ottila. Thoreau's influence on the character of Warwick is twofold: both natural and sexual. Thoreau's "prejudice for Adamhood" became well known, establishing a direct relationship with nature as one American model of manhood. He was the Alcott girls' favorite companion on cross-country nature rambles. Charming birds and chipmunks, telling stories of Indian history and natural geography, he attracted Louisa May Alcott as well. She recalled trailing behind Thoreau and her father as they discussed Thoreau's essays. In addition Thoreau provides a possible source for the fictional rivalry between Warwick and Moor; there were rumors of an attraction between Lidian Emerson and Thoreau. Even though critics found the triangle in *Moods* "impossible," Alcott confided to her *Journals,* in a postscript to the 1865 pages, that a case of the sort exists in Concord and the woman came and asked me how I knew it. I did *not* know or guess, but perhaps felt it without any other guide, and unconsciously put the thing into my book, for I changed the ending about that time. It was meant to show a life affected by *Moods*, not a discussion of marriage which I knew so little about, except to observe that very few were happy ones.

Sylvia Yule's heartfelt request to join the men's holiday party down the river is sanctioned not so much by her own brother as by his two friends, Moor and Warwick. The reader observes what the innocent Sylvia misses, that both men are courting her. Believing herself to be safely within the domestic circle, she is actually "on stage." Her protectors presume to make choices for her which, however well-meaning, keep her a dependent child. Sylvia's effort to gain self-respect ironically contributes to her desirability as a possession and is doomed to fail as the more dependent she becomes, the more she despises her own frailty. Her costume is a telling indication of the meaning this first sheltered trip out into the world has for her. In a kilted skirt and boots, she slings a pouch over her shoulder and so assures the men that she will not be a helpless decoration. Sylvia does, however, add a small decoration of great significance to herself; she "ornamented her hat pilgrim-wise with a cockle shell." She thus begins a voyage with the traditional emblem of Christian pilgrims. Moor immediately makes light of Sylvia's quest, calling it a "commonplace voyage," turned into a "pleasure pilgrimage with a lively lady to keep us knights and gentlemen wherever we are." His remark foreshadows a failure as lover and husband to understand and respect her true self. Warwick is more genuinely interested in Sylvia as a pilgrim, but he assumes the role of Mr. Greatheart, the Pilgrim's boatman, too early and with too much self-interest. Mark warns his sister that Moor is not really a potential friend for her, as he is "a young man still" and Sylvia, "a captivating little woman." He suggests that it would be better to "leave Platonics till you're forty." Mark has similar words of warning about Warwick, who is "restless, brilliant and violently virtuous."[3] Like Thoreau, who supported John Brown's Harper Ferry raid, denounced the Mexican War, and defended the cause of American Indians, Warwick is

a masterful soul, bent on living out his beliefs and aspirations at any cost, much given to denunciation of wrong-doing everywhere, and eager to execute justice upon all offenders high or low. Yet he possesses great nobility of character, great audacity of mind, and leads a life of the sternest integrity.

To Sylvia, Warwick's mind and heart seem open but he is not truthful with her. He does not tell her that he is pledged to Ottila. And he reserves the right to choose between Ottila and Sylvia while the inexperienced young woman waits in an agony of doubt about her lover's true feelings. After her marriage to Moor, Sylvia comes across his diary locked and when she finds its key, she discovers that her husband also has a hidden self. He has confided his disappointments and his hopes not to his "child-wife" but to the pages of a private journal. Thus, her simple revelation of her own hopes, weaknesses, and strengths in the courting period have not been matched by male openness.

Sylvia sees her single holiday adventure as a lovely world she cannot have. In both versions of the novel, but in different places, Alcott quotes Tennyson's "Lady of Shalott":

> The fairy lady of Shalott,
> She had left the web and left the loom,
> Had seen the water lilies bloom,
> Had seen the helmet and the plume,
> And had looked down to Camelot.

With her childhood home left behind, her alternative environments are nostalgic evocations of a world in which she, like many other Victorians, presume an Edenic harmony between the sexes. In *Jane Eyre,* after the destruction of the mansion and Rochester's permanent injuries, the lovers leave the civilized society in which they cannot live as equals for Ferndean, a wild country estate where, presumably, they can live in a state approaching their new equality, untroubled by the need to earn their bread or to bake it. Alcott, however, offers American impressionism at its most entrancing through Sylvia's own sun-drenched vision of the New World's Eden. Her eyes are newly open to scenes where

> Villages, like white flocks, slept on the hillsides; martinbox schoolhouses appeared here and there, astir with busy voices, alive with wistful eyes; and more than once they came upon little mermen bathing, who dived with sudden splashes, like a squad of turtles tumbling off a sunny rock.

She sees all the stages of life and all are sexually specific: the "white sleeved mowers," "rosy girls" who bring water for their sweethearts, and then "matrons tending babies in the doorway as they watched smaller selves playing keep house under the laylocks . . ." (ch. III).

In mid-nineteenth century Massachusetts neither the riverside landscape nor the woods where Sylvia and Warwick go berrying are wild or undomesticated, however. A forest fire set by men and fought by them interrupts the idyll. And then, in "A Golden Wedding," Alcott re-creates an American version of Jean Paul Richter's celebration in *Jubelsnoir*, a German Romantic novel she had just finished reading. *Moods* offers, only later to retract, America's arcadian myth in which true self and social role appear one and the same. In this domestic scene, it seems "natural" that Grandpa and Grandma have all their children and grandchildren about them and a homemade abundance teaches Sylvia lessons "not larned from books." The groaning table prefigures the cozy kitchen and delectable meals that made Alcott's later scenes of homelife famous. In *Moods,* objects bear the attributes of their owners. In the farmhouse,

> The women unpacked baskets, brooded over teapots and kept up a harmonious clack as the table was spread with pyramids of cake, regiments of pies, quagmires of jelly, snowbanks of bread, and gold mines of butter; every possible article of food, from baked beans to wedding cake, finding a place on that sacrificial altar.

Notice Alcott's expressive verb, "brooded," as if the women *were* their quilted tea cozies, often stitched in the shape of red hens. And, there are "regiments" of pies because Grandma is a general in her own kitchen. Alcott relentlessly impresses upon the reader that the visitors can don the costumes and play at family roles for a brief time only. She rings the curtain down with Sylvia's singing "John Anderson my Jo." For this scene even Warwick's heroic self is reduced to homely proportion when Grandma refers to him as "Wackett" and then mischievously asks Sylvia, "be you to be Mis' Wackett?" Richter is thus curiously quilted with Dickens in Alcott's own style. If Sylvia is not a boy, and not a world traveler, and not "Mis' Wackett," then who is she? Do women have selves, separate from their social roles as wives, sisters, daughters, seamstresses, cooks and so forth? The answer, at least according to Alcott, is yes. That selfhood is delicate, it must be nurtured and tempered with experience. And it must be balanced between passion and principle.

Introduction

In her sleepwalking scene (ch. XVII), reminiscent of Alcott's sensation stories, the author introduces a clue to what Sylvia will learn and accept about herself later in the novel. She sits in a chair and fondles an imaginary object. Moor, watching her, assumes it is his own hair she is touching, but the reader knows that Sylvia is stroking Warwick's gloves. We recall that only a chapter earlier she has noticed them with Warwick's traveling bag; like himself it is "simple and strong, no key . . ." And she longs to touch his gloves, "in the fond, foolish way which women have of endowing the possessions of those they love with the attractions of sentient things, and a portion of their owner's character or claim upon themselves." Moor even calls Sylvia "Lady Macbeth," and alternatively, "dear child." The point, of course, is that she cannot run away down the river, she does not belong in a patriarchal farmhouse, nor can she play at being a child. She does the bravest thing she can, with the help of Faith (aptly named); she tells her husband the truth about her feelings for him. Moor does the right thing, moving toward his own true self when he responds to Sylvia's truth-telling with, "We are as much divorced as if judge and jury had decided the righteous but hard separation for us." His startling, brave decision flies in the face of a parlor discussion of hypothetical divorce a few scenes earlier when Moor, confronted with a situation in which a wife has married the wrong man and left him for another, says that he would find it hard to say "go, my dear," to his wife because, "I love but few, and those few are my world; so do not try me too hardly, Sylvia" (ch. XV).

Faith Dane, who is not introduced in *Moods* until after Sylvia's marriage, gives the most sanguine advice during the parlor discussion, and it is she who assumes a major role as the confidante of all three lovers. Faith suggests that Geoffrey Moor, in particular, might need to go off on a quest for his own self. Moor must recognize his own ordinary human selfishness and anger, as well as his assumption of a masculine right to dominate Sylvia. These qualities stand in the way of self-reliance and principled selfhood. It is precisely through his humiliating rejection that Moor begins his journey to the Celestial City. Going off to fight in Italy, he will have Adam Warwick as Mr. Greatheart. Warwick is surely brave; tested in love and battle, he receives Garibaldi's red cloak, and a red scarf from a grateful peasant woman. Tellingly he gives them both away, casting off all earthly rewards; with his mother's picture around his neck, Adam will soon join her in heaven. Warwick entered the novel knowing that "a lean freeman is better than a fat slave," and he goes out of the story to a greater freedom, in the language of *The Pilgrim's Progress*. True feelings (sentiments) are passionate and they give energy and strength to freedom of the will and purposeful life.

Warwick, through a conversation with Faith Dane, understands before he leaves for Italy that Sylvia is not his equal and therefore that marrying her would, ultimately, enslave both of them. He accepts his heroic urge to carry her off as a weakness, and he avoids the temptation to confuse the idolization of his friends and comrades with more reliable self-knowledge and self-sacrifice. In both editions of *Moods* Sylvia's pilgrimage is the hardest of all. Poised between the end of childhood and the assumption of womanhood's rights and responsibilities, she has let her most important choice be made by men. She cannot retrace her steps but she can save her soul. The heroines of Alcott's sensation tales and antislavery stories frequently choose a liberating death over earthly bondage and so too does Sylvia Yule in *Moods*.

As it should be clear by now, *The Pilgrim's Progress* informs this novel and, in fact, resonates in all Alcott's subsequent fiction. It was Bronson Alcott's favorite book; Louisa Alcott heard the story, play acted it with her sisters, and read it herself many times. Modern readers might need a reminder of the particular spiritual equality Bunyan's classic offered to women. Each pilgrim's way is a lonely and gender specific journey. To be sure, the hero Christian, in Part 1 of the story, has allies as well as many temptors but he does travel alone toward the Celestial City, leaving behind his wife and four sons, knowing that his efforts break a path for them to follow. And so Christiana sets out in Part 2 with her sons, guided by the evidence of her husband's pilgrimage, and aided by Mr. Greatheart, the heavenly boatman, who knew her husband's trials. And Christiana has a friend of the heart, an honest, loving, young neighbor girl, Mercy.

Sylvia, like succeeding Alcott heroines, is a modern Mercy. In the preface to *Little Women*, Alcott, adapting John Bunyan to her own cause, addresses young readers:

> Go then, my little Book, and show to all
> That entertain, and bid thee welcome shall,
> What thou dost show them may be blest
> To them for good, may make them choose to be
> Pilgrims better, by far, than thee or me.
> Tell them of Mercy; she is one
> Who early hath her pilgrimage begun.
> Yea, let young damsels learn of her to prize

Introduction

The world which is to come, and so be wise;
For little tripping maids may follow God
Along the ways which saintly feet have trod.

Little Women is the American classic that made Alcott famous between the two editions of *Moods.* In *Little Women* she established a young woman's right to a trial period, testing herself in direct experience with life while enjoying the support of a democratic family. Nina Auerbach points out that Jo's refusal of Laurie in *Little Women* "remains the most talked-about part of the book from its day to ours . . ." (69). And she is even more insightful in pointing out that Alcott's fictional heroines repeatedly attest to a community of women as a cultural and political antidote to patriarchal families. Sylvia also says no, refusing Geoffrey Moor during his first proposal, and she means it. That she ultimately relents in loneliness and despair does not diminish her brave try.

In *Moods,* Faith is the predecessor to Marmee as a young woman's staunch ally in seeking independence. The "sad sisterhood of disappointed women" described in *Moods* can only become happier if Americans create both democratic families and a democratic society. It is the lack of both satisfactory marriages and societies in the real world that makes the endings so unsatisfactory in both editions of *Moods.* Like *Jane Eyre* (1847), *Wuthering Heights* (1850), and *The Scarlet Letter* (1850), *Moods* (1864) can only provide a romantic escape from the world. Eighteen years later Alcott severed the ties that bound Sylvia Yule to her father's home and her "old place." In the 1882 version of *Moods,* Mr. Yule dies painlessly and peacefully and Sylvia's year apart from her husband brings "the indescribable refinement of a deep inward life." Sylvia leaves her father's house, and with Faith, makes "a little pilgrimage through her Paradise Regained, lingering in many places to relive the sad or happy hours spent there." The pilgrimage is not merely a visit to the shrine of a departed husband. "As spring came on a great longing for a home of her own grew up in her, and where should she so naturally go as to the Manse, still waiting for its mistress" (ch. XX).

Awaiting her husband on the threshold of their home, Sylvia then tells him about her dream of Adam Warwick's death. Like Hester Prynne she sees a scarlet letter in the sky but Sylvia's heavenly sign says Amen as she bids a peaceful goodbye to Adam Warwick and lives on happily ever after. This 1882 ending, despite Sylvia's survival, is still unsatisfactory to modern readers. Alcott's brilliant depiction of romantic love and unequal marital roles was a genuine critique of patriarchal family life, but it never-theless suggested that equality within marriage could be accomplished by self-discipline and good faith. And her works have been criticized by many modern readers as promising more than any purely domestic institution could deliver. Nevertheless, generations of American women writers—from Sarah Orne Jewett and Kate Chopin to Willa Cather and Charlotte Perkins Gilman, and then Gertrude Stein and Ursula LeGuin—read the *Little Women* series whose important, adult genesis lies in *Moods*. *Little Women* became an American myth, and *Moods* was quickly forgotten, but Sylvia, like the March sisters, is a passionate woman who takes up her pilgrimage to principled womanhood.

Little Women's depiction of "Literary Lessons" (ch. 27) reveals the critical reception of the first *Moods*. Jo's first novel produced "a heap of notices, the perusal of which filled her with pride and joy one minute—wrath and dire dismay the next." The work was praised for spiritual values and damned for its metaphysics. Alcott's *Letters* and *Journals* provide a fuller record, though not a complete one, of readers' and reviewers' responses to the two versions of *Moods*.[4]

> Notices of Moods came from all directions, and though people didn't understand my ideas owing to my shortening the book so much, the notices were mostly favorable and gave quite as much praise as was good for me. I had letters from Mrs. Parker, Chadwick, Sanborn, Green the artist, T. Higginson and some others, all friendly and flat-tering. [. . .] People seem to think the book finely written, very promising, wise and interesting, but some fear that it isn't moral because it speaks freely of marriage. (*Journals,* Jan. 1865)

Then Alcott tucks in the patronizing criticism of Henry James, just after noting that Henry James, Sr., and Mrs. James had invited her to dinner and treated her "like the Queen of Sheba." She then allows herself only one restrained line: "Henry (Jr.) wrote a notice of *Moods* for the *North American* and it was very friendly, being a literary youth." James saw the novel as an unconvincing version of the old triangle, and he could not imagine that she proposed to be any more philosophical than that.[5]

Alcott was restrained and lightly ironical in her reporting of James's review, but her revisions of *Moods* for the 1882 edition certainly reflect some of his criticism. Sylvia is now firmly a young girl and not a disguised gardener's lad when she is first observed by Geoffrey Moor, and Alcott, having made her fame and fortune with *Little Women,* can rely upon her own observation and experience with enormous self-confidence. In 1865, however, she felt impelled to explain herself to friends and strangers. To Moncure Conway she wrote:

> Self abnegation is a noble thing but I think there is a limit to it, and though in a few rare cases it may work well yet half the misery of the world seems to come from unmated pairs trying to live their lie decorously to the end, and bringing children into the world to inherit the unhappiness and discord out of which they were born. There is discipline enough in the most perfect marriage and I don't agree to the doctrine of "marry in haste and repent at leisure" which seems to prevail. The book has been sharply criticized and I am glad of it, though I wish I had done better justice to my own idea. I heartily believe it, am willing to be blamed for it, and am not sorry I wrote it, for it has not only cleared and fixed many things in my own mind, but brought me thanks and good wishes from many whom I find have served better than I knew. (*Letters* 108)

Madeleine B. Stern notes that while the reviewer in *Harpers Weekly* (21 Jan. 1865) found "great power and absorbing interest" in *Moods,* Henry James stressed "the author's ignorance of human nature, and her self-confidence in spite of this ignorance" (*Letters* 108).

Like her *Journals* and *Letters,* Alcott's preface to the second edition, reprinted here, maintains that the first work was so altered for the "publisher that marriage appeared to be the theme instead of an attempt to show the mistakes of a moody nature, guided by impulse, not principle."

We do not have the drafts of *Moods* before the 1864 edition and can never know exactly what cuts Loring required of the author. Mrs. Caroline Dall read the printer's proofs with Louisa Alcott in 1864, and she reviewed the new edition of *Moods* in 1882,

> Before this new edition appeared the public seemed to think that friendly critics and an obstinate publisher had persuaded Miss Alcott to omit passages which changed the character of the book, and made its first publication very unsatisfactory to herself. Any one who will now compare the two editions will see that this did not take place. Mr. Loring was a man of business, paying a certain sum of money for the first novel of an almost unknown author. He wished to keep the size within a certain limit, and he omitted, with the author's reluc-

tant consent, the chapter now entitled "Sermons" and trimmed down the conversation in that called "What Next?" so as to secure this end. Examination will show that this in no respect changed the character of the story, nor did it interfere seriously with its purpose.

Dall praises the revisions because they strengthen the purpose of the novel. And she mentions the publication of Mrs. Ann Seemuller's *Emily Chester*, a novel remarkably similar to *Moods*, also published in 1864, which undoubtedly drew some sales that Alcott hoped for. Dropping the chapters, "In a Year" and "Holly," she notes, was a superficial change; Warwick's romance with Ottila was an unimportant element in the structure of the novel. Reformist Mrs. Dall thoroughly approved of the changed ending: artistic sense is reinforced by "a moral consciousness which has slowly been maturing ever since 1865." Sylvia, according to this critic, was, in the first edition, "a victim of Warwick's moods and goes contentedly out of the world. In the second (edition) she nobly conquers the weakness of her own and lives after her hero's death for the good man who has loved her."

Dall points out a very crucial change in Faith's discourse with Sylvia. In the first edition Sylvia asks which man she should discard and to which she should "cleave?" Faith answers "To neither." In the second edition, Sylvia asks which she should have married, "had fate given me the choice in time." Faith replies, "Neither." As a result of both heredity and an unhappy family, Sylvia's character, in Faith's judgment, was too fragile to survive the hardship of a wifely role.

Moods is about the other civil war, in which the conflicts were the inner struggle for modern individuality and the simultaneous battle to win for woman the rights of man. The battlefields were private homes as well as public workplaces, where the rights to own one's body and to enter the body politic were contested. *Moods* is therefore both romantic and realist in theme and structure; unevenly executed but valuable enough to be reworked by Louisa May Alcott and read once again by the descendants of *Little Women*. Jo March's first novel suffered the same fate as Alcott's first edition of *Moods*. The mature author still cared enough to memorialize her own painful experience of writing, rewriting, and searching for a publisher. *Moods,* as it was finally published in 1864, is a landmark in American literature and women's fiction. Revised, it tells us much about women writers' development and about the historical changes, often called a "silent revolution," which shaped modernity. Marked by demographic transformations including a decline in fertility, this silent revolution gave women a longer life expectancy (in large part a consequence of bearing fewer children), and facilitated women's entrance into the public world of work, culture, and politics. Louisa May Alcott's role in this revolution included her portrayals of female adolescence; she claimed "little women's" rights to passion, experience, self-reliance, and self-respect. Ironically the success of *Little Women,* a girl's book, slowly obscured Alcott's impressive production of women's fiction. Only recently, a generation of women writers and scholars, many of whom grew up reading Louisa May Alcott's fiction for girls, has rediscovered and reclaimed *Moods.* Sylvia Yule was Alcott's archetypal American Girl; in *Moods* she grows into generous, true-hearted womanhood, having learned that "none may live for love alone."

1. Louisa May Alcott, *The Journals of Louisa May Alcott,* ed. Joel Myerson, Daniel Shealy, and associate ed. Madeleine B. Stern (Boston: Little, 1989), Aug. 1860 (hereafter *Journals*). All references to Alcott's *Journals* are by date. I am grateful to the editors for sharing the manuscript of their edition before its publication. Alcott's journals and relevant letters and papers are deposited in the following institutions: Concord Free Public Library, Fruitlands Museums, Houghton Library of Harvard University, Massachusetts Historical Society, New York Historical Society, and University of Virginia (Louisa May Alcott Collection [No. 6255]). A complete list of Louisa May Alcott's letters and publishing history appears in "A Calendar of the Letters of Louisa May Alcott" in *Studies in the American Renaissance 1988* (Charlottesville: UP of Virginia). Selections from Alcott's correspondence are drawn from *The Selected Letters* of Louisa May Alcott, ed. Joel Myerson, Daniel Shealy, and assoc. ed. Madeleine B. Stern (Boston: Little, 1987; hereafter *Letters*).

2. Quoted in Madeleine B. Stern, *Imprints on History: Book Publishers and American Frontiers* (Bloomington, IN; U of Indiana P, 1956) 181, and Madeleine B. Stern, *Publishers for Mass Entertainment in Nineteenth Century America* (Boston: Hall, 1980) 192; from an undated letter, Alderman Library, University of Virginia. I am grateful to Madeleine B. Stern for calling this correspondence to my attention.

3. In the first edition of *Moods* (1864) Sylvia's brother is Mark Yule; his name is changed to Max Yule in the revised edition. In both versions Sylvia's brother is an artist who treats his fiancée as a favorite model. The question of dependency between artist and model, as between hero and heroine, is complex in all of Alcott's stories, and her psychology is close to that described by Marcia Westkott in *The Feminist Legacy of Karen Horney* (New Haven: Yale UP, 1986). Horney's view of the inner self and the social self were influenced by William James, a contemporary and a family friend of the Alcott sisters. Westkott argues that the dependent

xli

"feminine" woman feels anger toward the very individual upon whom she be-lieves she must rely: "Especially in intimate relationships this conflict is expressed both as a wish for the other to take charge of her life and protect her and as resentment of the power that the other exerts over her" (168). As in the case of *Jane Eyre,* contemporary romance novels, still feature female "fantasies of cruelly heroic men who magically become kindhearted partners" (ibid.). For a discussion of this issue and Westkott's treatment of it, see Janice Radway, chs. 3 and 4.

4. The letter to a "Mr. Ayer" of March 1865 gives perhaps the fullest statement of Alcott's intention in writing the first *Moods,* and her forthright rejec-tion of "Affinities, also Spiritualism and Free Love" as bases for marriage is then confirmed in her 1880s revision of *Moods.* Being true to oneself is the major theme of this letter. Alcott defends Sylvia on this score and insists that Warwick was "drawn from life" and was not "a base nor a treacherous man, but one possessing great faults as well as virtues and like better men most inconsistent, unwise and blind when in love . . ." She goes on to say, "These latter chapters were more carefully written than any others, and as the book has been underway for six years there has been no occasion for haste any where . . ." (*Letters* 109–10).

5. Evidence of Alcott's consistent radicalism in adult and children's fiction in the period between the two editions of *Moods* is found in a review of *Eight Cousins.* In *Eight Cousins* Alcott presented a very moody, young orphan girl, Rose Campbell, who is brought up by her uncle Alec Campbell in reform fashion, without corsets, fashionable clothes, coffee or "hot bread." Rose is taught to say what she thinks, bake her own bread, and exercise outdoors with her eight male cousins. Henry James hated *Eight Cousins,* and although he called Alcott "the novelist of children—the Thackery, the Trollope, of the nursery and the school room," he also credited her with, single-handedly, creating American children who are "without a certain charm usually possessed by the youngsters of the old world." Rose Campbell "is evidently a very subjective little girl, and certainly history will deepen the subjective tendency in the little girls who read it" ("Eight Cousins . . . ," *The Nation* 14 Oct. 1875). In other words, Alcott's girls will trust themselves.

Major Works by Louisa May Alcott

Short Stories

"Love and Self-Love." *Atlantic Monthly* 5.29 (Mar. 1860); "A Modern Cinderella: or, The Little Old Shoe." *Atlantic Monthly* 6.36 (Oct. 1860). Rpt. in *Camp and Fireside Stories*. Boston: Roberts Brothers, 1869.

"Pauline's Passion and Punishment." *Frank Leslie's Illustrated Newspaper* 15:379, 380 (3, 10 Jan. 1863). Pub. anon. Rpt. in *Behind a Mask: The Unknown Thrillers of Louisa May Alcott*. Ed. Madeleine B. Stern. New York: William Morrow, 1975.

"Hospital Sketches," *The Commonwealth* 1.38, 39, 41, 43 (22, 29 May; 12, 26 June 1863). Portion rpt. as "John" in *Merry's Museum* 2.8 (Aug. 1869). Rpt. as *Hospital Sketches*. Boston: James Redpath, 1863.

"A Whisper in the Dark." *Frank Leslie's Illustrated Newspaper* 16.401, 402 (6, 13 June 1863). Pub. anon. Rpt. in *A Modern Mephistopheles and A Whisper in the Dark*. Boston: Roberts Bros., 1889. Rpt. in *Plots and Counterplots: More Unknown Thrillers of Louisa May Alcott*. New York: William Morrow, 1976.

"Thoreau's Flute." *Atlantic Monthly* 12.71 (Sept. 1863).

"My Contraband" (first called "The Brothers"). *Atlantic Monthly* 12.73 (Nov. 1863). Rpt. in *Alternative Alcott*. Ed. Elaine Showalter. New Brunswick and London: Rutgers UP, 1988.

Selected Bibliography

"An Hour." *Commonwealth* 3.13, 14 (26 Nov., 3 Dec. 1864). Rpt. in *Hospital Sketches* and in *Camp and Fireside Stories.*

"A Pair of Eyes; or, Modern Magic." *Frank Leslie's Illustrated Newspaper* 17.11, 18 (25 Feb. 1865). Pub. anon. Rpt. in *A Double Life: Newly Discovered Thrillers of Louisa May Alcott.* Ed. Madeleine Stern, Joel Myerson, and Daniel Shealy. Boston: Little, 1988.

"V.V.: Or Plots and Counterplots." *Flag of Our Union* 20.5, 6, 7, 8 (4, 11, 18, 25 Feb. 1865). Rpt. in the *Ten Cent Novelettes of Standard American Authors* series (No. 80), pseud. A. M. Barnard, and in *Plots and Counterplots.*

"Diana and Persis," uncompleted, from manuscript, "An untitled romance." Alcott Papers, 59m–309 (21). Houghton Library, Harvard University. Rpt. as *Diana and Persis.* Ed. Sarah Elbert. New York: Arno, 1978. Rpt. in *Alternative Alcott.*

Novels

Moods. Boston: Loring, 1864. Rev. ed., Boston: Roberts Bros., 1882.

Little Women. Boston: Roberts Bros., 1868. Rpt. Boston: Little, 1915.

Little Men. Boston: Roberts Bros., 1871. Rpt. New York: Grosset and Dunlap, 1947.

Work: A Story of Experience. Boston: Roberts Bros., 1873. First serialized. *Christian Union,* Dec. 1871–June 1873. Rpt. New York: Schocken, 1977, and first six chaps. in *Alternative Alcott.*

Eight Cousins; or, The Aunt Hill. Boston: Roberts Bros., 1875.

An Old Fashioned Girl. Boston: Roberts Bros., 1876.

Rose in Bloom: A Sequel to Eight Cousins. Boston: Roberts Bros., 1876.

A Modern Mephistopheles. Boston: Roberts Bros., 1877. Pub. anon. in No Name Series. Rpt. in *A Modern Mephistopheles and Taming a Tartar.* Ed. Madeleine B. Stern. New York: Praeger, 1987.

Jo's Boys. Boston: Roberts Bros., 1886. Rpt. New York: Grosset and Dunlap, 1949.

Sources and Further Reading

Auerbach, Nina. *Communities of Women: An Idea in Fiction.* Cambridge, MA: Harvard UP, 1978.

Selected Bibliography

Baym, Nina. *Woman's Fiction: A Guide to Novels by and about Women in America,*
1820–1870. Ithaca: Cornell UP, 1978.

Bedell, Madelon. *The Alcotts: Biography of a Family.* New York: Clarkson
Potter, 1980.

Brontë, Charlotte. *Jane Eyre.* London, 1847. Rpt. ed. Richard J. Dunn. New
York: Norton, 1971.

Bunyan, John. *The Pilgrim's Progress.* London, 1659. Rpt. New York: Bar-
bour, 1972.

Cott, Nancy. *The Bonds of Womanhood: Woman's Sphere in New England, 1780–*
1835. New Haven: Yale UP, 1977.

————. "Passionlessness: An Interpretation of Victorian Sexual Ideol-
ogy, 1790–1850." *Signs: Journal of Women, Culture and Society* 4 (1978):
219–36.

Dahlstrad, Frederick C. *Amos Bronson Alcott: An Intellectual Biography.* London: Associated UP, 1986.

Dall, Caroline H. "Miss Alcott's First Novel: Its Two Editions Reviewed by
an Old Friend of the Author." Newspaper clipping, unidentified
source. Alcott Papers, 59m–309. Houghton Library, Harvard
University.

Davidoff, Leonore. *The Best Circles: Women and Society in Victorian England.*
Towanda, NJ: Rowan, 1973.

Douglas, Ann. *The Feminization of American Culture.* New York: Knopf, 1977).

————. "Mysteries of Louisa May Alcott." *New York Review of Books* 28
Sept. 1978: 60–63. Rpt. in *Critical Essays on Louisa May Alcott.* Ed.
Madeleine B. Stern. Boston: Hall, 1984.

Elbert, Sarah. *A Hunger for Home: Louisa May Alcott's Place in American Culture.*
New Brunswick: Rutgers UP, 1988.

————. Intro. *Work: A Story of Experience* (New York: Schocken, 1977).
ix–xliv.

Fetterley, Judith. "Impersonating 'Little Women': The Radicalism of Alcott's *Behind a Mask.*" *Women's Studies* 10 (1983): 1–14. Rpt. in *Critical*
Essays on Louisa May Alcott.

Fetterley, Judith. "*Little Women:* Alcott's Civil War." *Feminist Studies* 5
(1979): 369–83.

Frederickson, George M. *The Inner Civil War: Northern Intellectuals and the*
Crisis of Union. New York: Harper, 1965.

Gaskell, Elizabeth. *The Life of Charlotte Brontë.* 1857. Rpt. Penguin Books,
1975.

Gilbert, Sandra M., and Susan Gubar. *The Madwoman in the Attic: The Woman*

Writer and the Nineteenth-Century Literary Imagination. New Haven: Yale UP, 1979.

Gorsky, Susan. "Old Maids and New Women: Alternative to Marriages in Englishwomen's Novels, 1847–1915." *Journal of Popular Culture* 7 (Summer 1973): 68–85.

Haltunnen, Karen. *Confidence Men and Painted Women: A Study of Middle-Class Culture in America, 1830–1870*. New Haven: Yale UP, 1982.

————. "The Domestic Drama of Louisa May Alcott." *Feminist Studies* 10 (1984): 233–54.

Heilbrun, Carolyn. *Reinventing Womanhood*. New York: Norton, 1979.

Hollander, Anne. "Reflections on *Little Women*." *Children's Literature* 9:28–29.

Kaledin, Eugenia. "Louisa May Alcott: Success and the Sorrow of Self Denial." *Women's Studies* 5 (1983): 251–64.

Kelley, Mary. "The Sentimentalists: Promise and Betrayal in the Home." *Signs* 4 (Spring 1979): 434–44.

Keyser, Elizabeth. "Alcott's Portrait of the Artist as Little Woman." *International Journal of Women's Studies* 5.5 (1978): 445–59.

Lee, Eliza Buckminster. *Life of Jean Paul Richter*. Boston: Roberts Bros., 1864.

MacDonald, Ruth K. *Louisa May Alcott*. Boston: Twayne, 1983.

Marsella, Joy. *The Promise of Destiny: Children and Women in the Short Stories of Louisa May Alcott*. Westport, CT: Greenwood, 1983.

Myerson, Joel, Daniel Shealy, Madeleine Stern, eds. *The Selected Letters of Louisa May Alcott*. Boston: Little Brown, 1987.

Radway, Janice. *Reading the Romance: Women, Patriarchy, and Popular Literature*. Chapel Hill: U of North Carolina P, 1984.

Rose, Anne C. *Transcendentalism as a Social Movement, 1830–1850*. New Haven: Yale UP, 1981.

Rostenberg, Leona. "Some Anonymous and Pseudonymous Thrillers of Louisa May Alcott." *Papers of the Bibliographical Society of America* (1943).

Saxton, Martha. *Louisa May: A Modern Biography of Louisa May Alcott*. Boston: Houghton, 1977.

Showalter, Elaine. Intro. and ed. *Alternative Alcott*. New Brunswick and London: Rutgers UP, 1988.

Sklar, Kathryn Kish. *Catherine Beecher: A Study in American Domesticity*. New York: Norton, 1976.

Selected Bibliography

Smith-Rosenberg, Carroll. "Beauty, the Beast and the Militant Woman: A Study in Sex Roles and Social Stress in Jacksonian America." *American Quarterly* 22 (Winter 1971): 562–84.

Stern, Madeleine B. "Louisa Alcott, Trouper." *New England Quarterly* 16.2 (June 1943).

————. *Louisa May Alcott.* Norman: U of Oklahoma P, 1950, 1971, 1985.

————. *Purple Passage: The Life of Mrs. Frank Leslie.* Norman: U of Oklahoma P, 1953, 1970.

————. Ed. *Critical Essays on Louisa May Alcott.* Boston: Hall, 1984.

Stoehr, Taylor. *Nay Saying in Concord: Emerson, Alcott and Thoreau.* Hamden, CT: Scarecrow, 1971.

Tompkins, Jane. *Sensational Designs: The Cultural Work of American Fiction, 1790–1860.* New York: Oxford, 1985.

A NOTE ON THE TEXT

THIS NEW PUBLICATION of the 1864 edition of *Moods,* brought out by A. K. Loring, includes an appendix of excerpts from the second, revised edition published by Roberts Brothers in 1882. The excerpts are faithfully reset from the portions Alcott herself revised for the later edition. Typographical errors have been silently corrected. Nineteenth-century spellings and hyphenations have been preserved.

To present the textual changes between the two editions as clearly as possible, asterisked footnotes have been added to this 1864 text, describing Alcott's revisions. Short changes are given in these footnotes. The lengthier revisions, with page numbers from the 1882 edition, are reprinted in the appendix, in the order they appear in that edition. Two signs are used in these notes: *M1* stands for *Moods,* 1864 edition; *M2* indicates the revised edition of 1882.

Explanatory notes to this printing of *Moods* have been supplied and appear at the end of the volume.

MOODS

Life is a train of moods like a string of beads; and
as we pass through them they prove to be many
colored lenses, which paint the world their own
hue, and each shows us only what lies in its own focus.

—Emerson

CONTENTS

CHAPTER I

IN A YEAR*

✻✻✻✻✻✻

THE ROOM fronted the west, but a black cloud, barred with red, robbed the hour of twilight's tranquil charm. Shadows haunted it, lurking in corners like spies set there to watch the man who stood among them mute and motionless as if himself a shadow. His eye turned often to the window with a glance both vigilant and eager, yet saw nothing but a tropical luxuriance of foliage scarcely stirred by the sultry air heavy with odors that seemed to oppress not refresh. He listened with the same intentness, yet heard only the clamor of voices, the tramp of feet, the chime of bells, the varied turmoil of a city when night is defrauded of its peace by being turned to day. He watched and waited for something; presently it came. A viewless visitant, welcomed by longing soul and body as the man, with extended arms and parted lips received the voiceless greeting of the breeze that came winging its way across the broad Atlantic, full of healthful cheer for a home-sick heart. Far out he leaned; held back the thick-leaved boughs already rustling with a grateful stir, chid the shrill bird beating its flame-colored breast against its prison bars, and drank deep draughts of the blessed wind that seemed to cool the fever of his blood and give him back the vigor he had lost.

A sudden light shone out behind him filling the room with a glow that left no shadow in it. But he did not see the change, nor hear the step that broke the hush, nor turn to meet the woman who stood waiting for a

---

*Chapter I, "In a Year," is the first of several chapters omitted in *M2*.

5

lover's welcome. An indefinable air of sumptuous life surrounded her, and made the brilliant room a fitting frame for the figure standing there with warm-hued muslins, blowing in the wind. A figure full of the affluent beauty of womanhood in its prime, bearing unmistakable marks of the polished pupil of the world in the grace that flowed through every motion, the art which taught each feature to play its part with the ease of second nature and made dress the foil to loveliness. The face was delicate and dark as a fine bronze, a low forehead set in shadowy waves of hair, eyes full of slumberous fire, and a passionate yet haughty mouth that seemed shaped alike for caresses and commands.

A moment she watched the man before her, while over her countenance passed rapid variations of pride, resentment, and tenderness. Then with a stealthy step, an assured smile, she went to him and touched his hand, saying, in a voice inured to that language which seems made for lovers' lips—

"Only a month betrothed, and yet so cold and gloomy, Adam!"

With a slight recoil, a glance of soft detestation veiled and yet visible, Warwick answered like a satiric echo—

"Only a month betrothed, and yet so fond and jealous, Ottila!"

Unchilled by the action, undaunted by the look, the white arm took him captive, the beautiful face drew nearer, and the persuasive voice asked wistfully—

"Was it of me you thought when you turned with that longing in your eye?"

"No."

"Was it of a fairer or a dearer friend than I?"

"Yes."

The black brows contracted ominously, the mouth grew hard, the eyes glittered, the arm became a closer bond, the entreaty a command.

"Let me know the name, Adam."

"Self-respect."

She laughed low to herself, and the mobile features softened to their former tenderness as she looked up into that other face so full of an accusing significance which she would not understand.

"I have waited two long hours; have you no kinder greeting, love?"

"I have no truer one. Ottila, if a man has done unwittingly a weak, unwise, or wicked act, what should he do when he discovers it?"

"Repent and mend his ways; need I tell you that?"

"I have repented; will you help me mend my ways?"

"Confess, dear sinner; I will shrive you and grant absolution for the past, whatever it may be."

"How much would you do for love of me?"

"Anything for you, Adam."

"Then give me back my liberty."

He rose erect and stretched his hands to her with a gesture of entreaty, an expression of intense desire. Ottila fell back as if the forceful words and action swept her from him. The smile died on her lips, a foreboding fear looked out at her eyes, and she asked incredulously—

"Do you mean it?"

"Yes; now, entirely, and forever!"

If he had lifted his strong arm and struck her, it would not have daunted with such pale dismay. An instant she stood like one who saw a chasm widening before her, which she had no power to cross. Then as if disappointment was a thing impossible and unknown, she seized the imploring hands in a grasp that turned them white with its passionate pressure as she cried—

"No, I will not! I have waited for your love so long I cannot give it up; you shall not take it from me!"

But as if the words had made the deed irrevocable, Warwick put her away, speaking with the stern accent of one who fears a traitor in himself.

"I cannot take from you what you never had. Stand there and hear me. No; I will have no blandishments to keep me from my purpose, no soft words to silence the hard ones I mean to speak, no more illusions to hide us from each other and ourselves."

"Adam, you are cruel."

Better seem cruel than be treacherous; better wound your pride now than your heart hereafter, when too late you discover that I married you without confidence, respect, or love. For once in your life you shall hear the truth as plain as words can make it. You shall see me at my best as at my worst; you shall know what I have learned to find in you; shall look back into the life behind us, forward into the life before us, and if there be any candor in you I will wring from you an acknowledgment that you have led me into an unrighteous compact. Unrighteous, because you have deceived me in yourself, appealed to the baser, not the nobler instincts in me, and on such a foundation there can be no abiding happiness."

"Go on, I will hear you." And conscious that she could not control the will now thoroughly aroused, Ottila bent before it as if meekly ready to hear all things for love's sake.

A disdainful smile passed over Warwick's face, as with an eye that fixed and held her own, he rapidly went on, never passing to choose smooth phrases or soften facts, but seeming to find a relish in the utterance of bitter truths after the honeyed falsehood he had listened to so long. Yet through all the harshness glowed the courage of an upright soul, the fervor of a generous heart.

"I know little of such things and care less; but I think few lovers pass through a scene such as this is to be, because few have known lives like ours, or one such as we. You a woman stronger for good or ill than those about you, I a man untamed by any law but that of my own will. Strength is royal, we both possess it; as kings and queens drop their titles in their closets, let us drop all disguises and see each other as God sees us. This compact must be broken; let me show you why. Three months ago I came here to take the chill of an Arctic winter out of blood and brain. I have done so and am the worse for it. In melting frost I have kindled fire; a fire that will burn all virtue out of me unless I quench it at once. I mean to do so, because I will not keep the ten commandments, before men's eyes and break them every hour in my heart."

He paused a moment, as if hotter words rose to his lips than generosity would let him utter, and when he spoke again there was more reproach than anger in his voice.

"Ottila, till I knew you I loved no woman but my mother; I wooed no wife, bought no mistress, desired no friend, but led a life austere as any monk's asking only freedom and my work. Could you not let me keep my independence? Were there not men enough who would find no degradation in a spiritual slavery like this? Would nothing but my subjection satisfy your unconquerable appetite for power?"

"Did I seek you, Adam?"

"Yes! Not openly, I grant, your art was too fine for that; you shunned me that I might seek you to ask why. In interviews that seemed to come by chance, you tried every wile a woman owns, and they are many. You wooed me as such as you alone can woo the hearts they know are hardest to be won. You made your society a refreshment in this climate of the passions; you hid your real self and feigned that for which I felt most honor. You entertained my beliefs with largest hospitality; encouraged my ambitions with a sympathy so genial that I thought it genuine; professed my scorn for shammery, and seemed an earnest woman, eager to find the true, to do the right; a fit wife for any man who desired a helpmate, not a toy. It showed much strength of wit and will to conceive and execute the design. It proved your knowledge of the virtues you could counterfeit so well, else I never should have been where I am now."

"Your commendation is deserved, though so ungently given, Adam."

"There will be no more of it. If I am ungentle, it is because I despise deceit, and you possess a guile that has given me my first taste of self-contempt, and the draught is bitter. Hear me out; for this reminiscence is my justification; you must listen to the one and accept the other. You seemed all this, but under the honest friendliness you showed lurked the purpose you have since avowed, to conquer most entirely the man who denied your right to rule by the supremacy of beauty or of sex alone. You saw the unsuspected fascination that detained me here when my better self said 'Go.' You allured my eye with loveliness, my ear with music; piqued curiosity, pampered pride, and subdued will by flatteries subtly administered. Beginning afar off, you let all influences do their work till the moment came for the effective stroke. Then you made a crowning sacrifice of maiden modesty and owned you loved me."

Shame burned red as Ottila's dark cheek, and ire flamed up in her eyes, as the untamable spirit of the woman answered against her will—

"It was not made in vain; for, rebellious as you are, it subdued you, and with your own weapon, the bare truth."

He had said truly, "You shall see me at my best as at worst." She did, for putting pride underneath his feet he showed her a brave sincerity, which she could admire but never imitate, and in owning a defeat achieved a victory.

"You think I shall deny this. I do not, but acknowledge to the uttermost that, in spite of all resistance, I was conquered by a woman. If it affords you satisfaction to hear this, to know that it is hard to say, harder still to feel, take the ungenerous delight; I give it to you as an alms. But remember that if I have failed, no less have you. For in that stormy heart of yours there is no sentiment more powerful than that you feel for me, and through it you will receive the retribution you have brought upon yourself. You were elated with success, and forgot too soon the character you had so well supported. You thought love blinded me, but there was no love; and during this month I have learned to know you as you are. A woman of strong passions and weak principles; hungry for power and intent on pleasure; accomplished in deceit and reckless in trampling on the nobler instincts of a gifted but neglected nature. Ottila, I have no faith in you, feel no respect for the passion you inspire, own no allegiance to the dominion you assert."

"You cannot throw it off; it is too late."

It was a rash defiance; she saw that as it passed her lips, and would have given much to have recalled it. The stern gravity of Warwick's face flashed into a stern indignation. His eye shone like steel, but his voice dropped lower and his hand closed like a vice as he said, with the air of one who cannot conceal but can control sudden wrath at a taunt to which past weakness gives a double sting—

"It never is too late. If the priest stood ready, and I had sworn to marry you within the hour, I would break the oath, and God would pardon it, for no man has a right to embrace temptation and damn himself by a life-long lie. You choose to make it a hard battle for me; you are neither an honest friend nor a generous foe. No matter, I have fallen into an ambuscade and must cut my way out as I can, and as I will, for there is enough of this Devil's work in the world without our adding to it."

"You cannot escape with honor, Adam."

"I cannot remain with honor. Do not try me too hardly, Ottila. I am not patient, but I do desire to be just. I confess my weakness; will not that satisfy you? Blazon your wrong as you esteem it; ask sympathy of those who see not as I see; reproach, defy, lament. I will bear it all, will make any other sacrifice as an atonement, but I will 'hold fast mine integrity' and obey a higher law than your world recognizes, both for your sake and my own."

She watched him as he spoke, and to herself confessed a slavery more absolute than any he had known, for with a pang she felt that she had indeed fallen into the snare she spread for him, and in this man, who dared to own his weakness and her power, she had found a master. Was it too late to keep him? She knew that soft appeals were vain, tears like water on a rock, and with the skill that had subdued him once she endeavored to retrieve her blunder by an equanimity which had more effect than prayers or protestations. Warwick had read her well, had shown her herself stripped of all disguises, and left her no defence but tardy candor. She had the wisdom to see this, the wit to use it and restore the shadow of the power whose substance she had lost. Leaving her beauty to its silent work, she fixed on him eyes whose lustre was quenched in unshed tears, and said with an earnest, humble voice—

"I, too, desire to be just. I will not reproach, defy, or lament, but leave my fate to you. I am all you say, yet in your judgment remember mercy, and believe that at twenty-five there is still hope for the noble but neglected nature, still time to repair the faults of birth, education, and orphanhood. You say, I have a daring will, a love of conquest. Can I not will to overcome myself and do it? Can I not learn to be the woman I have seemed? Love has worked greater miracles; may it not work this? I have longed to be a truer creature than I am; have seen my wasted gifts, felt my capacity for better things, and looked for help from many sources, but never found it till you came. Do you wonder that I tried to make it mine? Adam, you are a self-elected missionary to the world's afflicted; you can look beyond external poverty and see the indigence of souls. I am a pauper in your eyes; stretch out your hand and save me from myself."

Straight through the one vulnerable point in the man's pride went this appeal to the man's pity. Indignation could not turn it aside, contempt blunt its edge, or wounded feeling lessen its force; and yet it failed: for in Adam Warwick justice was stronger than mercy, reason than impulse, head than heart. Experience was a teacher whom he trusted; he had weighed this woman and found her wanting; truth was not in her; the patient endeavor, the hard-won success so possible to many was hardly so to her, and a union between them could bring no lasting good to either. He knew this; had decided it in a calmer hour than the present, and by that decision he would now abide proof against all attacks from without or from within. More gently, but as inflexibly as before, he said—

"I do put out my hand and offer you the same bitter draught of self-contempt that proved a tonic to my own weak will. I can help, pity, and forgive you heartily, but I dare not marry you. The tie that binds us is a passion of the senses, not a love of the soul. You lack the moral sentiment that makes all gifts and graces subservient to the virtues that render womanhood a thing to honor as well as love. I can relinquish youth, beauty, worldly advantages, but I must reverence above all others the woman whom I marry, and feel an affection that elevates me by quickening all that is noblest and manliest in me. With you I should be either a tyrant or a slave. I will be neither, but go solitary all my life rather than rashly mortgage the freedom kept inviolate so long, or let the impulses of an hour mar the worth of coming years."

Bent and broken by the unanswerable accusations of what seemed a conscience in human shape, Ottila had sunk down before him with an abandonment as native to her as the indomitable will which still refused to relinquish hope even in despair.

"Go," she said, "I am not worthy of salvation. Yet it is hard, very hard, to lose the one motive strong enough to save me, the one sincere affection of my life."

Warwick had expected a tempestuous outbreak at his decision; this entire submission touched him, for in the last words of her brief lament he detected the accent of truth, and longed to answer it. He paused, searching for the just thing to be done. Ottila, with hidden face, watched while she wept, and waited hopefully for the relenting sign. In silence the two, a modern Samson and Delilah, waged the old war that has gone on ever since the strong locks were shorn and the temple fell; a war which fills the world with unmated pairs and the long train of evils arising from marriages made from impulse, and not principle. As usual, the most generous was worsted. The silence pleaded well for Ottila, and when Warwick spoke it was to say impetuously—

"You are right! It is hard that when two err one alone should suffer. I should have been wise enough to see the danger, brave enough to fly from it. I was not, and I owe you some reparation for the pain my folly brings you. I offer you the best, because the hardest, sacrifice that I can make. You say love can work miracles, and that yours is the sincerest affection of your life; prove it. In three months you conquered me; can you conquer yourself in twelve?"

"Try me!"

"I will. Nature takes a year for her harvests; I give you the same for yours. If you will devote one half the energy and care to this work that you devoted to that other,—will earnestly endeavor to cherish all that is womanly and noble in yourself, and through desire for another's respect earn your own,—I, too, will try to make myself a fitter mate for any woman, and keep our troth unbroken for a year. Can I do more?"

"I dared not ask so much! I have not deserved it, but I will. Only love me, Adam, and let me save myself through you."

Flushed and trembling with delight she rose, sure the trial was safely passed, but found that for herself a new one had begun. Warwick offered his hand.

"Farewell, then."

"Going? Surely you will stay and help me through my long probation?"

"No; if your desire has any worth you can work it out alone. We should be hindrances to one another, and the labor be ill done."

"Where will you go? Not far, Adam."

"Straight to the North. This luxurious life enervates me; the pestilence of slavery lurks in the air and infects me; I must build myself up anew and find again the man I was."

"When must you go? Not soon."

"At once."

"I shall hear from you?"

"Not till I come."

"But I shall need encouragement, shall grow hungry for a word, a thought from you. A year is very long to wait and work alone."

Eloquently she pleaded with voice and eyes and tender lips, but Warwick did not yield.

"If the test be tried at all it must be fairly tried. We must stand entirely apart and see what saving virtue lies in self-denial and self-help."

"You will forget me, Adam. Some woman with a calmer heart than mine will teach you to love as you desire to love, and when my work is done it will be all in vain."

"Never in vain if it be well done, for such labor is its own reward. Have no fear; one such lesson will last a lifetime. Do your part heartily, and I will keep my pledge until the year is out."

"And then, what then?"

"If I see in you the progress both should desire, if this tie bears the test of time and absence, and we find any basis for an abiding union, then, Ottila, I will marry you."

"But if meanwhile that colder, calmer woman comes to you, what then?"

"Then I will not marry you."

"Ah, your promise is a man's vow, made only to be broken. I have no faith in you."

"I think you may have. There will be no time for more folly; I must repair the loss of many wasted days,—nay, not wasted if I have learned this lesson well. Rest secure; it is impossible that I should love."

"You believed that three months ago and yet you are a lover now."

Ottila smiled an exultant smile, and Warwick acknowledged his proven fallibility by a haughty flush and a frank amendment.

"Let it stand, then, that if I love again I am to wait in silence till the year is out and you absolve me from my pledge. Does that satisfy you?"

"It must. But you will come, whatever changes may befall you? Promise me this."

"I promise it."

"Going so soon? Oh, wait a little!"

"When a duty is to be done, do it at once; delay is dangerous. Good night."

"Give me some remembrance of you. I have nothing, for you are not a generous lover."

"Generous in deeds, Ottila. I have given you a year's liberty, a dear gift from one who values it more than life. Now I add this."

He drew her to him, kissed the red mouth and looked down upon her with a glance that made his man's face as pitiful as any woman's as he let her lean there happy in the hope given at such cost. For a moment nothing stirred in the room but the soft whisper of the wind. For a moment Warwick's austere life looked hard to him, love seemed sweet, submission possible; for in all the world this was the only woman who clung to him, and it was beautiful to cherish and be cherished after years of solitude. A long sigh of desire and regret broke from him, and at the sound a stealthy smile touched Ottila's lips as she whispered, with a velvet cheek against his own—

"Love, you will stay?"

"I will not stay!"

And like one who cries out sharply within himself, "Get thee behind!" he broke away.

"Adam, come back to me! Come back!"

He looked over his shoulder, saw the fair woman in the heart of the warm glow, heard her cry of love and longing, knew the life of luxurious ease that waited for him, but steadily went out into the night, only answering—

"In a year."

CHAPTER II

WHIMS*

✸✸✸✸✸

"COME, Sylvia, it is nine o'clock! Little slug-a-bed, don't you mean to get up to-day?" said Miss Yule, bustling into her sister's room with the wide-awake appearance of one to whom sleep was a necessary evil, to be endured and gotten over as soon as possible.

"No, why should I?" And Sylvia turned her face away from the flood of light that poured into the room as Prue put aside the curtains and flung up the window.

"Why should you? What a question, unless you are ill; I was afraid you would suffer for that long row yesterday, and my predictions seldom fail."

"I am not suffering from any cause whatever, and your prediction does fail this time; I am only tired of everybody and everything, and see nothing worth getting up for; so I shall just stay here till I do. Please put the curtain down and leave me in peace."

Prue had dropped her voice to the foreboding tone so irritating to nervous persons whether sick or well, and Sylvia laid her arm across her eyes with an impatient gesture as she spoke sharply.

"Nothing worth getting up for," cried Prue, like an aggravating echo. "Why, child, there are a hundred pleasant things to do if you would only think so. Now don't be dismal and mope away this lovely day. Get up and

---

*Chapter II, "Whims," appears with important changes in *M2* as Chapter I, "Sylvia." Selections from it are reprinted in the appendix.

try my plan; have a good breakfast, read the papers, and then work in your garden before it grows too warm; that is wholesome exercise and you've neglected it sadly of late."

"I don't wish any breakfast; I hate newspapers, they are so full of lies; I'm tired of the garden, for nothing goes right this year; and I detest taking exercise merely because it's wholesome. No, I'll not get up for that."

"Then stay in the house and draw, read, or practise. Sit with Mark* in the studio; give Miss Hemming directions about your summer things, or go into town about your bonnet. There is a matinée, try that; or make calls, for you owe fifty at least. Now I'm sure there's employment enough and amusement enough for any reasonable person."

Prue looked triumphant, but Sylvia was not a "reasonable person," and went on in her former despondingly petulant strain.

"I'm tired of drawing; my head is a jumble of other people's ideas already, and Herr Pedalsturm has put the piano out of tune. Mark always makes a model of me if I go to him, and I don't like to see my eyes, arms, or hair in all his pictures. Miss Hemming's gossip is worse than fussing over new things that I don't need. Bonnets are my torment, and matinées are wearisome, for people whisper and flirt till the music is spoiled. Making calls is the worst of all; for what pleasure or profit is there in running from place to place to tell the same polite fibs over and over again, and listen to scandal that makes you pity or despise your neighbors. I shall not get up for any of these things."

Prue leaned on the bedpost meditating with an anxious face till a forlorn hope appeared which caused her to exclaim—

"Mark and I are going to see Geoffrey Moor, this morning, just home from Switzerland, where his poor sister died, you know. You really ought to come with us and welcome him, for though you can hardly remember him, he's been so long away, still, as one of the family, it is a proper compliment on your part. The drive will do you good, Geoffrey will be glad to see you, it is a lovely old place, and as you never saw the inside of the house you cannot complain that you are tired of that yet."

"Yes I can, for it will never seem as it has done, and I can no longer go where I please now that a master's presence spoils its freedom and solitude for me. I don't know him, and don't care to, though his name is so familiar. New people always disappoint me, especially if I've heard them praised

---

* Sylvia's brother, Mark Yule, becomes Max Yule in *M2*.

16

ever since I was born. I shall not get up for any Geoffrey Moor, so that bait fails."

Sylvia smiled involuntarily at her sister's defeat, but Prue fell back upon her last resource in times like this. With a determined gesture she plunged her hand into an abysmal pocket, and from a miscellaneous collection of treasures selected a tiny vial, presenting it to Sylvia with a half pleading, half authoritative look and tone.

"I'll leave you in peace if you'll only take a dose of chamomilla.[1] It is so soothing, that instead of tiring yourself with all manner of fancies, you'll drop into a quiet sleep, and by noon be ready to get up like a civilized being. Do take it, dear; just four sugar-plums, and I'm satisfied."

Sylvia received the bottle with a docile expression; but the next minute it flew out of the window, to be shivered on the walk below, while she said, laughing like a wilful creature as she was—

"I have taken it in the only way I ever shall, and the sparrows can try its soothing effects with me; so be satisfied."

"Very well. I shall send for Dr. Baum, for I'm convinced that you are going to be ill. I shall say no more, but act as I think proper, because it's like talking to the wind to reason with you in one of these perverse fits."

As Prue turned away, Sylvia frowned and called after her—

"Spare yourself the trouble, for Dr. Baum will follow the chamomilla, if you bring him here. What does he know about health, a fat German, looking lager beer and talking sauer-kraut? Bring me *bona fide* sugar-plums and I'll take them; but arsenic, mercury, and nightshade are not to my taste."[2]

"Would you feel insulted if I ask whether your breakfast is to be sent up, or kept waiting till you choose to come down?"

Prue looked rigidly calm, but Sylvia knew that she felt hurt, and with one of the sudden impulses which ruled her the frown melted to a smile, as drawing her sister down she kissed her in her most loving manner.

"Dear old soul, I'll be good by-and-by, but now I'm tired and cross, so let me keep out of every one's way and drowse myself into a cheerier frame of mind. I want nothing but solitude, a draught of water, and a kiss."

Prue was mollified at once, and, after stirring fussily about for several minutes gave her sister all she asked and departed to the myriad small cares that made her happiness. As the door closed, Sylvia sighed a long sigh of relief, and folding her arms under her head drifted away into the land of dreams, where ennui is unknown.

All the long summer morning she lay wrapt in sleeping and waking dreams, forgetful of the world about her, till her brother played the Wedding March upon her door on his way to lunch. The desire to avenge the sudden downfall of a lovely castle in the air roused Sylvia, and sent her down to skirmish with Mark. Before she could say a word, however, Prue began to talk in a steady stream, for the good soul had a habit of jumbling news, gossip, private opinions and public affairs into a colloquial hodge-podge, that was often as trying to the intellects as the risibles of her hearers.

"Sylvia, we had a charming call, and Geoffrey sent his love to you. I asked him over to dinner, and we shall dine at six, because then my father can be with us. I shall have to go to town first, for there are a dozen things suffering for attention. You can't wear a round hat and lawn jackets without a particle of set all summer. I want some things for dinner,—and the carpet must be got. What a lovely one Geoffrey had in the library! Then I must see if poor Mrs. Beck has had her leg comfortably off, find out if Freddy Lennox is dead, and order home the mosquito nettings. Now don't read all the afternoon, and be ready to receive any one who may come if I should get belated."

The necessity of disposing of a suspended mouthful produced a lull, and Sylvia seized the moment to ask in a careless way, intended to bring her brother out upon his favorite topic,—

"How did you find your saint, Mark?"

"The same sunshiny soul as ever, though he has had enough to make him old and grave before his time. He is just what we need in our neighborhood, and particularly in our house, for we are a dismal set at times, and he will do us all a world of good."

"What will become of me, with a pious, prosy, perfect creature eternally haunting the house and exhorting me on the error of my ways!" cried Sylvia.

"Don't disturb yourself; he is not likely to take much notice of you; and it is not for an indolent, freakish midge to scoff at a man whom she does not know, and couldn't appreciate if she did," was Mark's lofty reply.

"I rather liked the appearance of the saint, however," said Sylvia, with an expression of naughty malice, as she began her lunch.

"Why, where did you see him!" exclaimed her brother.

"I went over there yesterday to take a farewell run in the neglected garden before he came. I knew he was expected, but not that he was here; and when I saw the house open, I slipped in and peeped wherever I liked. You are right, Prue; it is a lovely old place."

"Now I know you did something dreadfully unladylike and improper. Put me out of suspense. I beg of you."

Prue's distressful face and Mark's surprise produced an inspiring effect upon Sylvia, who continued, with an air of demure satisfaction—

"I strolled about, enjoying myself, till I got into the library, and there I rummaged, for it was a charming place, and I was happy as only those are who love books, and feel their influence in the silence of a room whose finest ornaments they are."

"I hope Moor came in and found you trespassing."

"No, I went out and caught him playing. When I'd stayed as long as I dared, and borrowed a very interesting old book— *

"Sylvia! did you really take one without asking?" cried Prue, looking almost as much alarmed as if she had stolen the spoons.

"Yes; why not? I can apologize prettily, and it will open the way for more. I intend to browse over that library for the next six months."

"But it was such a liberty,—so rude, so—dear, dear; and he as fond and careful of his books as if they were his children! Well, I wash my hands of it, and am prepared for anything now!"

Mark enjoyed Sylvia's pranks too much to reprove, so he only laughed while one sister lamented and the other placidly went on—

When I had put the book nicely in my pocket, Prue, I walked into the garden. But before I'd picked a single flower, I heard little Tilly laugh behind the hedge and some strange voice talking to her. So I hopped upon a roller to see, and nearly tumbled off again; for there was a man lying on the grass, with the gardener's children rioting over him. Will was picking his pockets, and Tilly eating strawberries out of his hat, often thrusting one into the mouth of her long neighbor, who always smiled when the little hand came fumbling at his lips. You ought to have seen the pretty picture, Mark."

"Did he see the interesting picture on your side of the wall."

"No, I was just thinking what friendly eyes he had, listening to his pleasant talk with the little folks, and watching how they nestled to him as if he were a girl, when Tilly looked up and cried, 'I see Silver!' So I ran away, expecting to have them all come racing after. But no one appeared, and I only heard a laugh instead of the 'stop thief' that I deserved."

"If I had time I should convince you of the impropriety of such wild

---

* very interesting book *M2* (27)

actions; as I haven't, I can only implore you never to do so again on Geoffrey's premises," said Prue, rising as the carriage drove round.

"I can safely promise that," answered Sylvia, with a dismal shake of the head, as she leaned listlessly from the window till her brother and sister were gone.

At the appointed time Moor entered Mr. Yule's hospitably open door; but no one came to meet him, and the house was as silent as if nothing human inhabited it. He divined the cause of this, having met Prue and Mark going townward some hours before, and saying to himself, "The boat is late," he disturbed no one, but strolled into the drawing-rooms and looked about him. Being one of those who seldom find time heavy on their hands, he amused himself with observing what changes had been made during his absence. His journey round the apartments was not a long one, for, coming to an open window, he paused with an expression of mingled wonder and amusement.

A pile of cushions, pulled from chair and sofa, lay before the lone window, looking very like a newly deserted nest. A warm-hued picture lifted from the wall stood in a streak of sunshine; a half-cleared leaf of fruit lay on a taboret, and beside it, with a red stain on its title-page, appeared the stolen book. At sight of this Moor frowned, caught up his desecrated darling and put it in his pocket. But as he took another glance at the various indications of what had evidently been a solitary revel very much after his own heart, he relented, laid back the book, and, putting aside the curtain floating in the wind, looked out into the garden, attracted thither by the sound of a spade.

*A lad was at work near by, and wondering what new inmate the house had gained, the neglected guest waited to catch a glimpse of the unknown face. A slender boy, in a foreign-looking blouse of grey linen; a white collar lay over a ribbon at the throat, stout half boots covered a trim pair of feet, and a broad-brimmed hat flapped low on the forehead. Whistling softly he dug with active gestures; and, having made the necessary cavity, set a shrub, filled up the hole, trod it down scientifically, and then fell back to survey the success of his labors. But something was amiss, something had been forgotten, for suddenly up came the shrub, and seizing a wheelbarrow that stood near by, away rattled the boy round the corner

---

*The "lad" at work here becomes a girl in *M2*. The passage "A lad . . . play is done!" is replaced by two new paragraphs, reprinted in the appendix (18–19).

out of sight. Moor smiled at his impetuosity, and awaited his return with interest, suspecting from appearances that this was some *protégé* of Mark's employed as a model as well as gardener's boy.

Presently up the path came the lad, with head down and steady pace, trundling a barrow full of richer earth, surmounted by a watering-pot. Never stopping for breath he fell to work again, enlarged the hole, flung in the loam, poured in the water, reset the shrub, and when the last stamp and pat were given performed a little dance of triumph about it, at the close of which he pulled off his hat and began to fan his heated face. The action caused the observer to start and look again, thinking, as he recognized the energetic worker with a smile, "What a changeful thing it is! haunting one's premises unseen, and stealing one's books unsuspected; dreaming one half the day and masquerading the other half. What will happen next? Let us see but not be seen, lest the boy turn shy and run away before the pretty play is done!"

Holding the curtain between the window and himself, Moor peeped through the semi-transparent screen, enjoying the little episode immensely. Sylvia fanned and rested a few minutes, then went up and down among the flowers, often pausing to break a dead leaf, to brush away some harmful insect, or lift some struggling plant into the light; moving among them as if akin to them, and cognizant of their sweet wants. If she had seemed strong-armed and sturdy as a boy before, now she was tender fingered as a woman, and went humming here and there like any happy-hearted bee.

"Curious child!" thought Moor, watching the sunshine glitter on her uncovered head, and listening to the air she left half sung. "I've a great desire to step out and see how she will receive me. Not like any other girl, I fancy."

But, before he could execute his design, the roll of a carriage was heard in the avenue, and pausing an instant, with head erect like a startled doe, Sylvia turned and vanished, dropping flowers as she ran. Mr. Yule, accompanied by his son and daughter, came hurrying in with greetings, explanations, and apologies, and in a moment the house was full of a pleasant stir. Steps went up and down, voices echoed through the rooms, savory odors burst forth from below, and doors swung in the wind, as if the spell was broken and the sleeping palace had wakened with a word.

Prue made a hasty toilet and harassed the cook to the verge of spontaneous combustion, while Mark and his father devoted themselves to their guest. Just as dinner was announced Sylvia came in, as calm and cool as if wheelbarrows were myths and linen suits unknown. Moor was welcomed with a quiet hand-shake, a grave salutation, and a look that seemed to say, "Wait a little, I take no friends on trust."*

All through dinner, though she sat as silent as a well-bred child, she looked and listened with an expression of keen intelligence that children do not wear, and sometimes smiled to herself, as if she saw or heard something that pleased and interested her. When they rose from table she followed Prue up stairs, quite forgetting the disarray in which the drawing-room was left. The gentlemen took possession before either sister returned, and Mark's annoyance found vent in a philippic against oddities in general and Sylvia in particular; but his father and friend sat in the cushionless chairs, and pronounced the scene amusingly novel. Prue appeared in the midst of the laugh, and having discovered other delinquencies above, her patience was exhausted, and her regrets found no check in the presence of so old a friend as Moor.

"Something must be done about the child, father, for she is getting entirely beyond my control. If I attempt to make her study she writes poetry instead of her exercises, draws caricatures instead of sketching properly, and bewilders her music teacher by asking questions about Beethoven and Mendelssohn, as if they were personal friends of his. If I beg her to take exercise, she rides like an Amazon all over the Island, grubs in the garden as if for her living, or goes paddling about the bay till I'm distracted lest the tide should carry her out to sea. She is so wanting in moderation she gets ill, and when I give her proper medicines she flings them out of the window, and threatens to send that worthy, Dr. Baum, after them. Yet she must need something to set her right, for she is either overflowing with unnatural spirits or melancholy enough to break one's heart."

"What have you done with the little black sheep of my flock,—not banished her, I hope?" said Mr. Yule, placidly, ignoring all complaints.

"She is in the garden, attending to some of her disagreeable pets, I fancy. If you are going out there to smoke, please send her in, Mark; I want her."

As Mr. Yule was evidently yearning for his after-dinner nap, and Mark for his cigar, Moor followed his friend, and they stepped through the window into the garden, now lovely with the fading glow of summer sunset.

---

*In *M2* Alcott inserts here a one-paragraph description of Sylvia through the eyes of Geoffrey Moor, reprinted in the appendix (20–21).

Whims

"You must know that this peculiar little sister of mine clings to some of her childish beliefs and pleasures in spite of Prue's preaching and my raillery," began Mark, after a refreshing whiff or two. "She is overflowing with love and good will, but being too shy or too proud to offer it to her fellow-creatures, she expends it upon the necessitous inhabitants of earth, air, and water with the most charming philanthropy. Her dependents are neither beautiful nor very interesting, nor is she sentimentally enamored of them; but the more ugly and desolate the creature, the more devoted is she. Look at her now; most young ladies would have hysterics over any one of those pets of hers."

Moor looked, and thought the group a very pretty one, though a plump toad sat at Sylvia's feet, a roly-poly caterpillar was walking up her sleeve, a blind bird chirped on her shoulder, bees buzzed harmlessly about her head, as if they mistook her for a flower, and in her hand a little field mouse was breathing its short life away. Any tender-hearted girl might have stood thus surrounded by helpless things that pity had endeared, but few would have regarded them with an expression like that which Sylvia wore. Figure, posture, and employment were so childlike in their innocent unconsciousness, that the contrast was all the more strongly marked between them and the sweet thoughtfulness that made her face singularly attractive with the charm of dawning womanhood. Moor spoke before Mark could dispose of his smoke.

"This is a great improvement upon the boudoir full of lap-dogs, worsted-work and novels, Miss Sylvia. May I ask if you feel no repugnance to some of your patients; or is your charity strong enough to beautify them all?"

"I dislike many people, but few animals, because however ugly I pity them, and whatever I pity I am sure to love. It may be silly, but I think it does me good; and till I am wise enough to help my fellow-beings, I try to do my duty to these humbler sufferers, and find them both grateful and affectionate."

There was something very winning in the girl's manner as she spoke, touching the little creature in her hand almost as tenderly as if it had been a child. It showed the newcomer another phase of this many-sided character; and while Sylvia related the histories of her pets at his request, he was enjoying that finer history which every ingenuous soul writes on its owner's countenance for gifted eyes to read and love. As she passed, the little mouse lay stark and still in her gentle hand; and though they smiled at themselves, both young men felt like boys again as they helped her scoop a grave among the pansies, owning the beauty of compassion, though she showed it to them in such a simple shape.

Then Mark delivered his message, and Sylvia went away to receive Prue's lecture, with outward meekness, but such an absent mind that the words of wisdom went by her like the wind.

"Now come and take our twilight stroll, while Mark keeps Mr. Moor in the studio and Prue prepares another exhortation," said Sylvia, as her father woke, and taking his arm, they paced along the wide piazza that encircled the whole house.

"Will father do me a little favor?"

"That is all he lives for, dear."

"Then his life is a very successful one;" and the girl folded her other hand over that already on his arm. Mr. Yule shook his head with a regretful sigh, but asked benignly—

"What shall I do for my little daughter?"

"Forbid Mark to execute a plot with which he threatens me. He says he will bring every gentleman he knows (and that is a great many) to the house, and make it so agreeable that they will keep coming; for he insists that I need amusement, and nothing will be so entertaining as a lover or two. Please tell him not to, for I don't want any lovers yet."

"Why not?" asked her father, much amused at her twilight confidences.

"I'm afraid. Love is so cruel to some people, I feel as if it would be to me, for I am always in extremes, and continually going wrong while trying to go right. Love bewilders the wisest, and it would make me quite blind or mad, I know; therefore I'd rather have nothing to do with it, for a long, long while."

"Then Mark shall be forbidden to bring a single specimen. I very much prefer to keep you as you are. And yet you may be happier to do as others do; try it, if you like, my dear."

"But I can't do as others do; I've tried, and failed. Last winter, when Prue made me go about, though people probably thought me a stupid little thing, moping in corners, I was enjoying myself in my own way, and making discoveries that have been very useful ever since. I know I'm whimsical, and hard to please, and have no doubt the fault was in myself, but I was disappointed in nearly every one I met, though I went into what Prue calls 'our best society.' The girls seemed all made on the same pattern; they all said, did, thought, and wore about the same things, and knowing one was as good as knowing a dozen. Jessie Hope was the only one I cared much for, and she is so pretty, she seems made to be looked at and loved."

"How did you find the young gentlemen, Sylvia?"

"Still worse; for, though lively enough among them selves, they never found it worth their while to offer us any conversation but such as was very like the champagne and ice-cream they brought us,—sparkling, sweet, and unsubstantial. Almost all of them wore the superior air they put on before women, an air that says as plainly as words, 'I may ask you and I may not.' Now that is very exasperating to those who care no more for them than so many grasshoppers, and I often longed to take the conceit out of them by telling some of the criticisms passed upon them by the amiable young ladies who looked as if waiting to say meekly, 'Yes, thank you.'"

"Don't excite yourself, my dear; it is all very lamentable and laughable, but we must submit till the world learns better. There are often excellent young persons among the 'grasshoppers,' and if you cared to look you might find a pleasant friend here and there," said Mr. Yule, leaning a little toward his son's view of the matter.

"No, I cannot even do that without being laughed at; for no sooner do I mention the word friendship than people nod wisely and look as if they said, 'Oh, yes, every one knows what that sort of thing amounts to.' I should like a friend, father; some one beyond home, because he would be newer; a man (old or young, I don't care which), because men go where they like, see things with their own eyes, and have more to tell if they choose. I want a person simple, wise, and entertaining; and I think I should make a very grateful friend if such an one was kind enough to like me."

"I think you would, and perhaps if you try to be more like others you will find friends as they do, and so be happy, Sylvia."

"I cannot be like others, and their friendships would not satisfy me. I don't try to be odd; I long to be quiet and satisfied, but I cannot; and when I do what Prue calls wild things, it is not because I am thoughtless or idle, but because I am trying to be good and happy. The old ways fail, so I attempt new ones, hoping they will succeed; but they don't, and I still go looking and longing for happiness, yet always failing to find it, till sometimes I think I am a born disappointment."

"Perhaps love would bring the happiness, my dear?"

"I'm afraid not; but, however that may be, I shall never go running about for a lover as half my mates do. When the true one comes I shall know him, love him at once, and cling to him forever, no matter what may

25

happen. Till then I want a friend, and I will find one if I can. Don't you believe there may be real and simple friendships between men and women without falling into this everlasting sea of love?"

Mr. Yule was laughing quietly under cover of the darkness, but composed himself to answer gravely—

"Yes, for some of the most beautiful and famous friendships have been such, and I see no reason why there may not be again. Look about, Sylvia, make yourself happy; and, whether you find friend or lover, remember there is always the old Papa glad to do his best for you in both capacities."

Sylvia's hand crept to her father's shoulder, and her voice was full of daughterly affection, as she said—

"I'll have no lover but 'the old Papa' for a long while yet. But I will look about, and if I am fortunate enough to find and good enough to keep the person I want, I shall be very happy; for, father, I really think I need a friend."

Here Mark called his sister in to sing to them, a demand that would have been refused but for a promise to Prue to behave her best as an atonement for past pranks. Stepping in she sat down and gave Moor another surprise, as from her slender throat there came a voice whose power and pathos made a tragedy of the simple ballad she was singing.

"Why did you choose that plaintive thing, all about love, despair, and death? It quite breaks one's heart to hear it," said Prue, pausing in a mental estimate of her morning's shopping.

"It came into my head, and so I sung it. Now I'll try another, for I am bound to please you—if I can." And she broke out again with an airy melody as jubilant as if a lark had mistaken moonlight for the dawn and soared skyward, singing as it went. So blithe and beautiful were both voice and song they caused a sigh of pleasure, a sensation of keen delight in the listener, and seemed to gift the singer with an unsuspected charm. As she ended Sylvia turned about, and seeing the satisfaction of their guest in his face, prevented him from expressing it in words by saying, in her frank way—

"Never mind the compliments. I know my voice is good, for that you may thank nature; that it is well trained, for that praise Herr Pedalsturm; and that you have heard it at all, you owe to my desire to atone for certain trespasses of yesterday and to-day, because I seldom sing before strangers." [3]

"Allow me to offer my hearty thanks to Nature, Pedalsturm, and

Penitence, and also to hope that in time I may be regarded, not as a stranger, but a neighbor and a friend."

Something in the gentle emphasis of the last word struck pleasantly on the girl's ear, and seemed to answer an unspoken longing. She looked up at him with a searching glance, appeared to find some 'assurance given by looks,' and as a smile broke out over her face she offered her hand as if obeying a sudden impulse, and said, half to him, half to herself—

"I think I have found the friend already."

CHAPTER III

AFLOAT*

SYLVIA sat sewing in the sunshine with an expression on her face half mirthful, half melancholy, as she looked backward to the girlhood just ended, and forward to the womanhood just beginning, for on that midsummer day, she was eighteen. Voices roused her from her reverie, and, looking up, she saw her brother approaching with two friends, their neighbor Geoffrey Moor and his guest Adam Warwick. Her first impulse was to throw down her work and run to meet them, her second to remember her new dignity and sit still, awaiting them with well-bred composure, quite unconscious that the white figure among the vines added a picturesque finish to the quiet summer scene.

They came up warm and merry, with a brisk row across the bay, and Sylvia met them with a countenance that gave a heartier welcome than her words, as she greeted the neighbor cordially, the stranger courteously, and began to gather up her work when they seated themselves in the bamboo chairs scattered about the wide piazza.

"You need not disturb yourself," said Mark, "we are only making this

---

* "Afloat" appears in revised form as Chapter V in *M2;* it is preceded by Chapter IV, "Warwick," parts of which are reprinted in the appendix (50–58, 63–67). Alcott replaced the first paragraph of "Afloat" with a longer passage and made several changes in the second paragraph (see the appendix, 69–70). The two versions then continue in almost identical fashion for several pages.

A new chapter, "Moor," was added by Alcott as Chpater II of *M2;* it is reprinted in the appendix (31–42).

28

a way-station, *en route* for the studio. Can you tell me where my knapsack is to be found? after one of Prue's stowages, nothing short of a divining-rod will discover it, I'm afraid."

"I know where it is. Are you going away again so soon, Mark?"

"Only a two days' trip up the river with these mates of mine. No, Sylvia, it can't be done."

"I did not say anything."

"Not in words, but you looked a whole volley of 'Can't I goes?' and I answered it. No girl but you would dream of such a thing; you hate picnics, and as this will be a long and rough one, don't you see how absurd it would be for you to try it?"

"I don't quite see it, Mark, for this would not be an ordinary picnic; it would be like a little romance to me, and I had rather have it than any birthday present you could give me. We used to have such happy times together before we were grown up, I don't like to be so separated now. But if it is not best, I'm sorry that I even looked a wish."

Sylvia tried to keep both disappointment and desire out of her voice as she spoke, though a most intense longing had taken possession of her when she heard of a projected pleasure so entirely after her own heart. But there was an unconscious reproach in her last words a mute appeal in the wistful eyes that looked across the glittering bay to the green hills beyond. Now, Mark was both fond and proud of the young sister, who, while he was studying art abroad, had studied nature at home, till the wayward but winning child had bloomed into a most attractive girl. He remembered her devotion to him, his late neglect of her, and longed to make atonement. With elevated eyebrows and inquiring glances, he turned from one friend to another. Moor nodded and smiled, Warwick nodded and sighed privately, and having taken the sense of the meeting by a new style of vote, Mark suddenly announced—

"You can go if you like, Sylvia."*

"What!" cried his sister, starting up with a characteristic impetuosity

---

*The passage "Moor nodded . . . if you like, Sylvia." was reworked by Alcott to read in *M2*:

> "Why not?" asked Moor, with a smile of pleasure.
>
> "By all means," said Warwick, with a decided nod.
>
> Being satisfied on that point, though still very doubtful of the propriety of the step, Max relented, saying suddenly,—
>
> "You can go, Sylvia." (71)

that sent her basket tumbling down the steps, and crowned her dozing cat with Prue's nightcap frills. "Do you mean it, Mark? Wouldn't it spoil your pleasure, Mr. Moor? Shouldn't I be a trouble, Mr. Warwick? Tell me frankly, for if I can go I shall be happier than I can express."

The gentlemen smiled at her eagerness, but as they saw the altered face she turned toward them, each felt already repaid for any loss of freedom they might experience hereafter, and gave unanimous consent. Upon receipt of which Sylvia felt inclined to dance about the three and bless them audibly, but restrained herself, and beamed upon them in a state of wordless gratitude pleasant to behold. Having given a rash consent, Mark now thought best to offer a few obstacles to enhance its value and try his sister's mettle.

"Don't ascend into the air like a young balloon, child, but hear the conditions upon which you go, for if you fail to work three miracles it is all over with you. Firstly, the consent of the higher powers, for father will dread all sorts of dangers you are such a freakish creature, and Prue will be scandalized because trips like this are not the fashion for young ladies." [1]

*"Consider that point settled and go on to the next," said Sylvia, who, having ruled the house ever since she was born, had no fears of success with her father or sister.

"Secondly, you must do yourself up in as compact a parcel as possible; for though you little women are very ornamental on land, you are not very convenenient for transportation by water. Cambric gowns and French slippers are highly appropriate and agreeable at the present moment, but must be sacrificed to the stern necessities of the case. You must make a dowdy of yourself in some usefully short, scant, dingy costume, which will try the nerves of all beholders, and triumphantly prove that women were never meant for such excursions."

"Wait five minutes and I'll triumphantly prove to the contrary," answered Sylvia, as she ran into the house.

---

*Here Alcott adds the following to Sylvia's reply in *M2:*

"I beg your pardon, but they are. I went with a party of young people last year and camped out for a week. All were brothers and sisters or cousins, and we had a lovely time. Papa likes me to be happy, and Prue won't mind, as you are all so much older than I am, and two of you like brothers to me." (72)

Her five minutes was sufficiently elastic to cover fifteen, for she was ravaging her wardrobe to effect her purpose and convince her brother, whose artistic tastes she consulted, with a skill that did her good service in the end. Rapidly assuming a gray gown, with a jaunty jacket of the same, she kilted the skirt over one of green, the pedestrian length of which displayed boots of uncompromising thickness. Over her shoulder, by a broad ribbon, she slung a prettily wrought pouch, and ornamented her hat pilgrimwise with a cockle shell. Then taking her brother's alpenstock she crept down, and standing in the door-way presented a little figure all in gray and green, like the earth she was going to wander over, and a face that blushed and smiled and shone as she asked demurely—

"Please, Mark, am I picturesque and convenient enough to go?"

He wheeled about and stared approvingly, forgetting cause in effect till Warwick began to laugh like a merry bass viol, and Moor joined him, saying—

"Come, Mark, own that you are conquered, and let us turn our commonplace voyage into a pleasure pilgrimage, with a lively lady to keep us knights and gentlemen wherever we are."

"I say no more; only remember, Sylvia, if you get burnt, drowned, or blown away, I'm not responsible for the damage, and shall have the satisfaction of saying, 'There, I told you so.'"

"That satisfaction may be mine when I come home quite safe and well," replied Sylvia, serenely. "Now for the last condition."

Warwick looked with interest from the sister to the brother; for, being a solitary man, domestic scenes and relations possessed the charm of novelty to him.

"Thirdly, you are not to carry a boat-load of luggage, cloaks, pillows, silver forks, or a dozen napkins, but are to fare as we fare, sleeping in hammocks, barns, or on the bare ground, without shrieking at bats or bewailing the want of mosquito netting; eating when, where, and what is most convenient, and facing all kinds of weather regardless of complexion, dishevelment, and fatigue. If you can promise all this, be here loaded and ready to go off at six o'clock to-morrow morning."

After which cheerful picture of the joys to come, Mark marched away to his studio, taking his friends with him.

Sylvia worked the three miracles, and at half past-five, A.M. was discovered sitting on the piazza, with her hammock rolled into a twine sausage at her feet, her hat firmly tied on, her scrip packed, and her staff in her hand. "Waiting till called for," she said, as her brother passed her, late and yawning as usual. As the clock struck six the carriage drove round, and Moor and Warwick came up the avenue in nautical array. Then arose a delightful clamor of voices, slamming of doors, hurrying of feet and frequent peals of laughter; for every one was in holiday spirits, and the morning seemed made for pleasuring.

Mr. Yule regarded the voyagers with an aspect as benign as the summer sky overhead; Prue ran to and fro pouring forth a stream of counsels, warnings, and predictions; men and maids gathered on the lawn or hung out of upper windows; and even old Hecate, the cat, was seen chasing imaginary rats and mice in the grass till her yellow eyes glared with excitement. "All in," was announced at last, and as the carriage rolled away its occupants looked at one another with faces of blithe satisfaction that their pilgrimage was so auspiciously begun.

A mile or more up the river the large, newly-painted boat awaited them. The embarkation was a speedy one, for the cargo was soon stowed in lockers and under seats, Sylvia forwarded to her place in the bow; Mark, as commander of the craft, took the helm; Moor and Warwick, as crew, sat waiting orders; and Hugh, the coachman, stood ready to push off at word of command. Presently it came, a strong hand sent them rustling through the flags, down dropped the uplifted oars, and with a farewell cheer from a group upon the shore the Kelpie glided out into the stream.

Sylvia, too full of genuine content to talk, sat listening to the musical dip of well-pulled oars, watching the green banks on either side, dabbling her hands in the eddies as they rippled by, and singing to the wind, as cheerful and serene as the river that gave her back a smiling image of herself. What her companions talked of she neither heard nor cared to know, for she was looking at the great picturebook that always lies ready for the turning of the youngest or the oldest hands; was receiving the welcome of the playmates she best loved, and was silently yielding herself to the power which works all wonders with its benignant magic. Hour after hour she journeyed along that fluent road. Under bridges where early fishers lifted up their lines to let them through; past gardens tilled by unskilful townsmen who harvested an hour of strength to pay the daily tax the city levied on them; past honeymoon cottages where young wives walked with young husbands in the dew, or great houses shut against the morning. Lovers came floating down the stream with masterless rudder and trailing oars. College race-boats shot by with modern Greek choruses in full blast and the frankest criticisms from their scientific crews. Fathers went rowing to and fro with argosies of pretty children, who gave them gay good morrows. Sometimes they met fanciful nutshells manned by merry girls, who made for shore at sight of them with most erratic movements and novel commands included in their Art of Navigation. Now and then some poet or philosopher went musing by, fishing for facts or fictions, where other men catch pickerel or perch.

All manner of sights and sounds greeted Sylvia, and she felt as if she were watching a Panorama painted in water colors by an artist who had breathed into his work the breath of life and given each figure power to play its part. Never had human faces looked so lovely to her eye, for morning beautified the plainest with its ruddy kiss; never had human voices sounded so musical to her ear, for daily cares had not yet brought discord to the instruments tuned by sleep and touched by sunshine into pleasant sound; never had the whole race seemed so near and dear to her, for she was unconsciously pledging all she met in that genuine Elixir Vitae[2] which sets the coldest blood aglow and makes the whole world kin; never had she felt so truly her happiest self, for of all the costlier pleasures she had known not one had been so congenial as this, as she rippled farther and farther up the stream and seemed to float into a world whose airs brought only health and peace. Her comrades wisely left her to her thoughts, a smiling Silence for their figure-head, and none among them but found the day fairer and felt himself fitter to enjoy it for the innocent companionship of maidenhood and a happy heart.

At noon they dropped anchor under a wide-spreading oak that stood on the river's edge, a green tent for wanderers like themselves; there they ate their first meal spread among white clovers, with a pair of squirrels staring at them as curiously as human spectators ever watched royalty at dinner, while several meek cows courteously left their guests the shade and went away to dine at a side-table spread in the sun. They spent an hour or two talking or drowsing luxuriously on the grass; then the springing up of a fresh breeze roused them all, and weighing anchor they set sail for another port.

Now Sylvia saw new pictures, for, leaving all traces of the city behind them, they went swiftly countryward. Sometimes by hayfields, each an idyl in itself, with white-sleeved mowers all arow; the pleasant sound of whetted scythes; great loads rumbling up lanes, with brown-faced children shouting atop; rosy girls raising fragrant winrows or bringing water for thirsty sweethearts leaning on their rakes. Often they saw ancient farm-houses with mossy roofs, and long well-sweeps suggestive of fresh draughts, and the drip of brimming pitchers; orchards and cornfields rus-tling on either hand, and grandmotherly caps at the narrow windows, or stout matrons tending babies in the doorway as they watched smaller selves playing keep house under the "laylocks" by the wall. Villages, like white flocks, slept on the hillsides; martinbox schoolhouses appeared here and there, astir with busy voices, alive with wistful eyes; and more than once they came upon little mermen bathing, who dived with sudden splashes, like a squad of turtles tumbling off a sunny rock.

Then they went floating under vernal arches, where a murmurous rustle seemed to whisper, "Stay!" along shadowless sweeps, where the blue turned to gold and dazzled with its unsteady shimmer; passed islands so full of birds they seemed green cages floating in the sun, or doubled capes that opened long vistas of light and shade, through which they sailed into the pleasant land where summer reigned supreme. To Sylvia it seemed as if the inhabitants of these solitudes had flocked down to the shore to greet her as she came. Fleets of lilies unfurled their sails on either hand, and cardinal flowers waved their scarlet flags among the green. The sagitaria* lifted its blue spears from arrowy leaves; wild roses smiled at her with blooming faces; meadow lilies rang their flame-colored bells; and clematis and ivy hung garlands everywhere; as if hers were a floral progress, and each came to do her honor.

Her neighbors kept up a flow of conversation as steady as the river's, and Sylvia listened now. Insensibly the changeful scenes before them re-called others, and in the friendly atmosphere that surrounded them these reminiscences found free expression. Each of the three had been fortunate in seeing much of foreign life; each had seen a different phase of it, and all were young enough to be still enthusiastic, accomplished enough to serve up their recollections with taste and skill, and give Sylvia glimpses of the world through spectacles sufficiently rose-colored to lend it the warmth which even Truth allows to her sister Romance.

The wind served them till sunset, then the sail was lowered and the rowers took to their oars. Sylvia demanded her turn, and wrestled with one big oar while Warwick sat behind and did the work. Having blistered her hands and given herself as fine a color as any on her brother's palette,

---

*pontederia *M2*

she professed herself satisfied, and went back to her seat to watch the evening-red transfigure earth and sky, making the river and its banks a more royal pageant than splendor-loving Elizabeth ever saw along the Thames.[3]

Anxious to reach a certain point, they rowed on into the twilight, growing stiller and stiller as the deepening hush seemed to hint that Nature was at her prayers. Slowly the Kelpie floated along the shadowy way, and as the shores grew dim, the river dark with leaning hemlocks or an overhanging cliff, Sylvia felt as if she were making the last voyage across that fathomless stream where a pale boatman plies and many go lamenting.

The long silence was broken first by Moor's voice, saying—

"Adam, sing."

If the influences of the hour had calmed Mark, touched Sylvia, and made Moor long for music, they had also softened Warwick. Leaning on his oar he lent the music of a mellow voice to the words of a German Volkslied, and launched a fleet of echoes such as any tuneful vintager might have sent floating down the Rhine. Sylvia was no weeper, but as she listened, all the day's happiness which had been pent up in her heart found vent in sudden tears, that streamed down noiseless and refreshing as a warm south rain. Why they came she could not tell, for neither song nor singer possessed the power to win so rare a tribute, and at another time, she would have restrained all visible expression of this indefinable yet sweet emotion. Mark and Moor had joined in the burden of the song, and when that was done took up another; but Sylvia only sat and let her tears flow while they would, singing at heart, though her eyes were full and her cheeks wet faster than the wind could kiss them dry.

After frequent peerings and tackings here and there, Mark at last discovered the haven he desired, and with much rattling of oars, clanking of chains, and splashing of impetuous boots, a landing was effected, and Sylvia found herself standing on a green bank with her hammock in her arms and much wonderment in her mind whether the nocturnal experiences in store for her would prove as agreeable as daylight ones had been. Mark and Moor unloaded the boat and prospected for an eligible sleeping-place. Warwick, being an old campaigner, set about building a fire, and the girl began her sylvan housekeeping. The scene rapidly brightened into light and color as the blaze sprang up, showing the little kettle slung gipsywise on forked sticks, and the supper prettily set forth in a leafy table-service on a smooth, flat stone. Soon four pairs of wet feet surrounded the fire; an agreeable oblivion of *meum* and *tuum* concerning plates, knives, and cups did away with etiquette, and every one was in a comfortable state of weariness, which rendered the thought of bed so pleasant that they deferred their enjoyment of the reality, as children keep the best bite till the last.*

"What are you thinking of here all by yourself?" asked Mark, coming to lounge on his sister's plaid, which she had spread somewhat apart from the others, and where she sat watching the group before her with a dreamy aspect.†

"I was watching your two friends. See what a fine study they make with the red flicker of the fire on their faces and the background of dark pines behind them."

They did make a fine study, for both were goodly men yet utterly unlike, one being of the heroic type, the other of the poetic. Warwick was a head taller than his tall friend, broad-shouldered, strong-limbed, and bronzed by wind and weather. A massive head, covered with rings of ruddy brown hair; gray eyes, that seemed to pierce through all disguises, an eminent nose, and a beard like one of Mark's stout saints. Power, intellect, and courage were stamped on face and figure, making him the manliest man that Sylvia had ever seen. He leaned against the stone, yet nothing could have been less reposeful than his attitude, for the native unrest of the man asserted itself in spite of weariness or any soothing influence of time or place.‡ Moor was much slighter, and betrayed in every gesture the unconscious grace of the gentleman born. A most attractive face, with its broad brow, serene eyes, and the cordial smile about the mouth. A sweet, strong nature, one would say, which, having used life well had learned the secret of a true success. Inward tranquillity seemed his, and it was plain to see that no wave of sound, no wandering breath, no glimpse of color, no

---

* At this point in the "Afloat" chapter (ch. V) in *M2*, Sylvia performs a series of "dramatic pictures and pieces"; this passage is reprinted in the appendix (82–87).

† This paragraph and the next four pages are omitted in *M2*. Alcott continues the romance with: "Where are you going to hang me?" (*M2* 87); the chapters then conclude almost identically in both editions.

‡ In *M2* Warwick is introduced to Sylvia on a narrow strip of beach where the treacherous tide almost engulfs her. This takes place in Chapter IV, "Warwick"; see the appendix (50–58). Sylvia's "study" of Adam Warwick is identical in both editions, but in *M2* Alcott added a literary conversation between them which ended the chapter (63–68).

hint of night or nature was without its charm and its significance for him.

"Tell me about that man. Mark. I have heard you speak of him since you came home, but supposing he was some blowzy artist, I never cared to ask about him. Now I've seen. I want to know more," said Sylvia, as her brother laid himself down after an approving glance at the group opposite.

"I met him in Munich, when I first went abroad, and since then we have often come upon each other in our wanderings. He never writes, but goes and comes intent upon his own affairs; yet one never can forget him, and is always glad to feel the grip of his hand again, it seems to put such life and courage into one."

"Is he good? asked Sylvia, woman like, beginning with the morals.

"Violently virtuous. He is a masterful soul, bent on living out his beliefs and aspirations at any cost. Much given to denunciation of wrong-doing everywhere, and eager to execute justice upon all offenders high or low. Yet he possesses great nobility of character, great audacity of mind, and leads a life of the sternest integrity."

"Is he rich?"

"In his own eyes, because he makes his wants so few."

"Is he married?"

"No; he has no family, and not many friends, for he says what he means in the bluntest English, and few stand the test his sincerity applies."

"What does he do in the world?"

"Studies it, as we do books; dives into everything, analyzes character, and builds up his own with materials which will last. If that's not genius it's something better."

"Then he will do much good and be famous, wont he?"

"Great good to many, but never will be famous, I fear. He is too fierce an iconoclast to suit the old party, too individual a reformer to join the new, and being born a century too soon must bide his time, or play out his part before stage and audience are ready for him."

"Is he learned?"

"Very, in uncommon sorts of wisdom; left college after a year of it, because it could not give him what he wanted, and taking the world for his university, life for his tutor, says he shall not graduate till his term ends with days."

"I know I shall like him very much."

"I hope so, for my sake. He is a grand man in the rough, and an excellent tonic for those who have courage to try him."

Sylvia was silent, thinking over all she had just heard and finding

37

much to interest her in it, because, to her imaginative and enthusiastic nature, there was something irresistibly attractive in the strong, solitary, self-reliant man. Mark watched her for a moment, then asked with lazy curiosity—

"How do you like this other friend of mine?"

"He went away when I was such a child that since he came back I've had to begin again; but if I like him at the end of another month as much as I do now, I shall try to make your friend my friend, because I need such an one very much."

Mark laughed at the innocent frankness of his sister's speech but took it as she meant it, and answered soberly—

"Better leave Platonics till you're forty.[4] Though Moor is twelve years older than yourself he is a young man still, and you are grown a very captivating little woman."

Sylvia looked both scornful and indignant.

"You need have no fears. There *is* such a thing as true and simple friendship between men and women, and if I can find no one of my own sex who can give me the help and happiness I want, why may I not look for it anywhere and accept it in whatever shape it comes?"

"You may, my dear, and I'll lend a hand with all my heart, but you must be willing to take the consequences in whatever shape *they* come," said Mark, not ill pleased with the prospect his fancy conjured up.

"I will," replied Sylvia loftily, and fate took her at her word.

Presently some one suggested bed, and the proposition was unanimously accepted.

*"Where are you going to hang me?" asked Sylvia, as she laid hold of her hammock and looked about her with nearly as much interest as if her suspension was to be of the perpendicular order.

"You are not to be swung up in a tree to-night but laid like a ghost, and requested not to walk till morning. There is an unused barn close by, so we shall have a roof over us for one night longer," answered Mark, playing chamberlain while the others remained to quench the fire and secure the larder.

An early moon[†] lighted Sylvia to bed, and when shown her half the

---

*Here the two versions continue with only minor changes.
† The moon *M2* (88)

barn, which, as she was a Marine, was very properly the bay, Mark explained, she scouted the idea of being nervous or timid in such rude quarters, made herself a cosy nest and bade her brother a merry good night.

More weary than she would confess, Sylvia fell asleep at once, despite the novelty of her situation and the noises that fill a summer night with fitful rustlings and tones. How long she slept she did not know, but woke suddenly and sat erect with that curious thrill which sometimes startles one out of deepest slumber, and is often the forerunner of some dread or danger. She felt this hot tingle through blood and nerves, and stared about her thinking of fire. But everything was dark and still, and after waiting a few moments she decided that her nest had been too warm, for her temples throbbed and her cheeks were feverish with the close air of the barn half filled with new-made hay.

Creeping up a fragrant slope she spread her plaid* again and lay down where a cool breath flowed through wide chinks in the wall. Sleep was slowly returning when the rustle of footsteps scared it quite away and set her heart beating fast, for they came toward the new couch she had chosen. Holding her breath she listened. The quiet tread drew nearer and nearer till it paused within a yard of her, then some one seemed to throw themselves down, sigh heavily a few times and grow still as if falling asleep.

"It is Mark," thought Sylvia, and whispered his name, but no one answered, and from the other corner of the barn she heard her brother muttering in his sleep. Who was it, then? Mark had said there were no cattle near, she was sure neither of her comrades had left their bivouac, for there was her brother talking as usual in his dreams; some one seemed restless and turned often with decided motion, that was Warwick, she thought, while the quietest sleeper of the three betrayed his presence by laughing once with the low-toned merriment she recognized as Moor's. These discoveries left her a prey to visions of grimy strollers, maudlin farm-servants, and infectious emigrants in dismal array. A strong desire to cry out possessed her for a moment, but was checked; for with all her sensitiveness Sylvia had much common sense, and that spirit which hates to be conquered even by a natural fear. She remembered her scornful repudiation of the charge of timidity, and the endless jokes she would have to undergo if her mysterious neighbor should prove some harmless wan-

---

*her cloak M2 (88)

derer or an imaginary terror of her own, so she held her peace, thinking valiantly as the drops gathered on her forehead, and every sense grew painfully alert—

"I'll not call if my hair turns gray with fright, and I find myself an idiot to-morrow. I told them to try me, and I won't be found wanting at the first alarm. I'll be still, if the thing does not touch me till dawn, when I shall know how to act at once, and so save myself from ridicule at the cost of a wakeful night."

Holding fast to this resolve Sylvia lay motionless, listening to the cricket's chirp without, and taking uncomfortable notes of the state of things within, for the new comer stirred heavily, sighed long and deeply, and seemed to wake often, like one too sad or weary to rest. She would have been wise to have screamed her scream and had the rout over, for she tormented herself with the ingenuity of a lively fancy, and suffered more from her own terrors than at the discovery of a dozen vampires. Every tale of *diablerie* she had ever heard came most inopportunely to haunt her now, and though she felt their folly she could not free herself from their dominion.[5] She wondered till she could wonder no longer what the morning would show her. She tried to calculate in how many springs she could reach and fly over the low partition which separated her from her sleeping body-guard. She wished with all her heart that she had stayed in her nest which was nearer the door, and watched for dawn with eyes that ached to see the light.

In the midst of these distressful sensations the far-off crow of some vigilant chanticleer assured her that the short summer night was wearing away and relief was at hand. This comfortable conviction had so good an effect that she lapsed into what seemed a moment's oblivion, but was in fact an hour's restless sleep, for when her eyes unclosed again the first red streaks were visible in the east, and a dim light found its way into the barn through the great door which had been left ajar for air. An instant, Sylvia lay collecting herself, then rose on her arm, looked resolutely behind her, stared with round eyes a moment, and dropped down again, laughing with a merriment, which coming on the heels of her long alarm was rather hysterical. All she saw was a little soft-eyed Alderney,*[6] which lifted its stag-like head, and regarded her with a confiding aspect that won her pardon for its innocent offence.

---

*Alderney calf *M2* (91)

Through the relief of both mind and body which she experienced in no small degree, the first thought that came was a thankful "what a mercy I didn't call Mark, for I should never have heard the last of this;" and having fought her fears alone she enjoyed her success alone, and girl-like resolved to say nothing of her first night's adventures. Gathering herself up she crept nearer and caressed her late terror, which stretched its neck toward her with a comfortable sound, and munched her shawl like a cosset lamb. But before this new friendship was many minutes old, Sylvia's heavy lids fell together, her head dropped lower and lower, her hand lay still on the dappled neck, and with a long sigh of weariness she dropped back upon the hay, leaving little Alderney to watch over her much more tranquilly than she had watched over it.

CHAPTER IV

THROUGH FLOOD AND FIELD AND FIRE

VERY EARLY were they afloat again, and as they glided up the stream Sylvia watched the earth's awakening, seeing in it what her own should be. The sun was not yet visible above the hills, but the sky was ready for his coming, with the soft flush of color dawn gives only to her royal lover. Birds were chanting matins as if all the jubilance of their short lives must be poured out at once. Flowers stirred and brightened like children after sleep. A balmy wind came whispering from the wood, bringing the aroma of pines, the cool breath of damp nooks, the healthful kiss that leaves a glow behind. Light mists floated down the river like departing visions that had haunted it by night, and every ripple breaking on the shore seemed to sing a musical good morrow.

Sylvia could not conceal the weariness her long vigil left behind; and after betraying herself by a drowsy lurch that nearly took her overboard, she made herself comfortable, and slept till the grating of the keel on a pebbly shore woke her to find a new harbor reached under the lee of a cliff, whose deep shadow was very grateful after the glare of noon upon the water.

"How do you intend to dispose of yourself this afternoon, Adam?" asked Mark, when dinner was over and his sister busy feeding the birds.

"In this way," answered Warwick, producing a book and settling himself in a commodious cranny of the rock.

"Moor and I want to climb the cliff and sketch the view; but it is too rough a road for Sylvia. Would you mind mounting guard for an hour or two? Read away, and leave her to amuse herself; only pray don't let her get into any mischief by way of enjoying her liberty, for she fears nothing and is fond of experiments."

"I'll do my best," replied Warwick, with an air of resignation.

Having slung the hammock and seen Sylvia safely into it, the climbers departed, leaving her to enjoy the luxury of motion. For half an hour she swung idly, looking up into the green pavilion overhead, where many insect families were busy with their small joys and cares, or out over the still landscape basking in the warmth of a cloudless afternoon. Then she opened a book Mark had brought for his own amusement, and began to read as intently as her companion, who leaned against the boulder slowly turning his pages, with leafy shadows flickering over his uncovered head and touching it with alternate sun and shade. The book proved interesting, and Sylvia was rapidly skimming into the heart of the story, when an unguarded motion caused her swing to slope perilously to one side, and in saving herself she lost her book. This produced a predicament, for being helped into a hammock and getting out alone are two very different things. She eyed the distance from her nest to the ground, and fancied it had been made unusually great to keep her stationary. She held fast with one hand and stretched downward with the other, but the book insolently flirted its leaves just out of reach. She took a survey of Warwick; he had not perceived her plight, and she felt an unwonted reluctance to call for help, because he did not look like one used to come and go at a woman's bidding. After several fruitless essays she decided to hazard an ungraceful descent; and, gathering herself up, was about to launch boldly out, when Warwick cried, "Stop!" in a tone that nearly produced the catastrophe he wished to avert. Sylvia subsided, and coming up he lifted the book, glanced at the title, then keenly at the reader.

"Do you like this?"

"So far very much."

"Are you allowed to read what you choose?"

"Yes, sir. That is Mark's choice, however; I brought no book."

"I advise you to skim it into the river; it is not a book for you."

Sylvia caught a glimpse of the one he had been reading himself, and impelled by a sudden impulse to see what would come of it, she answered with a look as keen as his own—

"You disapprove of my book; would you recommend yours?"

"In this case, yes; for in one you will find much falsehood in purple and fine linen, in the other some truth in fig-leaves. Take your choice."

He offered both; but Sylvia took refuge in civility.

"I thank you, I'll have neither; but if you will please steady the hammock, I will try to find some more harmless amusement for myself."

He obeyed with one of the humorous expressions which often passed over his face. Sylvia descended as gracefully as circumstances permitted, and went roving up and down the cliffs. Warwick resumed his seat and the "barbaric yawp," but seemed to find Truth in demi-toilet less interesting than Youth in a gray gown and round hat, for which his taste is to be commended. The girl had small scope for amusement, and when she had gathered moss for pillows, laid out a white fungus to dry for a future pincushion, harvested penny-royal in little sheaves tied with grass-blades, watched a battle between black ants and red, and learned the landscape by heart; she was at the end of her resources, and leaning on a stone surveyed earth and sky with a somewhat despondent air.

"You would like something to do, I think."

"Yes, sir; for being rather new to this sort of life, I have not yet learned how to dispose of my time."

"I see that, and having deprived you of one employment will try to replace it by another."

Warwick rose, and going to the single birch that glimmered among the pines like a delicate spirit of the wood, he presently returned with strips of silvery bark.

"You were wishing for baskets to hold your spoils, yesterday; shall we make some now?" he asked.

"How stupid in me not to think of that! Yes, thank you, I should like it very much;" and producing her housewife, Sylvia fell to work with a brightening face.

Warwick sat a little below her on the rock, shaping his basket in perfect silence. This did not suit Sylvia, for feeling lively and loquacious she wanted conversation to occupy her thoughts as pleasantly as the birch rolls were occupying her hands, and there sat a person who, she was sure, could do it perfectly if he chose. She reconnoitered with covert glances, made sundry overtures, and sent out envoys in the shape of scissors, needles, and thread. But no answering glance met hers; her remarks received the briefest replies, and her offers of assistance were declined with an absent "No, thank you." Then she grew indignant at this seeming neglect, and thought, as she sat frowning over her work, behind his back—

"He treats me like a child,—very well, then, I'll behave like one, and beset him with questions till he is driven to speak; for he can talk, he ought to talk, he shall talk."

"Mr. Warwick, do you like children?" she began, with a determined aspect.

"Better than men or women."

"Do you enjoy amusing them?"

"Exceedingly, when in the humor."

"Are you in the humor now?"

"Yes, I think so."

"Then why don't you amuse me?"

"Because you are not a child."

"I fancied you thought me one."

"If I had, I probably should have put you on my knee, and told you fairy tales, or cut dolls for you out of this bark, instead of sitting respectfully silent and making a basket for your stores."

There was a curious smile about Warwick's mouth as he spoke, and Sylvia was rather abashed by her first exploit. But there was a pleasure in the daring, and choosing another topic she tried again.

"Mark was telling me last night about the great college you had chosen; I thought it must be a very original and interesting way to educate one's self, and wanted very much to know what you had been studying lately. May I ask you now?"

"Men and women," was the brief answer.

"Have you got your lesson, sir?"

"A part of it very thoroughly, I believe."

"Would you think me rude if I asked which part?"

"The latter."

"And what conclusions do you arrive at concerning this branch of the subject?" asked Sylvia, smiling and interested.

"That it is both dangerous and unsatisfactory."

He spoke so gravely; looked so stern, that Sylvia obeyed a warning instinct and sat silent till she had completed a canoe-shaped basket, the useful size of which produced a sudden longing to fill it. Her eye had already spied a knoll across the river covered with vines, and so suggestive of berries that she now found it impossible to resist the desire for an exploring trip in that direction. The boat was too large for her to manage alone, but an enterprising spirit had taken possession of her, and having made one voyage of discovery with small success she resolved to try again, hoping a second in another direction might prove more fruitful.

"Is your basket done, sir?" she asked.

"Yes; will you have it?"

"Why, you have made it as an Indian would, using grass instead of thread. It is much more complete than mine, for the green stitches ornament the white bark, but the black ones disfigure it. I should know a man made your basket and a woman mine."

"Because one is ugly and strong, the other graceful but unable to stand alone?" asked Warwick, rising, with a gesture that sent the silvery shreds flying away on the wind.

"One holds as much as the other, however; and I fancy the woman would fill hers soonest if she had the wherewithal to do it. Do you know there are berries on that hillside opposite?"

"I see vines, but consider fruit doubtful, for boys and birds are thicker than blackberries."

"I've a firm conviction that they have left some for us; and as Mark says you like frankness, I think I shall venture to ask you to row me over and help me fill the baskets on the other side."

Sylvia looked up at him with a merry mixture of doubt and daring in her face, and offered him his hat.

"Very good, I will," said Warwick, leading the way to the boat with an alacrity which proved how much pleasanter to him was action than repose.

There was no dry landing-place just opposite, and as he rowed higher, Adam fixed his eyes on Sylvia with a look peculiar to himself, a gaze more keen than soft, which seemed to search one through and through with its rapid discernment. He saw a face full of contradictions,— youthful, maidenly, and intelligent, yet touched with the unconscious melancholy which is born of disappointment and desire. The mouth was sweet and tender as a woman's should be, the brow spirited and thoughtful; but the eyes were by turns eager, absent, or sad, and there was much pride in the carriage of the small head with its hair of wavy gold gathered into a green snood, whence little tendrils kept breaking loose to dance upon her forehead, or hang about her neck. A most significant but not a beautiful face, because of its want of harmony. The dark eyes, among their fair surroundings, disturbed the sight as a discord in music jars upon the ear; even when the lips smiled the sombre shadow of black lashes seemed to fill them with a gloom that was never wholly lost. The voice, too, which should have been a girlish treble, was full and low as a matured woman's, with now and then a silvery ring to it, as if another and a blither creature spoke.

Sylvia could not be offended by the grave penetration of this glance, though an uncomfortable consciousness that she was being analyzed and tested made her meet it with a look intended to be dignified, but which was also somewhat defiant, and more than one smile passed over Warwick's countenance as he watched her. The moment the boat glided with a soft swish among the rushes that fringed the shore, she sprang up the bank, and leaving a basket behind her by way of hint, hurried to the sandy knoll, where, to her great satisfaction, she found the vines heavy with berries. As Warwick joined her she held up a shining cluster, saying with a touch of exultation in her voice—

"My faith is rewarded; taste and believe."

He accepted them with a nod, and said pleasantly—

"As my prophecy has failed, let us see if yours will be fulfilled."

"I accept the challenge." And down upon her knees went Sylvia among the vines, regardless of stains, rents, or wounded hands.

Warwick strolled away to leave her "claim" free, and silence fell between them; for one was too busy with thorns, the other with thoughts, to break the summer stillness. Sylvia worked with as much energy as if a silver cup was to be the reward of success. The sun shone fervently and the wind was cut off by the hill. Drops gathered on her forehead and her cheeks glowed; but she only pushed off her hat, thrust back her hair, and moved on to a richer spot. Vines caught at her by sleeve and skirt as if to dishearten the determined plunderer, but on she went with a wrench and a rip, an impatient "Ah!" and a hasty glance at damaged fabrics and fingers. Lively crickets flew up in swarms about her, surly wasps disputed her right to the fruit, and drunken bees blundered against her as they met zigzagging homeward much the worse for blackberry wine. She never heeded any of them, though at another time she would gladly have made friends with all, but found compensation for her discomforts in the busy twitter of sand swallows perched on the mullein-tops, the soft flight of yellow butterflies, and the rapidity with which the little canoe received its freight of "Ethiop sweets."[1] As the last handful went in she sprung up crying "Done!" with a suddenness that broke up the Long Parliament and sent its members skimming away as if a second "Noll" had appeared among them. "Done!" came back Warwick's answer like a deep echo from below, and hurrying down to meet him she displayed her success, saying archly—

"I am glad we both won, though, to be perfectly candid I think mine is decidedly the fullest." But as she swung up her birch pannier the handle broke, and down went basket, berries and all, into the long grass rustling at her feet.

Warwick could not restrain a laugh at the blank dismay that fell upon the exultation of Sylvia's face, and for a moment she was both piqued and petulant. Hot, tired, disappointed, and, hardest of all, laughed at, it was one of those times that try girls' souls. But she was too old to cry, too proud to complain, too well-bred to resent, so the little gust passed over unseen, she thought, and joining in the merriment she said, as she knelt down beside the wreck—

"This is a practical illustration of the old proverb, and I deserve it for my boasting. Next time I'll try to combine strength and beauty in my work."

To wise people character is betrayed by trifles. Warwick stopped laughing, and something about the girlish figure in the grass, regathering with wounded hands the little harvest lately lost, seemed to touch him. His face softened suddenly as he collected several broad leaves, spared them on the grass, and sitting down by Sylvia, looked under her hat-brim with a glance of mingled penitence and friendliness.

"Now, young philosopher, pile up your berries in that green platter while I repair the basket. Bear this in mind when you work in bark: make your handle the way of the grain, and choose a strip both smooth and broad."

Then drawing out his knife he fell to work, and while he tied green withes, as if the task were father to the thought, he told her something of a sojourn among the Indians, of whom he had learned much concerning their woodcraft, arts, and superstitions; lengthening the legend till the little canoe was ready for another launch. With her fancy full of war-trails and wampum, Sylvia followed to the river-side, and as they floated back dabbled her stained fingers in the water, comforting their smart with its cool flow till they swept by the landing-place, when she asked, wonderingly—

"Where are we going now? Have I been so troublesome that I must be taken home?"

"We are going to get a third course to follow the berries, unless you are afraid to trust yourself to me."

"Indeed, I'm not; take me where you like, sir."

Something in her frank tone, her confiding look, seemed to please Warwick; he sat a moment looking into the brown depths of the water, and let the boat drift, with no sound but the musical drip of drops from the oars.

"You are going upon a rock, sir."*

"I did that three months ago."†

He spoke as if to himself, his face darkened, and he shook the hair off his forehead with an impatient gesture. A swift stroke averted the shock, and the boat shot down the stream, leaving a track of foam behind it as Warwick rowed with the energy of one bent on outstripping some importunate remembrance or dogging care. Sylvia marvelled greatly at the change which came upon him, but held fast with flying hair and lips apart to catch the spray, enjoying the breezy flight along a path tessellated with broad bars of blue and gold. The race, ended as abruptly as it began, and Warwick seemed the winner, for when they touched the coast of a floating lily-island, the cloud was gone. As he shipped his oars he turned, saying, with very much the look and manner of a pleasant boy—

"You were asleep when we passed this morning; but I know you like lilies, so let us go a fishing."

"That I do!" cried Sylvia, capturing a great white flower with a clutch that nearly took her overboard. Warwick drew her back and did the gathering himself.

"Enough, sir, quite enough. Here are plenty to trim our table and ourselves with; leave the rest for other voyagers who may come this way."

As Warwick offered her the dripping nosegay he looked at the white hand scored with scarlet lines.

"Poor hand! let the lilies comfort it. You are a true woman, Miss Sylvia, for though your palm is purple there's not a stain upon your lips, and you have neither worked nor suffered for yourself it seems."

"I don't deserve that compliment, because I was only intent on outdoing you if possible; so you are mistaken again you see."

"Not entirely, I think. Some faces are so true an index of character

---

* "We are going upon a rock." *M2* (102)

† In *M2* this line and the following paragraph are changed to:

"Not if I can help it."

And a swift stroke averted the shock, to send them flying down the river till they reached the shore of a floating lilly island. Here Warwick shipped his oars, saying— (103)

that one cannot be mistaken. If you doubt this look down into the river, and such an one will inevitably smile back at you."

Pleased, yet somewhat abashed, Sylvia busied herself in knotting up the long brown stems and tinging her nose with yellow pollen as she inhaled the bitter-sweet breath of the lilies. But when Warwick turned to resume the oars, she said—

"Let us float out as we floated in. It is so still and lovely here I like to stay and enjoy it, for we may never see just such a scene again."

He obeyed, and both sat silent, watching the meadows that lay green and low along the shore, feeding their eyes with the beauty of the landscape, till its peaceful spirit seemed to pass into their own, and lend a subtle charm to that hour, which henceforth was to stand apart, serene and happy, in their memories forever. A still August day, with a shimmer in the air that veiled the distant hills with the mellow haze, no artist ever truly caught. Midsummer warmth and ripeness brooded in the verdure of field and forest. Wafts of fragrance went wandering by from newmown meadows and gardens full of bloom. All the sky wore its serenest blue, and up the river came frolic winds, ruffling the lily leaves until they showed their purple linings, sweeping shadowly ripples through the long grass, and lifting the locks from Sylvia's forehead with a grateful touch, as she sat softly swaying with the swaying of the boat. Slowly they drifted out into the current, slowly Warwick cleft the water with reluctant stroke, and slowly Sylvia's mind woke from its trance of dreamy delight, as with a gesture of assent she said—

"Yes, I am ready now. That was a happy little moment, and I am glad to have lived it, for such times return to refresh me when many a more stirring one is quite forgotten." A moment after she added, eagerly, as a new object of interest appeared: "Mr. Warwick, I see smoke. I know there is a wood on fire; I want to see it; please land again."

He glanced over his shoulder at the black cloud trailing away before the wind, saw Sylvia's desire in her face, and silently complied; for being a keen student of character, he was willing to prolong an interview that gave him glimpses of a nature in which the woman and the child were curiously blended.

"I love fire, and that must be a grand one, if we could only see it well. This bank is not high enough; let us go nearer and enjoy it," said Sylvia, finding that an orchard and a knoll or two intercepted the view of the burning wood.

"It is too far."

"Not at all. I am no helpless, fine lady. I can walk, run, and climb like any boy; so you need have no fears for me. I may never see such a sight again, and you know you'd go if you were alone. Please come, Mr. Warwick."

"I promised Mark to take care of you, and for the very reason that you love fire, I'd rather not take you into that furnace, lest you never come out again. Let us go back immediately."

The decision of his tone ruffled Sylvia, and she turned wilful at once, saying in a tone as decided as his own—

"No; I wish to see it. I am always allowed to do what I wish, so I shall go;" with which mutinous remark she walked straight away towards the burning wood.

Warwick looked after her, indulging a momentary desire to carry her back to the boat, like a naughty child. But the resolute aspect of the figure going on before him, convinced him that the attempt would be a failure, and with an amused expression he leisurely followed her.

Sylvia had not walked five minutes before she was satisfied that it *was* too far; but having rebelled, she would not own herself in the wrong, and being perverse, insisted upon carrying her point, though she walked all night. On she went over walls, under rails, across brooks, along the furrows of more than one ploughed field, and in among the rustling corn, that turned its broad leaves to the sun, always in advance of her companion, who followed with exemplary submission, but also with a satirical smile, that spurred her on as no other demonstration could have done. Six o'clock sounded from the church behind the hill; still the wood seemed to recede as she pursued, still close behind her came the steady footfalls, with no sound of weariness in them, and still Sylvia kept on, till breathless, but successful, she reached the object of her search.

Keeping to the windward of the smoke, she gained a rocky spot still warm and blackened by the late passage of the flames, and pausing there, forgot her own pranks in watching those which the fire played before her eyes. Many acres were burning, the air was full of the rush and roar of the victorious element, the crash of trees that fell before it, and the shouts of men who fought it unavailingly.

"Ah, this is grand! I wish Mark and Mr. Moor were here. Aren't you glad you came, sir?"

Sylvia glanced up at her companion, as he stood regarding the scene with the intent, alert expression one often sees in a fine hound when he scents danger in the air. But Warwick did not answer, for as she spoke a

51

long, sharp cry of human suffering rose above the tumult, terribly distinct and full of ominous suggestion.

"Some one was killed when that tree fell! Stay here till I come back;" and Adam strode away into the wood as if his place were where the peril lay.

For ten minutes Sylvia waited, pale and anxious; then her patience gave out, and saying to herself, "I can go where he does, and women are always more helpful than men at such times," she followed in the direction whence came the fitful sound of voices. The ground was hot underneath her feet, red eyes winked at her from the blackened sod, and fiery tongues darted up here and there, as if the flames were lurking still, ready for another outbreak. Intent upon her charitable errand, and excited by the novel scene, she pushed recklessly on, leaping charred logs, skirting still burning stumps, and peering eagerly into the dun veil that wavered to and fro. The appearance of an impassable ditch obliged her to halt, and pausing to take breath, she became aware that she had lost her way. The echo of voices had ceased, a red glare was deepening in front, and clouds of smoke enveloped her in a stifling atmosphere. A sense of bewilderment crept over her; she knew not where she was; and after a rapid flight in what she believed a safe direction had been cut short by the fall of a blazing tree before her, she stood still, taking counsel with herself. Darkness and danger seemed to encompass her, fire flickered on every side, and suffocating vapors shrouded earth and sky. A bare rock suggested one hope of safety, and muffling her head in her skirt, she lay down faint and blind, with a dull pain in her temples, and a fear at her heart fast deepening into terror, as her breath grew painful and her head began to swim.

"This is the last of the pleasant voyage! Oh, why does no one think of me?"

As the regret rose, a cry of suffering and entreaty broke from her. She had not called for help till now, thinking herself too remote, her voice too feeble to overpower the din about her. But some one had thought of her, for as the cry left her lips steps came crashing through the wood, a pair of strong arms caught her up, and before she could collect her scattered senses she was set down beyond all danger on the green bank of a little pool.

"Well, salamander, have you had fire enough?" asked Warwick, as he dashed a handful of water in her face with such energetic goodwill that it took her breath away.

"Yes, oh yes—and of water, too! Please stop, and let me get my breath!" gasped Sylvia, warding off a second baptism and staring dizzily about her.

"Why did you quit the place where I left you?" was the next question, somewhat sternly put.

"I wanted to know what happened."

"So you walked into a bonfire to satisfy your curiosity, though you had been told to keep out of it? You'd never make a Casabianca."[2]

"I hope not, for of all silly children, that boy was the silliest, and he deserved to be blown up for his want of common sense," cried the girl, petulantly.

"Obedience is an old-fashioned virtue, which you would do well to cultivate along with your common sense, young lady."

Sylvia changed the subject, for Warwick stood regarding her with an irate expression that was somewhat alarming. Fanning herself with the wet hat, she asked abruptly—

"Was the man hurt, sir?"

"Yes."

"Very much?"

"Yes."

"Can I not do something for him? He is very far from any house, and I have some experience in wounds."

"He is past all help, above all want now."

"Dead, Mr. Warwick?"

"Quite dead."

Sylvia sat down as suddenly as she had risen, and covered her face with a shiver, remembering that her own wilfulness had tempted a like fate, and she too, might now have been 'past help, above all want.' Warwick went down to the pool to bathe his hot face and blackened hands; as he returned Sylvia met him with a submissive—

"I will go back now if you are ready, sir."

If the way had seemed long in coming it was doubly so in returning, for neither pride nor perversity sustained her now, and every step cost an effort. "I can rest in the boat," was her sustaining thought; great therefore was her dismay when on reaching the river no boat was to be seen.

"Why, Mr. Warwick, where is it?"

"A long way down the river by this time, probably. Believing that we landed only for a moment, I did not fasten it, and the tide has carried it away."

"But what shall we do?"

"One of two things,—spend the night here, or go round by the bridge."

"Is it far?"

"Some three or four miles, I think."

"Is there no shorter way? no boat or carriage to be had?"

"If you care to wait, I can look for our runaway, or get a wagon from the town."

"It is growing late and you would be gone a long time, I suppose?"

"Probably."

"Which had we better do?"

"I should not venture to advise. Suit yourself, I will obey orders."

"If you were alone what would you do?"

"Swim across."

Sylvia looked disturbed, Warwick impenetrable, the river wide, the road long, and the cliffs the most inaccessible of places. An impressive pause ensued, then she said frankly—

"It is my own fault and I'll take the consequences. I choose the bridge and leave you the river. If I don't appear till dawn, tell Mark I sent him a good night," and girding up her energies she walked bravely off with much external composure and internal chagrin.

As before, Warwick followed in silence. For a time she kept in advance, then allowed him to gain upon her, and presently fell behind, plodding doggedly on through thick and thin, vainly trying to conceal the hunger and fatigue that were fast robbing her of both strength and spirits. Adam watched her with a masculine sense of the justice of the retribution which his wilful comrade had brought upon herself. But as he saw the elasticity leave her steps, the color fade from her cheeks, the resolute mouth relax, and the wistful eyes dim once or twice with tears of weariness and vexation, pity got the better of pique, and he relented. His steady tramp came to a halt, and stopping by a wayside spring, he pointed to a mossy stone, saying with no hint of superior powers—

"We are tired, let us rest."

Sylvia dropped down at once, and for a few minutes neither spoke, for the air was full of sounds more pertinent to the summer night than human voices. From the copse behind them, came the coo of wood-pigeons, from the grass, at their feet the plaintive chirp of crickets; a busy breeze whispered through the willow, the little spring dripped musically from the rock, and across the meadows came the sweet chime of a bell. Twilight was creeping over forest, hill, and stream, and seemed to drop refreshment and repose upon all weariness of soul and body, more grateful to Sylvia, than the welcome seat and leafy cup of water Warwick brought her from the spring.

The appearance of a thirsty sparrow gave her thoughts a pleasant turn, for, sitting motionless, she watched the little creature trip down to the pool, drink and bathe, then flying to a willow spray, dress its feathers, dry its wings, and sit chirping softly as if it sang its evening hymn. Warwick saw her interest, and searching in his pocket, found the relics of a biscuit, strewed a few bits upon the ground before him, and began a low, sweet whistle, which rose gradually to a varied strain, alluring, spirited, and clear as any bird voice of the wood. Little sparrow ceased his twitter, listened with outstretched neck and eager eye, hopping restlessly from twig to twig, until he hung just over the musician's head, agitated with a small flutter of surprise, delight, and doubt. Gathering a crumb or two into his hand, Warwick held it toward the bird, while softer, sweeter, and more urgent rose the invitation, and nearer and nearer drew the winged guest, fascinated by the spell.[3]

Suddenly a belated blackbird lit upon the wall, surveyed the group and burst into a jubilant song, that for a moment drowned his rival's notes. Then, as if claiming the reward, he fluttered to the grass, ate his fill, took a sip from the mossy basin by the way, and flew singing over the river, leaving a trail of music behind him. There was a dash and daring about this which fired little sparrow with emulation. His last fear seemed conquered, and he flew confidingly to Warwick's palm, pecking the crumbs with grateful chirps and friendly glances from its quick, bright eye. It was a pretty picture for the girl to see; the man, an image of power, in his hand the feathered atom, that, with unerring instinct, divined and trusted the superior nature which had not yet lost its passport to the world of innocent delights that Nature gives to those who love her best. Involuntarily Sylvia clapped her hands, and, startled by the sudden sound, little sparrow skimmed away.

"Thank you for the pleasantest sight I've seen for many a day. How did you learn this gentle art, Mr. Warwick?"

"I was a solitary boy, and found my only playmates in the woods and fields. I learned their worth, they saw my need, and when I asked their friendship, gave it freely. Now we should go; you are very tired, let me help you."

He held his hand to her, and she put her own into it with a confidence as instinctive as the bird's. Then, hand in hand they crossed the bridge and struck into the wilderness again; climbing slopes still warm and odorous, passing through dells full of chilly damps, along meadows spangled with fire-flies, and haunted by sonorous frogs; over rocks crisp with pale mosses, and between dark firs, where shadows brooded, and melancholy breezes rocked themselves to sleep. Speaking seldom, yet feeling no consciousness of silence, no sense of restraint, for they no longer seemed like strangers to one another, and this spontaneous friendliness lent an indefinable charm to the dusky walk. Warwick found satisfaction in the knowledge of her innocent faith in him, the touch of the little hand he held, the sight of the quiet figure at his side. Sylvia felt that it was pleasant to be the object of his care, fancied that they would learn to know each other better in three days of this free life than in as many months at home, and rejoiced over the discovery of unsuspected traits in him, like the soft lining of the chestnut burr, to which she had compared him more than once that afternoon. So, mutually and unconsciously yielding to the influence of the hour and the mood it brought them, they walked through the twilight in that eloquent silence which often proves more persuasive than the most fluent speech.

The welcome blaze of their own fire gladdened them at length, and when the last step was taken, Sylvia sat down with an inward conviction she never could get up again. Warwick told their mishap in the fewest possible words, while Mark, in a spasm of brotherly solicitude, goaded the fire to a roar that his sister's feet might be dried, administered a cordial as a preventive against cold, and prescribed her hammock the instant supper was done. She went away with him, but a moment after she came to Warwick with a box of Prue's ointment and a soft handkerchief stripped into bandages.

"What now?" he asked.

"I wish to dress your burns, sir."

"They will do well enough with a little water; go you and rest."

"Mr. Warwick, you know you ate your supper with your left hand, and put both behind you when you saw me looking at them. Please let me make them easier; they were burnt for me, and I shall get no sleep till I have had my way."

There was a curious mixture of command and entreaty in her manner, and before their owner had time to refuse or comply, the scorched hands were taken possession of, the red blisters covered with a cool bandage, and the frown of pain smoothed out of Warwick's forehead by the prospect of relief. As she tied the last knot, Sylvia glanced up with a look that mutely asked pardon for past waywardness, and expressed gratitude for past help; then, as if her heart were set at rest, she was gone before her patient could return his thanks.

She did not reappear, Mark went to send a lad after the lost boat, and the two friends were left alone; Warwick watching the blaze, Moor watching him, till, with a nod toward a pair of diminutive boots that stood turning out their toes before the fire, Adam said—

"The wearer of those defiant-looking articles is the most capricious piece of humanity it was ever my fortune to see. You have no idea of the life she has led me since you left."

"I can imagine it."

"She is as freakish, and wears as many shapes as Puck; a gnat, a will-o'-the-wisp, a Sister of Charity, a meek-faced child; and one does not know in which guise she pleases most. Hard the task of him who has and tries to hold her."

"Hard yet happy; for a word will tame the high spirit, a look touch the warm heart, a kind act be repaid with one still kinder. She is a woman to be studied well, taught tenderly, and, being won, cherished with an affection that knows no shadow of a change."

Moor spoke low, and on his face the fire-light seemed to shed a ruddier glow than it had done before. Warwick eyed him keenly for a moment, then said, with his usual abruptness—

"Geoffrey, you should marry."

"Set me the example by mortgaging your own heart, Adam."

*"I have."

"I thought so. Tell me the romance."

"It is the old story—a handsome woman, a foolish man; a few weeks of doubt, a few of happiness; then the two stand apart to view the leap before they take it; after that, peace or purgatory, as they choose well or ill."

---

*The remainder of the chapter is replaced in *M2* with the following:

"I hope to in good time. Will you follow my example?"

"When some woman is dearer to me than my liberty. It will be hard to find a mate, and I am in no haste. God bless your wooing, Geoffrey."

"And yours, Adam."

Then with a hearty handshake more expressive of affection than many a tenderer demonstration the friends parted, Warwick to watch the stars for hours, and Moor to muse beside the fire till the little boots were dry. (116–17)

"When is the probation over, Adam?"

"In June, God willing."

The hope of deliverance gave to Warwick's tone the fervor of desire, and led his friend to believe in the existence of a passion deep and strong as the heart he knew so well. No further confessions disturbed his satisfaction, for Warwick scorned complaint; pity he would not receive, sympathy was powerless to undo the past, time alone would mend it, and to time he looked for help. He rose presently as if bedward bound, but paused behind Moor, turned his face upward, and said, bending on it a look given to this friend alone—

"If my confidence were a good gift, you should have it. But my experience must not mar your faith in womankind. Keep it as chivalrous as ever, and may God send you the mate whom you deserve. Geoffrey, good night."

"Good night, Adam."

And with a hand-shake more expressive of affection than many a tenderer demonstration, they parted—Warwick to watch the stars for hours, and Moor to muse beside the fire till the little boots were dry.

CHAPTER V

A GOLDEN WEDDING

HITHERTO they had been a most decorous crew, but the next morning something in the air seemed to cause a general overflow of spirits, and they went up the river like a party of children on a merry-making. Sylvia decorated herself with garlands till she looked like a mermaid; Mark, as skipper, issued his orders with the true Marblehead twang; Moor kept up a fire of pun-provoking raillery; Warwick sung like a jovial giant; while the Kelpie danced over the water as if inspired with the universal gayety, and the very ripples seemed to lauch as they hurried by.*

"Mark, there is a boat coming up behind us with three gentlemen in it, who evidently intend to pass us with a great display of skill. Of course you won't let it," said Sylvia, welcoming the prospect of a race.

Her brother looked over his shoulder, took a critical survey, and nodded approvingly.

"They are worth a lesson, and shall have it. Easy, now, till they pass; then hard all, and give them a specimen of high art."

A sudden lull ensued on board the Kelpie while the blue shirts approached, caught, and passed with a great display of science, as Sylvia had prophesied, and as good an imitation of the demeanor of experienced watermen as could be assumed by a trio of studious youths not yet out of

---

*Alcott's structural revision of the "Golden Wedding" chapter (ch. VII in *M2*) begins here, with the omission of the boat race and therefore the encounter with Gabriel André.

their teens. As the foam of their wake broke against the other boat's side, Mark hailed them—

"Good morning, gentlemen! We'll wait for you above there, at the bend."

"All serene," returned the rival helmsman, with a bow in honor of Sylvia, while the other two caused a perceptible increase in the speed of the "Juanita," whose sentimental name was not at all in keeping with its rakish appearance.

"Short-sighted infants, to waste their wind in that style; but they pull well for their years," observed Mark paternally, as he waited till the others had gained sufficient advantage to make the race a more equal one. "Now. then!" he whispered a moment after; and, if suddenly endowed with life, the Kelpie shot away with the smooth speed given by strength and skill. Sylvia watched both boats, yearning to take an oar herself, yet full of admiration for the well-trained rowers, whose swift strokes set the river in a foam and made the moment one of pleasure and excitement. The blue shirts did their best against competitors who had rowed in many crafts and many waters. They kept the advantage till near the bend, then Mark's crew lent their reserved strength to a final effort, and bending to their oars with a will, gained steadily, till, with a triumphant stroke, they swept far ahead, and with oars at rest waited in magnanimous silence till the Juanita came up, gracefully confessing her defeat by a good-humored cheer from her panting crew.

For a moment the two boats floated side by side, while the young men interchanged compliments and jokes, for a river is a highway where all travellers may salute each other, and college boys are "Hail fellow! well met" with all the world.

Sylvia sat watching the lads, and one among them struck her fancy. The helmsman who had bowed to her was slight and swarthy, with Southern eyes, vivacious manners, and a singularly melodious voice. A Spaniard, she thought, and pleased herself with this picturesque figure till a traitorous smile about the young man's mouth betrayed that he was not unconscious of her regard. She colored as she met the glance of mingled mirth and admiration that he gave her, and hastily began to pull off the weedy decorations which she had forgotten. But she paused presently, for she heard a surprised voice exclaim—

"Why, Warwick! is that you or your ghost?"

Looking up Sylvia saw Adam lift the hat he had pulled over his brows, and take a slender brown hand extended over the boat-side with something like reluctance, as he answered the question in Spanish. A short conversation ensued, in which the dark stranger seemed to ask innumerable questions, Warwick to give curt replies, and the names Gabriel and Ottila to occur with familiar frequency. Sylvia knew nothing of the language, but received an impression that Warwick was not overjoyed at the meeting; that the youth was both pleased and perplexed by finding him there; and that neither parted with much regret as the distance slowly widened between the boats, and with a farewell salute parted company, each taking a different branch of the river, which divided just there.

For the first time Warwick allowed Mark to take his place at the oar, and sat looking into the clear depths below as if some scene lay there which other eyes could not discover.

"Who was the olive-colored party with the fine eyes and foreign accent?" asked Mark, lazily rowing.

"Gabriel André."

"Is he an Italian?"

"No; a Cuban."

"I forgot you had tried that mixture of Spain and Alabama. How was it?"

"As such climates always are to me,—intoxicating to-day, enervating to-morrow."

"How long were you there?"

"Three months."

"I feel tropically inclined, so tell us about it."

"There is nothing to tell."

"I'll prove that by a catechism. Where did you stay?"

"In Havana."

"Of course, but with whom?"

"Gabriel André."

"The father of the saffron youth?"

"Yes."

"Of whom did the family consist?"

"Four persons."

"Mark, leave Mr. Warwick alone."

"As long as he answers I shall question. Name the four persons, Adam."

"Gabriel, sen., Dolores his wife, Gabriel, jun., Catalina, his sister."

"Ah! now we progress. Was señorita Catalina as comely as her brother?"

"More so."

"You adored her, of course?"

"I loved her."

"Great heavens! what discoveries we make. He likes it, I know by the satirical glimmer in his eye; therefore I continue. She adored you, of course?"

"She loved me."

"You will return and marry her?"

"No."

"Your depravity appals me."

"Did I volunteer its discovery?"

"I demand it now. You left this girl believing that you adored her?"

"She knew I was fond of her."

"The parting was tender?"

"On her part."

"Iceberg! she wept in your arms?"

"And gave me an orange."

"You cherished, it of course?"

"I ate it immediately."

"What want of sentiment! You promised to return?"

"Yes."

"But will never keep the promise?"

"I never break one."

"Yet will not marry her?"

"By no means."

"Ask how old the lady was, Mark?"

"Age, Warwick?"

"Seven."

Mark caught a crab of the largest size at this reply, and remained where he fell, among the ruins of the castle in Spain, which he had erected with the scanty materials vouchsafed to him, while Warwick went back to his meditations.

A drop of rain roused Sylvia from the contemplation of an imaginary portrait of the little Cuban girl, and looking skyward she saw that the frolicsome wind had prepared a practical joke for them in the shape of a thunder-shower. A consultation was held, and it was decided to row on till a house appeared, in which they would take refuge till the storm was over. On they went, but the rain was in greater haste than they, and a summary drenching was effected before the toot of a dinner-horn guided them to shelter. Landing they marched over fields, a moist and mirthful company, toward a red farm-house standing under venerable elms, with a patriarchal air which promised hospitable treatment and good cheer.* A promise speedily fulfilled by the lively old woman, who appeared with an energetic "Shoo!" for the speckled hens congregated in the porch, and a hearty welcome for the weather-beaten strangers.

"Sakes alive!" she exclaimed; "you be in a mess, aint you? Come right in and make yourselves to home. Abel, take the men folks up chamber, and fit 'em out with anything dry you kin lay hands on. Phebe, see to this poor little creeter, and bring her down lookin' less like a drownded kitten. Nat, clear up your wittlin's, so 's't they kin toast their feet when they come down; and, Cinthy, don't dish up dinner jest yet."

These directions were given with such vigorous illustration, and the old face shone with such friendly zeal, that the four submitted at once, sure that the kind soul was pleasing herself in serving them, and finding something very attractive in the place, the people, and their own position. Abel, a staid farmer of forty, obeyed his mother's order regarding the "men folks;" and Phebe, a buxom girl of sixteen, led Sylvia to her own room, eagerly offering her best.

As she dried and redressed herself, Sylvia made sundry discoveries, which added to the romance and the enjoyment of the adventure. A smart gown lay on the bed in the low chamber, also various decorations upon chair and table, suggesting that some festival was afloat; and a few questions elicited the facts. Grandpa had seven sons and three daughters, all living, all married, and all blessed with flocks of children. Grandpa's birthday was always celebrated by a family gathering; but to-day, being the fiftieth anniversary of his wedding, the various households had resolved to keep it with unusual pomp; and all were coming for a supper, a dance, and a "sing" at the end. Upon receipt of which intelligence Sylvia proposed an immediate departure; but the grandmother and daughter cried out at this, pointed to the still falling rain, the lowering sky, the wet heap on the floor, and insisted on the strangers all remaining to enjoy the festival, and give an added interest by their presence.

Half promising what she wholly desired, Sylvia put on Phebe's second best blue gingham gown for the preservation of which she added a

---

*The revision ends here. The revised opening of this chapter is reprinted in the appendix (118–23).

white apron, and completing the whole with a pair of capacious shoes, went down to find her party and reveal the state of affairs. They were bestowed in the prim, best parlor, and greeted her with a peal of laughter; for all were *en costume*. Abel was a stout man, and his garments hung upon Moor with a melancholy air; Mark had disdained them, and with an eye to effect laid hands on an old uniform, in which he looked like a volunteer of 1812;[1] while Warwick's superior height placed Abel's wardrobe out of the question; and grandpa, taller than any of his seven goodly sons, supplied him with a sober suit,—roomy, square-flapped, and venerable,—which became him, and with his beard produced the curious effect of a youthful patriarch. To Sylvia's relief it was unanimously decided to remain, trusting to their own penetration to discover the most agreeable method of returning the favor; and regarding the adventure as a welcome change, after two days' solitude, all went out to dinner prepared to enact their parts with spirit.

The meal being despatched, Mark and Warwick went to help Abel with some out-door arrangements; and begging grandma to consider him one of her own boys, Moor tied on an apron and fell to work with Sylvia, laying the long table which was to receive the coming stores. True breeding is often as soon felt by the uncultivated as by the cultivated; and the zeal with which the strangers threw themselves into the business of the hour won the family, and placed them all in friendly relations at once. The old lady let them do what they would, admiring everything, and declaring over and over again that her new assistants "beat her boys and girls to nothin' with their tastiness and smartness." Sylvia trimmed the table with common flowers till it was an inviting sight before a viand appeared upon it, and hung green boughs about the room, with candles here and there to lend a festal light. Moor trundled a great cheese in from the dairy, brought milk-pans without mishap, disposed dishes, and caused Nat to cleave to him by the administration of surreptitious titbits and jocular suggestions; while Phebe tumbled about in every one's way, quite wild with excitement; and grandma stood in her pantry like a culinary general, swaying a big knife for a baton, as she issued orders and marshalled her forces, the busiest and merriest of them all.

When the last touch was given, Moor discarded his apron and went to join Mark. Sylvia presided over Phebe's toilet, and then sat herself down to support Nat through the trying half hour before, as he expressed it, "the party came in." The twelve years' boy was a cripple, one of those household blessings which, in the guise of an affliction, keep many hearts tenderly united by a common love and pity. A cheerful creature, always chirping like a cricket on the hearth as he sat carving or turning bits of wood into useful or ornamental shapes for such as cared to buy them of him, and hoarding up the proceeds like a little miser for one more helpless than himself.

"What are these, Nat?" asked Sylvia, with the interest that always won small people, because their quick instincts felt that it was sincere.

"Them are spoons—'postle spoons, they call 'em. You see I've got a cousin what reads a sight, and one day he says to me, 'Nat, in a book I see somethin' about a set of spoons with a 'postle's head on each of 'em; you make some and they'll sell I bet.' So I got gramper's Bible, found the picters of the 'postles, and worked and worked till I got the faces good; and now it's fun, for they do sell, and I'm savin' up a lot. It ain't for me, you know, but mother, 'cause she's wuss'n I be."

"Is she sick, Nat?"

"Oh, ain't she! Why she hasn't stood up this nine year. We was smashed in a wagon that tipped over when I was three years old. It done somethin' to my legs, but it broke her back, and made her no use, only jest to pet me, and keep us all kind of stiddy, you know. Ain't you seen her? Don't you want to?"

"Would she like it?"

"She admires to see folks, and asked about you at dinner; so I guess you'd better go see her. Look ahere, you like them spoons, and I'm agoin' to give you one; I'd give you all on 'em if they wasn't promised. I can make one more in time, so you jest take your pick, 'cause I like you, and want you not to forget me."

Sylvia chose Saint John, because it resembled Moor, she thought; bespoke and paid for a whole set, and privately resolved to send tools and rare woods to the little artist that he might serve his mother in his own pretty way. Then Nat took up his crutches and hopped nimbly before her to the room, where a plain, serene-faced woman lay knitting, with her best cap on, her clean handkerchief and large green fan laid out upon the coverlet. This was evidently the best room of the house; and as Sylvia sat taling to the invalid her eyes discovered many traces of that refinement which comes through the affections. Nothing seemed too good for "daughter Patience;" birds, books, flowers, and pictures were plentiful here though visible nowhere else. Two easy-chairs beside the bed showed where the old folks oftenest sat; Abel's home corner was there by the antique desk covered with farmers' literature and samples of seeds;

Phebe's work-basket stood in the window; Nat's lathe in the sunniest corner; and from the speckless carpet to the canary's clear water-glass all was exquisitely neat, for love and labor were the handmaids who served the helpless woman and asked no wages but her comfort.

Sylvia amused her new friends mightily, for finding that neither mother nor son had any complaints to make, any sympathy to ask, she exerted herself to give them what both needed, and kept them laughing by a lively recital of her voyage and its mishaps.

"Aint she prime, mother?" was Nat's candid commentary when the story ended, and he emerged red and shiny from the pillows where he had burrowed with boyish explosions of delight.

"She's very kind, dear, to amuse two stay-at-home folks like you and me, who seldom see what's going on outside four walls. You have a merry heart, miss, and I hope will keep it all your days, for it's a blessed thing to own."

"I think you have something better, a contented one," said Sylvia, as the woman regarded her with no sign of envy or regret.

"I ought to have; nine years on a body's back can teach a sight of things that are wuth knowin'. I've learnt patience pretty well I guess, and contentedness aint fur away, for though it sometimes seems ruther long to look forward to, perhaps nine more years layin' here, I jest remember it might have been wuss, and if I don't do much now there's all eternity to come."

Something in the woman's manner struck Sylvia as she watched her softly beating some tune on the sheet with her quiet eyes turning toward the light. Many sermons had been less eloquent to the girl than the look, the tone, the cheerful resignation of that plain face. She stooped and kissed it, saying gently—

"I shall remember this."

"Hooray! there they be; I hear Ben!"

And away clattered Nat to be immediately absorbed into the embraces of a swarm of relatives who now began to arrive in a steady stream. Old and young, large and small, rich and poor, with overflowing hands or trifles humbly given, all were received alike, all hugged by grandpa, kissed by grandma, shaken half breathless by Uncle Abel, welcomed by Aunt Patience, and danced round by Phebe and Nat till the house seemed a great hive of hilarious and affectionate bees. At first the strangers stood apart, but Phebe spread their story with such complimentary additions of her own that the family circle opened wide and took them in at once.

A Golden Wedding

Sylvia was enraptured with the wilderness of babies, and leaving the others to their own devices followed the matrons to "Patience's room," and gave herself up to the pleasant tyranny of the small potentates, who swarmed over her as she sat on the floor, tugging at her hair, exploring her eyes, covering her with moist kisses, and keeping up a babble of little voices more delightful to her than the discourse of the flattered mammas who benignly surveyed her admiration and their offspring's prowess.

The young people went to romp in the barn; the men, armed with unbrellas, turned out *en masse* to inspect the farm and stock, and compare notes over pig pens and garden gates. But Sylvia lingered where she was, enjoying a scene which filled her with a tender pain and pleasure, for each baby was laid on grandma's knee, its small virtues, vices, ailments, and accomplishments rehearsed, its beauties examined, its strength tested, and the verdict of the family oracle pronounced upon it as it was cradled, kissed, and blessed on the kind old heart which had room for every care and joy of those who called her mother. It was a sight the girl never forgot, because just then she was ready to receive it. Her best lessons did not come from books, and she learned one then as she saw the fairest success of a woman's life while watching this happy grandmother with fresh faces framing her withered one, daughterly voices chorusing good wishes, and the harvest of half a century of wedded life beautifully garnered in her arms.

The fragrance of coffee and recollections of Cynthia's joyful aberrations at such periods caused a breaking up of the maternal conclave. The babies were borne away to simmer between blankets until called for. The women unpacked baskets, brooded over teapots, and kept up an harmonious clack as the table was spread with pyramids of cake, regiments of pies, quagmires of jelly, snow-banks of bread, and gold mines of butter; every possible article of food, from baked beans to wedding cake, finding a place on that sacrificial altar.

Fearing to be in the way, Sylvia departed to the barn, where she found her party in a chaotic Babel; for the offshoots had been as fruitful as the parent tree, and some four dozen young immortals were in full riot. The bashful roosting with the hens on remote lofts and beams; the bold flirting or playing in the full light of day; the boys whooping, the girls screaming, all effervescing as if their spirits had reached the explosive point and must find vent in noise. Mark was in his element, introducing all manner of new games, the liveliest of the old and keeping the revel at its height; for rosy, bright-eyed girls were plenty, and the ancient uniform universally approved. Warwick had a flock of lads about him absorbed in the marvels he was producing with knife, stick, and string; and Moor a rival flock of little lasses breathless with interest in the tales he told. One on each knee, two at each side, four in a row on the hay at his feet, and the boldest of all with an arm about his neck and a curly head upon his shoulder, for Uncle Abel's clothes seemed to invest the wearer with a passport to their confidence at once. Sylvia joined this group and partook of a quiet entertainment with as childlike a relish as any of them, while the merry tumult went on about her.

The toot of the horn sent the whole barnful streaming into the house like a flock of hungry chickens, where, by some process known only to the mothers of large families, every one was wedged close about the table, and the feast began. This was none of your stand-up, wafery, bread and butter teas, but a thorough-going, sit-down supper, and all settled themselves with a smiling satisfaction, prophetic of great powers and an equal willingness to employ them. A detachment of half-grown girls was drawn up behind grandma, as waiters; Sylvia insisted on being one of them, and proved herself a neat-handed Phillis, though for a time slightly bewildered by the gastronomic performances she beheld. Babies ate pickles, small boys sequestered pie with a velocity that made her wink, women swam in the tea, and the men, metaphorically speaking, swept over the table like a swarm of locusts, while the host and hostess beamed upon one another and their robust descendants with an honest pride, which was beautiful to see.

"That Mr. Wackett ain't eat scursely nothin', he jest sets lookin' round kinder 'mazed like. Do go and make him fall to on somethin', or I shan't take a mite of comfort in my vittles," said grandma, as the girl came with an empty cup.

"He is enjoying it will all his heart and eyes, ma'am, for we don't see such fine spectacles every day. I'll take him something that he likes and make him eat it."

"Sakes alive! be you to be Mis' Wackett? I'd no idee of it, you look so young."

"Nor I; we are only friends, ma'am."

"Oh!" and the monosyllable was immensely expressive, as the old lady confided a knowing nod to the teapot, into whose depths she was just then peering. Sylvia walked away wondering why persons were always thinking and saying such things.

As she paused behind Warwick's chair with a glass of cream and a round of brown bread, he looked up at her with his blandest expression, though a touch of something like regret was in his voice.

"This is a sight worth living eighty hard years to see, and I envy that old couple as I never envied any one before. To rear ten virtuous children, put ten useful men and women into the world, and give them health and courage to work out their own salvation as these honest souls will do, is a better job done for the Lord, than winning a battle, or ruling a State. Here is all honor to them. Drink it with me."

He put the glass to her lips, drank what she left, and rising, placed her in his seat with the decisive air which few resisted.

"You take no thought of yourself and are doing too much; sit here a little, and let me take a few steps where you have taken many."

He served her, and standing at her back, bent now and then to speak, still with that softened look upon the face so seldom stirred by the gentler emotions that lay far down in that deep heart of his; for never had he felt so solitary.

All things must have an end, even a family feast, and by the time the last boys buttons peremptorily announced, 'Thus far shalt thou go and no farther,' all professed themselves satisfied, and a general uprising took place. The surplus population were herded in parlor and chambers, while a few energetic hands cleared away, and with much clattering of dishes and wafting of towels, left grandma's spandy clean premises as immaculate as ever. It was dark when all was done, so the kitchen was cleared, the candles lighted, Patience's door set open, and little Nat established in an impromptu orchestra, composed of a table and a chair, whence the first squeak of his fiddle proclaimed that the ball had begun.

Everybody danced; the babies stacked on Patience's bed, or penned behind chairs, sprawled and pranced in unsteady mimicry of their elders. Ungainly farmers, stiff with labor, recalled their early days and tramped briskly as they swung their wives about with a kindly pressure of the hard hands that had worked so long together. Little pairs toddled gravely through the figures, or frisked promiscuously in a grand conglomeration of arms and legs. Gallant cousins kissed pretty cousins at exciting periods, and were not rebuked. Mark wrought several of these incipient lovers to a pitch of despair, by his devotion to the comeliest damsels, and the skill with which he executed unheard-of evolutions before their admiring eyes; Moor led out the poorest and the plainest with a respect that caused their homely faces to shine, and their scant skirts to be forgotten. Warwick skimmed his five years partner through the air in a way that rendered her speechless with delight; and Sylvia danced as she never danced before. With sticky-fingered boys, sleepy with repletion, but bound to last it out; with rough-faced men who paid her paternal compliments; with smart youths who turned sheepish with that white lady's hand in their big brown ones, and one ambitious lad who confided to her his burning desire to work a sawmill, and marry a girl with black eyes and yellow hair. While, perched aloft, Nat bowed away till his pale face glowed, till all hearts warmed, all feet beat responsive to the good old tunes which have put so much health into human bodies, and so much happiness into human souls.

At the stroke of nine the last dance came. All down the long kitchen stretched two breathless rows; grandpa and grandma at the top, the youngest pair of grandchildren at the bottom, and all between fathers, mothers, uncles, aunts, and cousins, while such of the babies as were still extant, bobbed with unabated vigor, as Nat struck up the Virginia Reel, and the sturdy old couple led off as gallantly as the young one who came tearing up to meet them. Away they went, grandpa's white hair flying in the wind, grandma's impressive cap awry with excitement, as they ambled down the middle, and finished with a kiss when their tuneful journey was done, amid immense applause from those who regarded this as the crowning event of the day.

When all had had their turn, and twirled till they were dizzy, a short lull took place, with refreshments for such as still possessed the power of enjoying them. Then Phebe appeared with an armful of books, and all settled themselves for the family "sing."

Sylvia had heard much fine music, but never any that touched her like this, for though often discordant, it was hearty, with that undercurrent of feeling which adds sweetness to the rudest lay, and is often more attractive than the most florid ornament or faultless execution. Every one sang as every one had danced, with all their might; shrill children, soft-voiced girls, lullaby-singing mothers, gruff boys, and strong-lunged men; the old pair quavered, and still a few indefatigable babies crowed behind their little coops. Songs, ballads, comic airs, popular melodies, and hymns, came in rapid succession. And when they ended with that song which should be classed with sacred music for association's sake, and standing hand in hand about the room with the golden bride and bridegroom in their midst, sang "Home," Sylvia leaned against her brother with dim eyes and a heart too full to sing.

A Golden Wedding

Still standing thus when the last note had soared up and died, the old man folded his hands and began to pray. It was an old-fashioned prayer, such as the girl had never heard from the Bishop's lips; ungrammatical, inelegant, and long. A quiet talk with God, manly in its straightforward confession of short-comings, childlike in its appeal for guidance, fervent in its gratitude for all good gifts, and the crowning one of loving children. As if close intercourse had made the two familiar, this human father turned to the Divine, as these sons and daughters turned to him, as free to ask, as confident of a reply, as all afflictions, blessings, cares, and crosses, were laid down before him, and the work of eighty years submitted to his hand. There were not sounds in the room but the one voice often tremulous with emotion and with age, the coo of some dreaming baby, or the low sob of some mother whose arms were empty, as the old man stood there, rugged and white atop as the granite hills, with the old wife at his side, a circle of sons and daughters girdling them round, and in all hearts the thought that as the former wedding had been made for time this golden one at eighty must be for eternity.

While Sylvia looked and listened a sense of genuine devotion stole over her; the beauty and the worth of prayer grew clear to her through the earnest speech of that unlettered man, and for the first time she fully felt the nearness and the dearness of the Universal Father, whom she had been taught to fear, yet longed to love.

"Now, my children, you must go before the little folks are tuckered out," said Grandpa heartily. "Mother and me can't say enough toe thank you for the presents you have fetched us, the dutiful wishes you have give us, the pride and comfort you have allers ben toe us. I aint no hand at speeches, so I shan't make none, but jest say ef any 'fliction falls on any on you, remember mother's here toe help you bear it; ef any wordly loss comes toe you, remember father's house is yourn while it stans, and so the Lord bless and keep us all."

"Three cheers for gramper and grammer!" roared a six-foot scion as a safety valve for sundry unmasculine emotions, and three rousing hurras made the rafters ring, struck terror to the heart of the oldest inhabitant of the rat-haunted garret, and summarily woke all the babies.

Then the good-byes began, the flurry of wrong baskets, pails and bundles in wrong places; the sorting out of small folk too sleepy to know or care what became of them; the maternal cluckings, and paternal shouts for Kitty, Cy, Ben, Bill, or Mary Ann; the piling into vehicles with much

71

ramping of indignant horses unused to such late hours; the last farewells, the roll of wheels, as one by one the happy loads departed, and peace fell upon the household for another year.

"I declare for't, I never had sech an out an out good time sense I was born intoe the world. Ab'ram, you are fit to drop, and so be I; now let's set and talk it over along of Patience fore we go toe bed."

The old couple got into their chairs, and as they sat there side by side, remembering that she had given no gift, Sylvia crept behind them, and lending the magic of her voice to the simple air, sang the fittest song for time and place— "John Anderson my Jo." It was too much for grandma, the old heart overflowed, and reckless of the cherished cap she laid her head on her "John's" shoulder, exclaiming through her tears—

"That's the cap sheaf of the hull, and I can't bear no more to-night. Ab'ram, lend me your hankchif, for I dunno where mine is, and my face is all of a drip."

Before the red bandana had gently performed its work in grandpa's hand, Sylvia beckoned her party from the room, and showing them the clear moonlight night which followed the storm, suggested that they should both save appearances and enjoy a novel pleasure by floating home-ward instead of sleeping.* The tide against which they had pulled in coming-up would sweep them rapidly along, and make it easy to retrace in a few hours the way they had loitered over for three days.

The pleasant excitement of the evening had not yet subsided, and all applauded the plan as a fit finale to their voyage. The old lady strongly objected, but the young people overruled her, and being re-equipped in their damaged garments they bade the friendly family a grateful adieu, left their more solid thanks under Nat's pillow, and re-embarked, upon their shining road.

All night Sylvia lay under the canopy of boughs her brother made to shield her from the dew, listening to the soft sounds about her, the twitter of a restless bird, the bleat of some belated lamb, the ripple of a brook

---

M2 concludes "A Golden Wedding" with Sylvia falling asleep in Phoebe's garret room:

Before the red bandanna in grandpa's hand had gently performed its work, Sylvia slipped away to share Phoebe's bed in the old garret; lying long awake, full of new and happy thoughts, and lulled to sleep at last by the pleasant patter of the rain upon the roof. (139)

babbling like a baby in its sleep. All night she watched the changing shores, silvery green or dark with slumberous shadow, and followed the moon in its tranquil journey through the sky. When it set, she drew her cloak about her, and, pillowing her head upon her arm, exchanged the waking for a sleeping dream.

A thick mist encompassed her when she awoke. Above the sun shone dimly, below rose and fell the billows of the sea, before her sounded the city's fitful hum, and far behind her lay the green wilderness where she had lived and learned so much. Slowly the fog lifted, the sun came dazzling down upon the sea, and out in the open bay they sailed with the pennon streaming in the morning wind. But still with backward glance the girl watched the misty wall that rose between her and the charmed river, and still with yearning heart confessed how sweet that brief experience had been, for though she had not yet discovered it, like

> "The fairy Lady of Shalott,
> She had left the web and left the loom,
> Had seen the water lilies bloom,
> Had seen the helmet and the plume,
> And had looked down to Camelot." *[2]

---

*These lines from Tennyson conclude a new chapter, Chapter VIII, "Sermons," in *M2*, which ends with Sylvia's reverie as she is sailing down the river, through the night. "Sermons" is reprinted in the appendix (140–55).

CHAPTER VI

WHY SYLVIA WAS HAPPY

"I NEVER did understand you, Sylvia; and this last month you have been a perfect enigma to me."

With rocking-chair in full action, suspended needle, and thoughtful expression, Miss Yule had watched her sister for ten minutes as she sat with her work at her feet, her hands folded on her lap, and her eyes dreamily fixed on vacancy.

"I always was to myself, Prue, and am more so than ever now," answered Sylvia, waking out of her reverie with a smile that proved it had been a pleasant one.

"There must be some reason for this great change in you. Come, tell me, dear."

With a motherly gesture Miss Yule drew the girl to her knee, brushed back the bright hair, and looked into the face so freely turned to hers. Through all the years they had been together, the elder sister had never seen before the expression which the younger's face now wore. A vague expectancy sat in her eyes, some nameless content sweetened her smile, a beautiful repose replaced the varying enthusiasm, listlessness, and melancholy that used to haunt her countenance and make it such a study. Miss Yule could not read the secret of the change, yet felt its novel charm; Sylvia could not explain it, though penetrated by its power; and for a moment the sisters looked into each other's faces, wondering why each seemed altered. Then Prue, who never wasted much time in speculations of any kind, shook her head, and repeated—

"I don't understand it, but it must be right, because you are so improved in every way. Ever since that wild trip up the river you have been growing quiet, lovable, and cheerful, and I really begin to hope that you will become like other people."

"I only know that I am happy, Prue. Why it is so I cannot tell; but now I seldom have the old dissatisfied and restless feeling. Everything looks pleasant to me, every one seems kind, and life begins to be both sweet and earnest. It is only one of my moods, I suppose; but I am grateful for it, and pray that it may last."

So earnestly she spoke, so cheerfully she smiled, that Miss Yule blessed the mood and echoed Sylvia's wish, exclaiming in the next breath, with a sudden inspiration—

"My, dear, I've got it! You are growing up."

"I think I am. You tried to make a woman of me at sixteen, but it was impossible until the right time came. That wild trip up the river, as you call it, did more for me than I can ever tell, and when I seemed most like a child I was learning to be a woman."

"Well, my dear, go on as you've begun, and I shall be more than satisfied. What merry-making is on foot to-night? Mark and these friends of his keep you in constant motion with their riding, rowing, and rambling excursions, and if it did not agree with you so excellently, I really should like a little quiet after a month of bustle."

"They are only coming up as usual, and that reminds me that I must go and dress."

"There is another new change, Sylvia. You never used to care what you wore or how you looked, no matter how much time and trouble I expended on you and your wardrobe. Now you do care, and it does my heart good to see you always charmingly dressed, and looking your prettiest," said Miss Yule, with the satisfaction of a woman who heartily believed in costume as well as all the other elegances and proprieties of fashionable life.

"Am I ever that, Prue?" asked Sylvia, pausing on the threshold with a shy yet wistful glance.

"Ever what, dear?"

"Pretty?"

"Always so to me; and now I think every one finds you very attractive because you try to please, and seem to succeed delightfully."

Sylvia had never asked that question before, had never seemed to know or care, and could not have chosen a more auspicious moment for her frank inquiry than the present. The answer seemed to satisfy her, and smiling at some blithe anticipation of her own, she went away to make a lampless toilet in the dusk, which proved how slight a hold the feminine passion for making one's self pretty had yet taken upon her.

The September moon was up and shining clearly over garden, lawn, and sea, when the sound of voices called her down. At the stair-foot she paused with a disappointed air, for only one hat lay on the hall table, and a glance showed her only one guest with Mark and Prue. She strolled irresolutely through the breezy hall, looked out at either open door, sung a little to herself, but broke off in the middle of a line, and, as if following a sudden impulse, went out into the mellow moonlight, forgetful of uncovered head or dewy damage to the white hem of her gown. Half way down the avenue she paused before a shady nook, and looked in. The evergreens that enclosed it made the seat doubly dark to eyes inured to the outer light, and seeing a familiar seeming figure sitting with its head upon its hand, Sylvia leaned in, saying, with a daughterly caress—

"Why, what is my romantic father doing here?"

The sense of touch was quicker than that of sight, and with an exclamation of surprise she had drawn back before Warwick replied—

"It is not the old man, but the young one, who is romancing here."

"I beg your pardon! We have been waiting for you; what thought is so charming that you forgot us all?"

Sylvia was a little startled, else she would scarcely have asked so plain a question. But Warwick often asked much blunter ones, always told the naked truth without prevarication or delay, and straightway answered—*

"The thought of the woman whom I hope to make my wife."

Sylvia stood silent for a moment as if intent on fastening in her hair the delicate spray of hop-bells just gathered from the vine that formed a leafy frame for the graceful picture which she made standing, with uplifted arms, behind the arch. When she spoke it was to say, as she moved on toward the house—.

"It is too beautiful a night to stay in doors, but Prue is waiting for me, and Mark wants to plan with you about our ride to-morrow. Shall we go together?"

---

*Alcott changed Warwick's reply and the conversation that follows it in *M2*. The revised portion is reprinted in the appendix (160–64).

She beckoned, and he came out of the shadow showing her an expression which she had never seen before. His face was flushed, his eye unquiet, his manner eager yet restrained. She had seen him intellectually excited many times; never emotionally till now. Something wayward, yet warm, in this new mood attracted her, because so like her own. But with a tact as native as her sympathy she showed no sign of this, except in the attentive look she fixed upon him as the moonlight bathed him in its splendor. He met the glance, seemed to interpret it aright, but did not answer its unconscious inquiry; for pausing, he asked abruptly—

"Should a rash promise be considered binding when it threatens to destroy one's peace?"

Sylvia pondered an instant before she answered slowly—

"If the promise was freely given, no sin committed in its keeping, and no peace troubled but one's own, I should say yes."

Still pausing, he looked down at her with that unquiet glance as she looked up with her steady one, and with the same anxiety he asked—

"Would you keep such a promise inviolate, even though it might cost you the sacrifice of something dearer to you than your life?"

She thought again, and again looked up, answering with the sincerity that he had taught her—

"It might be unwise, but if the sacrifice was not one of principle or something that I ought to love more than life, I think I should keep the promise as religiously as an Indian keeps a vow of vengeance."

As she spoke, some recollection seemed to strike Warwick like a sudden stab. The flush died out of his face, the fire from his eyes, and an almost grim composure fell upon him as he said low to himself, with a forward step as if eager to leave some pain behind him—

"It is better so; for his sake I will leave all to time."

Sylvia saw his lips move, but caught no sound till he said with a gravity that was almost gloom—

"I think you would; therefore, beware how you bind yourself with such verbal bonds. Let us go in."

They went; Warwick to the drawing-room, but Sylvia ran up stairs for the Berlin wools, which in spite of heat and the sure staining of fingers were to be wound that night according to contract, for she kept a small promise as sacredly as she would have done a greater one.*

---

*Here the revision ends and the scene resumes with Sylvia and Warwick in the Yule's drawing room.

"What have you been doing to give yourself such an uplifted expression, Sylvia?" said Mark, as she came in.

"Feasting my eyes on lovely colors. Does not that look like a folded rainbow?" she answered, laying her brilliant burden on the table where Warwick sat examining a broken reel, and Prue was absorbed in getting a carriage blanket under way.

"Come, Sylvia, I shall soon be ready for the first shade," she said, clashing her formidable needles. "Is that past mending, Mr. Warwick?"

"Yes, without better tools than a knife, two pins, and a bodkin."

"Then you must put the skeins on a chair, Sylvia. Try not to tangle them, and spread your handkerchief in your lap, for that maroon color will stain sadly. Now don't speak to me, for I must count my stitches."

Sylvia began to wind the wools with a swift dexterity as natural to her hands as certain little graces of gesture which made their motions pleasant to watch. Warwick never rummaged work-baskets, gossiped, or paid compliments for want of something to do. If no little task appeared for them, he kept his hands out of mischief, and if nothing occurred to make words agreeable or necessary, he proved that he understood the art of silence, and sat with those vigilant eyes of his fixed upon whatever object attracted them. Just then the object was a bright band slipping round the chair-back, with a rapidity that soon produced a snarl, but no help till patient fingers had smoothed and wound it up. Then, with the look of one who says to himself, "I will!" he turned, planted himself squarely before Sylvia, and held out his hands.

"Here is a reel that will neither tangle nor break your skeins, will you use it?"

"Yes, thank you, and in return I'll wind your color first."

"Which is my color?"

"This fine scarlet, strong, enduring, and martial, like yourself."

"You are right."

"I thought so; Mr. Moor prefers blue, and I violet."

"Blue and red make violet," called Mark from his corner, catching the word "color," though busy with a sketch for a certain fair Jessie Hope.

Moor was with Mr. Yule in his study, Prue mentally wrapped in her blanket, and when Sylvia was drawn into an artistic controversy with her brother, Warwick fell into deep thought.

With the pride of a proud man once deceived, he had barred his heart against womankind, resolving that no second defeat should oppress him with that distrust of self and others, which is harder for a generous nature to bear, than the pain of its own wound. He had yet to learn that the shadow of love suggests its light; and that they who have been cheated of the food, without which none can truly live, long for it with redoubled hunger. Of late he had been discovering this, for a craving, stronger than his own strong will, possessed him. He tried to disbelieve and silence it; attacked it with reason, starved it with neglect, and chilled it with contempt. But when he fancied it was dead, the longing rose again, and with a clamorous cry, undid his work. For the first time, this free spirit felt the master's hand, confessed a need its own power could not supply, and saw that no man can live alone on even the highest aspirations without suffering for the vital warmth of the affections. A month ago he would have disdained the hope that now was so dear to him. But imperceptibly the influences of domestic life had tamed and won him. Solitude looked barren, vagrancy had lost its charm; his life seemed cold and bare, for, though devoted to noble aims, it was wanting in the social sacrifices, cares, and joys, that foster charity, and sweeten character. An impetuous desire to enjoy the rich experience which did so much for others, came over him to-night as it had often done while sharing the delights of this home, where he had made so long a pause. But with the desire came a memory that restrained him better than his promise. He saw what others had not yet discovered, and obeying the code of honor which governs a true gentlemen, loved his friend better than himself and held his peace.

The last skein came, and as she wound it, Sylvia's glance involuntarily rose from the strong hands to the face above them, and lingered there, for the penetrating gaze was averted, and an unwonted mildness inspired confidence as its usual expression of power commanded respect. His silence troubled her, and with curious yet respectful scrutiny, she studied his face as she had never done before. She found it full of a noble gravity and kindliness; candor and courage spoke in the lines of the mouth, benevolence and intellect in the broad arch of the forehead, ardor and energy in the fire of the eye, and on every lineament the stamp of that genuine manhood, which no art can counterfeit. Intent upon discovering the secret of the mastery he exerted over all who approached him, Sylvia had quite forgotten herself, when suddenly Warwick's eyes were fixed full open upon her own. What spell lay in them she could not tell, for human eye had never shed such sudden summer over her. Admiration was not in it, for it did not agitate; nor audacity, for it did not abash; but something that thrilled warm through blood and nerves, that filled her with a glad submission to some power, absolute yet tender, and caused her to turn her innocent face freely to his gaze, letting him read therein a sentiment for which she had not yet found a name.

It lasted but a moment; yet in that moment, each saw the other's heart, and each turned a new page in the romance of their lives. Sylvia's eyes fell first, but no blush followed, no sign of anger or perplexity, only a thoughtful silence, which continued till the last violet threat dropped from his hands, and she said almost regretfully—

"This is the end."

"Yes, this is the end."

As he echoed the words Warwick rose suddenly and went to talk with Mark, whose sketch was done. Sylvia sat a moment as if quite forgetful where she was, so absorbing was some thought or emotion. Presently she seemed to glow and kindle with an inward fire; over face and forehead, rushed an impetuous color, her eyes shone, and her lips trembled with the fluttering of her breath. Then a panic appeared to seize her, for, stealing noiselessly away, she hurried to her room, and covering up her face as if to hide it even from herself, whispered to that full heart of hers, with quick coming tears that belied the words—

"Now I know why I am happy!"*

How long she lay there weeping and smiling in the moonlight she never knew. Her sister's call broke in upon the first love dream she had ever woven for herself, and she went down to bid the friends good night. The hall was only lighted by the moon, and in the dimness of the shadow where she stood, no one saw traces of that midsummer shower on her cheeks, or detected the soft trouble in her eye, but for the first time Moor felt her hand tremble in his own and welcomed the propitious omen.

Being an old-fashioned gentleman, Mr. Yule preserved in his family the pleasant custom of hand-shaking, which gives such heartiness to the morning and evening greetings of a household. Moor liked and adopted it; Warwick had never done so, but that night he gave a hand to Prue and Mark with his most cordial expression, and Sylvia felt both her own taken in a warm lingering grasp, although he only said "good by!" Then they went; but while the three paused at the door held by the beauty of the night, back to them on the wings of the wind came Warwick's voice singing the song that Sylvia loved. All down the avenue, and far along the

---

*The ending of "Why Sylvia Was Happy" was revised for *M2;* Alcott's new version is reprinted in the appendix (169–70).

winding road they traced his progress, till the strain died in the distance leaving only the echo of the song to link them to the singer.

When evening came again Sylvia waited on the lawn to have the meeting over in the dark, for love made her very shy. But Moor came alone, and his first words were,

"Comfort me, Sylvia, Adam is gone. He went as unexpectedly as he came, and when I woke this morning a note lay at my door, but my friend was not there."

She murmured some stereotyped regret, but there was a sharp pain at her heart till there came to her the remembrance of Warwick's question, uttered on the spot where she was standing. Some solace she must have, and clinging to this one thought hopefully within herself—

"He has made some promise, has gone to get released from it, and will come back to say what he looked last night. He is so true I will believe in him and wait."

She did wait, but week after week went by and Warwick did not come.

CHAPTER VII

DULL BUT NECESSARY*

WHOEVER cares only for incident and action in a book had better skip this chapter and read on; but those who take an interest in the delineation of character will find the key to Sylvia's here.

John Yule might have been a poet, painter, or philanthropist, for Heaven had endowed him with fine gifts; he was a prosperous merchant with no ambition but to leave a fortune to his children and live down the memory of a bitter past. On the threshold of his life he stumbled and fell; for as he paused there, waiting for the first step to appear, Providence tested and found him wanting. On one side, Poverty offered the aspiring youth her meagre hand; but he was not wise enough to see the virtues hidden under her hard aspect, nor brave enough to learn the stern yet salutary lessons which labor, necessity, and patience teach, giving to those who serve and suffer the true success. On the other hand Opulence allured him with her many baits, and silencing the voice of conscience, he yielded to temptation and wrecked his nobler self.

A loveless marriage was the price he paid for his ambition; not a costly one, he thought, till time taught him that whosoever mars the integrity of his own soul by transgressing the great laws of life, even by so much as a hair's breadth, entails upon himself and heirs the inevitable retribution which proves their worth and keeps them sacred. The tie that

---

* "Dull, But Necessary" appears as Chapter III (43–49) in *M2*.

bound and burdened the unhappy twain, worn thin by constant friction, snapped at last, and in the solemn pause death made in his busy life, there rose before him those two ghosts who sooner or later haunt us all, saying with reproachful voices,—"This I might have been," and "This I am." Then he saw the failure of his life. At fifty he found himself poorer than when he made his momentous choice; for the years that had given him wealth, position, children, had also taken from him youth, self-respect, and many a gift whose worth was magnified by loss. He endeavored to repair the fault so tardily acknowledged, but found it impossible to cancel it when remorse, embittered effort, and age left him powerless to redeem the rich inheritance squandered in his prime.

If ever man received punishment for a self-inflicted wrong it was John Yule. A punishment as subtle as the sin; for in the children growing up about him every relinquished hope, neglected gift, lost aspiration, seemed to live again; yet on each and all was set the direful stamp of imperfection, which made them visible illustrations of the great law broken in his youth.

In Prudence, as she grew to womanhood, he saw his own practical tact and talent, nothing more. She seemed the living representative of the years spent in strife for profit, power, and place; the petty cares that fret the soul, the mercenary schemes that waste a life, the worldly formalities, frivolities, and fears, that so belittle character. All these he saw in this daughter's shape; and with pathetic patience bore the daily trial of an over active, over anxious, affectionate but most prosaic child.

In Mark he saw his ardor for the beautiful, his love of the poetic, his reverence for genius, virtue, heroism. But here too the subtle blight had fallen. This son, though strong in purpose was feeble in performance; for some hidden spring of power was wanting, and the shadow of that earlier defeat chilled in his nature the energy which is the first attribute of all success. Mark loved poetry, and "wrote in numbers for the numbers came;" but, whether tragic, tender, or devout, in each attempt there was enough of the divine fire to warm them into life, yet not enough to gift them with the fervor that can make a line immortal, and every song was a sweet lament for the loftier lays that might have been. He loved art and gave himself to it; but though studying all forms of beauty he never reached its soul, and every effort tantalized him with fresh glimpses of the fair ideal which he could not reach. He loved the true, but high thoughts seldom blossomed into noble deeds; for when the hour came the man was never ready, and disappointment was his daily portion. A sad fate for the son, a far sadder one for the father who had bequeathed it to him from the irrecoverable past.

In Sylvia he saw, mysteriously blended, the two natures that had given her life, although she was born when the gulf between regretful husband and sad wife was widest. As if indignant Nature rebelled against the outrage done her holiest ties, adverse temperaments gifted the child with the good and ill of each. From her father she received pride, intellect, and will; from her mother passion, imagination, and the fateful melancholy of a woman defrauded of her dearest hope. These conflicting temperaments, with all their aspirations, attributes, and inconsistencies, were woven into a nature fair and faulty; ambitious, yet not self-reliant; sensitive, yet not keen-sighted. These two masters ruled soul and body, warring against each other, making Sylvia an enigma to herself and her life a train of moods.

A wise and tender mother would have divined her nameless needs, answered her vague desires, and through the medium of the most omnipotent affection given to humanity, have made her what she might have been. But Sylvia had never known mother-love, for her life came through death; and the only legacy bequeathed her was a slight hold upon existence, a ceaseless craving for affection, and the shadow of a tragedy that wrung from the pale lips, that grew cold against her baby cheek, the cry, "Free at last, thank God for that!"

Prudence could not fill the empty place, though the good-hearted housewife did her best. Neither sister understood the other, and each tormented the other through her very love. Prue unconsciously exasperated Sylvia, Sylvia unconsciously shocked Prue, and they hitched along together each trying to do well and each taking diametrically opposite measures to effect her purpose. Mark briefly but truly described them when he said, "Sylvia trims the house with flowers, but Prudence dogs her with a dustpan."

Mr. Yule was now a studious, melancholy man,* who, having said one fatal "No" to himself, made it the satisfaction of his life to say a never varying "Yes" to his children. But though he left no wish of theirs ungratified, he seemed to have forfeited his power to draw and hold them to himself. He was more like an unobtrusive guest than a master in his house.

---

*busy, silent man *M2* (47)

Dull but Necessary

His children loved, but never clung to him, because unseen, yet impassible, rose the barrier of an instinctive protest against the wrong done their dead mother, unconscious on their part but terribly significant to him.

Mark had been years away; and though the brother and sister were tenderly attached, sex, tastes, and pursuits kept them too far apart, and Sylvia was solitary even in this social seeming home. Dissatisfied with herself, she endeavored to make her life what it should be with the energy of an ardent, aspiring nature; and through all experiences, sweet or bitter, all varying moods, successes and defeats, a sincere desire for happiness the best and highest, was the little rushlight of her soul that never wavered or went out.

She never had known friendship in its truest sense, for next to love it is the most abused of words. She had called many "friend," but was still ignorant of that sentiment, cooler than passion, warmer than respect, more just and generous than either, which recognizes a kindred spirit in another, and claiming its right, keeps it sacred by the wise reserve that is to friendship what the purple bloom is to the grape, a charm which once destroyed can never be restored. Love she had desired, yet dreaded, knowing her own passionate nature, and when it came to her, making that brief holiday the fateful point of her life, she gave herself to it wholly. Before that time she had rejoiced over a more tranquil pleasure, and believed that she had found her friend in the neighbor who after long absence had returned to his old place.

Nature had done much for Geoffrey Moor, but the wise mother also gave him those teachers to whose hard lessons she often leaves her dearest children. Five years spent in the service of a sister, who, through the sharp discipline of pain was fitting her meek soul for heaven, had given him an experience such as few young men receive. This fraternal devotion proved a blessing in disguise; it preserved him from any profanation of his youth, and the companionship of the helpless creature whom he loved had proved an ever present stimulant to all that was best and sweetest in the man. A single duty faithfully performed had set the seal of integrity upon his character, and given him grace to see at thirty the rich compensation he had received for the ambitions silently sacrificed at twenty-five. When his long vigil was over he looked into the world to find his place again. But the old desires were dead, the old allurements had lost their charm, and while he waited for time to show him what good work he should espouse, no longing was so strong as that for a home, where he might bless and be blessed in writing that immortal poem a virtuous and happy life.

Sylvia soon felt the power and beauty of this nature, and remembering how well he had ministered to a physical affliction, often looked into the face whose serenity was a perpetual rebuke, longing to ask him to help and heal the mental ills that perplexed and burdened her. Moor soon divined the real isolation of the girl, read the language of her wistful eyes, felt that he could serve her, and invited confidence by the cordial alacrity with which he met her least advance.

But while he served he learned to love her, for Sylvia, humble in her own conceit, and guarded by the secret passion that possessed her, freely showed the regard she felt, with no thought of misapprehension, no fear of consequences. Unconscious that such impulsive demonstration made her only more attractive, that every manifestation of her frank esteem was cherished in her friend's heart of hearts, and that through her he was enjoying the blossom time of life. So peacefully and pleasantly the summer ripened into autumn and Sylvia's interest into an enduring friendship.*

---

*The ending of "Dull, but Necessary" reads in *M2:*

So, peacefully and pleasantly, the spring ripened into summer, and Sylvia's interest into an enduring friendship, full of satisfaction till a stronger influence came to waken and disturb her. (49).

CHAPTER VIII

NO

DRAWN CURTAINS shut out the frosty night, the first fire of the season burned upon the hearth, and basking in its glow sat Sylvia, letting her thoughts wander where they would. As books most freely open at pages oftenest read, the romance of her summer life seldom failed to unclose at passages where Warwick's name appeared. Pleasant as were many hours of that time, none seemed so full of beauty as those passed with him, and sweetest of them all the twilight journey hand in hand. It now returned to her so freshly that she seemed to hear again the evening sounds, to feel the warm, fern-scented wind blow over her, to see the strong hand offered helpfully, and with an impulse past control she stretched her own to that visionary Warwick as the longing of her heart found vent in an eager *

"Come!"

"I am here."

A voice replied, a hand pressed hers, and springing up she saw, not Adam, but Moor, standing beside her with a beaming face. Concealing the thrill of joy, the pang of pain he had brought her, she greeted him cordially, and reseating herself, instinctively tried to turn the current of her thoughts.†

---

* In *M2* Alcott changed the opening paragraph of "No." It is reprinted in the appendix (171).

† In *M2* this paragraph reads:

A voice answered, a hand took hers, and starting up she saw Moor looking down at her. Hastening to compose herself, she smiled and leaned back in her chair, saying quietly,— (172).

"I am glad you came, for I have built castles in the air long enough, and you will give me more substantial entertainment, as you always do."

The broken dream had left tokens of its presence in the unwonted warmth of Sylvia's manner; Moor felt it, and for a moment did not answer. Much of her former shyness had crept over her of late; she sometimes shunned him, was less free in conversation, less frank in demonstration, and once or twice had colored deeply as she caught his eye upon her. These betrayals of Warwick's image in her thoughts seemed to Moor the happy omens he had waited eagerly to see, and each day his hope grew more assured. He had watched her unseen while she was busied with her mental pastime, and as he looked his heart had grown unspeakably tender, for never had her power over him been so fully felt, and never had he so longed to claim her in the name of his exceeding love. A pleasant peace reigned through the house, the girl sat watching at his side, the moment looked auspicious, the desire grew irresistible, and he yielded to it.

"You are thinking of something new and pleasant to tell me, I hope,—something in keeping with this quiet place and hour," said Sylvia, glancing up at him with the traitorous softness still in her eyes.

"Yes, and hoping you would like it."

"Then I have never heard it before?"

"Never from me."

"Go on, please; I am ready."

She folded her hands together on her knee, turned her face attentively to his, and unwittingly composed herself to listen to the sweet story so often told, and yet so hard to tell. Moor meant to woo her very gently, for he believed that love was new to her. He had planned many graceful illustrations for his tale, and rounded many smoothly-flowing sentences in which to unfold it. But the emotions are not well bred, and when the moment came nature conquered art. No demonstration seemed beautiful enough to grace the betrayal of his passion, no language eloquent enough to tell it, no power strong enough to hold in check the impulse that mastered him. He went to her, knelt down upon the cushion at her feet, and lifting to her a face flushed and fervent with the ardor of a man's first love, said impetuously—

"Sylvia, read it here!"

There was no need for her to look; act, touch, and tone told the story better than the most impassioned speech. The supplication of his attitude, the eager beating of his heart, the tender pressure of his hand, dispelled her blindness in the drawing of a breath, and showed her what she had done.

Now neglected warnings, selfish forgetfulness, and the knowledge of an unconscious but irremediable wrong frightened and bewildered her; she hid her face and shrunk back trembling with remorse and shame. Moor, seeing in her agitation only maiden happiness or hesitancy, accepted and enjoyed a blissful moment while he waited her reply. It was so long in coming that he gently tried to draw her hands away and look into her face, whispering like one scarcely doubtful of assent—

"You love me, Sylvia?"

"No."

Only half audible was the reluctant answer, yet he heard it, smiled at what he fancied a shy falsehood, and said tenderly—

"Will you let me love you, dear?"

"No."

Fainter than before was the one word, but it reached and startled him. Hurriedly he asked—

"Am I nothing to you but a friend?"

"No."

With a quick gesture he put down her hands and looked at her. Grief, regret, and pity, filled her face with trouble, but no love was there. He saw, yet would not believe the truth, felt that the sweet certainty of love had gone, yet could not relinquish the fond hope.

"Sylvia, do you understand me?"

"I do, I do! but I cannot say what you would have me, and I must tell the truth, although it breaks my heart. Geoffrey, I do not love you."

"Can I not teach you?" he pleaded eagerly.

"I have no desire to learn."

Softly she spoke, remorseful she looked; but the words wounded like a blow. All the glad assurance died, the passionate glow faded, the caress, half tender, half timid, fell away, and nothing of the happy lover remained in face or figure. He rose slowly as if the heavy disappointment oppressed both soul and body. He fixed on her a glance of mingled incredulity, reproach, and pain, and said, like one bent on ending suspense at once—

"Did you not see that I loved you? Can you have been trifling with me? Sylvia, I thought you too simple and sincere for heartless coquetry."

"I am! You shall not suspect me of that, though I deserve all other reproaches. I have been very selfish, very blind. I should have remembered that in your great kindness you might like me too well for your own peace. I should have believed Mark, and been less candid in my expressions of esteem. But I wanted a friend so much; I found all I could ask in you; I thought my youth, my faults, my follies, would make it impossible for you to see in me anything but a wayward girl, who frankly showed her regard, and was proud of yours. It was one of my sad mistakes; I see it now; and now it is too late for anything but penitence. Forgive me if you can; I've taken all the pleasure, and left you all the pain."

Sylvia spoke in a paraoxysm of remorseful sorrow. Moor listened with a sinking heart, and when she dropped her face into her hands again, unable to endure the pale expectancy of his, he turned away, saying with an accent of quiet despair—

"Then I have worked and waited all this summer to see my harvest fail at last. Oh, Sylvia, I so loved, so trusted you."

He leaned his arm on the low chimney piece, laid down his head upon it and stood silent, trying to forgive.

It is always a hard moment for any woman, when it demands her bravest sincerity to look into a countenance of eager love, and change it to one of bitter disappointment by the utterance of a monosyllable. To Sylvia it was doubly hard, for now her blindness seemed as incredible as cruel; her past frankness unjustifiable; her pleasure selfish; her refusal the blackest ingratitude, and her dream of friendship forever marred. In the brief pause that fell, every little service he had rendered her, rose freshly in her memory; every hour of real content and genuine worth that he had given her, seemed to come back and reproach her; every look, accent, action, of both happy past and sad present seemed to plead for him. Her conscience cried out against her, her heart overflowed with penitence and pity. She looked at him, longing to say something, do something that should prove her repentance, and assure him of the affection which she felt. As she looked, two great tears fell glittering to the hearth, and lay there such eloquent reproaches, that, had Sylvia's heart been hard and cold as the marble where they shone, it would have melted then. She could not bear it, she went to him, took in both her own the rejected hand that hung at his side, and feeling that no act could too tenderly express her sorrow, lifted it to her lips and softly kissed it.

An instant she was permitted to lay her cheek against it as a penitent child mutely imploring pardon might have done. Then it broke from her hold, and gathering her to himself, Moor looked up exclaiming with renewed hope, unaltered longing—

"You do care for me, then? You give yourself to me in spite of that hard No? Ah, Sylvia, you are capricious even in your love."

She could not answer, for if that first No had been hard to utter, this was impossible. It seemed like turning the knife in the wound, to disappoint the hope that had gathered strength from despair, and she could only lay her head down on his breast, weeping the saddest tears she had ever shed. Still happy in his new delusion, Moor softly stroked the shining hair, smiling so tenderly, so delightedly, that it was well for her she did not see the smile, the words were enough.

"Dear Sylvia, I have tried so hard to make you love me how could you help it?"

The reason sprung to her lips, but maiden pride and shame withheld it. What could she tell except that she had cherished a passion, based only on a look. She had deceived herself in her belief that Moor was but a friend, might she not also have deceived herself in believing Warwick was a lover? She could not own this secret, its betrayal could not alter her reply, nor heal Moor's wound, but the thought of Warwick strengthened her. It always did, as surely as the influence of his friend always soothed her, for one was an embodiment of power, the other of tenderness.

"Geoffery, let me be true to you and to myself," she said, so earnestly that it gave weight to her broken words. "I cannot be your wife, but I can be your dear friend forever. Try to believe this,—make my task easier by giving up your hope,—and oh, be sure that while I live I cannot do enough to show my sorrow for the great wrong I have done you."

"Must it be so? I find it very hard to accept the truth and give up the hope that has made my happiness so long. Let me keep it, Sylvia; let me wait and work again. I have a firm belief that you *will* love me yet, because I cleave to you with heart and soul, long for you continually, and think you the one woman of the world."

"Ah, if it were only possible!" she sighed.

"Let me make it so! In truth, I think I should not labor long. You are so young, dear, you have not learned to know your own heart yet. It was not pity nor penitence alone that brought you here to comfort me. Was it, Sylvia?"

"Yes. Had it been love, could I stand as I am now and not show it?"

She looked up at him, showed him that though her cheeks were wet there was no rosy dawn of passion there; though her eyes were as full of affection as of grief, there was no shy avoidance of his own, no dropping of the lids, lest they should tell too much; and though his arm encircled her, she did not cling to him as loving women cling when they lean on the strength which, touched by love, can both cherish and sustain. That look convinced him better than a flood of words. A long sigh broke from his lips, and, turning from her the eyes that had so wistfully searched and found not, they went wandering drearily hither and thither as if seeking the hope whose loss made life seem desolate. Sylvia saw it, groaned within herself, but still held fast to the hard truth, and tried to make it kinder.

"Geoffrey, I once heard you say to Mark, 'Friendship is the best college character can graduate from. Believe in it, seek for it, and when it comes keep it as sacredly as love.' All my life I have wanted a friend, have looked for one, and when he came I welcomed him. May I not keep him, and preserve the friendship dear and sacred still, although I cannot offer love?"

Softly, seriously, she spoke, but the words sounded cold to him; friendship seemed so poor now, love so rich, he could not leave the blessed sunshine which transfigured the whole earth and sit down in the little circle of a kindly fire without keen regret.

"I should say yes, I will try to do it if nothing easier remains to me. Sylvia, for five years I have longed and waited for a home. Duty forbade it then, because poor Marion had only me to make her sad life happy, and my mother left her to my charge. Now the duty is ended, the old house very empty, my heart very hungry for affection. You are all in all to me, and I find it so difficult to relinquish my dream that I must be importunate. I have spoken too soon, you have had no time to think, to look into yourself and question your own heart. Go, now, recall what I have said, remember that I will wait for you patiently, and when I leave, an hour hence, come down and give me my last answer."

Sylvia was about to speak, but the sound of an approaching step brought over her the shyness she had not felt before, and without a word she darted from the room. Then romance also fled, for Prue came bustling in, and Moor was called to talk of influenzas, while his thoughts were full of love.

Alone in her chamber Sylvia searched herself. She pictured the life that would be hers with Moor. The old house so full of something better than its opulence, an atmosphere of genial tranquillity which made it home-like to whoever crossed its threshold. Herself the daily companion and dear wife of the master who diffused such sunshine there; whose serenity soothed her restlessness; whose affection would be as enduring as his patience; whose character she so truly honored. She felt that no woman need ask a happier home, a truer or more tender lover. But when she looked into herself she found the cordial, unimpassioned sentiment he first inspired still unchanged, and her heart answered—

"This is friendship."

She thought of Warwick, and the other home that might be hers. Fancy painted in glowing colors the stirring life, the novelty, excitement, and ever new delight such wanderings would have for her. The joy of being always with him; the proud consciousness that she was nearest and dearest to such a man; the certainty that she might share the knowledge of his past, might enjoy his present, help to shape his future. There was no time to look into her heart, for up sprung its warm blood to her cheek, its hope to her eye, its longing to her lips, its answer glad and ready—

"Ah, this is love!"

The clock struck ten, and after lingering a little Sylvia went down. Slowly, because her errand was a hard one; thoughtfully, because she knew not where nor how she could best deliver it. No need to look for him or linger for his coming; he was already there. Alone in the hall, absently smoothing a little silken shawl she often wore, and waiting with a melancholy patience that smote her to the heart. He went to meet her, took both her hands in his, and looked into her face so tenderly, so wistfully!—

"Sylvia, is it good night or good by?"

Her eyes filled, her hands trembled, her color paled, but she answered steadily—

"Forgive me; it is good by."

CHAPTER IX

HOLLY*

"ANOTHER GIFT for you, Sylvia. I don't know the writing, but it smells like flowers," said Mark, as a smiling maid brought in a package on Christmas morning.

Sylvia tore off the wrapper, lifted a cover, and exclaimed with pleasure, though it was the simplest present she had received that day. Only an osier basket, graceful in design and shape, lined with moss, and filled with holly sprays, the scarlet berries glowing beautifully among the polished green. No note, no card, no hint of its donor anywhere appeared, for none of them recognized the boldly written address. Presently a thought came to Sylvia; in a moment the mystery seemed to grow delightfully clear, and she said to herself with a glow of joy, "This is so like Adam I know he sent it."

"I must say it is the most peculiar present I ever saw, and it is my belief that the boy who brought it stole whatever article of value it contained, for it was very carelessly done up. No person in their senses would send a few sprigs of common holly to a young lady in this odd way," said Prue, poking here and there in hopes of finding some clue.

"It is not common, but very beautiful; we seldom see any so large and green, and full of berries. Nor is it odd, but very kind, because from the worn look of the wrapper I know it has been sent a long way to please me. Look at the little ferns in the moss, and smell the sweet moist odor that

---

* "Holly" is one of several chapters omitted by Alcott in *M2*.

seems to take us into summer woods in spite of a snowstorm. Ah, he knew what I should like."

"Who knew?" asked Mark, quickly.

"You must guess." And fearing that she had betrayed herself, Sylvia hurried across the room to put the holly in water.

"Ah, ha, I see," said Mark, laughing.

"Who is it?" asked Prue, looking mystified.

"Geoffrey," whispered Mr. Yule, with an air of satisfaction.

Then all three looked at one another, all three nodded sagely, and all three glanced at the small person bending over the table with cheeks almost as rosy as the berries in her hand.

Every one knows what a Christmas party is when a general friendliness pervades the air, and good wishes fly about like *confetti* during Carnival. To such an one went Sylvia and Mark that night, the brother looking unusually blithe and debonair, because the beloved Jessie had promised to be there if certain aunts and uncles would go away in time; the sister in a costume as pretty as appropriate, for snow and holly made her a perfect Yule. Sylvia loved dancing, and knew "wall flowers" only by sight; therefore she was busy; her lover's gift shone greenly in bosom, hair, and fleecy skirts; therefore she was beautiful, and the thought that Adam had not forgotten her lay warm at her heart; therefore she was supremely happy. Mark was devoted, but disappointed, for Jessie did not come, and having doomed the detaining aunts and uncles to a most unblessed fate, he sought consolation among less fair damsels.

"Now go and enjoy yourself. I shall dance no more round dances, for I'd rather not with any one but you, and you have been a martyr long enough."

Mark roamed away, and finding a cool corner Sylvia watched the animated scene before her till her wandering glance was arrested by the sight of a new comer, and her mind busied with trying to recollect where she had seen him. The slender figure, swarthy face, and vivacious eyes all seemed familiar, but she could find no name for their possessor till he caught her eye, when he half bowed and wholly smiled. Then she remembered, and while still recalling that brief interview one of their young hosts appeared with the stranger, and Gabriel André was duly presented.

"I could hardly expect to be remembered, and am much flattered, I assure you. Did you suffer from the shower that day, Miss Yule?"

The speech was nothing, but the foreign accent gave a softness to the words, and the southern grace of manner gave an air of romance to the handsome youth. Sylvia was in the mood to be pleased with everybody, everything, and was unusually gracious as they merrily pursued the subject suggested by his question. Presently he asked—

"Is Warwick with you now?"

"He was not staying with us, but with his friend, Mr. Moor."

"He was the gentleman who pulled so well that day?"

"Yes."

"Is Warwick with him still?"

"Oh, no, he went away three months ago."

"I wonder where!"

"So do I!"

The wish had been impulsively expressed, and was as impulsively echoed. Young André smiled, and liked Miss Yule the better for forgetting that somewhat lofty air of hers.

"You have no conjecture, then? I wish to find him, much, very much, but cannot put myself upon his trail. He is so what you call peculiar that he writes no letters, leaves no address and roves here and there like a born gitano."

"Have you ill news for him?"

"I have the best a man could desire; but fear that while I look for him he has gone to make a disappointment for himself. You are a friend, I think?"

"I am."

"Then you know much of him, his life, his ways?"

"Yes, both from himself and Mr. Moor."

"Then you know of his betrothal to my cousin, doubtless, and I may speak of it, because if you will be so kind you may perhaps help us to find him."

"I did not know—perhaps he did not wish it—" began Sylvia, folding one hand tightly in the other, with a quick breath and a momentary sensation as if some one had struck her in the face.

"He thinks so little of us I shall not regard his wish just now. If you will permit me I would say a word for my cousin's sake, as I know you will be interested for her, and I do not feel myself strange with you."

Sylvia bowed, and standing before her with an air half mannish, half boyish, Gabriel went on in the low, rapid tone peculiar to him.

"See, then, my cousin was betrothed in May. A month after Adam cries out that he loves too much for his peace, that he has no freedom of his heart or mind, that he must go away and take his breath before he is made a happy slave forever. Ottila told me this. She implored him to stay; but no, he vows he will not come again till they marry, in the next June. He thinks it a weakness to adore a woman. Impertinente! I have no patience for him."

Gabriel spoke indignantly, and pressed his foot into the carpet with a scornful look. But Sylvia took no heed of his petulance, she only kept her eyes fixed upon him with an intentness which he mistook for interest. The eyes were fine, the interest was flattering, and though quite aware that he was both taking a liberty and committing a breach of confidence, the impulsive young gentleman chose to finish what he had begun, and trust that no harm would follow.

"He has been gone now more than half a year, but has sent no letter, no message, nothing to show that he still lives. Ottila waits, she writes, she grows too anxious to endure, she comes to look for him. I help her, but we do not find him yet, and meantime I amuse her. My friends are kind, and we enjoy much as we look about us for this truant Adam."

If Sylvia could have doubted the unexpected revelation, this last trait was so like Warwick it convinced her at once. Though the belief to which she had clung so long was suddenly swept from under her, she floated silently with no outward sign of shipwreck as her hope went down. Pride was her shield, and crowding back all other emotions she kept herself unnaturally calm behind it till she was alone. If Gabriel had been watching her he would only have discovered that she was a paler blonde than he had thought her; that her address was more coldly charming than before; and that her eye no longer met his, but rested steadily on the folded fan she held. He was not watching her, however, but glancing frequently over her head at something at the far end of the rooms which a crowd of assiduous gentlemen concealed. His eye wandered, but his thoughts did not; for still intent on the purpose that seemed to have brought him to her, he said, as if reluctant to be importunate, yet resolved to satisfy himself—

"Pardon me that I so poorly entertain you, and let me ask one other question in Ottila's name. This Moor, would he not give us some clue to Adam's haunts?"

"He is absent, and will be till spring, I think. Where I do not know, else I could write for you. Did Mr. Warwick promise to return in June?"

"Yes."

"Then, if he lives, he will come. Your cousin must wait; it will not be in vain."

"It shall not!"

The young man's voice was stern, and a passionate glitter made his black eyes fierce. Then the former suavity returned, and with his most gallant air he said—

"You are kind, Miss Yule; I thank you, and put away this so troublesome affair. May I have the honor?"

"If he had proposed to waltz over a precipice Sylvia felt as if she could have accepted, provided there was time to ask a question or two before the crash came. A moment afterward Mark was surprised to see her floating round the room on the air of "the olive-colored party," whom he recognized at once. His surprise soon changed to pleasure, for his beauty-loving eye as well as his brotherly pride was gratified as the whirling couples subsided and the young pair went circling slowly by, giving to the graceful pastime the enchantment few have skill to lend it, and making it a spectacle of life-enjoying youth to be remembered by the lookers on.

"Thank you! I have not enjoyed such a waltz since I left Cuba. It is the rudest of rude things to say, but to you I may confide it, because you dance like a Spaniard. The ladies here seem to me as cold as their own snow, and they make dancing a duty, not a pleasure. They should see Ottila; she is all grace and fire. I could kill myself dancing with her. Adam used to say it was like wine to watch her."

"I wish she was here to give us a lesson."

"She is, but will not dance tonight."

"Here!" cried Sylvia, stopping abruptly.

"Why not? Elyott is mad for her, and gave me no peace till I brought her. She is behind that wall of men; shall I make a passage for you? She will be glad to talk with you of Adam, and I to show you the handsomest woman in Habaña."

"Let us wait a little; I should be afraid to talk before so many. She is very beautiful, then."

"You will laugh and call me extravagant, as others do, if I say what I think; so I will let you judge for yourself. See, your brother stands on tiptoe to peep at her. Now he goes in, and there he will stay. You do not like that, perhaps. But Ottila cannot help her beauty, nor the power she has of making all men love her. I wish she could!"

"She is gifted and accomplished, as well as lovely?" asked Sylvia, glancing at her companion's gloomy face.

"She is everything a woman should be, and I could shoot Adam for his cruel neglect."

Gabriel's dark face kindled, as he spoke, and Sylvia drearily wished he would remember how ill-bred it was to tire her with complaints of her friend, and raptures over his cousin. He seemed to perceive this, turned a little haughty at her silence, and when he spoke was all the stranger again.

"This is a contra danza; shall we give the snow-ladies another lesson? First, may I do myself the pleasure of getting you an ice?"

"A glass of water, please; I am cool enough without more ice."

He seated her and went upon his errand. She *was* cool now; weary-footed, sick at heart, and yearning to be alone. But in these days women do not tear their hair and make scenes, though their hearts may ache and burn with the same sharp suffering as of old. Till her brother came she knew she must bear it, and make no sign. She did bear it, drank the water with a smile, danced the dance with spirit, and bore up bravely till Mark appeared. She was alone just then, and his first words were—

"Have you seen her?"

"No; take me where I can, and tell me what you know of her."

"Nothing, but that she is Andre's cousin, and he adores her, as boys always do a charming woman who is kind to them. Affect to be admiring these flowers, and look without her knowing it, or she will frown at you like an insulted princess, as she did at me."

Sylvia looked, saw the handsomest woman in Havana, and hated her immediately. It was but natural, for Sylvia was a very human girl, and Ottila one whom no woman would love, however much she might admire.

Hers was that type of character which every age has reproduced, varying externally with climates and conditions, but materially the same from fabled Circe[1] down to Lola Montes,[2] or some less famous syren whose subjects are not kings. The same passions that in ancient days broke out in heaven-defying crimes; the same power of beauty, intellect, or subtlety; the same untamable spirit and lack of moral sentiment are the attributes of all; latent or alert as the noble or ignoble nature may predominate. Most of us can recall some glimpse of such specimens of Nature's work in a daring mood. Many of our own drawing-rooms have held illustrations of the nobler type, and modern men and women have quailed before royal eyes whose possessors ruled all spirits but their own. Born in Athens, and endowed with a finer intellect, Ottila might have been an Aspasia;[3] or cast in that great tragedy the French Revolution, have played a brave part and died heroically like Roland and Corday.[4] But set down in uneventful times, the courage, wit, and passion that might have served high ends dwindled to their baser counterparts, and made her what she was,—a fair allurement to the eyes of men, a born rival to the peace of women, a rudderless nature absolute as fate.

Sylvia possessed no knowledge that could analyze for her the sentiment which repelled, even while it attracted her toward Warwick's betrothed. That he loved her she did not doubt, because she felt that even his pride would yield to the potent fascination of this woman. As Sylvia looked, her feminine eye took in every gift of face and figure, every grace of attitude or gesture, every daintiness of costume, and found no visible flaw in Ottila, from her haughty head to her handsome foot. Yet, when her scrutiny ended, the girl felt a sense of disappointment, and no envy mingled with her admiration.

As she stood, forgetting to assume interest in the camellias before her, she saw Gabriel join his cousin, saw her pause and look up at him with an anxious question. He answered it, glancing toward that part of the room where she was standing. Ottila's gaze was fixed upon her instantly; a rapid, but keen survey followed, and then the lustrous eyes turned away with such supreme indifference, that Sylvia's blood tingled as if she had received an insult.

"Mark, I am going home," she said, abruptly.

"Very well, I'm ready."

When safe in her own room Sylvia's first act was to take off the holly wreath, for her head throbbed with a heavy pain that forbade hope of sleep that night. Looking at the little chaplet so happily made, she saw that all the berries had fallen, and nothing but the barbed leaves remained. A sudden gesture crushed it in both her hands, and standing so, she gathered many a scattered memory to confirm that night's discovery.

Warwick had said, with such a tender accent in his voice, "I thought of the woman I would make my wife." That was Ottila. He had asked so anxiously, "If one should keep a promise when it disturbed one's peace?" That was because he repented of his hasty vow to absent himself till June. It was not love she saw in his eyes the night they parted, but pity. He read her secret before that compassionate glance revealed it to herself, and he had gone away to spare her further folly. She had deceived herself, had blindly cherished a baseless hope, and this was the end. Even for the nameless gift she found a reason, with a woman's skill, in self-torture. Moor had met Adam, had told his disappointment, and still pitying her Warwick had sent the pretty greeting to console her for the loss of both friend and lover.

This thought seemed to sting her into sudden passion. As if longing to destroy every trace of her delusion, she tore away the holly wreaths and flung them in the fire; took down the bow and arrow Warwick had made her from above the *étagère,* where she had arranged the spoils of her happy voyage, snapped them across her knee and sent them after the holly; followed by the birch canoe, and every pebble, moss, shell, or bunch of headed grass he had given her then. The osier basket was not spared, the box went next, and even the wrapper on its way to immolation, when, as she rent it apart, with a stern pleasure in the sacrifice it was going to complete, from some close fold of the paper hitherto undisturbed a card dropped at her feet.

She caught it up and read in handwriting almost as familiar as her own: "To Sylvia—A merry Christmas and best wishes from her friend, Geoffrey Moor." The word "friend" was underscored, as if he desired to assure her that he still cherished the only tie permitted him, and sent the green token to lighten her regret that she could give no more.

Warm over Sylvia's sore heart rushed the tender thought and longing, as her tears began to flow. "He cares for me! he remembered me! I wish he would come back and comfort me!"

CHAPTER X

YES

꒯꒯꒯꒯꒯꒯

*IT IS EASY to say, "I will forget," but perhaps the hardest task given us is to lock up a natural yearning of the heart, and turn a deaf ear to its plaint, for captive and jailer must inhabit the same small cell. Sylvia was proud, with that pride which is both sensitive and courageous, which can not only suffer but wring strength from suffering. While she struggled with a grief and shame that aged her with their pain, she asked no help, made no complaint; but when the forbidden passion stretched its arms to her, she thrust it back and turned to pleasure for oblivion.

Those who knew her best were troubled and surprised by the craving for excitement which now took possession of her, the avidity with which she gratified it, regardless of time, health, and money. All day she hurried here and there, driving, shopping, sight-seeing, or entertaining guests, at home. Night brought no cessation of her dissipation, for when balls, masquerades, and concerts failed, there still remained the theatre. This soon became both a refuge and a solace, for believing it to be less harmful than other excitements, her father indulged her new whim. But, had she known

---

*Here in M2 Alcott added the following lines to her opening of Chapter XI, "Yes" (182):

> Moor went away to live down his disappointment. The houses by the sea were shut, and the Yules went to town for the winter. No word came from Warwick, and Sylvia ceased to hope. The rest of the chapter remains the same in both editions.

it, this was the most dangerous pastime she could have chosen. Calling for no exertion of her own, it left her free to passively receive a stimulant to her unhappy love in watching its mimic semblance through all phases of tragic suffering and sorrow, for she would see no comedies, and Shakespeare's tragedies became her study.

This lasted for a time, then the reaction came. A black melancholy fell upon her, and energy deserted soul and body. She found it a weariness to get up in the morning and weariness to lie down at night. She no longer cared even to seem cheerful, owned that she was spiritless, hoped she should be ill, and did not care if she died to-morrow. When this dark mood seemed about to become chronic she began to mend, for youth is wonderfully recuperative, and the deepest wounds soon heal even against the sufferer's will. A quiet apathy replaced the gloom, and she let the tide drift her where it would, hoping nothing, expecting nothing, asking nothing but that she need not suffer any more.

She lived fast; all processes with her were rapid; and the secret experience of that winter taught her many things. She believed it had only taught her to forget, for now the outcast love lay very still, and no longer beat despairingly against the door of her heart, demanding to be taken in from the cold. She fancied that neglect had killed it, and that its grave was green with many tears. Alas for Sylvia! how could she know that it had only sobbed itself to sleep, and would wake beautiful and strong at the first sound of its master's voice.

Mark became eventful. In his fitful fashion he had painted a picture of the Golden Wedding, from sketches taken at the time. Moor had suggested and bespoken it, that the young artist might have a motive for finishing it, because, though he excelled in scenes of that description, he thought them beneath him, and tempted by more ambitious designs, neglected his true branch of the art. In April it was finished, and at his father's request Mark reluctantly sent it with his Clytemnestra to the annual exhibition.[1] One morning at breakfast Mr. Yule suddenly laughed out behind his paper, and with a face of unmixed satisfaction passed it to his son, pointing to a long critique upon the Exhibition. Mark prepared himself to receive with becoming modesty the praises lavished upon his great work, but was stricken with amazement to find Clytemnestra disposed of in a single sentence, and the Golden Wedding lauded in a long enthusiastic paragraph.

"What the deuce does the man mean!" he ejaculated, staring at his father.

"He means that the work which warms the heart is greater than that which freezes the blood, I suspect. Moor knew what you could do and has made you do it, sure that if you worked for fame unconsciously you should achieve it. This is a success that I can appreciate, and I congratulate you heartily, my son."

"Thank you, sir. But upon my word I don't understand it, and if this wasn't written by the best Art critic in the country I should feel inclined to say the writer was a fool. Why that little thing was a daub compared to the other."

He got no farther in his protest against this unexpected freak of fortune, for Sylvia seized the paper and read the paragraph aloud with such happy emphasis amid Prue's outcries and his father's applause, that Mark began to feel that he really had done something praiseworthy, and that the "daub" was not so despicable after all.

"I'm going to look at it from this new point of sight," was his sole comment as he went away.

Three hours afterward he appeared to Sylvia as she sat sewing alone, and startled her with the mysterious announcement.

"I've done it!"

"Done what? Have you burnt poor Clytemnestra?"

"Hang Clytemnestra! I'll begin at the beginning and prepare you for the grand finale. I went to the Exhibition, and stared at Father Blake and his family for an hour. Decided that wasn't bad, though I still admire the other more. Then people began to come and crowd up, so that I slipped away for I couldn't stand the compliments. Dahlmann, Scott, and all the rest of my tribe were there, and, as true as my name is Mark Yule, every man of them ignored the Greek party and congratulated me upon the success of that counfounded Golden Wedding."

"My dearest boy, I am so proud! so glad! What is the matter? Have you been bitten by a tarantula?"

She might well ask, for Mark was dancing all over the carpet in a most extraordinary style, and only stopped long enough to throw a little case into Sylvia's lap, asking as a whole faceful of smiles broke loose—

"What does that mean?"

She opened it, and a suspicious circlet of diamonds appeared, at sight of which she clapped her hands, and cried out—

"You're going to ask Jessie to wear it!"

"I have! I have!" sung Mark, dancing more wildly than ever. Sylvia chased him into a corner and held him there, almost as much excited as he, while she demanded a full explanation, which he gave her, laughing like a boy, and blushing like a girl.

"You have no business to ask, but of course I'm dying to tell you. I went from that Painter's Purgatory as we call it, to Mr. Hope's, and asked for Miss Jessie. My angel came down; I told her of my success, and she smiled as never a woman did before; I added that I'd only waited to make myself more worthy of her, by showing that I had talent, as well as love and money to offer her, and she began to cry, whereat I took her in my arms and ascended straight into heaven."

"Please be sober, Mark, and tell me all about it. Was she glad? Did she say she would? And is everything as we would have it?"

"It is all perfect, divine, and rapturous, to the last degree. Jessie has liked me ever since she was born, she thinks; adores you and Prue for sisters; yearns to call my parent father; allowed me to say and do whatever I liked; and gave me a ravishing kiss just there. Sacred spot; I shall get a mate to it when I put this on her blessed little finger. Try it for me, I want it to be right, and your hands are of a size. That fits grandly. When shall I see a joyful sweetheart doing this on his own behalf, Sylvia?"

"Never!"

She shook off the ring as if it burned her, watching it roll glittering away, with a somewhat tragical expression. Then she calmed herself, and sitting down to her work, enjoyed Mark's raptures for an hour.

The distant city bells were ringing nine that night as a man paused before Mr. Yule's house, and attentively scrutinized each window. Many were alight, but on the drawn curtain of one a woman's shadow came and went. He watched it a moment, passed up the steps, and noiselessly went in. The hall was bright and solitary; from above came the sound of voices, from a room to the right, the stir of papers and the scratch of a pen, from one on the left, a steady rustle as of silk, swept slowly to and fro. To the threshold of this door the man stepped and looked in.

Sylvia was just turning in her walk, and as she came musing down the room, Moor saw her well. With some women dress has no relation to states of mind; with Sylvia it was often an indication of the mental garb she wore. Moor remembered this trait, and saw in both countenance and costume the change that had befallen her in his long absence. Her face was neither gay nor melancholy, but serious and coldly quiet, as if some inward twilight reigned. Her dress, a soft, sad grey, with no decoration but a knot of snowdrops in her bosom.[2] On these pale flowers her eyes were fixed, and as she walked with folded arms and drooping head, she sang low to herself—

> 'Upon the convent roof, the snows
>   Lie sparkling to the moon;
> My breath to heaven like incense goes,
>   May my soul follow soon.
> Lord, make my spirit pure and clear,
>   As are the frosty skies,
> Or this first snowdrop of the year,
>   That in my bosom lies.'

"Sylvia!"

Very gentle was the call, but she started as if it had been a shout, looked an instant while light and color flashed into her face, then ran to him exclaiming joyfully—

"Oh, Geoffrey! I am glad! I am glad!"

There could be but one answer to such a welcome, and Sylvia received it as she stood there, not weeping now, but smiling with the sincerest satisfaction, the happiest surprise. Moor shared both emotions, feeling as a man might feel when, parched with thirst, he stretches out his hand for a drop of rain, and receives a brimming cup of water. He drank a deep draught gratefully, then, fearing that it might be as suddenly withdrawn, asked anxiously—

"Sylvia, are we friends or lovers?"

"Anything, if you will only stay."

She looked up as she spoke, and her face betrayed that a conflict between desire and doubt was going on within her. Impulse had sent her there, and now it was so sweet to know herself beloved, she found it hard to go away. Her brother's happiness had touched her heart, roused the old craving for affection, and brought a strong desire to fill the aching void her lost love had left with this recovered one. Sylvia had not learned to reason yet, she could only feel, because, owing to the unequal development of her divided nature, the heart grew faster than the intellect. Instinct was her surest guide, and when she followed it unblinded by a passion, unthwarted by a mood, she prospered. But now she was so blinded and so thwarted, and now her great temptation came. Ambition, man's idol, had tempted the father; love, woman's god, tempted the daughter; and, as if the father's atonement was to be wrought out through his dearest child, the daughter also made the fatal false step of her life.

"Then you *have* learned to love me, Sylvia?"

"No, the old feeling has not changed except to grow more remorseful, more eager to prove its truth. Once you asked me if I did not wish to love you; then I did not, now I sincerely do. If you still want me with my many faults, and will teach me in your gentle way to be all I should to you, I will gladly learn, because I never needed love as I do now. Geoffrey, shall I stay or go?"

"Stay, Sylvia. Ah, thank God for this!"

If she had ever hoped that Moor would forget her for his own sake, she now saw how vain such hope would have been, and was both touched and troubled by the knowledge of her supremacy which that hour gave her. She was as much the calmer as friendship is than love, and was the first to speak again, still standing there content although her words expressed a doubt.

"Are you very sure you want me? Are you not tired of the thorn that has fretted you so long? Remember, I am so young, so ignorant, and unfitted for a wife. Can I give you real happiness? make home what you would have it? and never see in your face regret that some wiser, better woman was not in my place?"

"I am sure of myself, and satisfied with you, as you are no wiser, no better, nothing but my Sylvia."

"It is very sweet to hear you say that with such a look. I do not deserve it but I will. Is the pain I once gave you gone now, Geoffrey?"

"Gone forever."

"Then I am satisfied, and will begin my life anew by trying to learn well the lesson my kind master is to teach me."

When Moor went that night Sylvia followed him, and as they stood together this happy moment seemed to recall that other sad one, for taking her hands again he asked, smiling now—

"Dear, is it good night or good by?"

"It is good by and come to-morrow."

CHAPTER XI

WOOING

NOTHING could have been more unlike than the two pairs of lovers who from April to August haunted Mr. Yule's house. One pair was of the popular order, for Mark was tenderly tyrannical, Jessie adoringly submissive, and at all hours of the day they were to be seen making tableaux of themselves. The other pair were of the peculiar order, undemonstrative and unsentimental, but quite as happy. Moor knew his power, but used it generously, asking little while giving much. Sylvia as yet found nothing to regret, for so gently was she taught, the lesson could not seem hard, and when her affection remained unchanged in kind, although it deepened in degree, she said within herself—

"That strong and sudden passion was not true love, but an unwise, unhappy delusion of my own. I should be glad that it is gone, because I know I am not fit to be Warwick's wife. This quiet feeling which Geoffrey inspires must be a safer love for me, and I should be grateful that in making his happiness I may yet find my own."

She tried heartily to forget herself in others, unconscious that there are times when the duty we owe ourselves is greater than that we owe to them. In the atmosphere of cheerfulness that now surrounded her she could not but be cheerful, and soon it would have been difficult to find a more harmonious household than this. One little cloud alone remained to mar the general sunshine. Mark was in a frenzy to be married, but had set his heart on a double wedding, and Sylvia would not fix the time, always pleading—

Wooing

"Let me be quite sure of myself before I take this step, and do not wait."

Matters stood thus till Mark, having prepared his honeymoon cottage, as a relief to his impatience, found it so irresistible that he announced his marriage for the first of August, and declared no human power should change his purpose. Sylvia promised to think of it, but gave no decided answer, for though she would hardly own it to herself she longed to remain free till June was past. It came and went without a sign and July began before the longing died a sudden death, and she consented to be married.*

Mark and Jessie came in from the city one warm morning and found Sylvia sitting idly in the hall. She left her preparations all to Prue, who revelled in such things, and applied herself diligently to her lesson as if afraid she might not learn it as she should. Half way up stairs Mark turned and said, laughing—

"Sylvia, I saw Searle to-day,—one of the fellows whom we met on the river last summer,—and he began to tell me something about André and the splendid cousin, who is married and gone abroad it seems. I did not hear much, for Jessie was waiting; but you remember the handsome Cubans we saw at Christmas, don't you?†

'Yes, I remember.'

'Well, I thought you'd like to know that the lad had gone home to Cleopatra's wedding, so you cannot have him to dance at yours. Have you forgotten how you waltzed that night?"

"No, I've not forgotten."

Mark went off to consult Prue, and Jessie began to display her purchases before eyes that only saw a blur of shapes and colors, and expatiate upon their beauties to ears that only heard the words—"The splendid cousin is married and gone abroad."

---

*In *M2*:

Sylvia promised to think of it, but would give no decided answer, because, though she hardly owned it to herself, she longed to hear some news of Warwick before it was too late. (194)

† In *M2* Alcott removed all references to the Cuban cousins and therefore to Warwick's engagement. Instead, Max brings news of another kind to Sylvia; the passage is reprinted in the appendix (195). The scene resumes with "All took care that Miss Caprice should not have time to change her mind."

"I should enjoy these pretty things a thousand times more if you would please us all by being married when we are," sighed Jessie, looking at her pearls.

"I will."

"What, really? Sylvia, you are a perfect darling! Mark! Prue! she says she will!"

Away flew Jessie to proclaim the glad tidings, and Sylvia, with a curious expression of relief, regret, and ressolve, repeated to herself that decided—

"I will."

Every one took care that Miss Caprice should not have time to change her mind. The whole house was soon in a bustle, for Prue ruled supreme. Mr. Yule fled from the din of women's tongues, the bridegrooms were kept on a very short allowance of bride, and Sylvia and Jessie were almost invisible, for milliners and mantua-makers swarmed about them till they felt like animated pin-cushions. The last evening came at length, and Sylvia was just planning an escape into the garden when Prue, whose tongue wagged as rapidly as her hands worked, exclaimed—

"How can you stand staring out of window when there is so much to do? Here are all these trunks to pack, Maria in her bed with every tooth in a frightful state of inflammation, and that capable Jane What's-her-name gone off while I was putting a chamomile poultice on her face. If you are tired sit down and try on all your shoes, for though Mr. Peggit has your measure, those absurd clerks seem to think it a compliment to send children's sizes to grown women. I'm sure my rubbers were a perfect insult."

Sylvia sat down, tugged on one boot and fell into a reverie with the other in her hand, while Prue clacked on like a wordmill in full operation.

"How I'm ever to get all these gowns into that trunk passes my comprehension. There's a tray for each, of course; but a ball dress is such a fractious thing. I could shake that Antoinette Roche for disappointing you at the last minute; and what you are to do for a maid, I don't know. You'll have so much dressing to do you will be quite worn out; and I want you to look your best on all occasions, for you will meet everybody. This collar won't wear well; Clara hasn't a particle of judgment, though her taste is sweet. These hose, now, are a good, firm article; I chose them myself. Do be sure you get all your things from the wash. At those great hotels there's a deal of pilfering, and you are so careless."

Here Sylvia came out of her reverie with a sigh that was almost a groan.

"Don't they fit? I knew they wouldn't!" said Prue, with an air of triumph.

"The boots suit me, but the hotels do not; and if it was not ungrateful, after all your trouble, I should like to make a bonfire of this roomful of haberdashery, and walk quietly away to my new home by the light of it."

As if the bare idea of such an awful proceeding robbed her of all strength, Miss Yule sat suddenly down in the trunk by which she was standing. Fortunately it was nearly full, but her appearance was decidedly ludicrous as she sat with the collar in one uplifted hand, the hose in the other, and the ball dress laid over her lap like a fainting lady; while she said, with imploring solemnity, which changed abruptly from the pathetic to the comic at the end of her speech—

"Sylvia, if I ever cherished a wish in this world of disappointment, it is that your wedding shall have nothing peculiar about it, because every friend and relation you've got expects it. Do let me have the comfort of knowing that every one was surprised and pleased; for if the expression was elegant (which it isn't, and only suggested by my trials with those dressmakers), I should say I was on pins and needles till it's all over. Bless me! and so I am, for here are three on the floor and one in my shoe." Prue paused to extract the appropriate figure of speech which she had chosen, and Sylvia said—

"If we have everything else as you wish it, would you mind if we did n't go the journey?"

"Of course I should. Every one goes a wedding trip, its part of the ceremony; and if two carriages and two bridal pairs don't leave here to-morrow, I shall feel as if all my trouble had been thrown away."

"I'll go, Prue, I'll go; and you shall be satisfied. But I thought we might go from here in style, and then slip off on some quieter trip. I am so tired I dread the idea of frolicking for a whole month, as Mark and Jessie mean to do."

It was Prue's turn to groan now, and she did so dismally. But Sylvia had never asked a favor in vain, and this was not the moment to refuse to her anything, so worldly pride yielded to sisterly affection, and Prue said with resignation, as she fell to work more vigorously than ever, because she had wasted five good minutes—

"Do as you like, dear, you shall not be crossed on your last day at home. Ask Geoffrey, and if you are happy I'm satisfied."

Before Sylvia could thank her sister there came a tap and a voice asking—

"Might I come in?"

"If you can get in," answered Prue, as, reversing her plan in her hurry, she whisked the collar into a piecebag and the hose into a bandbox.

Moor paused on the threshold in a masculine maze, that one small person could need so much drapery.

"May I borrow Sylvia for a little while? A breath of air will do her good, and I want her bright and blooming for to-morrow, else young Mrs. Yule will outshine young Mrs. Moor."

"What a thoughtful creature you are, Geoffrey. Take her and welcome, only pray put on a shawl, Sylvia, and don't stay out late, for a bride with a cold in her head is the saddest of spectacles."

Glad to be released Sylvia went away, and, dropping the shawl as soon as she was out of Prue's sight, paced up and down the garden walks upon her lover's arm. Having heard her wish and given a hearty assent Moor asked—

"Where shall we go? Tell me what you would like best and you shall have it. You will not let me give you many gifts, but this pleasure you will accept from me I know."

"You give me yourself, that is more than I deserve. But I should like to have you take me to the place you like best. Don't tell me beforehand, let it be a surprise."

"I will, it is already settled, and I know you will like it. Is there no other wish to be granted, no doubt to be set at rest, or regret withheld that I should know. Tell me, Sylvia, for if ever there should be confidence between us it is now."

As he spoke the desire to tell him of her love for Adam rose within her, but with the desire came a thought that modified the form in which impulse prompted her to make confession. Moor was both sensitive and proud, would not the knowledge of the fact mar for him the friendship that was so much to both? From Warwick he would never learn it, from her he should have only a half confidence, and so love both friend and wife with an untroubled heart. Few of us can always control the rebellious nature that so often betrays and then reproaches, few always weigh the moment and the act that bans or blesses it, and where is the life that has not known some turning-point when a fugitive emotion has decided great issues for good or ill? Such an emotion came to Sylvia then, and another temptation, wearing the guise of generosity, urged her to another false step, for when the first is taken a second inevitably follows.

"I have no wish, no regret, nothing but the old doubt of my unstable self, and the fear that I may fail to make you happy. But I should like to tell you something. I don't know that you will care for it, or that there is any need to tell it, but when you said there should be confidence between us, I felt that I wanted you to know that I had loved some one before I loved you."

He did not see her face, he only heard her quiet voice. He had no thought of Adam, whom she had known so short a time, who was already bound; he only fancied that she spoke of some young lover who had touched her heart, and while he smiled at the nice sense of honor that prompted the innocent confession, he said, with no coldness, no curiosity in voice or face—

"No need to tell it, dear. I have no jealousy of any one who has gone before me. Rest assured of this, for if I could not share so large a heart with one who will never claim my share I should not deserve it."

"That is so like you! Now I am quite at ease."

He looked down at her as she went beside him, thinking that of all the brides he had ever seen his own looked least like one.

"I always thought that you would make a very ardent lover, Sylvia. That you would be excited, gay, and brilliant at a time like this. But you are so quiet, so absorbed, and so unlike your former self that I begin to think I do not know you yet."

"You will in time. I am passionate and restless by nature, but I am also very sensitive to all influences, personal or otherwise, and were you different from your tranquil, sunshiny self, I too should change. I am quiet because I seem in a pleasant state, half waking, half dreaming, from which I never wish to wake. I am tired of the past, contented with the present, and to you I leave the future."

"It shall be a happy one if I can make it so, and to-morrow you will give me the dear right to try."

"Yes," she said, and thinking of the solemn promises to be then made, she added, thoughtfully, "I think I love, I know I honor, I will try to obey. Can I do more?"

Well for them both if they could have known that friendship is love's twin, and the gentle sisters are too often mistaken for each other. That Sylvia was innocently deceiving both her lover and herself, by wrapping her friendship in the garb her lost love had worn, forgetting that the wanderer might return and claim its own, leaving the other to suffer for the borrowed warmth. They did not know it, and walked tranquilly together in the summer night, planning the new life as they went, and when they parted Moor pointed to a young moon hanging in the sky.

"See, Sylvia, our honeymoon has risen."

"May it be a happy one!"

"It will be, and when the anniversary of this glad night comes round it shall be shining still. God bless my little wife."

CHAPTER XII

WEDDING

SYLVIA was awakened on her wedding morning by a curious choking sound, and starting up found Prue crying over her as if her heart were broken.

"What has happened? Is Geoffrey ill? Is all the silver stolen? Can't the Bishop come?" she asked, wondering what calamity could move her sister to tears at such a busy time.

Prue took Sylvia in her arms, and rocking to and fro as if she were still a baby, poured forth a stream of words and tears together.

"Nothing has happened; I came to call you and broke down because it was the last time I should do it. I've been awake all night, thinking of you and all you've been to me since I took you in my arms nineteen years ago, and said you should be mine. My little Sylvia, I've been neglectful of so many things, and now I see them all; I've fretted you with my ways, and haven't been patient enough with yours; I've been selfish even about your wedding, and it won't be as you like it; you'll reproach me in your heart, and I shall hate myself for it when you are gone never to be my care and comfort any more. And—oh, my dear, my dear, what shall I do without you?"

This unexpected demonstration from her prosaic sister touched Sylvia more than the most sentimental lamentations from another. It brought to mind all the past devotion, the future solitude of Prue's life, and she clung about her neck tearless but very tender.

"I never shall reproach you, never cease to love and thank you for all you've been to me, my dear old girl. You mustn't grieve over me, or think I shall forget you, for you never shall be forsaken; and very soon I shall be back, almost as much your Sylvia as ever. Mark will live on one side, I shall live on the other, and we'll be merry and cosy together. And who knows but when we are both out of your way you will learn to think of yourself and marry also."

At this Prue began to laugh hysterically, and exlaimed, with more than her usual incoherency—

"I must tell you, it was so very odd! I didn't mean to do so, because you children would tease me; but now I will to make you laugh, for it's a bad omen to cry over a bride, they say. My dear, that gouty Mr. Mac-Gregor, when I went in with some of my nice broth last week (Hugh slops so, and he's such a fidget, I took it myself), after he had eaten every drop before my eyes, wiped his mouth and asked me to marry him."

"And you would not, Prue?"

"Bless me, child, how could I? I must take care of my poor dear father, and he isn't pleasant in the least, you know, but would wear my life out in a week. I really pitied him, however, when I refused him, with a napkin round his neck, and he tapped his waistcoat with a spoon so comically, when he offered me his heart, as if it were something good to eat."

"How very funny! What made him do it, Prue?"

"He said he'd watched the preparations from his window, and got so interested in weddings that he wanted one himself, and felt drawn to me I was so sympathetic. That means a good nurse and cook, my dear. I understand these invalid gentlemen, and will be a slave to no man so fat and fussy as Mr. Mac, as my brother calls him. It's not respectful, but I like to refresh myself by saying it just now."

"Never mind the old soul, Prue, but go and have your breakfast comfortably for there's much to be done, and no one is to dress me but your own dear self."

At this Prue relapsed into the pathetic again, and cried over her sister as if, despite the omen, brides were plants that needed much watering.

The appearance of the afflicted Maria, with her face still partially eclipsed by the chamomile comforter, and an announcement that the waiters had come and were "ordering round dreadful," caused Prue to pocket her handkerchief and descend to turn the tables in every sense of the word.

Wedding

The prospect of the wedding breakfast made the usual meal a mere mockery. Every one was in a driving hurry, every one was very much excited, and nobody but Prue and the colored gentlemen brought anyting to pass. Sylvia went from room to room bidding them good-by as the child who had played there so long. But each looked unfamiliar in its state and festival array, and the old house seemed to have forgotten her already. She spent an hour with her father, paid Mark a little call in the studio where he was bidding adieu to the joys of bachelorhood, and preparing himself for the jars of matrimony by a composing smoke, and then Prue claimed her.

The agonies she suffered during that long toilet are beyond the powers of language to portray, for Prue surpassed herself and was the very essence of fussiness. But Sylvia bore it patiently as a last sacrifice, because her sister was very tender-hearted still, and laughed and cried over her work till all was done, when she surveyed the effect with pensive satisfaction.

"You are very sweet, my dear, and so delightfully calm, you really do surprise me. I always thought you'd have hysterics on your wedding-day, and got my *vinaigrette* all ready. Keep your hands just as they are, with the handkerchief and bouquet, it looks very easy and rich. Dear me, what a spectacle I've made of myself! But I shall cry no more, not even during the ceremony as many do. Such displays of feeling are in very bad taste, and I shall be firm, perfectly firm, so if you hear any one sniff you'll know it is n't me. Now I must go and scramble on my dress; first, let me arrange you smoothly in a chair. There, my precious, now think of soothing things, and don't stir till Geoffrey comes for you."

Too tired to care what happened just then, Sylvia sat as she was placed, feeling like a fashion-plate of a bride, and wishing she could go to sleep. Presently the sound of steps as fleet as Mark's but lighter, waked her up, and forgetting orders, she rustled to the door with an expression which fashion-plates have not yet attained.

"Good morning, little bride."

"Good morning, bonny bridegroom."

Then they looked at one another, and both smiled. But they seemed to have changed characters, for Moor's usually tranquil face was full of pale excitement; Sylvia's usually vivacious one, full of quietude, and her eyes wore the unquestioning content of a child who accepts some friendly hand, sure that it will lead it right.

"Prue desire me to take you out into the upper hall, and when Mr. Deane beckons, we are to go down at once. The rooms are full, and Jessie is ready. Shall we go?"

"One moment: Geoffrey, are you quite happy now?"

"Supremely happy!"

"Then it shall be the first duty of my life to keep you so," and with a gesture soft yet solemn, Sylvia laid her hand in his, as if endowing him with both gift and giver. He held it fast and never let it go until it was his own.

In the upper hall they found Mark hovering about Jessie like an agitated bee, about a very full-blown flower, and Clara Deane flapping him away, lest he should damage the effect of this beautiful white rose. For ten minutes, ages they seemed, the five stood together listening to the stir below, looking at one another, till they were tired of the sight and scent of orange blossoms, and wishing that the whole affair was safely over. But the instant a portentous "Hem!" was heard, and a white glove seen to beckon from the stair foot, every one fell into a flutter. Moor turned paler still, and Sylvia felt his heart beat hard against her hand. She, herself was seized with a momentary desire to run away and say "No" again; Mark looked as if nerving himself for immediate execution, and Jessie feebly whispered—

"Oh, Clara, I'm going to faint!"

"Good-heavens, what shall I do with her? Mark support her! My darling girl, smell this and bear up. For mercy sake do something, Sylvia, and don't stand there looking as if you'd been married every day for a year."

In his excitement, Mark gave his bride a little shake. Its effect was marvellous. She rallied instantly, with a reproachful glance at her crumpled veil and a decided—"Come quick, I can go now."

Down they went, through a wilderness of summer silks, black coats, and bridal gloves. How they reached their places none of them ever knew; Mark said afterward, that the instinct of self preservation, led him to the only means of extrication that circumstances allowed. The moment the Bishop opened his book, Prue took out her handkerchief and cried steadily through the entire ceremony, for dear as were the proprieties, the "children" were dearer still.

At Sylvia's desire, Mark was married first, and as she stood listening to the sonorous roll of the service falling from the Bishop's lips, she tried to feel devout and solemn, but failed to do so. She tried to keep her thoughts from wandering, but continually found herself wondering if that sob came from Prue, if her father felt it very much, and when it would be done. She tried to keep her eyes fixed timidly upon the carpet as she had been told to do, but they would rise and glance about against her will.

One of these derelictions from the path of duty, nearly produced a catastrophe. Little Tilly, the gardener's pretty child, had strayed in from among the servants peeping at a long window in the rear, and established herself near the wedding group, looking like a small ballet girl in her full white frock and wreath pushed rakishly askew on her curly pate. As she stood regarding the scene with dignified amazement, her eye met Sylvia's. In spite of the unusual costume, the baby knew her playmate, and running to her, thrust her head under the veil with a delighted "Peep a bo!" Horror seized Jessie, Mark was on the brink of a laugh, and Moor looked like one fallen from the clouds. But Sylvia drew the little marplot close to her with a warning word, and there she stayed, quietly amusing herself with "pooring" the silvery dress, smelling the flowers and staring at the bishop.

After this, all prospered. The gloves came smoothly off, the rings went smoothly on; no one cried but Prue, no one laughed but Tilly; the brides were admired, the grooms envied; the service pronounced impressive, and when it ended, a tumult of congratulations arose.

Sylvia always had a very confused idea of what happened during the next hour. She remembered being kissed till her checks burned, and shaken hands with till her fingers tingled; bowing in answer to toasts, and forgetting to reply when addressed by the new name; trying to eat and drink, and discovering that everything tasted of wedding cake; finding herself up stairs hurrying on her travelling dress, then down stairs saying good by; and when her father embraced her last of all, suddenly realizing with a pang, that she was married and going away, never to be little Sylvia any more.

Prue *was* gratified to her heart's content, for, when the two bridal carriages had vanished with handkerchiefs flying from their windows, in answer to the white whirlwind on the lawn, Mrs. Grundy, with an approving smile on her aristocratic countenance, pronounced this the most charming affair of the season.

CHAPTER XIII

SYLVIA'S HONEYMOON

IT BEGAN with a pleasant journey. Day after day they loitered along country roads that led them through many scenes of summer beauty; pausing at old-fashioned inns and wayside farmhouses, or gipsying at noon in some green nook where their four-footed comrades dined off their tablecloth while they made merry over the less simple fare their last hostess had provided for them. When the scenery was uninteresting, as was sometimes the case, for Nature will not disturb her domestic arrangements for any bridal pair, one or the other read aloud, or both sang, while conversation was a never-failing pastime and silence had charms which they could enjoy. Sometimes they walked a mile or two, ran down a hillside, rustled through a grain field, strolled into an orchard, or feasted from fruitful hedges by the way, as care-free as the squirrels on the wall, or the jolly brown bees lunching at the sign of "The Clover-top." They made friends with sheep in meadows, cows at the brook, travellers morose or bland, farmers full of a sturdy sense that made their chat as wholesome as the mould they delved in; school children bare-footed and blithe, and specimens of womankind, from the buxom house-wife who took them under her motherly wing at once, to the sour, snuffy, shoe-binding spinster with "No Admittance" written all over her face.

To Moor the world was glorified with the purple light which sel-dom touches it but once for any of us; the journey was a wedding march, made beautiful by summer, victorious by joy; his young wife the queen of women, and himself an equal of the gods because no longer conscious of a want. Sylvia could not be otherwise than happy, for finding unbounded liberty and love her portion, she had nothing to regret, and regarded marriage as an agreeable process which had simply changed her name and given her protector, friend, and lover all in one. She was therefore her sweetest and sincerest self, miraculously docile, and charmingly gay; interested in all she saw, and quite overflowing with delight when the last days of the week betrayed the secret that her destination was the mountains.

Loving the sea so well, her few flights from home had given her only marine experiences, and the flavor of entire novelty was added to the feast her husband had provided for her. It came to her not only when she could enjoy it most, but when she needed it most, soothing the unquiet, stimulating the nobler elements which ruled her life by turns and fitting her for what lay before her. Choosing the quietest roads, Moor showed her the wonders of a region whose wild grandeur and beauty make its memory a lifelong satisfaction. Day after day they followed mountain paths, studying the changes of an ever-varying landscape, watching the flush of dawn redden the granite fronts of these Titans scared with centuries of storm, the lustre of noon brood over them until they smiled, the evening purple wrap them in its splendor, or moonlight touch them with its magic; till Sylvia always looking up at that which filled her heart with reverence and awe, was led to look beyond, and through the medium of the friend beside her learned that human love brings us nearer to the Divine, and is the surest means to that great end.

The last week of the honeymoon came all too soon, for then they had promised to return. The crowning glory of the range was left until the last, and after a day of memorable delights Sylvia sat in the sunset feasting her eyes upon the wonders of a scene which is indescribable, for words have limits and that is apparently illimitable. Presently Moor came to her asking—

"Will you join a party to the great ice palace, and see three acres of snow in August, worn by a waterfall into a cathedral, as white if not as durable as any marble?"

"I sit so comfortably here I think I had rather not. But you must go because you like such wonders, and I shall rest till you come back."

"Then I shall take myself off and leave you to muse over the pleasures of the day, which for a few hours has made you one of the most eminent woman this side the Rocky Mountains. There is a bugle at the house here with which to make the echoes, I shall take it with me, and from time to time send up a sweet reminder that you are not to stray away and lose yourself."

Sylvia sat for half an hour, then wearied by the immensity of the wide landscape she tried to rest her mind by examining the beauties close at hand. Strolling down the path the sight-seers had taken, she found herself in a rocky basin, scooped in the mountain side like a cup for a little pool, so clear and bright it looked a diamond set in jet. A fringe of scanty herbage had collected about its brim, russet mosses, purple heath, and delicate white flowers, like a band of tiny hill people keeping their revels by some fairy well. The spot attracted her, and remembering that she was not to stray away, she sat down beside the path to wait for her husband's return.

In the act of bending over the pool to sprinkle the thirsty little company about it, her hand was arrested by the tramp of approaching feet, and looking up to discover who was the disturber of her retreat, she saw a man pausing at the top of the path opposite to that by which she had come. He seemed scrutinizing the solitary occupant of the dell before descending; but as she turned her face to him he flung away knapsack, hat, and staff, and then with a great start she saw no stranger, but Adam Warwick. Coming down to her so joyfully, so impetuously, she had only time to recognise him, and cry out, when she was swept up in an embrace as tender as irresistible, and lay there conscious of nothing, but that happiness like some strong swift angel had wrapt her away into the promised land so long believed in, hungered for, and despaired of, as forever lost. Soon she heard his voice, breathless eager, but so fond it seemed another voice than his.

"My darling! did you think I should never come?"

"I thought you had forgotten me, I knew you were married. Adam, put me down."*

But he only held her closer, and laughed such a happy laugh that Sylvia felt the truth before he uttered it.

"How could I marry, loving you? How could I forget you even if I had never come to tell you this? Sylvia, I know much that has passed. Geoffrey's

---

* "I knew you were married." Cut from *M2*.

failure gave me courage to hope for success, and that the mute betrothal made with a look so long ago had been to you all it has been to me." *

Adam, you are both right and wrong,—you do not know all,—let me tell you,'—began Sylvia, as these proofs of ignorance brought her to herself with a shock of recollection and dismay. But Warwick was as absolute in his happiness as he had been in his self-denial, and took possession of her mentally as well as physically with a despotism too welcome and entire to be at once resisted.

"You shall tell me nothing till I have shown the cause of my hard-seeming silence. I must throw off that burden first, then I will listen to you until morning if you will. I have earned this moment by a year of effort, let me keep you here and enjoy it without alloy."

The old charm had lost none of its power, for absence seemed to have gifted it with redoubled potency, the confirmation of that early hope to grace it with redoubled warmth. Sylvia let him keep her, feeling that he had earned that small reward for a year's endeavor, resolving to grant all now left her to bestow, a few moments more of blissful ignorance, then to show him his loss and comfort him, sure that her husband would find no disloyalty in a compassion scarcely less deep and self-forgetful than his own would have been had he shared their secret. Only pausing to place himself upon the seat she had left, Warwick put off her hat, and turning her face to his regarded it with such unfeigned and entire content her wavering purpose was fixed by a single look. Then as he began to tell the story of the past she forgot everything but the rapid words she listened to, the countenance she watched, so beautifully changed and softened, it seemed as if she had never seen the man before† or saw him now as we sometimes see familiar figures glorified in dreams. In the fewest, kindest words Warwick told her of Ottila, the promise and the parting; then, as if the dearer theme deserved less brevity, he lingered on it as one lingers at a friend's door, enjoying in anticipation the welcome he is sure awaits him.

"The night we walked together by the river—such a wilful yet

---

* Alcott cut "How could I marry, loving you?" and revised the opening line of Warwick's response thus: "How could I forget you even if I had never come to tell you this?" (215).

† The paragraph is cut off here in the *M2* and Warwick resumes his speech to Sylvia with the same recollection of their walk by the river in both editions of *Moods* (216).

winning comrade as I had that day, and how I enjoyed it all!—that night I suspected that Geoffrey loved you, Sylvia, and was glad to think it. A month later I was sure of it, and found in that knowledge the great hardship of my life, because I loved you myself. Audacious thing! how dared you steal into my heart and take possession when I had turned my last guest out and barred the door? I thought I had done with the sentiment that had so nearly wrecked me once, but see how blind I was—the false love only made me readier for the true. You never seemed a child to me, Sylvia, because you have an old soul in a young body, and your father's trials and temptations live again in you. This first attracted me. I liked to watch, to question, to study the human enigma to which I had found a clue from its maker's lips. I liked your candor and simplicity, your courage and caprice. Even your faults found favor in my eyes; for pride, will, impetuosity were old friends of mine, and I liked to see them working in another shape. At first you were a curiosity, then an amusement, then a necessity. I wanted you, not occasionally, but constantly. You put salt and savor into life for me; for whether you spoke or were silent, were sweet or sour, friendly or cold, I was satisfied to feel your nearness, and always took away an inward content which nothing else could give me. This affection was so unlike the other that I deceived myself for a time—not long. I soon knew what had befallen me, soon felt that this sentiment was good to feel, because I forgot my turbulent and worser self and felt the nobler regenerated by the innocent companionship you gave me. I wanted you, but it was not the touch of hands or lips, the soft encounter of eyes, the tones of tenderness, I wanted most. It was that something beyond my reach, vital and vestal, invisible, yet irresistible; that something, be it heart, soul, or mind, which drew me to you by an attraction genial and genuine as itself. My Sylvia, that was love, and when it came to me I took it in, sure that whether its fruition was granted or denied I should be a manlier man for having harbored it even for an hour. Why turn your face away? Well, hide it if you will, but lean here as you did once so long ago."

She let him lay it on his shoulder, still feeling that Moor was one to look below the surface of these things and own that she did well in giving so pure a love a happy moment before its death, as she would have cherished Warwick had he laid dying.*

---

*This paragraph is shortened in *M2:* "Still silent, Sylvia listened, as she would have done to one about to die" (218).

"On that September evening, as I sat alone, I had been thinking of what might be and what must be. Had decided that I would go away for Geoffrey's sake. He was fitter than I to have you, being so gentle, and in all ways ready to possess a wife. I was so rought, such a vagrant, so full of my own purposes and plans, how could I dare to take into my keeping such a tender little creature as yourself? I thought you did not care for me; I knew any knowledge of my love would only mar his own; so it was best to go at once and leave him to the happiness he so well deserved. Just then you came to me, as if the wind had blown my desire to my arms. Such a loving touch that was! it nearly melted my resolve, it seemed hard not to take the one thing I wanted when it came to me so opportunely. I yearned to break that idle promise, made when I was vain in my own conceit, and justly punished for its folly; but you said keep it, and I did.* You could not understand my trouble, and when I sat before you so still, perhaps looking grim and cold, you did not know how I was wrestling with my unruly self. I am not truly generous, for the relinquishment of any cherished object always costs a battle, and I too often find I am worsted. For the first time I dared not meet your eyes till you dived into mine with that expression wistful and guileless, which has often made me feel as if we stood divested of our bodies, soul to soul.

"Tongue I could control, heart I could not. Up it sprung stronger than will, swifter than thought, and answered you. Sylvia, had there been one ray of self-consciousness in those steady eyes of yours, one atom of maiden shame, or fear, or trouble, I should have claimed you as my own. There was not; and though you let me read your face like an open book, you never dreamed what eloquence was in it. Innocent heart, that loved and had not learned to know it. I saw this instantly, saw that a few more such encounters would show it to you likewise, and felt more strongly than before that if ever the just deed to you, the generous one to Geoffrey were done, it should be then. For that was the one moment when your half-awakened heart could fall painlessly asleep again, if I did not disturb it, and dream on till Geoffrey woke it, to find a gentler master than I could be to it."

"It could not, Adam; you had wholly roused it, and it cried for you so long, so bitterly, oh, why did you not come to answer it before?"

---

*Warwick's evocation of his promise to Ottila is excised from his speech in *M2*.

*How could I till the year was over? Was I not obeying you in keeping that accursed promise? God knows I have made many blunders, but I think the most senseless was that promise; the most short-sighted, that belief. What right had I to fetter my tongue, or try to govern love? Shall I ever learn to do my own work aright, and not meddle with the Lord's? Sylvia, take this presumptuous and domineering devil out of me in time, lest I blunder as blindly after you are mine as I have before. Now let me finish before Mark comes to find us. I went away, you know, singing the farewell I dared not speak, and for nine months kept myself sane and steady with whatever my hands found to do. If ever work of mine is blessed it will be that, for into it I put the best endeavor of my life. Though I had renounced you, I kept my love; let it burn day and night, fed it with labor and with prayer, trusting that this selfish heart of mine might be recast and made a fitter receptacle for an enduring treasure. In May, far at the West, I met a woman who knew Geoffrey; had seen him lately, and learned that he had lost you. She was his cousin, I his friend, and through our mutual interest in him this confidence naturally came about. When she told me this hope blazed up, and all manner of wild fancies haunted me. Love is arrogant, and I nourished a belief that even I might succeed where Geoffrey failed. You were so young, you were not likely to be easily won by any other, if such a man had asked in vain, and a conviction gradually took possession of me that you *had* understood, *had* loved, and were yet waiting for me. A month seemed an eternity to wait, but I left myself no moment for despair, and soon turned my face to Cuba, finding renewed hope on the way. Gabriel went with me, told me how Ottila had searched for me, and failing to find me had gone back to make ready for my coming. How she had tried to be all I desire, and unworthy I was of her. This was well, but the mention of your name was better, and much close questioning gave me the scene, which he remembered, because Ottila had chidden him sharply for his disclosures to yourself. Knowing you so well, I gathered much from trifles which were nothing in Gabriel's eyes. I felt that regard for me, if nothing warmer, had prompted your interest in them; and out of the facts given me by Faith and Gabriel I built myself a home, which I have inhabited as a

---

*An extended revision begins here in *M2* and replaces several pages. The tragic end of Sylvia's honeymoon is thus not substantially altered in *M2;* instead there is a new description of Warwick's conflict between love and friendship. This revision is reprinted in the appendix (219–21).

guest till now, when I know myself its master, and welcome its dear mistress, so my darling."

He bent to give her tender greeting, but Sylvia arrested him.

"Not yet, Adam! not yet! Go on, before it is too late to tell me as you wish."

He thought it was some maidenly scruple, and though he smiled at it he respected it, for this same coyness in the midst of all her whims had always been one of her attractions in his eye.

"Shy thing! I will tame you yet, and draw you to me as confidingly as I drew the bird to hop into my hand and eat. You must not fear me, Sylvia, else I shall grow tyrannical; for I hate fear, and like to trample on whatever dares not fill its place bravely, sure that it will receive its due as trustfully as these little mosses sit among the clouds and find a spring to feed them even in the rock. Now I will make a speedy end of this, pleasant as it is to sit here feeling myself no longer a solitary waif. I shall spare you the stormy scenes I passed through with Ottila, because I do not care to think of my Cleopatra while I hold "my fine spirit Ariel" in my arms.[1] She had done her best, but had I been still heart-free I never could have married her. She is one of those tameless natures which only God can govern; I dared not, even when I thought I loved her, for much as I love power I love truth more. I told her this, heard prayers, reproaches, threats, and denunciations; tried to leave her kindly, and then was ready for my fate with you. But I was not to have my will so easily. I had fallen into the net, and was not to leave it till the scourging had been given. So like that other wandering Christian, I cried out, submitted, and was the meeker for it. I had to wait a little before the ship sailed; I would not stay at El Labarinto, Gabriel's home, for Ottila was there; and though the fever raged at Havana, I felt secure in my hitherto unbroken health. I returned there, and paid the penalty; for weeks of suffering taught me that I could not trifle with this body of mine, sturdy as it seemed."

"Oh, Adam, who took care of you? Where did you lie and suffer all that time?"

"Never fret yourself concerning that; I was not neglected. A sister of the 'Sacred Heart' took excellent care of me, and a hospital is as good as a palace when one neither knows nor cares where he is. It went hardly with me, I believe; but being resolved to live, I fought it through. Death looked at me, had compassion, and passed by. There is a Haytien proverb which must comfort you if I am a gaunt ghost of my former self: 'A lean freeman is

better than a fat slave.' There comes the first smile I have seen; but my next
bit of news will bring a frown, I think. When I was well enough to creep
out, I learned that Ottila was married. You heard the rumor, doubtless, but
not the name, for Gabriel's and mine were curiously blended in many
minds by the suddenness of my disappearance and his appearance as the
bridegroom. It was like her,—she had prepared for me as if sure I was to
fill the place I had left, hoping that this confidence of hers would have its
due effect upon me. It did try me sorely, but an experience once over is as if
it had never been, as far as regret or indecision is concerned; therefore
wedding gowns and imperious women failed to move me. To be left a
groomless bride stung that fiery pride of hers more than many an actual
shame or sin would have done. People would pity her, would see her loss,
deride her wilful folly. Gabriel loved her as she desired to be loved, blindly
and passionately; few knew of our later bond, many of our betrothal, why
not let the world believe me the rejected party come back for a last appeal?
I had avoided all whom I once knew, for I loathed the place; no one had
discovered me at the hospital, she thought me gone, she boldly took the
step, married the poor boy, left Cuba before I was myself again, and won
herself an empty victory which I never shall disturb."

"How strange! Yet I can believe it of her, she looked a woman who
would dare do anything. Then you came back Adam, to find me? What led
you here, hoping so much and knowing so little?"

"Did you ever know me do anything in the accustomed way? Do I
not always aim straight at the thing I want and pursue it by the shortest
road? It fails often, and I go back to the slower surer way; but my own is
always tried first, as involuntarily as I hurled myself down that slope, as if
storming a fort instead of meeting my sweetheart. That is a pretty old word
beloved of better men than I, so let me use it once. Among the first persons
I met on landing was a friend of your father's; he was just driving away in
hot haste, but catching a glimpse of the familiar face, I bethought me that it
was the season for summer travel, you might be away, and no one else
would satisfy me; he might know, and time be saved.* I asked one question, "Where are the Yules?" He answered, as he vanished, "The young
people are all at the mountains." That was enough, and congratulating
myself on the forethought which would save me some hundred miles of

---

*Here the two editions are the same again.

needless delay, away I went, and for days have been searching for you every where on that side of these hills which I know so well. But no Yules had passed, and feeling sure you were on this side I came, not around, but straight over, for this seemed a royal road to my love, and here I found her waiting for me by the way. Now Sylvia, are your doubts all answered, your fears all laid, your heart at rest on mine?

As the time drew nearer Sylvia's task daunted her. Warwick was so confident, so glad and tender over her, it seemed like pronouncing the death doom to say those hard words, "It is too late." While she struggled to find some expression that should tell all kindly yet entirely, Adam, seeming to read some hint of her trouble, asked, with that gentleness which now overlaid his former abruptness, and was the more alluring for the contrast—

"Have I been too arrogant a lover? too sure of happiness, too blind to my small deserts? Sylvia, have I misunderstood the greeting you have given me?"

"Yes, Adam, utterly."*

He knit his brows, his eye grew anxious, his content seemed rudely broken, but still hopefully he said—

"You mean that absence has changed you, that you do not love me as you did, and pity made you kind? Well, I receive the disappointment, but I do not relinquish my desire. What has been may be; let me try again to earn you; teach me to be humble, patient, all that I should be to make myself more dear to you. Something disturbs you, be frank with me; I have shown you all my heart, what have you to show me in return?"

"Only this."

She freed herself entirely from his hold and held up her hand before him. He did not see the ring; he thought she gave him all he asked, and with a glow of gratitude extended both his own to take it. Then she saw that delay was worse than weak, and though she trembled she spoke out bravely ending his suspense at once.

"Adam, I do *not* love you as I did, nor can I wish or try to bring it back, because—I am married."

He sprung up as if shot through the heart, nor could a veritable bullet from her hand have daunted him with a more intense dismay than those

---

* "utterly" omitted in *M2* (222)

129

three words. An instant's incredulity, then conviction came to him, and he met it like a man, for though his face whitened and his eye burned with an expression that wrung her heart, he demanded steadily,—

"To whom?" *

This was the hardest question of all, for well she knew the name would wound the deeper for its dearness, and while it lingered pitifully upon her lips its owner answered for himself. Clear and sweet came up the music of the horn, bringing them a familiar air they all loved, and had often sung together. Warwick knew it instantly, felt the hard truth but rebelled against it, and put out his arm as if to ward it off as he exclaimed, with real anguish in countenance and voice—"Oh, Sylvia! it is not Geoffrey?" †

'Yes.'

Then, as if all strength had gone out of her, she dropped down upon the mossy margin of the spring and covered up her face, feeling that the first sharpness of a pain like this was not for human eyes to witness. How many minutes passed she could not tell, the stillness of the spot remained unbroken by any sound but the whisper of the wind, and in this silence Sylvia found time to marvel at the calmness which came to her. Self had been forgotten in surprise and sympathy, and still her one thought was how to comfort Warwick. She had expected some outburst of feeling, some gust of anger or despair, but neither sigh nor sob, reproach nor regret reached her, and soon she stole an anxious glance to see how it went with him. He was standing where she left him, both hands locked together till they were white with the passionate pressure. His eyes fixed on some distant object with a regard as imploring as unseeing, and through those windows of the soul he looked out darkly, not despairingly; but as if sure that somewhere there was help for him, and he waited for it with a stern patience more terrible to watch than the most tempestuous grief. Sylvia could not bear it, and remembering that her confession had not yet been made, seized that instant for the purpose, prompted by an instinct which assured her that the knowledge of her pain would help him to bear his own.

She told him all, and ended saying—‡

---

* In *M2:* "To whom if not to Geoffrey?" (223)

† In *M2:* "Sylvia, it *is* he?" (223)

‡ . . . and ended, saying imploringly,—

"Adam, how can I comfort you?" *M2* (224)

"Now, Adam, come to me and let me try to comfort you."

Sylvia was right; for through the sorrowful bewilderment that brought a brief eclipse of hope and courage, sympathy reached him like a friendly hand to uphold him till he found the light again. While speaking, she had seen the immobility that frightened her break up, and Warwick's whole face flush and quiver with the rush of emotions controllable no longer. But the demonstration which followed was one she had never thought to see from him, for when she stretched her hands to him with that tender invitation,* she saw the deep eyes fill and overflow. Then he threw himself down before her, and for the first time in her short life showed her that sad type of human suffering, a man weeping like a woman.

Warwick was one of those whose passions, as his virtues, were in unison with the powerful body they inhabited, and in such a crisis as the present but one of two reliefs were possible to him; either wrathful denunciation, expostulation and despair, or the abandon of a child. Against the former he had been struggling dumbly till Sylvia's words had turned the tide, and too entirely natural to feel a touch of shame at that which is not a weakness but a strength, too wise to reject so safe an outlet for so dangerous a grief, he yielded to it, letting the merciful magic of tears quench the fire, wash the first bitterness away, and leave reproaches only writ in water. It was better so, and Sylvia acknowledged it within herself as she sat mute and motionless, softly touching the brown hair scattered on the moss,† her poor consolation silenced by the pathos of the sight, while through it all rose and fell the fitful echo of the horn, in very truth "a sweet reminder not to stray away and lose herself." An hour ago it would have been a welcome sound, for peak after peak gave back the strain, and airy voices whispered it until the faintest murmur died. But now she let it soar and sigh half heard, for audible to her alone still came its sad accompaniment was far more; for music, the comforter, laid her balm on his sore heart as no mortal pity could have done, and wrought the miracle which changed the friend who seemed to have robbed him of his love to an unconscious Orpheus, who subdued the savage and harmonized the man. Soon he was himself again, for to those who harbor the strong virtues with patient zeal, no lasting ill can come, no affliction can wholly crush, no temptation wholly vanquish. He rose with eyes the clearer for their stormy rain, twice

---

*M2: with that remorseful cry (225)
†M2: brown head lying on the moss, (225)

a man for having dared to be a child again. Humbler and happier for the knowledge that neither vain resentment nor unjust accusation had defrauded of its dignity, the heavy hour that left him desolate but not degraded.

"I *am* comforted, Sylvia, rest assured of that. And now there is little more to say, but one thing to do. I shall not see your husband yet, and leave you to tell him what seems best, for, with the instinct of an animal, I always go away to outlive my hurts alone. But remember that I acquit you of blame, and believe that I will yet be* happy in your happiness. I know if Geoffrey were here, he would let me do this, because he has suffered as I suffer now."

Bending, he gathered her to an embrace as different from that other as despair is from delight, and while he held her there, crowding into one short minute, all the pain and passion of a year, she heard a low, but exceeding bitter cry—"Oh, my Sylvia! it is hard to give you up." Then, with a solemn satisfaction, which assured her as it did himself, he spoke out clear and loud—

"Thank God for the merciful Hereafter, in which we may retrieve the blunders we make here."

With that he left her, never turning till the burden so joyfully cast down had been resumed. Then, staff and hat in hand, he paused on the margin of that granite cup, to him a cup of sorrow, and looked into its depths again. Clouds were trooping eastward, but in that pause the sun glanced full on Warwick's figure, lifting his powerful head into a flood of light, as he waved his hand to Sylvia with a gesture of courage and good cheer. The look, the act, the memories they brought her, made her heart ache with a sharper pang than pity, and filled her eyes with tears of impotent regret, as she turned her head as if to chide the blithe clamor of the horn. When she looked again, the figure and the sunshine were both gone, leaving her alone and in the shadow.†

---

*M2: can yet be (226)

†M2 adds three new paragraphs to this ending. They are reprinted in the appendix (227).

CHAPTER XIV

A FIRESIDE FETE*

"*NO COUSIN FAITH* to-night. The rain has prevented her from taking this boat, and she is not likely to come later as she comes alone," said Moor, returning from a fruitless drive to meet his expected guest one October evening.

"It always rains when I want anything very much. I seem to have a great deal of bad weather in my life," answered Sylvia, despondingly.

"Never mind the rain; let us make sunshine for ourselves, and forget it as children do."

"I wish I was a child again, they are always happy."

"Let us play at being children, then. Let us sit down upon the rug, parch corn, crack nuts, roast apples, and be merry in spite of wind or weather."

Sylvia's face brightened, for the fancy pleased her, and she wanted something new and pleasant to divert her thoughts from herself. Glancing at her dress, which was unusually matronly in honor of the occasion, she said smiling—

"I don't look much like a child, but I should like to try and feel like one again if I can."

"Let us both look and feel so as much as possible. You like

---

*"A Fireside Fête" (with accent added) becomes Chapter XV in *M2*. It opens with Sylvia and Moor in their new home; the first page of *M1* is omitted, and the narrative resumes with "No lad could have spoken . . ." The revised opening of the chapter is reprinted in the appendix (228–33).

masquerading; go make a little girl of yourself, while I turn boy, and prepare for our merry making."

No lad could have spoken with a blither face, for Moor had preserved much of the boy in spite of his thirty years. His cheerfulness was so infectious, that Sylvia already began to forget her gloom, and hurried away to do her part. Putting on a short, girlish gown, kept for scrambles among the rocks, she improvised a pinafore, and braided her long hair a la Morlena Kenwigs, with butterfly bows at the ends. When she went down, she found her husband in garden jacket, collar turned over a ribbon, hair in a curly tumble, and jackknife in hand, seated on the rug before a roaring fire, and a semicircle of apples, whittling and whistling like a very boy. They examined one another with mirthful commendations, and Moor began his part by saying—

"Isn't this jolly? Now come and cuddle down here beside me, and see which will keep it up the longest."

"What would Prue say? and who would recognize the elegant Mr. Moor in this big boy? Putting dignity and broadcloth aside makes you look about eighteen, and very charming I find you," said Sylvia, looking about twelve herself, and also very charming.

"Here is a wooden fork for you to tend the roast with, while I see to the corn laws and prepare a vegetable snowstorm. What will you have, little girl, you look as if you wanted something?"

"I was only thinking that I should have a doll to match your knife. I feel as if I should enjoy trotting a staring fright on my knee, and singing Hush-a-by. But I fancy even your magic cannot produce such a thing,— can it, my lad?"

"In exactly five minutes a lovely doll will appear, though such a thing has not been seen in my bachelor establishment for years."

With which mysterious announcement Moor ran off, blundering over the ottomans and slamming the doors as a true boy should. Sylvia pricked chestnuts, and began to forget her bosom trouble as she wondered what would appear with the impatient curiosity appropriate to the character she had assumed. Presently her husband reappeared with much breeziness of aspect, rain drops in his hair, and a squirming bundle in his arms. Triumphantly unfolding many wraps, he displayed little Tilly in her night-gown.

"There is sorcery for you, and a doll worth having; being one of the sort that can shut its eyes; it was going to bed, but its mamma relented and lends it to us for the night. I told Mrs. Dodd you wanted her, and could n't wait, so she sent her clothes; but the room is so warm let the dear play in her pretty bed-gown."

Sylvia received her lovely plaything with enthusiasm, and Tilly felt herself suddenly transported to a baby's Paradise, where beds were unknown and fruit and freedom were her welcome portion. Merrily popped the corn, nimbly danced the nuts upon the shovel, lustily remonstrated the rosy martyrs on the hearth, and cheerfully the minutes slipped away. Sylvia sung every jubilant air she knew, Moor whistled astonishing accompaniments, and Tilly danced over the carpet with nutshells on her toes, and tried to fill her little gown with "pitty flowers" from its garlands and bouquets. Without the wind lamented, the sky wept, and the sea thundered on the shore; but within, youth, innocence, and love held their blithe revel undisturbed.

"How are the spirits now?" asked one playmate of the other.

"Quite merry, thank you; and I should think I was little Sylvia again but for the sight of this."

She held up the hand that wore a single ornament; but the hand had grown so slender since it was first put on, that the ring would have fallen had she not caught it at her finger-tip. There was nothing of the boy in her companion's face, as he said, with an anxious look—

"If you go on thinning so fast I shall begin to fear that the little wife is not happy with her old husband. Is she, dear?"

"She would be a most ungrateful woman if she were not. I always get thin as winter comes on, but I'm so careless I'll find a guard for my ring to-morrow."

"No need to wait till then; wear this to please me, and let Marion's cipher signify that you are *mine*."

With a gravity that touched her more than the bestowal of so dear a relic, Moor unslung a signet ring from his watchguard, and with some difficulty pressed it to its place on Sylvia's finger, a most effectual keeper for that other ring whose tenure seemed so slight. She shrunk a little and glanced up at him because his touch was more firm than tender, and his face wore a masterful expression seldom seen there; for instinct, subtler than perception, prompted both act and aspect. Then her eye fell and fixed upon the dark stone with the single letter engraved upon its tiny oval, and to her it took a double significance as her husband held it there, claiming her again, with that emphatic "Mine." She did not speak, but something in her manner caused the fold between his brows to smooth itself away as he regarded the small land lying passively in his, and said, half playfully, half earnestly—

"Forgive me if I hurt you, but you know my wooing is not over yet; and till you love me with a perfect love I cannot feel that my wife is wholly mine."

"I am so young, you know; when I am a woman grown I can give you a woman's love; now it is a girl's, you say. Wait for me, Geoffrey, a little longer, for indeed I do my best to be all you would have me."

Something brought tears into her eyes and made her lips tremble, but in a breath the smile came back, and she added gayly—

"How can I help being grave sometimes, and getting thin, with so many housekeeping cares upon my shoulders, and such an exacting, tyrannical husband to wear upon my nerves. Don't I look like the most miserable of wives?"

She did not certainly as she shook the popper laughingly, and looked over her shoulder at him, with the bloom of firelight on her cheeks, its cheerfulness in her eyes.

"Keep that expression for every day wear, and I am satisfied. I want no tame Griselda, but the little girl who once said she was always happy with me. Assure me of that, and, having won my Leah, I can work and wait still longer for my Rachel.[1] Bless the baby! what has she done to herself now?"

Tilly had retired behind the sofa, after she had swarmed over every chair and couch, examined everything within her reach, on *étagère* and table, embraced the Hebe in the corner, played a fantasia on the piano, and choked herself with the stopper of the odor bottle. A doleful wail betrayed her hiding-place, and she now emerged with a pair of nutcrackers, ditto of pinched fingers, and an expression of great mental and bodily distress. Her woes vanished instantaneously, however, when the feast was announced, and she performed an unsteady *pas seul* about the banquet, varied by skirmishes with her long night-gown and darts at any unguarded viand that tempted her.

No ordinary table service would suit the holders of this fireside *fête*. The corn was heaped in a bronze urn, the nuts in a graceful basket, the apples lay on a plate of curiously ancient china, and the water turned to wine through the medium of a purple flagon of Bohemian glass. The refection was spread upon the rug as on a flowery table, and all the lustres were lighted, filling the room with a festal glow. Prue would have held up her hands in dismay, like the benighted piece of excellence she was, but Mark would have enjoyed the picturesque group and sketched a mate to the Golden Wedding. For Moor, armed with the wooden fork, did the honors; Sylvia, leaning on her arm, dropped corn after corn into a baby mouth that bird-like always gaped for more; and Tilly lay luxuriously between them, warming her little feet as she ate and babbled to the flames.

The clock was on the stroke of eight, the revel at its height, when the door opened and a servant announced—

"Miss Dane and Mr. Warwick."

An impressive puase followed, broken by a crow from Tilly, who seized this propitious moment to bury one hand in the nuts and with the other capture the big red apple which had been denied her. The sound seemed to dissipate the blank surprise that had fallen on all parties, and brought both host and hostess to their feet, the former exclaiming heartily—

"Welcome, friends, to a modern saturnalia and the bosom of the Happy Family!"

"I fear you did not expect me so late," said Miss Dane. "I was detained at the time fixed upon and gave it up, but Mr. Warwick came, and we set off together. Pray don't disturb yourselves, but let us enjoy the game with you."*

"You and Adam are guests who never come too early or too late. We are playing children to-night, so just put yourselves back a dozen years and let us all be merry together. Sylvia, this our cousin, Faith here is your new kinswoman. Please love one another as little people are commanded to do."†

A short stir ensued while hands were shaken, wraps put off, and some degree of order restored to the room, then they all sat down and began to talk. With well bred oblivion of the short gown and long braids of her bashfullooking hostess, Miss Dane suggested and discussed various subjects of mutual interest, while Sylvia tried to keep her eyes from wandering to the mirror opposite, which reflected the figures of her husband and his friend.

Warwick sat erect in the easy-chair, for he never lounged; and Moor,

---

* This and the following paragraph are cut in *M2* and Alcott replaced them with a new version, reprinted in the appendix (238–39).

† The chapter resumes here in *M2* with minor changes from the 1864 *Moods*.

still supporting his character, was perched upon the arm, talking with boyish vivacity. Every sense being unwontedly alert, Sylvia found herself listening to both guests at once, and bearing her own part in one conversation so well that occasional lapses were only attributed to natural embarrassment. What she and Miss Dane said she never remembered; what the other talked of she never forgot. The first words she caught were her husband's.

"You see I have begun to live for myself, Adam."

"I also see that it agrees with you excellently."

"Better than with you, for you are not looking like your old self, though June made you happy, I hope?"

"If freedom is happiness it did."

"Are you still alone?"

"More so than ever."

Sylvia lost the next words, for a look showed her Moor's hand on Adam's shoulder, and that for the first time within her memory Warwick did not meet his friend's glance with one as open, but bent his eyes upon the ground, while his hand went to and fro across his lips as if to steady them. It was a gesture she remembered well, for though self-control could keep the eye clear, the voice firm, that half-hidden mouth of his sometimes rebelled and grew tremulous as a woman's. The sight and the answer set her heart beating with the thought, "Why has he come?" The repetition of a question by Miss Dane recalled her from a dangerous memory, and when that friendly lady entered upon another long sentence to relieve her young hostess, she heard Moor say—

"You have had too much solitude, Adam; I am sure of it, for no man can live long alone and not get the uncanny look you have. What have you been at?"

"Fighting the old fight with this unruly self of mine, and getting ready for another tussle with the Adversary, in whatever shape he may appear."

"And now you are come to your friend for the social solace which the haughtiest heart hungers for when most alone. You shall have it. Stay with us, Adam, and remember that whatever changes come to me my house is always yours."

"I know it, Geoffrey. I wanted to see your happiness before I go away again, and should like to stay with you a day or so if you are sure that—that she would like it."

Moor laughed and pulled a lock of the brown mane, as if to tease the lion into a display of the spirit he seemed to have lost.

"How shy you are of speaking the new name! 'She' will like it, I assure you, for she makes my friends hers. Sylvia, come here, and tell Adam he is welcome; he dares to doubt it. Come and talk over old times, while I do the same with Faith."

She went, trembling inwardly, but outwardly composed, for she took refuge in one of those commonplace acts which in such moments we gladly perform, and bless in our secret souls. She had often wondered where they would next meet, and how she should comport herself at such a trying time. She had never imagined that he would come in this way, or that a heart-brush would save her from the betrayal of emotion. So it was, however, and an involuntary smile passed over her face as she managed to say quite naturally, while brushing the nutshells tidily out of sight—

"You know you are always welcome, Mr. Warwick. 'Adam's Room,' as we call it, is always ready, and Geoffrey was wishing for you only yesterday."

"I am sure of his satisfaction at my coming, can I be equally sure of yours. May I, ought I to stay?"

He leaned forward as he spoke, with an eager yet submissive look, that Sylvia dared not meet, and in her anxiety to preserve her self-possession, she forgot that to this listener every uttered word became a truth, because his own were always so.

"Why not, if you can bear our quiet life, for we are a Darby and Joan already, though we do not look so to-night, I acknowledge."

Men seldom understand the subterfuges women instinctively use to conceal many a natural emotion which they are not strong enough to control, not brave enough to confess. To Warwick, Sylvia seemed almost careless, her words a frivolous answer to the real meaning of his question, her smile one of tranquil welcome. Her manner wrought an instant change in him, and when he spoke again he was the Warwick of a year ago.

"I hesitated, Mrs. Moor, because I have sometimes heard young wives complain that their husbands' friends were marplots, and I have no desire to be one."

This speech, delivered with frosty gravity, made Sylvia as cool and quiet as itself. She put her ally down, looked full at Warwick, and said with a blending of dignity and cordiality which even the pinafore could not destroy—

"Please to consider yourself a specially invited guest, now and always. Never hesitate, but come and go as freely as you used to do, for nothing need be changed between us three because two of us have one home to offer you."

"Thanks; and now that the hearth is scrupulously clean may I offer you a chair?"

The old keenness was in his eye, the old firmness about the mouth, the old satirical smile on his lips as Warwick presented the seat, with an inclination that to her seemed ironical. She sat down, but when she cast about her mind for some safe and easy topic to introduce, every idea had fled; even memory and fancy turned traitors; not a lively sally could be found, not a pleasant remembrance returned to help her, and she sat dumb. Before the dreadful pause grew awkward, however, rescue came in the form of Tilly. Nothing daunted by the severe simplicity of her attire she planted herself before Warwick, and shaking her hair out of her eyes stared at him with an inquiring glance and cheeks as red as her apple. She seemed satisfied in a moment, and climbing to his knee established herself there, coolly taking possession of his watch, and examining the brown beard curiously as it parted with the white flash of teeth, when Warwick smiled his warmest smile.

"This recalls the night you fed the sparrow in your hand. Do you remember, Adam?" and Sylvia looked and spoke like her old self again.

"I seldom forget anything. But pleasant as that hour was this is more to me, for the bird flew away, the baby stays and gives me what I need."

He wrapt the child closer in his arms, leaned his dark head on the bright one, and took the little feet into his hand with a fatherly look that caused Tilly to pat his cheek and begin an animated recital of some nursery legend, which ended in a sudden gape, reminding Sylvia that one of her guests was keeping late hours.

"What comes next?" asked Warwick.

"Now I lay me and byelow in the trib," answered Tilly, stretching herself over his arm with a great yawn.

Warwick kissed the rosy half-open mouth and seemed loth to part with the pious baby, for he took the shawl Sylvia brought and did up the drowsy bundle himself. While so busied she stole a furtive glance at him, having looked without seeing before. Thinner and browner, but stronger than ever was the familiar face she saw, yet neither sad nor stern, for the grave gentleness which had been a fugitive expression before now seemed habitual. This, with the hand at the lips and the slow dropping of the eyes, were the only tokens of the sharp experience he had been passing through. Born for conflict and endurance, he seemed to have manfully accepted the sweet uses of adversity and grown the richer for his loss.

Those who themselves are quick to suffer, are also quick to see the marks of suffering in others; that hasty scrutiny assured Sylvia of all she had yearned to know, yet wrung her heart with a pity the deeper for its impotence. Tilly's heavy head drooped between her bearer and the light as they left the room, but in the dusky hall a few hot tears fell on the baby's hair, and her new nurse lingered long after the lullaby was done. When she reappeared the girlish dress was gone, and she was Madam Moor again, as her husband called her when she assumed her stately air. All smiled at the change, but he alone spoke of it.

"I win the applause, Sylvia; for I sustain my character to the end, while you give up before the curtain falls. You are not so good an actress as I thought you."

Sylvia's smile was sadder than her tears as she briefly answered—"No, I find I cannot be a child again."

CHAPTER XV

EARLY AND LATE

ONE of Sylvia's first acts when she rose was most significant. She shook down her abundant hair, carefully arranged a part in thick curls over cheeks and forehead, gathered the rest into its usual coil, and said to herself, as she surveyed her face half hidden in the shining cloud—

"It looks very sentimental, and I hate the weakness that drives me to it, but it must be done, because my face is such a traitor. Poor Geoffrey! he said I was no actress; I am learning fast."

Why every faculty seemed sharpened, every object assumed an unwonted interest, and that quiet hour possessed an excitement that made her own room and countenance look strange to her, she would not ask herself, as she paused on the threshold of the door to ascertain if her guests were stirring. Nothing was heard but the sound of regular footfalls on the walk before the door, and with an expression of relief she slowly went down. Moor was taking his morning walk bareheaded in the sun. Usually Sylvia ran to join him, but now she stood musing on the steps, until he saw and came to her. As he offered the flower always ready for her, he said smiling—

"Did the play last night so captivate you, that you go back to the curls, because you cannot keep the braids?"

"A sillier whim than that, even. I am afraid of those two people; and as I am so quick to show my feelings in my face, I intend to hide behind this veil if I get shy or troubled. Did you think I could be so artful?"

"Your craft amazes me. But, dearest child, you need not be afraid of Faith and Adam. Both already love you for my sake, and soon will for your own. Both are so much older, that they can easily overlook any little short-coming, in consideration of your youth. Sylvia, I want to tell you some-thing about Adam.* I never spoke of it before, because, although no prom-ise of silence was asked or given, I knew he considered it a confidence. Now that it is all over, I know that I may tell my wife, and she will help me comfort him."

"Tell on, Geoffrey, I hear you."

"Well, dear, when we went gypsying long ago, on the night you and Adam lost the boat, as I sat drying your boots, and privately adoring them in spite of the mud, I made a discovery. Adam loved, was on some sort of probation, and would be married in June. He was slow to speak of it, but I understood, and last night when I went to his room with him, I asked how he had fared. Sylvia, it would have your heart ache to have seen his face, as he said in that brief way of his—"Geoffrey, the woman I loved is married, ask me nothing more." I never shall; but I know, by the change I see in him, that the love was very dear, the wound very deep."

"Poor Adam! how can we help him?"

"Let him do as he likes. I will take him to his old haunts, and busy him with my affairs till he forgets his own. In the evenings we will have Prue, Mark, and Jessie over here, will surround him with social influences, and make the last hours of the day the cheerfullest; then he wont lie awake and think all night, as I suspect he has been doing of late. Sylvia, I should like to see that woman; though I could find it in my heart to hate her for her perfidy to such a man."

Sylvia's head was bent as if to inhale the sweetness of the flower she held, and all her husband saw was the bright hair blowing in the wind.

"I pity her for her loss as well as hate her. Now, let us talk of some-thing else, or my tell-tale face will betray that we have been talking of him, when we meet Adam."

†They did so, and when Warwick put up his curtain, the first sight he saw, was his friend walking with his young wife under the red-leaved

---

*Alcott altered this sentence and omitted Moor's confidence that follows about Warwick's unhappy love affair with Ottila in *M2* and added a tender plot by Moor to pair his friend Adam with his cousin Faith Dane. This new section is reprinted in the appendix (247–49).

†The two versions come together here and are nearly identical for several pages.

maples, in the sunshine. The look Moor had spoken of, came into his eyes, darkening them with the shadow of despair. A moment it gloomed there, then passed, for Honor said reproachfully to Love—"They are happy, should not that content you?"

"It shall!" answered the master of both, as he dropped the curtain and turned away.

In pursuance of his kindly plan, Moor took Adam out for a long tramp soon after breakfast, and Sylvia and Miss Dane sat down to sew. In the absence of the greater fear, Sylvia soon forgot the lesser one, and began to feel at ease, to study her new relative and covet her esteem.

Faith was past thirty, shapely and tall, with much natural dignity of carriage, and a face never beautiful, but always singularly attractive from its mild and earnest character. Looking at her, one felt assured that here was a right womanly woman, gentle, just, and true; possessed of a well-balanced mind, a self-reliant soul, and that fine gift which is so rare, the power of acting as a touchstone to all who approached, forcing them to rise or fall to their true level, unconscious of the test applied. Her presence was comfortable, her voice had motherly tones in it, her eyes a helpful look. Even the soft hue of her dress, the brown gloss of her hair, the graceful industry of her hands, had their attractive influence. Sylvia saw and felt these things with the quickness of her susceptible temperament, and found herself so warmed and won, that soon it cost her an effort to withhold anything that tried or troubled her, for Faith was a born consoler, and Sylvia's heart was full.

However gloomy her day might have been she always brightened in the evening as naturally as moths begin to flutter when candles come. On the evening of this day the friendly atmosphere about her, and the excitement of Warwick's presence so affected her, that though the gayety of girlhood was quite gone she looked as softly brilliant as some late flower that has gathered the summer to itself and gives it out again in the bloom and beauty of a single hour.

When tea was over, for heroes and heroines must eat if they are to do anything worth the paper on which their triumphs and tribulations are recorded, the women gathered about the library table, work in hand, as female tongues go easier when their fingers are occupied. Sylvia left Prue and Jessie to enjoy Faith, and while she fabricated some trifle with scarlet silk and an ivory shuttle, she listened to the conversation of the gentlemen who roved about the room till a remark of Prue's brought the party together.

"Helen Chesterfield has run away from her husband in the most disgraceful manner."

Mark and Moor drew near, Adam leaned on the chimneypiece, the workers paused, and having produced her sensation, Prue proceeded to gratify their curiosity as briefly as possible, for all knew the parties in question and all waited anxiously to hear particulars.

"She married a Frenchman old enough to be her father, but very rich. She thought she loved him, but when she got tired of her fine establishment, and the novelties of Paris, she found she did not, and was miserable. Many of her new friends had lovers, so why should not she; and presently she began to amuse herself with this Louis Gustave Isadore Theodule de Roueville—There's a name for a Christian man! Well, she began in play, grew in earnest, and when she could bear her domestic trouble no longer she just ran away, ruining herself for this life, and really I don't know but for the next also."

"Poor soul! I always thought she was a fool, but upon my word I pity her," said Mark.

"Remember she was very young, so far away from her mother, with no real friend to warn and help her, and love is so sweet. No wonder she went."

"Sylvia, how can you excuse her in that way? She should have done her duty whether she loved the old gentleman or not, and kept her troubles to herself in a proper manner. You young girls think so much of love, so little of moral obligations, decorum, and the opinions of the world, you are not fit judges of the case. Mr. Warwick agrees with me, I am sure."

"Not in the least."

"Do you mean to say that Helen should have left her husband?"

"Certainly, if she could not love him."

"Do you also mean to say that she did right to run off with that Gustave Isadore Theodule creature?"

"By no means. It is worse than folly to attempt the righting of one wrong by the commission of another."

"Then what in the world should she have done?"

"She should have honestly decided what she loved, have frankly told the husband the mistake both had made, and demanded her liberty. If the lover was worthy, have openly married him and borne the world's censures. If not worthy, have stood alone, an honest woman in God's eyes, whatever the blind world might have thought."

Prue was scandalized to the last degree, for with her marriage was more a law than a gospel; a law which ordained that a pair once yoked should abide by their bargain, be it good or ill, and preserve the proprieties in public no matter how hot a hell their home might be for them and for their children.

"What a dreadful state society would be in if your ideas were adopted! People would constantly be finding out that they were mismatched, and go running about as if playing that game where every one changes places. I'd rather die at once than live to see such a state of things as that," said the worthy spinster.

"So would I, and recommend prevention rather than a dangerous cure."

"I really should like to hear your views, Mr. Warwick, for you quite take my breath away."

Much to Sylvia's surprise Adam appeared to like the subject, and placed his views at Prue's disposal with alacrity.

"I would begin at the beginning, and teach young people that marriage is not the only aim and end of life, yet would fit them for it as for a sacrament too high and holy to be profaned by a light word or thought. Show them how to be worthy of it and how to wait for it. Give them a law of life both cheerful and sustaining; a law that shall keep them hopeful if single, sure that here or hereafter they will find that other self and be accepted by it; happy if wedded, for their own integrity of heart will teach them to know the true god when he comes, and keep them loyal to the last."

"That is all very excellent and charming, but what are the poor souls to do who have n't been educated in this fine way?" asked Prue.

"Unhappy marriages are the tragedies of our day, and will be, till we learn that there are truer laws to be obeyed than those custom sanctions, other obstacles than inequalities of fortune, rank, and age. Because two persons love, it is not always safe or wise for them to marry, nor need it necessarily wreck their peace to live apart. Often what seems the best affection of our hearts does more for us by being thwarted than if granted its fulfilment and prove a failure which embitters two lives instead of sweetening one."

He paused there, but Prue wanted a clearer answer, and turned to Faith, sure that the woman would take her own view of the matter.

"Which of us is right, Miss Dane, in Helen's case?"

"I cannot venture to judge the young lady, knowing so little of her character or the influences that have surrounded her, and believing that a certain divine example is best for us to follow at such times. I agree with Mr. Warwick, but not wholly, for his summary mode of adjustment would not be quite just nor right in all cases. If both find that they do not love, the sooner they part the wiser; if one alone makes the discovery the case is sadder still, and harder for either to decide. But as I speak from observation only my opinions are of little worth."

"Of great worth, Miss Dane; for to women like yourself observation often does the work of experience, and despite your modesty I wait to hear the opinions."

Warwick spoke, and spoke urgently, for the effect of all this upon Sylvia was too absorbing a study to be relinquished yet. As he turned to her, Faith gave him an intelligent glance, and answered like one speaking with intention and to some secret but serious issue—

"You shall have them. Let us suppose that Helen was a woman possessed of a stronger character, a deeper nature; the husband a younger, nobler man; the lover truly excellent, and above even counselling the step this pair have taken. In a case like that the wife, having promised to guard another's happiness, should sincerely endeavor to do so, remembering that in making the joy of others we often find our own, and that having made so great a mistake the other should not bear all the loss. If there be a strong attachment on the husband's part, and he a man worthy of affection and respect, who has given himself confidingly, believing himself beloved by the woman he so loves, she should leave no effort unmade, no self-denial unexacted, till she has proved beyond all doubt that it is impossible to be a true wife. Then, and not till then, has she the right to dissolve the tie that has become a sin, because where no love lives inevitable suffering and sorrow enter in, falling not only upon guilty parents, but the innocent children who may be given them."

"And the lover, what of him?" asked Adam, still intent upon his purpose, for, though he looked steadily at Faith, he knew that Sylvia drove the shuttle in and out with a desperate industry that made her silence significant to him.

"I would have the lover suffer and wait; sure that, however it may fare with him, he will be the richer and the better for having known the joy and pain of love."

"Thank you." And to Mark's surprise Warwick bowed gravely, and Miss Dane resumed her work with a preoccupied air.

"Well, for a confirmed celibate, it strikes me you take a remarkable interest in matrimony," said Mark. "Or is it merely a base desire to speculate upon the tribulations of your fellow-beings, and congratulate yourself upon your escape from them?"

"Neither; I not only pity and long to alleviate them, but have a strong desire to share them, and the wish and purpose of my life for the last year has been to marry."

Outspoken as Warwick was at all times and on sll subjects, there was something in this avowal that touched those present, for with the words a quick rising light and warmth illuminated his whole countenance, and the energy of his desire tuned his voice to a key which caused one heart to beat fast, one pair of eyes to fill with sudden tears. Moor could not see his friend's face, but he saw Mark's, divined the indiscreet inquiry hovering on his lips, and arrested it with a warning gesture.

A pause ensued, during which each person made some mental comment on the last speech, and to several of the group that little moment was a memorable one.* Remembering the lost love Warwick had confessed to him, Moor thought with friendliest regret—"Poor Adam, he finds it impossible to forget." Reading the truth in the keen delight the instant brought her, Sylvia cried out within herself, "Oh, Geoffrey, forgive me, for I love him!" and Warwick whispered to that impetuous heart of his, "Be still, we have ventured far enough."

Prue spoke first, very much disturbed by having her prejudices and opinions opposed, and very anxious to prove herself in the right.

"Mark and Geoffrey look as if they agreed with Mr. Warwick in his—excuse me if I say, dangerous ideas; but I fancy the personal application of them would change their minds. Now, Mark, just look at it; suppose some one of Jessie's lovers should discover an affinity for her, and she for him, what would you do?"

"Shoot him or myself, or all three, and make a neat little tragedy of it."

"There is no getting a serious answer from you, and I wonder I ever try. Geoffrey, I put the case to you; if Sylvia should find she adored Julian Haize, who fell sick when she was married, you know, and should inform you of that agreeable fact some fine day, should you think it quite reasonable and right to say, "Go, my dear, I'm very sorry, but it can't be helped."

The way in which Prue put the case made it impossible for her hearers not to laugh. But Sylvia held her breath while waiting for her

---

*The remainder of this paragraph is excised in *M2* (257).

husband's answer. He was standing behind her chair, and spoke with the smile still on his lips, too confident to harbor even a passing fancy.

"Perhaps I ought to be generous enough to do so, but not being a Jaques, with a convenient glacier to help me out of the predicament, I am afraid I should be hard to manage. I love but few, and those few are my world; so do not try me too hardly, Sylvia."

"I shall do my best, Geoffrey."

She dropped her shuttle as she spoke, and stooping to pick it up, down swept the long curls over either cheek; thus, when she fell to work again, nothing of her face was visible but a glimpse of forehead, black lashes and faintly smiling mouth. Moor led the conversation to other topics, and was soon deep in an art discussion with Mark and Miss Dane, while Prue and Jessie chatted away on that safe subject, dress. But Sylvia worked silently, and Warwick still leaned there watching the busy hand as if he saw something more than a pretty contrast between the white fingers and the scarlet silk.

When the other guests had left, and Faith and himself had gone to their rooms, Warwick, bent on not passing another sleepless night full of unprofitable longings, went down again to get a book. The library was still lighted, and standing there alone he saw Sylvia, wearing an expression that startled him. Both hands pushed back and held her hair away as if she scorned concealment from herself. Her eyes seemed fixed with a despairing glance on some invisible disturber of her peace. All the light and color that made her beautiful were gone, leaving her face worn and old, and the language of both countenance and attitude was that of one suddenly confronted with some hard fact, some heavy duty, that must be accepted and performed.

This revelation lasted but a moment, Moor's step came down the hall, the hair fell, the anguish passed, and nothing but a wan and weary face remained. But Warwick had seen it, and as he stole away unperceived he pressed his hands together, saying mournfully within himself, "I was mistaken. God help us all."

CHAPTER XVI

IN THE TWILIGHT

IF SYLVIA needed another trial to make that hard week harder, it soon
came to her in the knowledge that Warwick watched her. She well knew
why, and vainly endeavored to conceal from him that which she had suc-
ceeded in concealing entirely from others. But he possessed the key to her
variaable moods; he alone knew that now painful forethought, not caprice
dictated many of her seeming whims, and ruled her simplest action. To
others she appeared busy, gay, and full of interest in all about her; to him,
the industry was a preventive of forbidden thoughts; the gayety a daily
endeavor to forget; the interest, an anxiety concerning the looks and words
of her companions, because she must guard her own.

Sylvia felt something like terror in the presence of this penetrating
eye, this daring will, for the vigilance was unflagging and unobtrusive, and
with all her efforts she could not read his heart as she felt her own was
being read. Adam could act no part, but bent on learning the truth for the
sake of all, he surmounted the dangers of the situation by no artifice, no
rash indulgence, but by simply shunning solitary interviews with Sylvia as
carefully as the courtesy due his hostess would allow. In walks and drives,
and general conversation, he bore his part, surprising and delighting those
who knew him best by the genial change which seemed to have softened
his rugged nature. But the instant the family group fell apart and Moor's
devotion to his cousin left Sylvia alone, Warwick was away into the wood
or out upon the sea, lingering there till some meal, some appointed pleasure, or the evening lamp brought all together. Sylvia understood this, and
loved him for it even while she longed to have it otherwise. But Moor

reproached him for his desertion, doubly felt since the gentler acquirements made him dearer to his friend. Hating all disguises, Warwick found it hard to withhold the fact which was not his own to give, and sparing no blame to himself, answered Moor's playful complaint with a sad sincerity that freed him from all further pleadings.

"Geoffrey, I have a heavy heart which even you cannot heal. Leave it to time, and let me come and go as of old, enjoying the social hour when I may, flying to solitude when I must."

Much as Sylvia had longed to see these friends, she counted the hours of their stay, for the presence of one was a daily disquieting, because spirits would often flag, conversation fail, and an utter weariness creep over her when she could least account for or yield to it. More than once during that week she longed to lay her head on Faith's kind bosom and ask help. Deep as was her husband's love it did not possess the soothing power of a woman's sympathy, and though it cradled her as tenderly as if she had been a child, Faith's compassion would have been like motherly arms to fold and foster. But friendly as they soon became, frank as was Faith's regard for Sylvia, earnest as was Sylvia's affection for Faith, she never seemed to reach that deeper place where she desired to be. Always when she thought she had found the innermost that each of us seek for in our friend, she felt that Faith drew back, and a reserve as delicate as inflexible barred her approach with chilly gentleness. This seemed so foreign to Faith's nature that Sylvia pondered and grieved over it till the belief came to her that this woman, so truly excellent and loveworthy, did not desire to receive her confidence, and sometimes a bitter fear assailed her that Warwick was not the only reader of her secret trouble.

All things have an end, and the last day came none too soon for one dweller under that hospitable roof. Faith refused all entreaties to stay, and looked somewhat anxiously at Warwick as Moor turned from herself to him with the same urgency.

"Adam, you will stay? Promise me another week?"

"I never promise, Geoffrey."

Believing that, as no denial came, his request was granted, Moor gave his whole attention to Faith, who was to leave them in an hour.

"Sylvia, while I help our cousin to select and fasten up the books and prints she likes to take with her, will you run down into the garden and fill your prettiest basket with our finest grapes? You will like that better than fumbling with folds and string; and you know one's servants should not perform these pleasant services for one's best friends."

Glad to be away, Sylvia ran through the long grape walk to its sunniest nook, and standing outside the arch, began to lay the purple clusters in her basket. Only a moment was she there alone; Warwick's shadow, lengthened by the declining sun, soon fell black along the path. He did not see her, nor seem intent on following her; he walked slowly, hat in hand, so slowly that he was but midway down the leafy lane when Faith's voice arrested him. She was in haste, as her hurried step and almost breathless words betrayed; and losing not an instant, she cried before they met—

"Adam, you will come with me? I cannot leave you here."·

"Do you doubt me, Faith?"

"No; but loving women are so weak."

"So strong, you mean; men are weakest when they love."

"Adam, *will* you come?"

"I will follow you; I shall speak with Geoffrey first."

"Must you tell him so soon?"

"I must."

Faith's hand had been on Warwick's arm; as he spoke the last words she bent her head upon it for an instant, then without another word turned and hurried back as rapidly as she had come, while Warwick stood where she left him, motionless as if buried in some absorbing thought.

All had passed in a moment, a moment too short, too full of intense surprise to leave Sylvia time for recollection and betrayal of her presence. Half hidden and wholly unobserved she had seen the unwonted agitation of Faith's countenance and manner, had heard Warwick's softly spoken answers to those eager appeals, and with a great pang had discovered that some tender confidence existed between these two of which she had never dreamed. Sudden as the discovery was its acceptance and belief; for, knowing her own weakness, Sylvia found something like relief in the hope that a new happiness for Warwick had ended all temptation, and in time perhaps all pain for herself. Impulsive as ever she leaned upon the seeming truth, and making of the fancy a fact, passed into a perfect passion of self-abnegation, thinking, in the brief pause that followed Faith's departure—

"This is the change we see in him; this made him watch me, hoping I had forgotten, as I once said and believed. I should be glad, I will be glad, and let him see that even while I suffer I can rejoice in that which helps us both."

Full of her generous purpose, yet half doubtful how to execute it, Sylvia stepped from the recess where she had stood, and slowly passed toward Warwick, apparently intent on settling her fruity burden as she went. At the first sound of her light step on the gravel he turned, feeling at once that she must have heard, and eager to learn what significance that short dialogue possessed for her. Only a hasty glance did she give him as she came, but it showed him flushed cheeks, excited eyes, and lips a little tremulous as they said—

"These are for Faith; will you hold the basket while I cover it with leaves?"

He took it, and as the first green covering was deftly laid, he asked, below his breath—

"Sylvia, did you hear us?"

To his unutterable amazement she looked up clearly, and all her heart was in her voice, as she answered with a fervency he could not doubt—

"Yes; and I was glad to hear, to know that a nobler woman filled the place I cannot fill. Oh, believe it, Adam; and be sure that the knowledge of your great content will lighten the terrible regret which you have seen as nothing else ever could have done."

Down fell the basket at their feet, and taking her face between his hands, Warwick bent and searched with a glance that seemed to penetrate to her heart's core. For a moment she struggled to escape, but the grasp that held her was immovable. She tried to oppose a steadfast front and baffle that perilous inspection, but quick and deep rushed the traitorous color over cheek and forehead with its mute betrayal. She tried to turn her eyes away, but those other eyes, dark and dilated with intensity of purpose, fixed her own, and the confronting countenance wore an expression which made its familiar features look awfully large and grand to her panic-stricken sight. A sense of utter helplessness fell on her, courage deserted her, pride changed to fear, defiance to despair; as the flush faded, the fugitive glance was arrested and the upturned face became a pale blank, ready to receive the answer that strong scrutiny was slowly bringing to the light, as invisible characters start out upon a page when fire passes over them. Neither spoke, but soon through all opposing barriers the magnetism of an indomitable will drew forth the truth, set free the captive passion pent so long, and wrung from those reluctant lineaments a full confession of that power which heaven has gifted with eternal youth.

The instant this assurance was his own beyond a doubt, Warwick released her, snatched up his hat, and hurrying down the path vanished in the wood. Spent as with an hour's excitement, and bewildered by emotions which she could not longer master, Sylvia lingered in the grape walk till her husband called her. Then hastily refilling her basket, she shook her hair about her face and went to bid Faith good by. Moor was to accompany her to the city, and they left early, that Faith might pause for adieux to Mark and Prudence.

"Where is Adam? Has he gone before, or been inveigled into staying?"

Moor spoke to Sylvia, but busied in fastening the basket-lid, she seemed not to hear, and Faith replied for her.

"He will take a later boat, we need not wait for him."

When Faith embraced Sylvia, all the coldness had melted from her manner, and her voice was tender as a mother's as she whispered low in her ear—

"Dear child, if ever you need any help that Geoffrey cannot give, remember cousin Faith."

For two hours Sylvia sat alone, not idle, for in the first real solitude she had enjoyed for seven days she looked deeply into herself, and putting by all disguises owned the truth, and resolved to repair the past if possible, as Faith had counselled in the case which she had now made her own. Like so many of us, Sylvia often saw her errors too late to avoid committing them, and failing to do the right thing at the right moment, kept herself forever in arrears with that creditor who must inevitably be satisfied. She had been coming to this decision all that weary week, and these quiet hours left her both resolute and resigned.

As she sat there while the early twilight began to gather, her eye often turned to Warwick's travelling bag, which Faith, having espied it ready in his chamber, had brought down and laid in the library, as a reminder of her wish. As she looked at it, Sylvia's heart yearned toward it in the fond, foolish way which women have of endowing the possessions of those they love with the attractions of sentient things, and a portion of their owner's character or claim upon themselves. It was like Warwick, simple and strong, no key, and every mark of the long use which had tested its capabilities and proved them durable. A pair of gloves lay beside it on the chair, and though she longed to touch anything of his, she resisted the temptation till, pausing near them in one of her journeys to the window, she saw a rent in the glove that lay uppermost,—that appeal was irresistible,—"Poor Adam! there has been no one to care for him so long, and Faith does not yet know how; surely I may perform so small a service for him if he never knows how tenderly I do it?"

Standing ready to drop her work at a sound, Sylvia snatched a brief satisfaction which solaced her more than an hour of idle lamentation, and as she kissed the glove with a long, sad kiss, and put it down with eyes that dimly saw where it should be, perhaps there went as much real love and sorrow into that little act as ever glorified some greater deed. Then she went to lie in the "Refuge," as she had named an ancient chair, with her head on its embracing arm. Not weeping, but quietly watching the flicker of the fire, which filled the room with warm duskiness, making the twilight doubly pleasant, till a sudden blaze leaped up, showing her that her watch was over and Warwick come. She had not heard him enter, but there he was close before her, his face glowing with the frosty air, his eye clear and kind, and in his aspect that nameless charm which won for him the confidence of whosoever read his countenance. Scarce knowing why, Sylvia felt reassured that all was well, and looked up with more welcome in her heart than she dared betray in words.

"Come at last! where have you been so long, Adam?"

"Round the Island I suspect, for I lost my way, and had no guide but instinct to lead me home again. I like to say that word, for though it is not home it seems so to me now. May I sit here before I go, and warm myself at your fire, Sylvia?"

Sure of his answer he established himself on the stool at her feet, stretched his hands to the grateful blaze, and went on with some inward resolution lending its power and depth to his voice.

"I had a question to settle with myself and went to find my best counsellors in the wood. Often when I am harassed by some perplexity or doubt to which I can find no wise or welcome answer, I walk myself into a belief that it will come; then it appears. I stoop to break a handsome flower, to pick up a cone, or watch some little creature happier than I, and there lies my answer, like a good luck penny, ready to my hand."

"Faith has gone, but Geoffrey hopes to keep you for another," said Sylvia, ignoring the unsafe topic.

"Shall he have his wish?"

"Faith expects you to follow her."

"And you think I ought?"

"I think you will."

"When does the next boat leave?"

"An hour hence."

"I'll wait for it here. Did I wake you coming in?"

"I was not asleep; only lazy, warm, and quiet."

"And deadly tired;—dear soul, how can it be otherwise, leading the life you lead."

There was such compassion in his voice, such affection in his eye, such fostering kindliness in the touch of the hand he laid upon her own that Sylvia cried within herself,—"Oh, if Geoffrey would only come!" and hoping for that help to save her from herself, she hastily replied—

"You are mistaken, Adam,—my life is easier than I deserve,—my husband makes me very—"

"Miserable,—the truth to me, Sylvia."

Warwick rose as he spoke, closed the door and came back wearing an expression which caused her to start up with a gesture of entreaty—

"No, no, I will not hear you! Adam, you must not speak!"

He paused opposite her, leaving a little space between them, which he did not cross through all that followed, and with that look, inflexible yet pitiful, he answered steadily—

"I *must* speak and you *will* hear me. But understand me, Sylvia, I desire and design no French sentiment nor sin like that we heard of, and what I say now I would say if Geoffrey stood between us. I have settled this point after long thought and the heartiest prayers I ever prayed; and much as I have at stake, I speak more for your sake than my own. Therefore do not entreat nor delay, but listen and let me show you the wrong you are doing yourself, your husband, and your friend."

"Does Faith know all the past? does she desire you to do this that her happiness may be secure?" demanded Sylvia.

"Faith is no more to me, nor I to Faith, than the friendliest regard can make us. She suspected that I loved you long ago; she now believes that you love me; she pities her cousin tenderly, but will not meddle with the tangle we have made of our three lives. Forget that folly, and let me speak to you as I should. When we parted I thought that you loved Geoffrey; so did you. When I came here I was sure of it for a day; but on that second night I saw your face as you stood here alone, and then I knew what I have since assured myself of. God knows, I think my gain dearly purchased by his loss. I see your double trial; I know the tribulations in store for all of us; yet, as an honest man, I must speak out, because you ought not to delude yourself or Geoffrey another day."

"What right have you to come between us and decide my duty, Adam?" Sylvia spoke passionately, roused to resistance by his manner and the turmoil of emotions warring within her.

"The right of a sane man to save the woman he loves from destroying her own peace forever, and undermining the confidence of the friend dearest to them both. I know this is not the world's way in such matters; but I care not; because I believe on human creature has a right to speak to another in times like these as if they two stood alone. I will not command, I will appeal to you, and if you are the candid soul I think you, your own words shall prove the truth of what I say. Sylvia, do you love your husband?"

"Yes, Adam, dearly."

"More than you love me?"

"I wish I did! I wish I did!"

"Are you happy with him?"

"I was till you came; I shall be when you are gone."

"Never!* It is impossible to go back to the blind tranquillity you once enjoyed. Now a single duty lies before you; delay is weak, deceit is wicked; utter sincerity alone can help us. Tell Geoffrey all; then, whether you live your life alone, or one day come to me, there is no false dealing to repent of, and looking the hard fact in the face robs it of one half its terrors. Will you do this, Sylvia?"

"No, Adam. Remember what he said that night: 'I love but few, and those few are my world,'—I am chief in that world; shall I destroy it, for my selfish pleasure? He waited for me very long, is waiting still; can I for a second time disappoint the patient heart that would find it easier to give up life than the poor possession which I am. No, I ought not, dare not do it yet."

"If you dare not speak the truth to your friend, you do not deserve him, and the name is a lie. You ask me to remember what he said that night,—I ask you to recall the look with which he begged you not to try him too hardly. Put it to yourself,—which is the kinder justice, a full confession now, or a late one hereafter, when longer subterfuge has made it harder for you to offer, bitterer for him to receive? I tell you, Sylvia, it were more merciful to murder him outright than to slowly wear away his faith, his peace, and love by a vain endeavor to perform as a duty what should be your sweetest pleasure, and what will soon become a burden heavier than you can bear."

"You do not see as I see; you cannot understand what I am to him, nor can I tell you what he is to me. It is not as if I could dislike or despise

---

*Never! omitted in *M2*

him for any unworthiness of his own; nor as if he were a lover only. Then I could do much which now is worse than impossible, for I have married him, and it is too late."

"Oh, Sylvia! why could you not have waited?"

"Why? because I am what I am, too easily led by circumstances, too entirely possessed by whatever hope, belief, or fear rules me for the hour. Give me a steadfast nature like your own and I will be as strong. I know I am weak, but I am not wilfully wicked; and when I ask you to be silent, it is because I want to save him from the pain of doubt, and try to teach myself to love him as I should. I must have time, but I can bear much and endeavor more persistently than you believe. If I forgot you once, can I not again? and should I not? I am all in all to him, while you, so strong, so self-reliant, can do without my love as you have-done till now, and will soon outlive your sorrow for the loss of that which might have made us happy had I been more patient."

"Yes, I shall outlive it, else I should have little faith in myself. But I shall not forget; and if you would remain forever what you now are to me, you will so act that nothing may mar this memory, if it is to be no more. I doubt your power to forget an affection which has survived so many changes and withstood assaults such as Geoffrey must unconsciously have made upon it. But I have no right to condemn your beliefs, to order your actions, or force you to accept my code of morals if you are not ready for it. You must decide, but do not again deceive yourself, and through whatever comes hold fast to that which is better worth preserving than husband, happiness, or friend."

His words fell cold on Sylvia's ear, for with the inconsistency of a woman's heart she thought he gave her up too readily, yet honored him more truly for sacrificing both himself and her to the principle that ruled his life and made him what he was. His seeming resignation steadied her, for now he waited her decision, while before he was only bent on executing the purpose wherein he believed salvation lay. She girded up her strength, collected her thoughts, and tried to show him what she believed to be her duty.

"Let me tell you how it is with me, Adam, and be patient if I am not wise and brave like you, but far too young, too ignorant to bear such troubles well. I am not leaning on my own judgment now, but on Faith's, and though you do not love her as I hoped, you feel she is one to trust. She said the wife, in that fictitious case which was so real to us, the wife should leave no effort unmade, no self-denial unexacted, till she had fairly proved that she could not be what she had promised. Then, and then only, had she a right to undo the tie that had bound her. I must do this before I think of your love or my own, for on my marriage morning I made a vow within myself that Geoffrey's happiness should be the first duty of my life. I shall keep that vow as sacredly as I will those I made before the world, until I find that it is utterly beyond my power, then I will break all together."

"You have tried that once, and failed."

"No, I have never tried it as I shall now. At first, I did not know the truth, then I was afraid to believe, and struggled blindly to forget. Now I see clearly, I confess it, I resolve to conquer it, and I will not yield until I have done my best. You say you must respect me. Could you do so if I no longer respected myself? I should not, if I forgot all Geoffrey had borne and done for me, and could not bear and do this thing for him. I must make the effort, and make it silently; for he is very proud with all his gentleness, and would reject the seeming sacrifice though he would make one doubly hard for love of me. If I am to stay with him, it spares him the bitterest pain he could suffer; if I am to go, it gives him a few more months of happiness, and I may so prepare him that the parting will be less hard. How others would act I cannot tell, I only know that this seems right to me; and I must fight my fight alone, even if I die in doing it."

She was so earnest, yet so humble; so weak in all but the desire to do well; so young to be tormented with such fateful issues, and withal so steadfast in the grateful yet remorseful tenderness she bore her husband, that though sorely disappointed and not one whit convinced, Warwick could only submit to this woman-hearted child, and love her with re-doubled love, both for what she was and what she aspired to be.

"Sylvia, what would you have me do?"*

"You must go away, and for a long time, Adam; because when you are near me my will is swayed by yours, and what you desire I long to give you. Go quite away, and through Faith you may learn whether I succeed or fail. It is hard to say this, yet you know it is a truer hospitality in me to send you from my door than to detain and offer you temptation for your daily bread."

How strangely Ottila came back to him, and all the scenes he had passed through with her!—a perilous contrast just then. Yet, despite his

---

*M2 revises this line strategically: "Sylvia, what can I do to help you?" (276).

pride in the loving little creature who put him from her that she might be worthy of him, one irrepressible lament swelled his heart and passed his lips—*

"Ah, Sylvia! I thought that parting on the mountain was the hardest I could ever know, but this is harder; for now I have but to say come to me, and you would come."

But the bitter moment had its drop of honey, whose sweetness nourished him when all else failed. Sylvia answered with a perfect confidence in that integrity which even her own longing could not bribe—

"Yes, Adam, but you will not say it, because feeling as I feel, you know I must not come to you."

He did know it, and confessed his submission by folding fast the arms half opened for her, and standing dumb with the words trembling on his lips. It was the bravest action of a life full of real valor, for the sacrifice was not made with more than human fortitude. The man's heart clamored for its right, patience was weary, hope despaired, and all natural instincts mutinied against the command that bound them. But no grain of virtue ever falls wasted to the ground; it drops back upon its giver a regathered strength, and cannot fail of its reward in some kindred soul's approval, imitation, or delight. It was so then, as Sylvia went to him; for though she did not touch nor smile upon him, he felt her nearness; and the parting assured him that its power bound them closer than the happiest union. In her face there shone a look half fervent, half devout, and her voice had no falter in it now.

"You show me what I should be. All my life I have desired strength of heart and stability of soul; may I not hope to earn for myself a little of the integrity I love in you? If courage, self-denial, and self-help, make you what you are, can I have a more effectual guide? You say you shall outlive this passion; why should not I imitate your brave example, and find the consolations you shall find? Oh, Adam, let me try."

"You shall."

"Then go; go now, while I can say it as I should."

"The good Lord bless and help you, Sylvia."

---

*This paragraph is omitted in *M2* and Alcott substituted:

It was hard to submit; for though he asked nothing for himself, he longed intensely to share in some way the burden that he could not lighten. (276)

She gave him both her hands, but though he only pressed them silently, that pressure nearly destroyed the victory she had won, for the strong grasp snapped the slender guard-ring Moor had given her a week ago. She heard it drop with a golden tinkle on the hearth, saw the dark oval, with its doubly significant character, roll into the ashes, and felt Warwick's hold tighten as if he echoed the emphatic word uttered when the ineffectual gift was first bestowed. Superstition flowed in Sylvia's blood, and was as unconquerable as the imagination which supplied its food. This omen startled her. It seemed a forewarning that endeavor would be vain, that submission was wisdom, and that the husband's charm had lost its virtue when the stronger power claimed her. The desire to resist began to waver as the old passionate longing sprang up more eloquent than ever; she felt the rush of a coming impulse, knew that it would sweep her into Warwick's arms, there to forget her duty, to forfeit his respect. With the last effort of a sorely tried spirit she tore her hands away, fled up to the room which had never needed lock or key till now, and stifling the sound of those departing steps among the cushions of the little couch where she had wept away childish woes and dreamed girlish dreams, she struggled with the great sorrow of her too early womanhood, uttering with broken voice that petition oftenest quoted from the one prayer which expresses all our needs—

"Lead me not into temptation, but deliver me from evil."

CHAPTER XVII

ASLEEP AND AWAKE

MARCH WINDS were howling round the house, the clock was striking two, the library lamp still burned, and Moor sat writing with an anxious face. Occasionally, he paused to look backward through the leaves of the book in which he wrote; sometimes he sat with suspended pen, thinking deeply; and once or twice he laid it down, to press his hand over eyes more weary than the mind that compelled them to this late service.

Returning to his work after one of these pauses, he was a little startled to see Sylvia standing on the threshold of the door. Rising hastily to ask if she were ill, he stopped half way across the room, for, with a thrill of apprehension and surprise, he saw that she was asleep. Her eyes were open, fixed and vacant, her face reposeful, her breathing regular, and every sense apparently wrapt in the profoundest unconsciousness. Fearful of awakening her too suddenly, Moor stood motionless, yet full of interest, for this was his first experience of somnambulism, and it was a strange, almost an awful sight, to witness the blind obedience of the body to the soul that ruled it.

For several minutes she remained where she first appeared. Then, as if the dream demanded action, she stooped, and seemed to take some object from a chair beside the door, held it an instant, kissed it softly and laid it down. Slowly and steadily she went across the room, avoiding all obstacles with the unerring instinct that often leads the sleepwalker through dangers that appall his waking eyes, and sat down in the great chair he had left, leaned her cheek upon its arm, and rested tranquilly for several minutes. Soon the dream disturbed her, and lifting her head, she bent forward, as if addressing or caressing some one seated at her feet. Involuntarily her husband smiled; for often when they were alone he sat there reading or talking to her, while she played with his hair, likening its brown abundance to young Milton's curling locks in the picture overhead. The smile had hardly risen when it was scared away, for Sylvia suddenly sprung up with both hands out, crying in a voice that rent the silence with its imploring energy—

"No, no, you must not speak! I will not hear you!"

Her own cry woke her. Consciousness and memory returned together, and her face whitened with a look of terror, as her bewildered eyes showed her not Warwick, but her husband. This look, so full of fear, yet so intelligent, startled Moor more than the apparition or the cry had done, for a conviction flashed into his mind that some unsuspected trouble had been burdening Sylvia, and was now finding vent against her will. Anxious to possess himself of the truth, and bent on doing so, he veiled his purpose for a time, letting his unchanged manner reassure and compose her.

"Dear child, don't look so lost and wild. You are quite safe, and have only been wandering in your sleep. Why, Mrs. Macbeth, have you murdered some one, that you go crying out in this uncanny way, frightening me as much as I seem to have frightened you?"

"I have murdered sleep.[1] What did I do? what did I say?" she asked, trembling and shrinking as she dropped into her chair.

Hoping to quiet her, he took his place on the footstool, and told her what had passed. At first, she listened with a divided mind, for so strongly was she still impressed with the vividness of the dream, she half expected Warwick to rise like Banquo, and claim the seat that a single occupancy seemed to have made his own.[2] An expression of intense relief replaced that of fear, when she had heard all, and she composed herself with the knowledge that her secret was still hers. For, dreary bosom-guest as it was, she had not yet resolved to end her trial.

"What set you walking, Sylvia?"

"I recollect hearing the clock strike one, and thinking I would come down to see what you were doing so late, but must have dropped off and carried out my design asleep. You see I put on wrapper and slippers as I always do, when I take nocturnal rambles awake. How pleasant the fire feels, and how cosy you look here; no wonder you like to stay and enjoy it."

She leaned forward warming her hands in unconscious imitation of Adam, on the night which she had been recalling before she slept. Moor watched her with increasing disquiet; for never had he seen her in a mood like this. She evaded his question, she averted her eyes, she half hid her face, and with a gesture that of late had grown habitual, seemed to try to hide her heart. Often had she baffled him, sometimes grieved him, but never before showed that she feared him. This wounded both his love and pride, and this fixed his resolution, to wring from her an explanation of the changes which had passed over her within those winter months, for they had been many and mysterious. As if she feared silence, Sylvia soon spoke again.

"Why are you up so late? This is not the first time I have seen your lamp burning when I woke. What are you studying so deeply?"

"My wife."

Leaning on the arm of her chair he looked up wistfully, tenderly, as if inviting confidence, sueing for affection. The words, the look, smote Sylvia to the heart, and but for the thought, "I have not tried long enough," she would have uttered the confession that leaped to her lips. Once spoken, it would be too late for secret effort or success, and this man's happiest hopes would vanish in a breath. Knowing that his nature was almost as sensitively fastidious as a woman's, she also knew that the discovery of her love for Adam, innocent as it had been, self-denying as it tried to be, would forever mar the beauty of his wedded life for Moor. No hour of it would seem sacred, no act, look, or word of hers entirely his own, nor any of the dear delights of home remain undarkened by the shadow of his friend. She could not speak yet, and turning her eyes to the fire, she asked—

"Why study me? Have you no better book?"

"None that I love to read so well or have such need to understand; because, though nearest and dearest as you are to me, I seem to know you less than any friend I have. I do not wish to wound you, dear, nor be exacting; but since we were married you have grown more shy than ever, and the act which should have drawn us tenderly together seems to have estranged us. You never talk now of yourself, or ask me to explain the working of that busy mind of yours; and lately you have sometimes shunned me, as if solitude were pleasanter than my society. Is it, Sylvia?"

"Sometimes; I always liked to be alone, you know."

She answered as truly as she could, feeling that his love demanded every confidence but the one cruel one which would destroy its peace past help.

"I knew I had a most tenacious heart, but I hoped it was not a selfish one," he sorrowfully said. "Now I see that it is, and deeply regret that my hopeful spirit, my impatient love, has brought disappointment to us both. I should have waited longer, should have been less confident of my own power to win you, and never let you waste your life in vain endeavors to be happy when I was not all to you that you expected. I should not have consented to your wish to spend the winter here so much alone with me. I should have known that such a quiet home and studious companion could not have many charms for a young girl like you. Forgive me, I will do better, and this one-sided life of ours shall be changed; for while I have been supremely content you have been miserable."

It was impossible to deny it, and with a tearless sob she laid her arm about his neck; her head on his shoulder, and mutely confessed the truth of what he said. The trouble deepened in his face, but he spoke out more cheerfully, believing that he had found the secret sorrow.

"Thank heaven, nothing is past mending, and we will yet be happy. An entire change shall be made; you shall no longer devote yourself to me, but I to you. Will you go abroad, and forget this dismal home until its rest grows inviting, Sylvia?"

"No, Geoffrey, not yet. I will learn to make the home pleasant, I will work harder, and leave no time for ennui and discontent. I promised to make your happiness, and I can do it better here than anywhere. Let me try again."

"No, Sylvia, you work too hard already; you do everything with such vehemence you wear out your body before your will is weary, and that brings melancholy. I am very credulous, but when I see that acts belie words I cease to believe. These months assure me that you are not happy; have I found the secret thorn that frets you?"

She did not answer, for truth she could not, and falsehood she would not, give him. He rose, went walking to and fro, searching memory, heart, and conscience for any other cause, but found none, and saw only one way out of his bewilderment. He drew a chair before her, sat down, and looking at her with the masterful expression dominant in his face, asked briefly—

"Sylvia, have I been tyrannical, unjust, unkind, since you came to me?"

"Oh, Geoffrey, too generous, too just, too tender!"

"Have I claimed any rights but those you gave me, entreated or demanded any sacrifices knowingly and wilfully?"

"Never."

"Now I do claim the right to know your heart; I do entreat and demand one thing, your confidence."

Then she felt that the hour had come, and tried to prepare to meet it as she should by remembering that she had endeavored prayerfully, desperately, despairingly, to do her duty, and had failed. Warwick was right, she could not forget him. There was such vitality in the man and in the sentiment he inspired, that it endowed his memory with a power more potent than the visible presence of her husband. The knowledge of his love now undid the work that ignorance had helped patience and pride to achieve before. The more she struggled to forget, the deeper, dearer, grew the yearning that must be denied, till months of fruitless effort convinced her that it was impossible to outlive a passion more indomitable than will, or penitence, or perserverance.* Now she saw the wisdom of Adam's warning, and felt that he knew both his friend's heart and her own better than herself. Now she bitterly regretted that she had not spoken out when he was there to help her, and before the least deceit had taken the dignity from sorrow. Nevertheless, though she trembled she resolved; and while Moor spoke on, she made ready to atone for past silence by a perfect loyalty to truth.

"My wife, concealment is not generosity, for the heaviest trouble shared together could not so take the sweetness from my life, the charm from home, or make me more miserable than this want of confidence. It is a double wrong, because you not only mar my peace but destroy your own by wasting health and happiness in vain endeavors to bear some grief alone. Your eye seldom meets mine now, your words are measured, your actions cautious, your innocent gayety all gone. You hide your heart from me, you hide your face; I seem to have lost the frank girl whom I loved, and found a melancholy woman, who suffers silently till her honest nature rebels, and brings her to confession in her sleep. There is no page of my life which I have not freely shown you; do I do not deserve an equal candor? Shall I not receive it?"

"Yes."

"Sylvia, what stands between us?"

"Adam Warwick."

Earnest as a prayer, brief as a command had been the question, in-

---

*This sentence is omitted in *M2* and the text is revised to read:

Once she had held the secret, now it held her; the hidden wound was poisoning her life, and tempting her to escape by thoughts of death. (285–86)

stantaneous was the reply, as Sylvia knelt down before him, put back the veil that should never hide her from him any more, looked up into her husband's face without one shadow in her own, and steadily told all.

The revelation was too utterly unexpected, too difficult of belief to be at once accepted or understood. Moor started at the name, then leaned forward, breathless and intent, as if to seize the words before they left her lips; words that recalled incidents and acts dark and unmeaning till the spark of intelligence fired a long train of memories and enlightened him with terrible rapidity. Blinded by his own devotion, the knowledge of Adam's love and loss seemed gages of his fidelity; the thought that he loved Sylvia never had occurred to him, and seemed incredible even when her own lips told it. She had been right in fearing the effect this knowledge would have upon him. It stung his pride, wounded his heart, and forever marred his faith in love and friendship. As the truth broke over him, cold and bitter as a billow of the sea, she saw gathering in his face the still white grief and indignation of an outraged spirit, suffering with all a woman's pain, with all a man's intensity of passion. His eye grew fiery and stern, the veins rose dark upon his forehead, the lines about the mouth showed hard and grim, the whole face altered terribly. As she looked, Sylvia thanked heaven that Warwick was not there to feel the sudden atonement for an innocent offence which his friend might have exacted before this natural but unworthy temptation had passed by.

"Now I have given all my confidence though I may have broken both our hearts in doing it. I do not hope for pardon yet, but I am sure of pity, and I leave my fate in your hands. Geoffrey, what shall I do?"

"Wait for me," and putting her away, Moor left the room.

Suffering too much in mind to remember that she had a body, Sylvia remained where she was, and leaning her head upon her hands tried to recall what had passed, to nerve herself for what was to come. Her first sensation was one of unutterable relief. The long struggle was over; the haunting care was gone; there was nothing now to conceal; she might be herself again, and her spirit rose with something of its old elasticity as the heavy burden was removed. A moment she enjoyed this hard-won freedom, then the memory that the burden was not lost but laid on other shoulders, filled her with an anguish too sharp to find vent in tears, too deep to leave any hope of cure except in action. But how act? She had performed the duty so long, so vainly delayed, and when the first glow of satisfaction passed, found redoubled anxiety, regreat, and pain before her. Clear and hard the truth stood there, and no power of hers could recall the words that showed it to her husband, could give them back the early blindness, or the later vicissitudes of hope and fear. In the long silence that filled the room she had time to calm her perturbation and comfort her remorse by the vague but helpful belief which seldom deserts sanguine spirits, that something, as yet unseen and unsuspected, would appear to heal the breach, to show what was to be done, and to make all happy in the end.

Where Moor went or how long he stayed Sylvia never knew, but when at length he came, her first glance showed her that pride is as much to be dreaded as passion. No gold is without alloy, and now she saw the shadow of a nature which had seemed all sunshine. She knew he was very proud, but never thought to be the cause of its saddest manifestation; one which showed her that its presence could make the silent sorrow of a just and gentle man a harder trial to sustain than the hottest anger, the bitterest reproach. Scarcely paler than when he went, there was no sign of violent emotion in his countenance. His eye shone keen and dark, an anxious fold crossed his forehead, and a melancholy gravity replaced the cheerful serenity his face once wore. Wherein the alteration lay Sylvia could not tell, but over the whole man some subtle change had passed. The sudden frost which had blighted the tenderest affection of his life seemed to have left its chill behind, robbing his manner of its cordial charm, his voice of its heartsome ring, and giving him the look of one who sternly said—"I must suffer, but it shall be alone."

Cold and quiet, he stood regarding her with a strange expression, as if endeavoring to realize the truth, and see in her not his wife but Warwick's lover. Oppressed by the old fear, now augmented by a measureless regret, she could only look up at him feeling that her husband had become her judge. Yet as she looked she was conscious of a momentary wonder at the seeming transposition of character in the two so near and dear to her. Strong-hearted Warwick wept like any child, but accepted his disappointment without complaint and bore it manfully. Moor, from whom she would sooner have expected such demonstration, grew stormy first, then stern, as she once believed his friend would have done. She forgot that Moor's pain was the sharper, his wound the deeper, for the patient hope cherished so long; the knowledge that he never had been, never could be loved as he loved; the sense of wrong that could not but burn even in the meekest heart at such a later discovery such an entire loss.

Sylvia spoke first, not audibly, but with a little gesture of supplica-

tion, a glance of sorrowful submission. He answered both, not by lamentation or reproach, but by just enough of his accustomed tenderness in touch
and tone to make her tears break forth, as he placed her in the ancient chair
so often occupied together, took the one opposite, and sweeping a clear
space on the table between them, looked across it with the air of a man
bent on seeing his way and following it any cost.

"Now Sylvia, I can listen as I should."

"Oh, Geoffrey, what can I say?"

"Repeat all you have already told me. I only gathered one fact then,
now I want the circumstances, for I find this confession difficult of belief."

Perhaps no sterner expiation could have been required of her than to
sit there, face to face, eye to eye, and tell again that little history of
thwarted love and fruitless endeavor. Excitement had given her courage
for the first confession, now it was torture to carefully repeat what had
poured freely from her lips before. But she did it, glad to prove her penitence by any test he might apply. Tears often blinded her, uncontrollable
emotion often arrested her; and more than once she turned on him a
beseeching look, which asked as plainly as words, "Must I go on?"

Intent on learning all, Moor was unconscious of the trial he imposed,
unaware that the change in himself was the keenest reproach he could have
made, and still with a persistency as gentle as inflexible, he pursued his
purpose to the end. When great drops rolled down her cheeks he dried
them silently; when she paused, he waited till she calmed herself; and
when she spoke he listened with few interruptions but a question now and
then. Occasionally a sudden flush of passionate pain swept across his face,
as some phrase, implying rather than expressing Warwick's love or Sylvia's
longing, escaped the narrator's lips, and when she described their parting
on that very spot, his eye went from her to the hearth her words seemed to
make desolate, with a glance she never could forget. But when the last
question was answered, the last appeal for pardon brokenly uttered, nothing but the pale pride remained; and his voice was cold and quiet as
his mien.

"Yes, it is this which has baffled and kept me groping in the dark so
long, for I wholly trusted what I wholly loved."

"Alas, it was that very confidence that made my task seem so necessary and so hard. How often I longed to go to you with my great trouble as
I used to do with lesser ones. But here you would suffer more than I; and
having done the wrong, it was for me to pay the penalty. So like many

another weak yet willing soul, I tried to keep you happy at all costs."

"One frank word before I married you would have spared us this. Could you not foresee the end and dare to speak it, Sylvia?"

"I see it now, I did not then, else I would have spoken as freely as I speak to-night. I thought I had outlived my love for Adam; it seemed kind to spare you a knowledge that would disturb your friendship, so though I told the truth, I did not tell it all. I thought temptations came from without; I could withstand such, and I did, even when it wore Adam's shape. This temptation came so suddenly, seemed so harmless, generous and just, that I yielded to it unconscious that it was one. Surely I deceived myself as cruelly as I did you, and God knows I have tried to atone for it when time taught me my fatal error."

"Poor child, it was too soon for you to play the perilous game of hearts. I should have known it, and left you to the safe and simple joys of girlhood. Forgive me that I have kept you a prisoner so long; take off the fetter I put on, and go, Sylvia."

"No, do not put me from you yet; do not think that I can hurt you so, and then be glad to leave you suffering alone. Look like your kind self if you can; talk to me as you used to; let me show you my heart and you will see how large a place you fill in it. Let me begin again, for now the secret is told there is no fear to keep out love; and I can give my whole strength to learning the lesson you have tried so patiently to teach."

"You cannot, Sylvia. We are as much divorced as if judge and jury had decided the righteous but hard separation for us. You can never be a wife to me with an unconquerable affection in your heart; I can never be your husband while the shadow of a fear remains. I will have all or nothing."

"Adam foretold this. He knew you best, and I should have followed the brave counsel he gave me long ago. Oh, if he were only here to help us now!"

The desire broke from Sylvia's lips involuntarily as she turned for strength to the strong soul that loved her. But it was like wind to smouldering fire; a pang of jealousy wrung Moor's heart, and he spoke out with a flash of the eye that startled Sylvia more than the rapid change of voice and manner.

"Hush! Say anything of yourself or me, and I can bear it, but spare me the sound of Adam's name to-night. A man's nature is not forgiving like a woman's, and the best of us harbor impulses you know nothing of. If I am to lose wife, friend, and home, for God's sake leave me my self-respect."

All the coldness and pride passed from Moor's face as the climax of his sorrow came; with an impetuous gesture he threw his arms across the table, and laid down his head in a paroxysm of tearless suffering such as men only know.

How Sylvia longed to speak! But what consolation could the tenderest words supply? She searched for some alleviating suggestion, some happier hope; none came. Her eye turned imploringly to the pictured Fates above her as if imploring them to aid her. But they looked back at her inexorably dumb, and instinctively her thought passed beyond them to the Ruler of all fates, asking the help which never is refused. No words embodied her appeal, no sound expressed it, only a voiceless cry from the depths of a contrite spirit, owning its weakness, making known its want. She prayed for submission, but her deeper need was seen, and when she asked for patience to endure, Heaven sent her power to act, and out of this sharp trial brought her a better strength and clearer knowledge of herself than years of smoother experience could have bestowed. A sense of security, of stability, came to her as that entire reliance assured her by its all-sustaining power that she had found what she most needed to make life clear to her and duty sweet. With her face in her hands, she sat, forgetful that she was not alone, as in that brief but precious moment she felt the exceeding comfort of a childlike faith in the one Friend who, when we are deserted by all, even by ourselves, puts forth His hand and gathers us tenderly to Himself.

Her husband's voice recalled her, and looking up she showed him such an earnest, patient countenance, it touched him like an unconscious rebuke. The first tears she had seen rose to his eyes, and all the old tenderness came back into his voice, softening the dismissal which had been more coldly begun.

"Dear, silence and rest are best for both of us to-night. We cannot treat this trouble as we should till we are calmer; then we will take counsel how soonest to end what never should have been begun. Forgive me, pray for me, and in sleep forget me for a little while."

He held the door for her, but as she passed Sylvia lifted her face for the good night caress without which she had never left him since she became his wife. She did not speak, but her eye humbly besought this token of forgiveness; nor was it denied. Moor laid his hand upon her lips, saying, "these are Adam's now," and kissed her on the forehead.

Such a little thing: But it overcame Sylvia with the sorrowful certainty of the loss which had befallen both, and she crept away, feeling herself an exile from the heart and home whose happy mistress she could never be again.

Moor watched the little figure going upward, and weeping softly as it went, as if he echoed the sad "never any more," which those tears expressed, and when it vanished with a backward look, shut himself in alone with his great sorrow.

CHAPTER XVIII

WHAT NEXT?

SYLVIA laid her head down on her pillow, believing that this night would be the longest, saddest she had ever known. But before she had time to sigh for sleep it wrapt her in its comfortable arms, and held her till day broke. Sunshine streamed across the room, and early birds piped on the budding boughs that swayed before the window. But no morning smile saluted her, no morning flower awaited her, and nothing but a little note lay on the unpressed pillow at her side.

"Sylvia, I have gone away to Faith, because this proud, resentful spirit of mine must be subdued before I meet you. I leave that behind me which will speak to you more kindly, calmly than I can now, and show you that my effort has been equal to my failure. There is nothing for me to do but submit; manfully if I must, meekly if I can; and this short exile will prepare me for the longer one to come. Take counsel with those nearer and dearer to you than myself, and secure the happiness which I have so ignorantly delayed, but cannot wilfully destroy. God be with you and through all that is and is to come, remember that you remain beloved forever in the heart of Geoffrey Moor."

Sylvia had known many sad uprisings, but never a sadder one than this, and the hours that followed aged her more than any year had done. All day she wandered aimlessly to and fro, for the inward conflict would not let her rest. The house seemed home no longer when its presiding genius was gone, and everywhere some token of his former presence touched her with its mute reproach.

She asked no counsel of her family, for well she knew the outburst of condemnation, incredulity, and grief that would assail her there. They could not help her yet; they would only augment perplexities, weaken convictions, and distract her mind. When she was sure of herself she would tell them, endure their indignation and regret, and steadily execute the new purpose, whatever it should be.

To many it might seem an easy task to break the bond that burdened and assume the tie that blessed. But Sylvia had grown wise in self-knowledge, timorous through self-delusion; therefore the greater the freedom given her the more she hesitated to avail herself of it. The nobler each friend grew as she turned from one to the other, the more impossible seemed the decision, for generous spirit and loving heart contended for the mastery, yet neither won. She knew that Moor had put her from him never to be recalled till some miracle was wrought that should make her truly his. This renunciation showed her how much he had become to her, how entirely she had learned to lean upon him, and how great a boon such perfect love was in itself. Even the prospect of a life with Warwick brought forebodings with its hope. Reason made her listen to many doubts which hitherto passion had suppressed. Would she never tire of his unrest? Could she fill so large a heart and give it power as well as warmth? Might not the two wills clash, the ardent natures inflame one another, the stronger intellect exhaust the weaker, the disappointment come again? And as she asked these questions, conscience, the monitor whom no bribe can tempt, no threat silence, invariably answered "Yes."

But chief among the cares that beset her was one that grew more burdensome with thought. By her own will she had put her liberty into another's keeping; law confirmed the act, gospel sanctioned the vow, and it could only be redeemed by paying the costly price demanded of those who own that they have drawn a blank in the lottery of marriage. Public opinion is a grim ghost that daunts the bravest, and Sylvia knew that trials lay before her from which she would shrink and suffer, as only a woman sensitive and proud as she could shrink and suffer. Once apply this remedy and any tongue would have the power to wound, any eye to insult with pity or contempt, any stranger to criticise or condemn, and she would have no means of redress, no place of refuge, even in that stronghold, Adam's heart.

All that dreary day she wrestled with these stubborn facts, but could neither mould nor modify them as she would, and evening found her spent, but not decided. Too excited for sleep, yet too weary for exertion, she turned bedward, hoping that the darkness and the silence of night would bring good counsel, if not rest.

Till now she had shunned the library as one shuns the spot where one has suffered most. But as she passed the open door the gloom that reigned within seemed typical of that which had fallen on its absent master, and following the impulse of the moment Sylvia went in to light it with the little glimmer of her lamp. Nothing had been touched, for no hand but her own preserved the order of this room, and all household duties had been neglected on that day. The old chair stood where she had left it, and over its arm was thrown the velvet coat, half dressing-gown, half blouse, that Moor liked to wear at this household trysting-place. Sylvia bent to fold it smoothly as it hung, and feeling that she must solace herself with some touch of tenderness, laid her cheek against the soft garment, whispering "Good night." Something glittered on the cushion of the chair, and looking nearer she found a steel-clasped book, upon the cover of which lay a dead heliotrope, a little key.

It was Moor's Diary, and now she understood that passage of the note which had been obscure before. "I leave that behind me which will speak to you more kindly, calmly, than I can now, and show you that my effort has been equal to my failure." She had often begged to read it, threatened to pick the lock, and felt the strongest curiosity to learn what was contained in the long entries that he daily made. Her requests had always been answered with the promise of entire possession of the book when the year was out. Now he gave it, though the year was not gone, and many leaves were yet unfilled. He thought she would come to this room first, would see her morning flower laid ready for her, and, sitting in what they called their Refuge, would draw some comfort for herself, some palliation for his innocent offence, from the record so abruptly ended.

She took it, went away to her own room, unlocked the short romance of his wedded life, and found her husband's heart laid bare before her.

It was a strange and solemn thing to look so deeply into the private experience of a fellow-being; to trace the birth and progress of purposes and passions, the motives of action, the secret aspirations, the besetting sins that made up the inner life he had been leading beside her. Moor wrote with an eloquent sincerity because he had put himself into his book, as if feeling the need of some *confidante* he had chosen the only one that pardons egotism. Here, too, Sylvia saw her chameleon self, etched with loving care, endowed with all gifts and graces, studied with unflagging zeal, and made the idol of a life.

Often a tuneful spirit seemed to assert itself, and passing from smooth prose to smoother poetry, sonnet, song, or psalm, flowed down the page in cadences stately, sweet, or solemn, filling the reader with delight at the discovery of a gift so genuine, yet so shyly folded up within itself, unconscious that its modesty was the surest token of its worth. More than once Sylvia laid her face into the book, and added her involuntary comment on some poem or passage made pathetic by the present; and more than once paused to wonder, with exceeding wonder, why she could not give such genius and affection its reward. Had she needed any confirmation of the fact so hard to teach herself, this opening of his innermost would have given it. For while she bitterly grieved over the death-blow she had dealt his happy hope, it no longer seemed a possibility to change her stubborn heart, or lessen by a fraction the debt which she sadly felt could only be repaid in friendship's silver, not love's gold.

All night she lay there like some Magdalene, purer but as penitent as Correggio's Mary, with the book, the lamp, the melancholy eyes, the golden hair that painters love. All night she read, gathering courage, not consolation, from those pages, for seeing what she was not showed her what she might become; and when she turned the little key upon that story without an end, Sylvia the girl was dead, but Sylvia the woman had begun to live.

Lying in the rosy hush of dawn, there came to her a sudden memory—

"If ever you need help that Geoffrey cannot give, remember cousin Faith."

This was the hour Faith foresaw; Moor had gone to her with his trouble, why not follow, and let this woman, wise, discreet, and gentle, show her what should come next?

The newly risen sun saw Sylvia away upon her journey to Faith's home among the hills. She lived alone, a cheerful, busy, solitary soul, demanding little of others, yet giving freely to whomsoever asked an alms of her.

Sylvia found the gray cottage nestled in a hollow of the mountain side; a pleasant hermitage, secure and still. Mistress and maid composed the household, but none of the gloom of isolation darkened the sunshine that pervaded it; peace seemed to sit upon its threshold, content to brood beneath its eaves, and the atmosphere of home to make it beautiful.

When some momentous purpose or event absorbs us we break

through fears and formalities, act out ourselves forgetful of reserve, and use the plainest phrases to express emotions which need no ornament and little aid from language. Sylvia illustrated this fact, then; for, without hesitation or embarrassment, she entered Miss Dane's door, called no servant to announce her, but went, as if by instinct, straight to the room where Faith sat alone, and with the simplest greeting asked—

"Is Geoffrey here?"

"He was an hour ago, and will be an hour hence. I sent him out to rest, for he cannot sleep. I am glad you came to him; he has not learned to do without you yet."

With no bustle of surprise or sympathy Faith put away her work, took off the hat and cloak, drew her guest beside her on the couch before the one deep window looking down the valley, and gently chafing the chilly hands in warm ones, said nothing more till Sylvia spoke.

"He has told you all the wrong I have done him?"

"Yes, and found a little comfort here. Do you need consolation also?"

"Can you ask? But I need something more, and no one can give it to me so well as you. I want to be set right, to hear things called by their true names, to be taken out of myself and made to see why I am always doing wrong while trying to do well."

"Your father, sister, or brother are fitter for that task than I. Have you tried them?"

"No, and I will not. They love me, but they could not help me; for they would beg me to conceal if I cannot forget, to endure if I cannot conquer, and abide by my mistake at all costs. That is not the help I want. I desire to know the one just thing to be done, and to be made brave enough to do it, though friends lament, gossips clamor, and the heavens fall. I am in earnest now. Rate me sharply, drag out my weaknesses, shame my follies, show no mercy to my selfish hopes; and when I can no longer hide from myself put me in the way I should go, and I will follow it though my feet bleed at every step."

She was in earnest now, terribly so, but still Faith drew back, though her compassionate face belied her hesitating words.

"Go to Adam; who wiser or more just than he?"

"I cannot. He, as well as Geoffrey, loves me too well to decide for me. You stand between them, wise as the one, gentle as the other, and you do not care for me enough to let affection hoodwink reason. Faith, you bade me come; do not cast me off, for if you shut your heart against me I know not where to go."

Despairing she spoke, disconsolate she looked, and Faith's reluctance vanished. The maternal aspect returned, her voice resumed its warmth, her eye its benignity, and Sylvia was reassured before a word was spoken.

"I do not cast you off, nor shut my heart against you. I only hesitated to assume such responsibility, and shrunk from the task because of compassion, not coldness. Sit here, and tell me all your trouble, Sylvia?"

"That is so kind! It seems quite natural to turn to you as if I had a claim upon you. Let me have, and if you can, love me a little, because I have no mother, and need one very much."

"My child, you shall not need one any more."

*"I feel that, and am comforted already. Faith, if you were me, and stood where I stand, beloved by two men, either of whom any woman might be proud to call husband, putting self away, to which should you cleave?"

"To neither."

Sylvia paled and trembled, as if the oracle she had invoked was an unanswerable voice pronouncing the inevitable. She watched Faith's countenance a moment, groping for her meaning, failed to find it, and whispered below her breath—

"Can I know why?"

"Because your husband *is,* your lover *should be* your friend and nothing more. You have been hardly taught the lesson many have to learn, that friendship cannot fill love's place, yet should be kept inviolate, and served as an austerer mistress who can make life very beautiful to such as feel her worth and deserve her delight. Adam taught me this, for though Geoffrey took you from him, he still held fast his friend, letting no disappointment sour, no envy alienate, no resentment destroy the perfect friendship years of mutual fidelity have built up between them."

"Yes!" cried Sylvia, "how I have honored Adam for that steadfastness, and how I have despised myself, because I could not be as wise and faithful in the earlier, safer sentiment I felt for Geoffrey."

"Be wise and faithful now; cease to be the wife, but remain the friend; freely give all you can with honesty, not one jot more."

"Never did man possess a truer friend than I will be to him—if he

---

*Alcott's considerable revisions of this chapter begin with this speech; see the appendix (304–05).

will let me. But, Faith, if I may be that to Geoffrey, may I not be something nearer and dearer to Adam? Would not you dare to hope it, were you me?"

"No, Sylvia, never."

"Why not?"

"If you were blind, a cripple, or cursed with some incurable infirmity of body, would not you hesitate to bind yourself and your affliction to another?"

"You know I should not only hesitate, but utterly refuse."

"I do know it, therefore I venture to show you why, according to my belief, you should not marry Adam. I cannot tell you as I ought, but only try to show you where to seek the explanation of my seeming harsh advice. There are diseases more subtle and dangerous than any that vex our flesh; diseases that should be as carefully cured if curable, as inexorably prevented from spreading as any malady we dread. A paralyzed will, a morbid mind, a mad temper, a tainted heart, a blind soul, are afflictions to be as much regarded as bodily infirmities. Nay, more, inasmuch as souls are of greater value than perishable flesh. * Where this is religiously taught, believed, and practised, marriage becomes in truth a sacrament blessed of God; children thank parents for the gift of life; parents see in children living satisfactions and rewards, not reproaches or retributions doubly heavy to be borne, for the knowledge that where two sinned, many must inevitably suffer."

"You try to tell me gently, Faith, but I see that you consider me one of the innocent unfortunates, who have no right to marry till they be healed, perhaps never. I have dimly felt this during the past year, now I know it, and thank God that I have no child to reproach me hereafter, for bequeathing it the mental ills I have not yet outlived."

"Dear Sylvia, you are an exceptional case in all respects, because an extreme one. The ancient theology of two contending spirits in one body, is strangely exemplified in you, for each rules by turns, and each helps or hinders as moods and circumstances lead. Even in the great event of a woman's life, you were thwarted by conflicting powers; impulse and ignorance, passion and pride, hope and despair. Now you stand at the parting of the ways, looking wistfully along the pleasant one where Adam seems to

---

*Here the two versions become almost identical again for several paragraphs.

beckon, while I point down the rugged one where I have walked,* and though my heart aches as I do it, counsel you as I would a daughter of my own."

"I thank you, I fill follow you, but my life looks very barren if I must relinquish my desire."†

"Not as barren as if you possessed your desire, and found in it another misery and mistake. Could you have loved Geoffrey, it might have been safe and well with you; loving Adam, it is neither.‡ Let me show you why. He is an exception like yourself; perhaps that explains your attraction for each other. In him the head rules, in Geoffrey the heart. The one criticises, the other loves mankind. Geoffrey is proud and private in all that lies nearest him, clings to persons, and is faithful as a woman. Adam has only the pride of an intellect which tests all things, and abides by its own insight. He clings to principles; persons are but animated facts or ideas; he seizes, searches, uses them, and when they have no more for him, drops them like the husk, whose kernel he has secured; passing on to find and study other samples without regret, but with unabated zeal. For life to him is perpetual progress, and he obeys the law of his nature as steadily as sun or sea. Is not this so?"

"All true; what more, Faith?"

"Few women, if wise, would dare to marry this man, noble and loveworthy as he is,§ till time has tamed and experience developed him. Even then the risk is great, for he demands and unconsciously absorbs into himself the personality of others, making large returns, but of a kind which only those as strong, sagacious, and steadfast as himself can receive and adapt to their individual uses, without being overcome and possessed. That none of us should be, except by the Spirit stronger than man, purer than woman. You feel, though you do not understand this power. You know that his presence excites, yet wearies you; that, while you love him, you fear him, and even when you long to be all in all to him, you doubt your ability to make his happiness. Am I not right?"

---

*The words "where Adam . . . walked," are replaced in *M2* by "where love seems to beckon, while I point down the rugged one that leads to duty," (306).

†*M2:* ". . . but life looks very barren." (306)

‡This sentence is replaced in *M2* with: "Could you love Geoffrey, it would be safe and well with you; loving Adam, it would be neither." (306)

§*M2:* noble as he is, (307)

"I must say, yes."

*"Then, it is scarcely necessary for me to tell you that I think this unequal marriage would be but a brief one for you; bright at its beginning, dark at its end. With him you would exhaust yourself in passionate endeavors to follow where he led. He would not know this, you would not confess it, but too late you might both learn that you were too young, too ardent, too frail in all but the might of love, to be his wife. It is like a woodbird mating with an eagle, straining its little wings to scale the sky with him, blinding itself with gazing at the sun, striving to fill and warm the wild eyrie which becomes its home, and perishing in the stern solitude the other loves. Yet, too fond and faithful to regret the safer nest among the grass, the gentler mate it might have had, the summer life and winter flitting to the south for which it was designed."

"Faith, you frighten me; you seem to see and show me all the dim forebodings I have hidden away within myself, because I could not understand or dared not face them. How have you learned so much? How can you read me so well? and who told you these things of us all?"

"I had an unhappy girlhood in a discordant home; early cares and losses made me old in youth, and taught me to observe how others bore their burdens. Since then solitude has led me to study and reflect upon the question toward which my thoughts inevitably turned. Concerning yourself and your past Geoffrey told me much but Adam more."

"Have you seen him? Has he been here? When, Faith, when?"

Light and color flashed back into Sylvia's face, and the glad eagerness of her voice was a pleasant sound to hear after the despairing accents gone before. Faith sighed, but answered fully, carefully, while the compassion of her look deepened as she spoke.

†"I saw him but a week ago, vehement and vigorous as ever. He has come hither often during the winter, has watched you unseen, and brought me news of you which made Geoffrey's disclosure scarcely a surprise. He said you bade him hear of you through me, that he preferred to come, not write, for letters were often false interpreters, but face to face one gets the real thought of one's friend by look, as well as word, and the result is satisfactory."

"That is Adam! But what more did he say? How did you advise him? I know he asked counsel of you, as we all have done."

---

*Here Alcott makes several changes in *M2*. See the appendix (307–09).
†At this point Alcott made only minor revisions for several pages.

"He did, and I gave it as frankly as to you and Geoffrey. He made me understand you, judge you leniently, see in you the virtues you have cherished despite drawbacks such as few have to struggle with. Your father made Adam his confessor during the happy month when you first knew him. I need not tell you how he received and preserved such a trust. He betrayed no confidence, but in speaking of you I saw that his knowledge of the father taught him to understand the daughter. It was well and beautifully done, and did we need anything to endear him to us this trait of character would do it, for it is a rare endowment, the power of overcoming all obstacles of pride, age, and the sad reserve self-condemnation brings us, and making confession a grateful healing."

"I know it; we tell our sorrows to such as Geoffrey, our sins to such as Adam. But, Faith, when you spoke of me, did you say to him what you have been saying to me about my unfitness to be his wife because of inequality, and my unhappy inheritance?"

"Could I do otherwise when he fixed that commanding eye of his upon me asking, 'Is my love as wise as it is warm?' He is one of those who force the hardest truths from us by the simple fact that they can bear it, and would do the same for us. He needed it then, for though instinct was right,—hence his anxious question,—his heart, never so entirely roused as now, made it difficult for him to judge of your relations to one another, and there my woman's insight helped him."

"What did he do when you told him? I see that you will yet hesitate to tell me. I think you have been preparing me to hear it. Speak out. Though my cheeks whiten and my hands tremble I can bear it, for you shall be the law by which I will abide."

"You shall be a law to yourself, my brave Sylvia. Put your hands in mine and hold fast to the friend who loves and honors you for this. I will tell you what Adam did and said. He sat in deep thought many minutes; but with him to see is to do, and soon he turned to me with the courageous expression which in him signifies that the fight is fought, the victory won. 'It is necessary to be just, it is not necessary to be happy. I shall never marry Sylvia, even if I may,'*—and with that paraphrase of words, whose mean-

---

* Adam's reply as quoted by Faith was changed somewhat in *M2:*

'It is necessary to be true, it is not necessary to be happy. I would never marry Sylvia, even if I might,' (311).

ing seemed to fit his need, he went away. I think he will not come again either to me—or you."

How still the room grew as Faith's reluctant lips uttered the last words! Sylvia sat motionless looking out into the sunny valley, with eyes that saw nothing but the image of that beloved friend leaving her perhaps forever. Well she knew that with this man to see *was* to do, and with a woful sense of desolation falling cold upon her heart, she felt that there was nothing more to hope for but a brave submission like his own. Yet in that pause there came a feeling of relief after the first despair. The power of choice was no longer left her, and the help she needed was bestowed by one who could decide against himself, inspired by a sentiment which curbed a strong man's love of power,* and made it subject to a just man's love of right. Great examples never lose their virtue; what Pompey was to Warwick that Warwick became to Sylvia, and in the moment of supremest sorrow she felt the fire of a noble emulation kindling within her from the spark he left behind.†

"Faith, what comes next?"

"This," and she was gathered close while Faith confessed how hard her task had been by letting tears fall fast upon the head which seemed to have found its proper resting-place, as if despite her courage and her wisdom the woman's heart was half broken with its pity. Better than any words was the motherly embrace, the silent shower, the blessed balm of sympathy which soothed the wounds it could not heal. Leaning against each other the two hearts talked together in the silence, feeling the beauty of the tie kind Nature weaves between the hearts that should be knit. Faith often turned her lips to Sylvia's forehead, brushed back her hair with a lingering touch, and drew her nearer as if it was very pleasant to see and feel the little creature in her arms. Sylvia lay there, tearless and tranquil; thinking thoughts for which she had no words, and trying to prepare herself for the life to come, a life that now looked very desolate. Her eye still rested on the valley where the river flowed, the elms waved their budding boughs in the bland air, and the meadows wore their earliest tinge

---

*love of self, *M2* (312)

† . . . emulation kindled in her from the spark he left behind. *M2* (312).

Here Alcott adds a page in *M2* and resumes with "Faith, what comes next?" The following paragraph, however, contains many small changes. See the appendix for this entire passage (312–14).

of green. But she was not conscious of these things till the sight of a solitary figure coming slowly up the hill recalled her to the present and the duties it still held for her.

"Here is Geoffrey! How wearily he walks,—how changed and old he looks,—oh, why was I born to be a curse to all who love me!"

"Hush, Sylvia, say anything but that, because it casts reproach upon your father. Your life is but just begun; make it a blessing, not a curse, as all of us have power to do; and remember that for every affliction there are two helpers, who can heal or end the heaviest we know—Time and Death. The first we may invoke and wait for; the last God alone can send when it is better not to live."

"I will try to be patient. Will you meet and tell Geoffrey what has passed? I have no strength left but for passive endurance."

Faith went; Sylvia heard the murmur of earnest conversation; then steps came rapidly along the hall, and Moor was in the room. She rose involuntarily, but for a moment neither spoke, for never had they met as now. Each regarded the other as if a year had rolled between them since they parted, and each saw in the other the changes that one day had wrought. Neither the fire of resentment nor the frost of pride now rendered Moor's face stormy or stern. Anxious and worn it was, with newly graven lines upon the forehead and melancholy curves about the mouth, but the peace of a conquered spirit touched it with a pale serenity, and some perennial hope shone in the glance he bent upon his wife. For the first time in her life Sylvia was truly beautiful,—not physically, for never had she looked more weak and wan, but spiritually, as the inward change made itself manifest in an indescribable expression of meekness and of strength. With suffering came submission, with repentance came regeneration, and the power of the woman yet to be, touched with beauty the pathos of the woman now passing through the fire.

*"Faith has told you what has passed between us, and you know that my loss is a double one," she said. "Let me add that I deserve it, that I clearly see my mistakes, will amend such as I can, bear the consequences of such as are past help, try to profit by all, and make no new ones. I cannot be your wife, I ought not to be Adam's; but I may be myself, may live my life

---

*"Faith has told you" up to "I shall still hope and wait": this passage was reworked by Alcott in *M2;* see the appendix (315).

alone, and being friends with both wrong neither. This is my decision; in it I believe, by it I will abide, and if it be a just one God will not let me fail."

"I submit, Sylvia; I can still hope and wait."

So humbly he said it, so heartily he meant it, she felt that his love was as indomitable as Warwick's will, and the wish that it were right and possible to accept and reward it woke with all its old intensity. It was not possible; and though her heart grew heavier within her, Sylvia answered steadily—

"No, Geoffrey, do not hope, do not wait; forgive me and forget me. Go abroad as you proposed; travel far and stay long away. Change your life, and learn to see in me only the friend I once was and still desire to be."

"I will go, will stay till you recall me, but while you live your life alone I shall still hope and wait."

This invincible fidelity, so patient, so persistent, impressed the listener like a prophecy, disturbed her conviction, arrested the words upon her lips and softened them.

"It is not for one so unstable as myself to say, 'I shall never change.' I do not say it, though I heartily believe it, but will leave all to time. Surely I may do this; may let separation gently, gradually convince you or alter me; and as the one return which I can make for all you have given me, let this tie between us remain unbroken for a little longer. Take this poor consolation with you; it is the best that I can offer now. Mine is the knowledge that however I may thwart your life in this world, there is a beautiful eternity in which you will forget me and be happy."

She gave him comfort, but he robbed her of her own as he drew her to him, answering with a glance brighter than any smile—

"Love is immortal, dear, and even in the 'beautiful eternity' I shall still hope and wait."

*HOW SOON it was all over! the return to separate homes, the disclosures, and the storms; the preparations for the solitary voyage,[†] the last charges and farewells.

Mark would not, and Prue could not, go to see the traveller off; the

---

    *The ending of the chapter remains basically the same in both versions of *Moods*.

    [†] In *M2* Alcott inserts here: "for Moor decided to go abroad," (316).

former being too angry to lend his countenance to what he termed a barbarous banishment, the latter, being half blind with crying, stayed to nurse Jessie, whose soft heart was nearly broken at what seemed to her the most direful affliction under heaven.

But Sylvia and her father followed Moor till his foot left the soil, and still lingered on the wharf to watch the steamer out of port. An uncongenial place in which to part; carriages rolled up and down, a clamor of voices filled the air, the little steamtug snorted with impatience, and the waves flowed seaward with the ebbing of the tide. But father and daughter saw only one object, heard only one sound, Moor's face as it looked down upon them from the deck, Moor's voice as he sent cheery messages to those left behind. Mr. Yule was endeavoring to reply as cheerily, and Sylvia was gazing with eyes that saw very dimly through their tears, when both were aware of an instantaneous change in the countenance they watched. Something beyond themselves seemed to arrest Moor's eye; a moment he stood intent and motionless, then flushed to the forehead with the dark glow Sylvia remembered well, waved his hand to them and vanished down the cabin stairs.

"Papa, what did he see?"

There was no need of any answer; Adam Warwick came striding through the crowd, saw them, paused with both hands out, and a questioning glance as if uncertain of his greeting. With one impulse the hands were taken; Sylvia could not speak, her father could, and did approvingly—

"Welcome, Warwick; you are come to say good by to Geoffrey?"

"Rather to you, sir; he needs none, I go with him."

"With him!" echoed both hearers.

"Ay, that I will. Did you think I would let him go away alone feeling bereaved of wife and home, and friend?"

"We should have known you better. But, Warwick, he will shun you; he hid himself just now as you approached; he has tried to forgive, but he cannot so soon forget."

"All the more need of my helping him to do both. He cannot shun me long with no hiding-place to fly to but the sea, and I will so gently constrain him by the old-time love we bore each other, that he must relent and take me back into his heart again."

"Oh, Adam! go with him, stay with him, and bring him safely back to me when time has helped us all."

"I shall do it, God willing."

What Next?

Unmindful of all else Warwick bent and took her to him as he gave the promise, seemed to put his whole heart into a single kiss and left her trembling with the stress of his farewell. She saw him cleave his way through the throng, leap the space left by the gangway just withdrawn, and vanish in search of that lost friend. Then she turned her face to her father's shoulder, conscious of nothing but the fact that Warwick had come and gone.

A cannon boomed, the crowd cheered, the last cable was flung off, and the steamer glided from her moorings with the surge of water and the waft of wind like some seamonster eager to be out upon the ocean free again.

"Look up, Sylvia; she will soon pass from sight."

"Are they there?"

"No."

"Then I do not care to see. Look for me, father, and tell me when they come."

"They will not come, dear; both have said good by, and we have seen the last of them for many a long day."

"They will come! Adam will bring Geoffrey to show me they are friends again. I know it; you shall see it. Lift me to that block and watch the deck with me that we may see them the instant they appear."

Up she sprung, eyes clear now, nerves steady, faith strong. Leaning forward so utterly forgetful of herself, she would have fallen into the green water tumbling there below, had not her father held her fast. How slowly the minutes seemed to pass, how rapidly the steamer seemed to glide away, how heavily the sense of loss weighed on her heart as wave after wave rolled between her and her heart's desire.

"Come down, Sylvia, it is giving yourself useless pain to watch and wait. Come home, my child, and let us comfort one another."

She did not hear him, for as he spoke the steamer swung slowly round to launch itself into the open bay, and with a cry that drew many eyes upon the young figure with its face of pale exceptancy, Sylvia saw her hope fulfilled.

"I knew they would come! See, father, see! Geoffrey is smiling as he waves his handkerchief, and Adam's hand is on his shoulder. Answer them! oh, answer them! I can only look."

The old man did answer them enthusiastically, and Sylvia stretched her arms across the widening space as if to bring them back again. Side by side the friends stood now; Moor's eye upon his wife, while from his hand the little flag of peace streamed in the wind. But Warwick's glance was turned upon his friend, and Warwick's hand already seemed to claim the charge he had accepted.

Standing thus they passed from sight, never to come sailing home together as the woman on the shore was praying God to let her see them come.

CHAPTER XIX

SIX MONTHS*

THE ENSUING half† year seemed fuller of duties and events than any Sylvia had ever known. At first she found it very hard to live her life alone; for inward solitude‡ oppressed her, and external trials were not wanting. Only to the few who had a right to know, had the whole trouble been confided. They were discreet from family pride, if from no tenderer feeling; but the curious world outside of that small circle was full of shrewd surmises, of keen eyes for discovering domestic breaches, and shrill tongues for proclaiming them. Warwick escaped suspicion, being so little known, so seldom seen; but for the usual nine days matrons and venerable maids wagged their caps, lifted their hands, and sighed as they sipped their dish of scandal and of tea—

"Poor young man! I always said how it would be, she was so peculiar. My dear creature, haven't you heard that Mrs. Moor isn't happy with her husband, and that he has gone abroad quite broken-hearted?"

Sylvia felt this deeply, but received it as her just punishment, and bore herself so meekly that public opinion soon turned a somersault, and the murmur changed to—

"Poor young thing! what could she expect? My dear, I have it from

---

*This chapter becomes "A Year" in *M2*. Alcott adds a new beginning page, reprinted in the appendix (320).

†The ensuing year *M2* (321).

‡ cares *M2* (321).

the best authority, that Mr. Moor has made her miserable for a year, and now left her broken-hearted." After that, the gossips took up some newer tragedy, and left Mrs. Moor to mend her heart as best she could, a favor very gratefully received.

As Hester Prynne seemed to see some trace of her own sin in every bosom, by the glare of the Scarlet Letter burning on her own; so Sylvia, living in the shadow of a household grief, found herself detecting various phases of her own experience in others. She had joined that sad sisterhood called disappointed women; a larger class than many deem it to be, though there are few of us who have not seen members of it. Unhappy wives; mistaken or forsaken lovers; meek souls, who make life a long penance for the sins of others; gifted creatures kindled into fitful brilliancy by some inward fire that consumes but cannot warm. These are the women who fly to convents, write bitter books, sing songs full of heartbreak, act splendidly the passion they have lost or never won. Who smile, and try to lead brave uncomplaining lives, but whose tragic eyes betray them, whose voices, however sweet or gay, contain an undertone of hopelessness, whose faces sometimes startle one with an expression which haunts the observer long after it is gone.

Undoubtedly Sylvia would have joined the melancholy chorus, and fallen to lamenting that ever she was born, had she not possessed a purpose that took her out of herself and proved her salvation. Faith's words took root and blossomed. Intent on making her life a blessing, not a reproach to her father, she lived for him entirely. He had taken her back to him, as if the burden of her unhappy past should be upon his shoulders, the expiation of her faults come from him alone. Sylvia understood this now, and nestled to him so gladly, so confidingly, he seemed to have found again the daughter he had lost and be almost content to have her all his own.

How many roofs cover families or friends who live years together, yet never truly know each other; who love, and long and try to meet, yet fail to do so till some unexpected emotion or event performs the work. In the weeks that followed the departure of the friends, Sylvia discovered this and learned to know her father. No one was so much to her as he; no one so fully entered into her thoughts and feelings; for sympathy drew them tenderly together, and sorrow made them equals. As man and woman they talked, as father and daughter they loved; and the beautiful relation became their truest solace and support.

Miss Yule both rejoiced at and rebelled against this; was generous, yet mortally jealous; made no complaint, but grieved in private, and one fine day amazed her sister by announcing, that, being of no farther use at home, she had decided to be married. Both Mr. Yule and Sylvia had desired this event, but hardly dared to expect it in spite of sundry propitious signs and circumstances.

A certain worthy widower had haunted the house of late, evidently on matrimonial thoughts intent. A solid gentleman, both physically and financially speaking; possessed of an ill-kept house, bad servants, and nine neglected children. This prospect, however alarming to others, had great charms for Prue; nor was the Reverend Gamaliel Bliss repugnant to her, being a rubicund, bland personage, much given to fine linen, long dinners, and short sermons. His third spouse had been suddenly translated, and though the years of mourning had not yet expired, things went so hardly with Gamaliel, that he could no longer delay casting his pastoral eyes over the flock which had already given three lambs to his fold, in search of a fourth. None appeared whose meek graces were sufficiently attractive, or whose dowries were sufficiently large. Meantime the nine olive-branches grew wild, the servants revelled, the ministerial digestion suffered, the sacred shirts went buttonless, and their wearer was wellnigh distraught. At this crisis he saw Prudence, and fell into a way of seating himself before the well-endowed spinster, with a large cambric pocket-handkerchief upon his knee, a frequent tear meandering down his florid countenance, and volcanic sighs agitating his capacious waistcoat as he poured his woes into her ear. Prue had been deeply touched by these moist appeals, and was not much surprised when the reverend gentleman went ponderously down upon his knee before her in the good old-fashioned style which frequent use had endeared to him, murmuring with an appropriate quotation and a subterranean sob—

"Miss Yule, 'a good wife is a crown to her husband;' be such an one to me, unworthy as I am, and a mother to my bereaved babes, who suffer for a tender woman's care."

She merely upset her sewing-table with an appropriate start, but speedily recovered, and with a maidenly blush murmured in return—

"Dear me, how very unexpected! pray speak to papa,—oh, rise, I beg."

"Call me Gamaliel, and I obey!" gasped the stout lover, divided between rapture and doubts of his ability to perform the feat alone.

"Gam-aliel," sighed Prue, surrendering her hand.

"My Prudence, blessed among woman!" responded the blissful Bliss. And having saluted the fair member, allowed it to help him rise; when, after a few decorous endearments, he departed to papa, and the bride elect rushed up to Sylvia with the incoherent announcement—

"My dearest child, I have accepted him! It was such a surprise, though so touchingly done. I was positively mortified; Maria had swept the room so ill, his knees were white with lint, and I'm a very happy woman, bless you, love!"

"Sit down, and tell me all about it," cried her sister. "Don't try to sew, but cry if you like, and let me pet you, for indeèd I am rejoiced."

But Prue preferred to rock violently, and boggle down a seam as the best quietus for her fluttered nerves, while she told her romance, received congratulations, and settled a few objections made by Sylvia, who tried to play the prudent matron.

"I am afraid he is too old for you, my dear."

"Just the age; a man should always be ten years older than his wife. A woman of thirty-five is in the prime of life, and if she hasn't arrived at years of discretion then, she never will. Shall I wear pearl-colored silk and a white bonnet, or just a very handsome travelling dress?"

"Whichever you like. But, Prue, is n't he rather stout, I won't say corpulent?"

"Sylvia, how can you! Because papa is a shadow, you call a fine, manly person like Gam—Mr. Bliss, corpulent. I always said I would *not* marry an invalid, (Macgregor died of apoplexy last week, I heard, at a small dinner party; fell forward with his head upon the cheese, and expired without a groan,) and where can you find a more robust and healthy man than Mr. Bliss? Not a gray hair, and gout his only complaint. So aristocratic. You know I've loads of fine old flannel, just the thing for him."

Sylvia commanded her countenance with difficulty, and went on with her maternal inquiries.

"He is a personable man, and an excellent one, I believe, yet I should rather dread the responsibility of nine small children, if I were you."

"They are my chief inducement to the match. Just think of the state those dears must be in, with only a young governess, and half a dozen giddy maids to see to them. I long to be among them, and named an early day, because measles and scarlatina are coming round again, and only Fanny, and the twins, Gus and Gam, have had either. I know all their names and ages, dispositions, and characters and love them like a mother already. He perfectly adores them, and that is very charming in a learned man like Mr. Bliss."

"If that is your feeling it will all go well I have no doubt. But, Prue—I don't wish to be unkind, dear,—do you quite like the idea of being the fourth Mrs. Bliss?"

"Bless me, I never thought of that! Poor man, it only shows how much he must need consolation, and proves how good a husband he must have been. No, Sylvia, I don't care a particle. I never knew those estimable ladies, and the memory of them shall not keep me from making Gamaliel happy if I can. What he goes through now is almost beyond belief. My child, just think!—the coachman drinks; the cook has tea-parties whenever she likes, and supports her brother's family out of her perquisites, as she calls her bare-faced thefts; the house maids romp with the indoor man, and have endless followers; three old maids set their caps at him, and that hussy, (I must use a strong expression,) that hussy of a governess makes love to him before the children. It is my duty to marry him; I shall do it, and put an end to this fearful state of things."

Sylvia asked but one more question—

"Now, seriously, do you love him very much? Will he make you as happy as my dear old girl should be?"

"Prue dropped her work, and hiding her face on Sylvia's shoulder, answered with a plaintive sniff or two, and much real feeling—

"Yes, my dear, I do. I tried to love him, and I did not fail. I shall be happy, for I shall be busy. I am not needed here any more, and so I am glad to go away into a home of my own, feeling sure that you can fill my place; and Maria knows my ways too well to let things go amiss. Now, kiss me, and smooth my collar, for papa may call me down."

The sisters embraced and cried a little, as women usually find it necessary to do at such interesting times; then fell to planning the wedding outfit, and deciding between the "light silk and white bonnet," or the "handsome travelling suit."

Miss Yule made a great sacrifice to the proprieties by relinquishing her desire for a stately wedding, and much to Sylvia's surprise and relief, insisted that, as the family was then situated, it was best to have no stir or parade, but to be married quietly at church and slip unostentatiously out of the old life into the new. Her will was law, and as the elderly bridegroom felt that there was no time to spare, and the measles continued to go about seeking whom they might devour, Prue did not keep him waiting long. "Three weeks is very little time, and nothing will be properly done, for one must have everything new when one is married of course, and mantua-makers are but mortal women (exorbitant in their charges this season, I assure you), so be patient, Gamaliel, and spend the time in teaching my little ones to love me before I come."

"My dearest creature, I will." And well did the enamored gentleman perform his promise.

Prue kept hers so punctually that she was married with the bastings in her wedding gown and two dozen pocket-handkerchiefs still unhemmed; facts which disturbed her even during the ceremony. A quiet time throughout; and after a sober feast, a tearful farewell, Mrs. Gamaliel Bliss departed, leaving a great void behind and carrying joy to the heart of her spouse, comfort to the souls of the excited nine, destruction to the "High Life Below Stairs," and order, peace, and plenty to the realm over which she was to know a long and prosperous reign.

Hardly had the excitement of this event subsided when another occurred to keep Sylvia from melancholy and bring an added satisfaction to her lonely days. Across the sea there came to her a little book, bearing her name upon its title-page. Quaintly printed, and bound in some foreign style, plain and unassuming without, but very rich within, for there she found Warwick's Essays, and between each of these one of the poems from Moor's Diary. Far away there in Switzerland they had devised this pleasure for her, and done honor to the woman whom they both loved, by dedicating to her the first fruits of their lives. "Alpen Rosen" was its title, and none could have better suited it in Sylvia's eyes, for to her Warwick was the Alps and Moor the roses. Each had helped the other; Warwick's rugged prose gathered grace from Moor's poetry, and Moor's smoothly flowing lines acquired power from Warwick's prose. Each had given her his best, and very proud was Sylvia of the little book, over which she pored day after day, living on and in it, eagerly collecting all praises, resenting all censures, and thinking it the one perfect volume in the world.

Others felt and acknowledged its worth as well, for though fashionable libraries were not besieged by inquiries for it, and no short-lived enthusiasm welcomed it, a place was found for it on many study tables, where real work was done. Innocent girls sang the songs and loved the poet, while thoughtful women, looking deeper, honored the man. Young men received the Essays as brave protests against the evils of the times, and old men felt their faith in honor and honesty revive. The wise saw great promise in it, and the most critical could not deny its beauty and its power.

Early in autumn arrived a fresh delight; and Jessie's little daughter became peacemaker as well as idol. Mark forgave his enemies, and swore eternal friendship with all mankind the first day of his baby's life; and when his sister brought it to him he took both in his arms, making atonement for many hasty words and hard thoughts by the broken whisper—

"I have two little Sylvias now."

This wonderful being absorbed both households, from grandpapa to the deposed sovereign Tilly, whom Sylvia called her own, and kept much with her; while Prue threatened to cause a rise in the price of stationery by the daily and copious letters full of warning and advice which she sent, feeling herself a mother in Israel among her tribe of nine, now safely carried through the Red Sea of scarlatina. Happy faces made perpetual sunshine round the little Sylvia, but to none was she so dear a boon as to her young god-mother. Jessie became a trifle jealous of "old Sylvia," as she now called herself, for she almost lived in baby's nursery; hurrying over in time to assist at its morning ablutions, hovering about its crib when it slept, daily discovering beauties invisible even to its mother's eyes, and working early and late on dainty garments, rich in the embroidery which she now thanked Prue for teaching her against her will. The touch of the baby hands seemed to heal her sore heart; the sound of the baby voice, even when most unmusical, had a soothing effect upon her nerves; the tender cares its helplessness demanded absorbed her thoughts, and kept her happy in a new world whose delights she had never known till now.

From this time a restful expression replaced the patient hopelessness her face had worn before, and in the lullabys she sang the listeners caught echoes of the cheerful voice they had never thought to hear again. Gay she was not, but serene. Quiet was all she asked; and shunning society seemed happiest to sit at home with baby and its gentle mother, with Mark, now painting as if inspired, or with her father, who relinquished business and devoted himself to her. A pleasant pause seemed to have come after troublous days; a tranquil hush in which she sat waiting for what time should bring her. But as she waited the woman seemed to bloom more beautifully than the girl had done. Light and color revisited her countenance clearer and deeper than of old; fine lines ennobled features faulty in themselves; and the indescribable refinement of a deep inward life made itself manifest in look, speech, and gesture, giving promise of a gracious womanhood.*

Mr. Yule augured well from this repose, and believed the dawning

---

*Alcott rewrites the ending of "A Year" following this paragraph. The passage is reprinted in the appendix (332–34).

loveliness to be a herald of returning love. He was thinking hopeful thoughts one day as he sat writing to Moor, whose faithful correspondent he had become, when Sylvia came in with one of the few notes she sent her husband while away.

"Just in time. God bless me, child! what is it?"

Well might he exclaim, for in his daughter's face he saw an expression which caused his hope to suddenly become a glad belief. Her lips smiled, though in her eyes there lay a shadow which could not comprehend, and her answer did not enlighten him as she put her arm about his neck and laid her slip of paper in his hand.

"Enclose my note, and send the letter; then, father, we will talk."

CHAPTER XX

COME*

※※※※※※

IN A SMALL Italian town not far from Rome, a traveller stood listening to an account of a battle lately fought near by, in which the town had suffered much, yet been forever honored in the eyes of its inhabitants, by having been the headquarters of the Hero of Italy.[1] An inquiry of the traveller's concerning a countryman of whom he was in search, created a sensation at the little inn, and elicited the story of the battle, one incident of which was still the all-absorbing topic with the excited villagers. This was the incident which one of the group related with the dramatic effects of a language composed almost as much of gesture as of words, and an audience as picturesque as could well be conceived.

While the fight was raging on the distant plain, a troop of marauding Croats dashed into the town, whose defenders, although outnumbered, contested every inch of ground, while slowly driven back toward the convent, the despoiling of which was the object of the attack. This convent was both hospital and refuge, for there were gathered women and children, the sick, the wounded, and the old. To secure the safety of these rather than of the sacred relics, the Italians were bent on holding the town till the reinforcement for which they had sent could come up. It was a question of time, and every moment brought nearer the destruction of the helpless garrison, trembling behind the convent walls. A brutal massacre was in store for them if no help came; and remembering this the

---

*Chapter XX, "Come," is changed to Chapter XXI, "Adam Keeps His Promise," in *M2*.

red-shirted Garibaldians fought as if they well deserved their sobriquet of "Scarlet Demons."

Help did come, not from below, but from above. Suddenly a cannon thundered royally, and down the narrow street rushed a deathful defiance, carrying disorder and dismay to the assailants, joy and wonder to the nearly exhausted defenders. Wonder, for well they knew the gun had stood silent and unmanned since the retreat of the enemy two days before, and this unexpected answer to their prayers seemed Heaven-sent. Those below looked up as they fought, those above looked down as they feared, and midway between all saw that a single man held the gun. A stalwart figure, bareheaded, stern faced, sinewy armed, fitfully seen through clouds of smoke and flashes of fire, working with a silent energy that seemed almost superhuman to the eyes of the superstitious souls, who believed they saw and heard the convent's patron saint proclaiming their salvation with a mighty voice.

This belief inspired the Italians, caused a panic among the Croats, and saved the town. A few rounds turned the scale, the pursued became the pursuers, and when the reinforcement arrived there was little for it to do but join in the rejoicing and salute the brave cannoneer, who proved to be no saint, but a stranger come to watch the battle, and thus opportunely lend his aid.

Enthusiastic were the demonstrations; vivas, blessings, tears, hand-kissing, and invocation of all the saints in the calendar, till it was discovered that the unknown gentleman had a bullet in his breast and was in need of instant help. Whereupon the women, clustering about him like bees, bore him away to the wounded ward, where the inmates rose up in their beds to welcome him, and the clamorous crowd were with difficulty persuaded to relinquish him to the priest, the surgeon, and the rest he needed. Nor was this all; the crowning glory of the event to the villagers was the coming of the Chief at nightfall, and the scene about the stranger's bed. Here the narrator glowed with pride, the women in the group began to sob, and the men took off their caps, with black eyes glittering through their tears.

"Excellenza, he who had fought for us like a tempest, an angel of doom, lay there beside my cousin Beppo, who was past help and is now in holy Paradise—Speranza was washing the smoke and powder from him, the wound was easy—death of my soul! may he who gave it die unconfessed! See you, I am there, I watch him, the friend of Excellenza, the great still man who smiled but said no word to us. Then comes the Chief,—

silenzio, till I finish!—he comes, they have told him, he stays at the bed, he looks down, the fine eye shines, he takes the hand, he says low—'I thank you,'—he lays his cloak,—the gray cloak we know and love so well— over the wounded breast, and so goes on. We cry out, but what does the friend? Behold! he lifts himself, he lays the cloak upon my Beppo, he says in that so broken way of his—'Comrade, the honor is for you who gave your life for him, I give but a single hour.' Beppo saw, heard, comprehended; thanked him with a glance, and rose up to die crying, 'Viva Italia! Viva Garibaldi!'

The cry was caught up by all the listeners in a whirlwind of enthusiastic loyalty, and the stranger joined in it, thrilled with an equal love and honor for the Patriot Soldier, whose name upon Italian lips means liberty.

"Where is he now, this friend of mine, so nearly lost, so happily found?"

A dozen hands pointed to the convent, a dozen brown faces lighted up, and a dozen eager voices poured out directions, messages, and benedictions in a breath. Ordering his carriage to follow presently, the traveller rapidly climbed the steep road, guided by signs he could not well mistake. The convent gate stood open, and he paused for no permission to enter, for looking through it, down the green vista of an orchard path, he saw his friend and sprang to meet him.

"Adam!"

"Geoffrey!"

"Truant that you are, to desert me for ten days, and only let me find you when you have no need of me."

"I always need you, but am not always needed. I went away because the old restlessness came upon me in that dead city Rome. You were happy there, but I scented war, followed and found it by instinct, and have had enough of it. Look at my hands."

He laughed as he showed them, still bruised and blackened with the hard usage they had received; nothing else but a paler shade of color from loss of blood, showed that he had passed through any suffering or danger.

"Brave hands, I honor them for all their grime. Tell me about it, Adam; show me the wound; describe the scene, I want to hear it in calm English."

But Warwick was slow to do so being the hero of the tale, and very brief was the reply Moor got.

"I came to watch, but found work ready for me. It is not clear to me even now what I did, nor how I did it. One of my Berserker rages possessed me I fancy; my nerves and muscles seemed made of steel and gutta percha; the smell of powder intoxicated, and the sense of power was grand. The fire, the smoke, the din were all delicious, and I felt like a giant, as I wielded that great weapon, dealing many deaths with a single pair of hands."

"The savage in you got the mastery just then; I've seen it, and have often wondered how you managed to control it so well. Now it has had a holiday and made a hero of you."

"The savage is better out than in, and any man may be a hero if he will. What have you been doing since I left you poring over pictures in a mouldy palace?"

"You think to slip away from the subject, do you? and after facing death at a cannon's breach expect me to be satisfied with an ordinary greeting? I won't have it; I insist upon asking as many questions as I like, hearing about the wound and seeing if it is doing well. Where is it?"

Warwick showed it, a little purple spot above his heart. Moor's face grew anxious as he looked, but cleared again as he examined it, for the ball had gone upward and the wholesome flesh was already healing fast.

"Too near, Adam, but thank God it was no nearer. A little lower and I might have looked for you in vain."

"This heart of mine is a tough organ, bullet-proof, I dare say, though I wear no breastplate."

"But this!" Involuntarily Moor's eye asked the question his lips did not utter as he touched a worn and faded case hanging on the broad breast before him. Silently Warwick opened it, showing not Sylvia's face but that of an old woman, rudely drawn in sepia; the brown tints bringing out the marked features as no softer hue could have done, and giving to each line a depth of expression that made the serious countenance singularly lifelike and attractive.

Now Moor saw where Warwick got both keen eyes and tender mouth, as well as all the gentler traits that softened his strong character; and felt that no other woman ever had or ever would hold so dear a place as the old mother whose likeness he had drawn and hung where other men wear images of mistress or of wife. With a glance as full of penitence as the other had been of disquiet, Moor laid back the little case, drew bandage and blouse over both wound and picture, and linked his arm in Warwick's as he asked—

"Who shot you?"

"How can I tell? I knew nothing of it till that flock of women fell to kissing these dirty hands of mine; then I was conscious of a stinging pain in my shoulder, and a warm stream trickling down my side. I looked to see what was amiss, whereat the good souls set up a shriek, took possession of me, and for half an hour wept and wailed over me in a frenzy of emotion and good-will that kept me merry in spite of the surgeon's probes and the priest's prayers. The appellations showered upon me would have startled even your ears, accustomed to soft words. Were you ever called 'core of my heart,' 'sun of my soul,' or 'cup of gold'?"

"Cannonading suits your spirits excellently; I remember your telling me that you had tried and liked it. But there is to be no more of it, I have other plans for you. Before I mention them tell me of the interview with Garibaldi."

"That now is a thing to ask one about; a thing to talk of and take pride in all one's days. I was half asleep and thought myself dreaming till he spoke. A right noble face, Geoffrey—full of thought and power; the look of one born to command others because master of himself. A square strong frame; no decorations, no parade; dressed like his men, yet as much the chief as if he wore a dozen orders on his scarlet shirt."

"Where is the cloak? I want to see and touch it; surely you kept it as a relic?"

"Not I. Having seen the man, what do I care for the garment that covered him. I keep the hand shake, the 'Grazia, grazia,' for my share. Poor Beppo lies buried in the hero's cloak."

"I grudge it to him, every inch of it, for not having seen the man *I* do desire the garment. Who but you would have done it?"

Warwick smiled, knowing that his friend was well pleased with him for all his murmuring. They walked in silence till Moor abruptly asked—

"When can you travel, Adam?"

"I was coming back to you to-morrow."

"Are you sure it is safe?2

"Quite sure; ten days is enough to waste upon a scratch like this."

"Come now, I cannot wait till to-morrow."

"Very good. Can you stop till I get my hat?"

"You don't ask me why I am in such haste."

Moor's tone caused Warwick to pause and look at him. Joy, impatience, anxiety, contended with each other in his countenance; and as if unable to tell the cause himself he put a little paper into the other's hand.

Only three words were contained in it, but they caused Warwick's face to kindle with all the joy betrayed in that of his friend, none of the impatience nor anxiety.

"What can I say to show you my content?* The months have seemed very long to you, but now comes the reward. The blessed little letter! so like herself; the slender slip, the delicate handwriting, the three happy words,—'Geoffrey, come home.'"†

Moor did not speak, but still looked up anxiously, inquiringly; and Warwick answered with a glance he could not doubt.

"Have no fears for me. I share the joy as heartily as I shared the sorrow; neither can separate us any more."

"Thank heaven for that! But, Adam, may I accept this good gift and be sure I am not robbing you again? You never speak of the past, how is it with you now?"

"Quite well and happy; the pain is gone, the peace remains. I would not have it otherwise. Six months‡ have cured the selfishness of love, and left the satisfaction which nothing can change or take away."

"But Sylvia, what of her, Adam?"

"Henceforth, Sylvia and Ottila are only fair illustrations of the two extremes of love. I am glad to have known both; each has helped me, and each will be remembered while I live. But having gained the experience I can relinquish the unconscious bestowers of it, if it is not best to keep them. Believe that I do this without regret, and freely enjoy the happiness that comes to you."§

"I will, but not as I once should; for though I feel that you need neither sympathy nor pity, still, I seem to take so much and leave you nothing."

"You leave me myself, better and humbler than before. In the fierce half hour I lived not long ago, I think a great and needful change was wrought in me. All lives are full of such, coming when least looked for,

---

* *M2* reads: "What can I say to show you my pleasure?" (343)

† Instead of "Geoffrey, come home," *M2* reads: "each saying volumes" (343).

‡ *M2* substitutes "Time and suffering" for "Six months" (343).

§ References to Sylvia and Ottila (the lines "But Sylvia . . . to keep them") are removed from *M2,* and the text resumes with: "Believe that I say this without regret, and freely enjoy the happiness that comes to you" (343).

working out the end through unexpected means. The restless, domineering devil that haunted me was cast out then; and during the quiet time that followed a new spirit entered in and took possession."

"What is it, Adam?"

"I cannot tell, yet I welcome it. This peaceful mood may not last perhaps, but it brings me that rare moment—pity that it is so rare, and but a moment—when we seem to see temptation at our feet; when we are conscious of a willingness to leave all in God's hand, ready for whatever He may send; feeling that whether it be suffering or joy we shall see the Giver in the gift, and when He calls can answer cheerfully 'Lord here am I.'"

It *was* a rare moment, and in it Moor for the first time clearly saw the desire and design of his friend's life; saw it because it was accomplished, and for the instant Adam Warwick was what he aspired to be. A goodly man, whose stalwart body seemed a fit home for a strong soul, wise with the wisdom of a deep experience, genial with the virtues of an upright life, devout with that humble yet valiant piety which comes through hard-won victories over "the world, the flesh, and the devil." Despite the hope that warmed his heart, Moor felt poor beside him, as a new reverence warmed the old affection. His face showed it though he did not speak, and Warwick laid an arm about his shoulders as he had often done of late when they were alone, drawing him gently on again, as he said, with a touch of playfulness to set both at ease—

"Tell me your plans, 'my cup of gold,' and let me lend a hand toward filling you brimful of happiness. You are going home?"

"At once; you also."

"Is it best?"

"Yes; you came for me, I stay for you, and Sylvia waits for both."

"She says nothing of me in this short, sweet note of hers;" and Warwick smoothed it carefully in his large hand, eyeing it as if he wished there were some little word for him.

"True, but in the few letters she has written there always comes a message to you, though you never write a line; nor would you go to her now had she sent for you alone; she knew that, and sends for me, sure that you will follow."

"Being a woman she cannot quite forgive me for loving her too well to make her miserable. Dear soul, she will never know how much it cost me, but I knew that my only safety lay in flight. Tell her so a long while hence."

"You shall do it yourself, for you are coming home with me."

"What to do there?"

"All you ever did; walk up and down the face of the earth, waxing in power and virtue, and coming often to us when we get fairly back into our former ways, for you are still the house friend."

"I was wondering, as I walked here, what my next summons would be, when lo, you came. Go on, I'll follow you; one could hardly have a better guide."*

"You are sure you are able, Adam?"

"Shall I uproot a tree or fling you over the wall to convince you, you motherly body? I am nearly whole again, and a breath of sea air will complete the cure. Let me cover my head, say farewell to the good Sisters, and I shall be glad to slip away without further demonstrations from the volcanoes below there."

Laying one hand on the low wall, Warwick vaulted over with a backward glance at Moor, who followed to the gateway, there to wait till the adieux were over. Very brief they were, and presently Warwick reappeared, evidently touched yet ill-pleased at something, for he both smiled and frowned as he paused on the threshold as if loth to go. A little white goat came skipping from the orchard, and seeing the stranger took refuge at Warwick's knee. The act of the creature seemed to suggest a thought to the man. Pulling off the gay handkerchief some grateful woman had knotted round his neck, he fastened it about the goat's, having secured something in one end, then rose as if content.

"What are you doing?" called Moor, wondering at this arrangement.

"Widening the narrow entrance into heaven set apart for rich men unless they leave their substance behind, as I am trying to do. The kind creatures cannot refuse it now; so trot away to your mistress, little Nanna, and tell no tales as you go."

As the goat went tapping up the steps a stir within announced the dreaded demonstration. Warwick did not seem to hear it; he stood looking

---

*For this paragraph *M2* substitutes:

   I shall not disturb you yet. I'll see you safe across, and then vanish for another year. I was wondering, as I walked here, what my next summons would be, when lo, you came. Go on, I'll follow you; one could hardly have a better guide." (346)

far across the trampled plain and ruined town toward the mountains shining white against the deep Italian sky. A rapt, far-reaching look, as if he saw beyond the purple wall, and seeing forgot the present in some vision of the future.

"Come, Adam! I am waiting."

His eye came back, the lost look passed, and cheerily he answered—

"I am ready."

A fortnight later in that dark hour before the dawn, with a murky sky above them, a hungry sea below them, the two stood together the last to leave a sinking ship.

"Room for one more, choose quick!" shouted a hoarse voice from the boat tossing underneath, freighted to the water's edge with trembling lives.

"Go, Geoffrey, Sylvia is waiting."

"Not without you, Adam."

"But you are exhausted; I can bear a rough hour better than yourself, and morning will bring help."

"It may not. Go, I am the lesser loss."

"What folly! I will force you to it; steady there, he is coming."

"Push off, I am *not* coming."

In times like that, few pause for pity or persuasion; the instinct of self-preservation rules supreme, and each is for himself, except those in whom love of another is stronger than love of life. Even while the friends generously contended the boat was swept away, and they were left alone in the deserted ship, swiftly making its last voyage downward. Spent with a day of intense excitement, and sick with hope deferred, Moor leaned on Warwick, feeling that it was adding bitterness to death to die in sight of shore. But Warwick never knew despair; passive submission was not in his power while anything remained to do or dare, and even then he did not cease to hope. It was certain death to linger there; other boats less heavily laden had put off before, and might drift across the track; wreckers waiting on the shore might hear and help; at least it were better to die bravely and not "strike sail to a fear." About his waist still hung a fragment of the rope which had lowered more than one baby to its mother's arms; before them the shattered taffrail rose and fell as the waves beat over it. Wrenching a spar away he lashed Moor to it, explaining his purpose as he worked. There was only rope enough for one, and in the darkness Moor believed that Warwick had taken equal precautions for himself.

"Now Geoffrey your hand, and when the next wave ebbs let us follow it. If we are parted and you see her first tell her I remembered, and give her this."

In the black night with only Heaven to see them the men kissed tenderly as women, then hand in hand sprang out into the sea. Drenched and blinded they struggled up after the first plunge, and struck out for the shore, guided by the thunder of the surf they had listened to for twelve long hours, as it broke against the beach, and brought no help on its receding billows. Soon Warwick was the only one who struggled, for Moor's strength was gone, and he clung half conscious to the spar, tossing from wave to wave, a piteous plaything for the sea.

"I see a light!—they must take you in—hold fast, I'll save you for the little wife at home."

Moor heard but two words, "wife" and "home;" strained his dim eyes to see the light, spent his last grain of strength to reach it, and in the act lost consciousness, whispering—"She will thank you," as his head fell against Warwick's breast and lay there, heavy and still. Lifting himself above the spar, Adam lent the full power of his voice to the shout he sent ringing through the storm. He did not call in vain, a friendly wind took the cry to human ears, a relenting wave swept them within the reach of human aid, and the boat's crew, pausing involuntarily, saw a hand clutch the suspended oar, a face flash up from the black water, and heard a breathless voice issue the command—

"Take in this man! he saved you for your wives, save him for his."

One resolute will can sway a panic stricken multitude; it did so then. The boat was rocking in the long swell of the sea; a moment and the coming wave would sweep them far apart. A woman sobbed, and as if moved by one impulse four sturdy arms clutched and drew Moor in. While loosening his friend Warwick had forgotten himself, and the spar was gone. He knew it, but the rest believed that they left the strong man a chance of life equal to their own in that overladen boat. Yet in the memories of all who caught that last glimpse of him there long remained the recollection of a dauntless face floating out into the night, a steady voice calling through the gale, "A good voyage, comrades!" as he turned away to enter port before them.

Wide was the sea and pitiless the storm, but neither could dismay the unconquerable spirit of the man who fought against the elements as bravely as if they were adversaries of mortal mould, and might be vanquished in the end. But it was not to be; soon he felt it, accepted it, turned his face upward toward the sky, where one star shone, and when Death whispered "Come!" answered as cheerily as to that other friend, "I am ready." Then with a parting thought for the man he had saved, the woman he had loved, the promise he had kept, a great and tender heart went down into the sea.

SOMETIMES the Sculptor, whose workshop is the world, fuses many metals and casts a noble statue; leaves it for humanity to criticise, and when time has mellowed both beauties and blemishes, removes it to that inner studio, there to be carved in enduring marble.

Adam Warwick was such an one; with much alloy and many flaws; but beneath all defects the Master's eye saw the grand lines that were to serve as models for the perfect man, and when the design had passed through all necessary processes,—the mould of clay, the furnace fire, the test of time,—He washed the dust away, and pronounced it ready for the marble.

CHAPTER XXI

OUT OF THE SHADOW*

THEY had been together for an hour, the husband and wife. The first excitement was now over, and Sylvia stood behind him tearless and tranquil, while Moor, looking like a man out of whom the sea had drenched both strength and spirit, leaned his weary head against her, trying to accept the great loss, enjoy the great gain which had befallen him. Hitherto all their talk had been of Warwick, and as Moor concluded the history of the months so tragically ended, for the first time he ventured to express wonder at the calmness with which his hearer received the sad story.

"How quietly you listen to words which it wrings my heart to utter. Have you wept your tears dry, or do you still cling to hope?"

"No, I feel that we shall never see him any more; but I have no desire to weep, for tears and lamentations to not belong to him. He died a beautiful, a noble death; the sea is a fitting grave for him, and it is pleasant to think of him asleep there, quiet at last."

"I cannot feel so; I find it hard to think of him as dead; he was so full of life, so fit to live."

"And therefore fit to die. Imagine him as I do, enjoying the larger life he longed for, and growing to be the strong, sweet soul whose foreshadowing we saw and loved so here."

"Sylvia, I have told you of the beautiful change which befell him in

---

*Chapter XXI, "Out of the Shadow," becomes Chapter XXIII, "At Last," in *M2*. The entire revised chapter, almost completely new, is reprinted in the appendix (352–59).

those last days, and now I see the same in you. Are you, too, about to leave me when I have just recovered you?"

"I shall stay with you all my life."

"Then Adam was less to you than you believed, and I am more?"

"Nothing is changed. Adam is all he ever was to me, you are all you ever can be; but I——"

"Then why send for me? Why say you will stay with me all your life? Sylvia, for God's sake, let there be no more delusion or deceit!"

"Never again! I will tell you; I meant to do it at once, but it is so hard——"

She turned her face away, and for a moment neither stirred. Then drawing his head to its former resting-place she touched it very tenderly, seeing how many white threads shone among the brown; and as her hand went to and fro with an inexpressibly soothing gesture, she said, in a tone whose quietude controlled his agitation like a spell——

"Long ago, in my great trouble, Faith told me that for every human effort or affliction there were two friendly helpers, Time and Death. The first has taught me more gently than I deserved; has made me humble, and given me hope that through my errors I may draw virtue from repentance. But while I have been learning the lessons time can teach, that other helper has told me to be ready for its coming. Geoffrey, I sent for you because I knew you would love to see me again before we must say the long good by."

"Oh, Sylvia! not that; anything but that. I cannot bear it now!"

"Dear heart, be patient; lean on me, and let me help you bear it, for it is inevitable."

"It shall not be! There must be some help, some hope. God would not be so pitiless as to take both."

"I shall not leave you yet. He does not take me; it is I, who, by wasting life, have lost the right to live."

"But is it so? I cannot make it true. You look so beautiful, so blooming, and the future seemed so sure. Sylvia, show it to me, if it must be."

She only turned her face to him, only held up her transparent hand, and let him read the heavy truth. He did so, for now he saw the beauty and the bloom were transitory as the glow of leaves that frost makes fairest as they fall, and felt the full significance of the great change which had come. He clung to her with a desperate yet despairing hold, and she could only let the first passion of his grief have way, soothing and sustaining, while her heart bled and the draught was very bitter to her lips.

"Hush, love; be quiet for a little; and when you can bear it better, I will tell you how it is with me."

"Tell me now; let me hear everything at once. When did you know? How are you sure? Why keep it from me all this time?"

"I have only known it for a little while, but I am very sure, and I kept it from you that you might come happily home, for knowledge of it would have lengthened every mile, and made the journey one long anxiety. I could not know that Adam would go first, and so make my task doubly hard."

"Come to me, Sylvia; let me keep you while I may. I will not be violent; I will listen patiently, and through everything remember you."

He did remember her, so thoughtfully, so tenderly, that her little story flowed on uninterrupted by sigh or sob; and while he held his grief in check, the balm of submission comforted his sore heart. Sitting by him, sustaining and sustained, she told the history of the last six months, till just before the sending of the letter. She paused there a moment, then hurried on, gradually losing the consciousness of present emotion in the vivid memory of the past.

"You have no faith in dreams; I have; and to a dream I owe my sudden awakening to the truth. Thank and respect it, for without its warning I might have remained in ignorance of my state until it was too late to find and bring you home."

"God bless the dream and keep the dreamer!"

"This was a strange and solemn vision; one to remember and to love for its beautiful interpretation of the prophecy that used to awe and sadden me, but never can again. I dreamed that the last day of the world had come. I stood on a shadowy house-top in a shadowy city, and all around me far as eye could reach thronged myriads of people, till the earth seemed white with human faces. All were mute and motionless, as if fixed in a trance of expectation, for none knew how the end would come. Utter silence filled the world, and across the sky a vast curtain of the blackest cloud was falling, blotting out face after face and leaving the world a blank. In that universal gloom and stillness, far above me in the heavens I saw the pale outlines of a word stretching from horizon to horizon. Letter after letter came out full and clear, till all across the sky, burning with a ruddy glory stronger than the sun, shone the great word Amen. As the last letter reached its bright perfection, a long waft of wind broke over me like a universal sigh of hope from human hearts. For far away on the horizon's edge all saw a line of light that widened as they looked, and through that rift, between the dark earth and the darker sky, rolled in a softly flowing sea. Wave after wave came on, so wide, so cool, so still. None trembled at their approach, none shrunk from their embrace, but all turned toward that ocean with a mighty rush, all faces glowed in its splendor, and million after million vanished with longing eyes fixed on the arch of light through which the ebbing sea would float them when its work was done. I felt no fear, only the deepest awe, for I seemed such an infinitesimal atom of the countless host that I forgot myself. Nearer and nearer came the flood, till its breath blew on my cheeks, and I, too, leaned to meet it, longing to be taken. A great wave rolled up before me, and through its soft glimmer I saw a beautiful, benignant face regarding me. Then I knew that each and all had seen the same, and losing fear in love were glad to go. The joyful yearning woke me as the wave seemed to break at my feet, and ebbing leave me still alive."

"And that is all? Only a dream, a foreboding fancy, Sylvia?"

"When I woke my hair was damp on my forehead, my breath quite still, my heart so cold I felt as if death had indeed been near me and left its chill behind. So strong was the impression of the dream, so perfect was the similitude between the sensations I had experienced then, and more than once awake, that I felt that something was seriously wrong with me."

"You had been ill then?"

"Not consciously, not suffering any pain, but consumed with an inward fever that would not burn itself away. I used to have a touch of it in the evenings, you remember; but now it burned all day, making me look strong and rosy, yet leaving me so worn out at night that no sleep seemed to restore me. A few weak and weary hours, then the fire was rekindled and the false strength, color, spirits, returned to deceive myself, and those about me, for another day."

"Did you tell no one of this, Sylvia?"

"Not at first, because I fancied it a mental ill. I had thought so much, so deeply, it seemed but natural that I should be tired. I tried to rest myself by laying all my cares and sorrows in God's hand, and waiting patiently to be shown the end. I see it now, but for a time I could only sit and wait; and while I did so my soul grew strong but my ill-used body failed. The dream came, and in the stillness of that night I felt a strange assurance that I should see my mother soon."

"Dear, what did you do?"

"I determined to discover if I had deceived myself with a superstitious fancy, or learned a fateful fact in my own mysterious way. If it were false, no one would be made anxious by it; if true, possessing the knowledge of it would enable me to comfort others. I went privately to town and consulted the famous physician who has grown gray in the study of disease."

"Did you go alone, Sylvia?"

"Yes, alone. I am braver than I used to be, and have learned never to feel quite alone. I found a grave, stern-looking man; I told him that I wished to know the entire truth whatever it might be, and that he need not fear to tell me because I was prepared for it. He asked many questions, thought a little, and was very slow to speak. Then I saw how it would be, but urged him to set my mind at rest. His stern old face grew very pitiful as he took my hand and answered gently—"My child, go home and prepare to die."

"Good God, how cruel! Sylvia, how did you bear it?"

"At first the earth seemed to slip away from under me, and time to stand still. Then I was myself again, and could listen steadily to all he said. It was only this,—I had been born with a strong nature in a feeble frame, had lived too fast, wasted health ignorantly, and was past help."

"Could he do nothing for you?"

"Nothing but tell me how to husband my remaining strength, and make the end easy by the care that would have kept me longer had I known this sooner."

"And no one saw your danger; no one warned you of it; and I was away!"

"Father could not see it, for I looked well and tried to think I felt so. Mark and Jessie were absorbed in baby Sylvia, and Prue was gone. You might have seen and helped me, for you have the intuitions of a woman in many things, but I could not send for you then because I could not give you what you asked. Was it wrong to call you when I did, and try to make the hard fact easier to bear by telling it myself?"

"Heaven bless you for it, Sylvia. It was truly generous and kind. I never could have forgiven you had you denied me the happiness of seeing you again, and you have robbed the truth of half of its bitter pain by telling it yourself."

A restful expression came into her face, and a sigh of satisfaction proved how great was the relief of feeling that for once her heart had prompted her aright. Moor let her rest a little, then asked with a look more pathetic than his words—

"What am I to you now? Where is my home to be?"

"My friend forever, no more, no less; and your home is here with us until I leave my father to your care. All this pain and separation were in vain if we have not learned that love can neither be forced nor feigned. While I endeavored to do so, God did not help me, and I went deeper and deeper into sorrow and wrong doing. When I dropped all self-delusion and desperate striving, and stood still, asking to be shown the right, then he put out his hand and through much tribulation led me to convictions that I dare not disobey. Our friendship may be a happy one if we accept and use it as we should. Let it be so, and for the little while that I remain, let us live honestly before heaven and take no thought for the world's opinion."

Adam might have owned the glance she bent upon her husband, so clear, so steadfast was it; but the earnestness was all her own, and blended with it a new strength that seemed a late compensation for lost love and waning life. Remembering the price both had paid for it, Moor gratefully accepted the costly friendship offered him, and soon acknowledged both its beauty and its worth.

"One question more; Sylvia, how long?"

It was very hard to answer, but folding the sharp fact in the gentlest fancy that appeared to her she gave him the whole truth.

"I shall not see the spring again, but it will be a pleasant time to lay me underneath the flowers."

Sylvia had not known how to live, but now she proved that she did know how to die. So beautifully were the two made one, the winning girl, the deep-hearted woman, that she seemed the same beloved Sylvia, yet Sylvia strengthened, purified, and perfected by the hard past, the solemn present. Those about her felt and owned the unconscious power, which we call the influence of character, and which is the noblest that gives sovereignty to man or woman.

So cheerfully did she speak of it, so tranquilly did she prepare to meet it, that death soon ceased to be an image of grief or fear to those about her, and became a benignant friend, who, when the mortal wearies, blesses it with a brief sleep, that it may wake immortal. She would have no sad, sick-chamber, no mournful faces, no cessation of the wholesome household cares and joys, that do so much to make hearts strong and spirits happy. While strength remained, she went her round of daily duties, doing each so lovingly, that the most trivial became a delight, and taking unsuspected thought for the comfort or the pleasure of those soon to be left behind, so tenderly, that she could not seem lost to them, even when she was gone.

Faith came to her, and as her hands became too weak for anything but patient folding, every care slipped so quietly into Faith's, that few perceived how fast she was laying down the things of this world, and making ready to take up those of the world to come. Her father was her faithful shadow; bent and white-haired now, but growing young at heart in spite of sorrow, for his daughter had in truth become the blessing of his life. Mark and Jessie brought their offering of love in little Sylvia's shape, and the innocent consoler did her sweet work by making sunshine in a shady place. But Moor was all in all to Sylvia, and their friendship proved an abiding strength, for sorrow made it very tender, sincerity ennobled it, and the coming change sanctified it to them both.

April came; and on her birthday, with a grateful heart, Moor gathered the first snow-drops of the year. All day they stood beside her couch, as fragile and as pale as she, and many eyes had filled as loving fancies likened her to the slender, transparent vase, the very spirit of a shape, and the white flowers that had blossomed beautifully through the snow. When the evening lamp was lighted, she took the little posy in her hand, and lay with her eyes upon it, listening to the book Moor read, for this hour always soothed the unrest of the day. Very quiet was the pleasant room, with no sounds in it but the soft flicker of the fire, the rustle of Faith's needle, and the subdued music of the voice that patiently went reading on, long after Sylvia's eyes had closed, lest she should miss its murmur. For an hour she seemed to sleep, so motionless, so colorless, that her father, always sitting at her side, bent down at last to listen at her lips. The lips smiled, the eyes unclosed, and she looked up at him, with an expression as tender as tranquil.

"A long sleep and pleasant dreams that wake you smiling?" he asked.

"Beautiful and happy thoughts, father; let me tell you some of them. As I lay here, I fell to thinking of my life, and at first it seemed the sorrowfullest failure I had ever known. Whom had I made happy? What had I done worth the doing? Where was the humble satisfaction that should come hand in hand with death? At first I could find no answers to my questions, and though my one and twenty years do not seem long to live, I felt as if it would have been better for us all if I had died, a new-born baby in my mother's arms."

"My child, say anything but that, because it is I who have made your life a failure."

"Wait a little, father, and you will see that it is a beautiful success. I *have* given happiness, *have* done something worth the doing; now I see a compensation for all seeming loss, and heartily thank God that I did not die till I had learned the true purpose of all lives. He knows that I say these things humbly, that I claim no virtue for myself, and have been a blind instrument in His hand, to illustrate truths that will endure when I am forgotten. I have helped Mark and Jessie, for, remembering me, they will feel how blest they are in truly loving one another. They will keep little Sylvia from making mistakes like mine, and the household joys and sorrows we have known together, will teach Mark to make his talent a delight to many, by letting art interpret nature."

Her brother standing behind her stooped and kissed her, saying through his tears—

"I shall remember, dear."

"I have helped Geoffrey, I believe. He lived too much in the affections, till through me he learned that none may live for love alone. Genius will be born of grief, and he will put his sorrow into song to touch and teach other hearts more gently than his own has been, so growing a nobler and a richer man for the great cross of his life."

Calm, with the calmness of a grief too deep for tears, and strong in a devout belief, Moor gave his testimony as she paused.

"I shall endeavor, and now I am as grateful for the pain as for the joy, because together they will show me how to live, and when I have learned that I shall be ready to come to you."

"I think I have served Adam. He needed gentleness as Geoffrey needed strength, and I, unworthy as I am, woke that deep heart of his and made it a fitter mate for his great soul. To us it seems as if he had left his work unfinished, but God knew best, and when he was needed for a better work he went to find it. Yet I am sure that he was worthier of eternal life for having known the discipline of love."

There was no voice to answer now, but Sylvia felt that she would receive it very soon and was content.

"Have you no lesson for your father? The old man needs it most."

She laid her thin hand tenderly on his, that if her words should bring reproach, she might seem to share it with him.

"Yes, father, this. That if the chief desire of the heart is for the right, it is possible for any human being, through all trials, temptations, and mistakes, to bring good out of evil, hope from despair, success from defeat, and come at last to know an hour as beautiful and blest as this."

Who could doubt that *she* had learned the lesson, when from the

ruins of the perishable body the imperishable soul rose steadfast and serene, proving that after the long bewilderment of life and love it had
attained the eternal peace.

The room grew very still, and while those about her pondered her
words with natural tears, Sylvia lay looking up at a lovely picture that
seemed leaning down to offer her again the happiest memory of her youth.
It was a painting of the moonlight voyage down the river. Mark had given it
that day, and now when the longer, sadder voyage was nearly over, she
regarded it with a tender pleasure. The moon shone full on Warwick,
looking out straight and strong before him with the vigilant expression
native to his face; a fit helmsman to guide the boat along that rapid stream.
Mark seemed pausing to watch the oars silvered by the light, and their
reflections wavy with the current. Moor, seen in shadow, leaned upon his
hand, as if watching Sylvia, a quiet figure, full of grace and color, couched
under the green arch. On either hand the summer woods made vernal
gloom, behind the cliffs rose sharply up against the blue, and all before
wound a shining road, along which the boat seemed floating like a bird on
slender wings between two skies.

So long she lay forgetful of herself and all about her, that Moor saw
she needed rest, for the breath fluttered on her lips, the flowers had fallen
one by one, and her face wore the weary yet happy look of some patient
child waiting for its lullaby.

"Dear, you have talked enough; let me take you up now, lest the
pleasant day be spoiled by a sleepless night."

"I am ready, yet I love to stay among you all, for in my sleep I seem to
drift so far away I never quite come back. Good night, good night; I shall
see you in the morning."

With a smile, a kiss for all, they saw her fold her arms about her
husband's neck, and lay down her head as if she never cared to lift it up
again. The little journey was both a pleasure and pain to them, for each
night the way seemed longer to Sylvia, and though the burden lightened
the bearer grew more heavy-hearted. It was a silent passage now, for
neither spoke, except when one asked tenderly, "Are you easy, love?" and
the other answered, with a breath that chilled his cheek, "Quite happy,
quite content."

So, cradled on the heart that loved her best, Sylvia was gently carried
to the end of her short pilgrimage, and when her husband laid her down
the morning had already dawned.

REVIEW OF MOODS

REVIEW OF MOODS BY HENRY JAMES

Miss Alcott's "Moods"

UNDER the above title, Miss Alcott has given us her version of the old story of the husband, the wife, and the lover. This story has been told so often that an author's only pretext for telling it again is his consciousness of an ability to make it either more entertaining or more instructive; to invest it with incidents more dramatic, or with a more pointed moral. Its interest has already been carried to the furthest limits, both of tragedy and comedy, by a number of practised French writers: under this head, therefore, competition would be superfluous. Has Miss Alcott proposed to herself to give her story a philosophical bearing? We can hardly suppose it.

We have seen it asserted that her book claims to deal with the "doctrine of affinities." What the doctrine of affinities is, we do not exactly know; but we are inclined to think that our author has been somewhat maligned. Her book is, to our perception, innocent of any doctrine whatever.

The heroine of "Moods" is a fitful, wayward, and withal most amiable young person, named Sylvia. We regret to say that Miss Alcott takes her up in her childhood. We are utterly weary of stories about precocious little girls. In the first place, they are in themselves disagreeable and unprofitable objects of study; and in the second, they are always the precursors of a not less unprofitable middle-aged lover. We admit that, even to the middle-aged, Sylvia must have been a most engaging little person. One of her means of fascination is to disguise herself as a boy and work in the garden with a hoe and wheelbarrow; under which circumstances she is clandestinely watched by one of the heroes, who then and there falls in love with her. Then she goes off on a camping-out expedition of a week's duration, in company with three gentlemen, with no superfluous luggage, as far as we can ascertain, but a cockle-shell stuck "pilgrim-wise" in her hat. It is hard to say whether the impropriety of this proceeding is the greater or the less from the fact of her extreme youth. This fact is at any rate kindly overlooked by two of her companions, who become desperately enamored of her before the week is out. These two gentlemen are Miss Alcott's heroes. One of them, Mr. Geoffrey Moor, is unobjectionable enough; we shall have something to say of him hereafter: but the other, Mr. Adam Warwick, is one of our oldest and most inveterate foes. He is the inevitable *cavaliere servente* of the precocious little girl; the laconical, satirical, dogmatical lover, of about thirty-five, with the "brown mane", the "quiet smile", the "masterful soul", and the "commanding eye." Do not all novel-readers remember a figure, a hundred figures, analogous to this? Can they not, one of his properties being given,—the "quiet smile" for instance,—reconstruct the whole monstrous shape? When the "quiet smile" is suggested, we know what is coming: we foresee the cynical bachelor or widower, the amateur of human nature, "Full of strange oaths, and bearded like the pard", who has travelled all over the world, lives on a mysterious patrimony, and spends his time in breaking the hearts and the wills of demure little school-girls, who answer him with "Yes, sir", and "No, sir."

Mr. Warwick is plainly a great favorite with the author. She has for him that affection which writers entertain, not for those figures whom they have well known, but for such as they have much pondered. Miss Alcott has probably mused upon Warwick so long and so lovingly that she has lost all sense of his proportions. There is a most discouraging good-will in the manner in which lady novelists elaborate their impossible heroes. There are, thank Heaven, no such men at large in society. We speak thus devoutly, not because Warwick is a vicious person,—on the contrary, he exhibits the sternest integrity; but because, apparently as a natural result of being thoroughly conscientious, he is essentially disagreeable. Women appear to delight in the conception of men who shall be insupportable to men. Warwick is intended to be a profoundly serious person. A species of prologue is prefixed to the tale, in which we are initiated into his passion for one Ottila, a beautiful Cuban lady. This chapter is a literary curiosity. The relations of the two lovers are illustrated by means of a dialogue between them. Considering how bad this dialogue is, it is really very good.

Review of *Moods*

We mean that, considering what nonsense the lovers are made to talk, their conversation is quite dramatic. We are not certain of the extent to which the author sympathizes with her hero; but we are pretty sure that she has a secret "Bravo" in store for him upon his exit. He talks to his mistress as no sane man ever talked to a woman. It is not too much to say that he talks like a brute. Ottila's great crime has been, that, after three months' wooing, he has not found her so excellent a person as he at first supposed her to be. This is a specimen of his language: "You allured my eye with loveliness, my ear with music; piqued curiosity, pampered pride, and subdued will by flatteries subtly administered. Beginning afar off, you let all influences do their work, till the moment came for the effective stroke. Then you made a crowning sacrifice of maiden modesty, and owned you loved me." What return does she get for the sacrifice, if sacrifice it was? To have her favors thrown back in her teeth on the day that her lover determines to jilt her. To jilt a woman in an underhand fashion is bad enough; but to break your word to her and at the same time load her with outrage, to call her evil names because she is so provokingly in the right, to add the foulest insult to the bitterest injury,—these things may be worthy of a dissolute adventurer, but they are certainly not worthy of a model hero. Warwick tells Ottila that he is "a man untamed by any law but that of [his] own will." He is further described as "violently virtuous, a masterful soul, bent on living out his aspirations at any cost"; and as possessed of "great nobility of character, great audacity of mind"; as being "too fierce an iconoclast to suit the old party, too individual a reformer to join the new", and "a grand man in the rough, an excellent tonic for those who have courage to try him." Truly, for her courage in trying him, poor Ottila is generously rewarded. His attitude towards her may be reduced to this:— Three months ago, I fell in love with your beauty, your grace, your wit. I took them as a promise of a moral elevation which I now find you do not possess. And yet, the deuse take it, I am engaged to you. *Ergo,* you are false, immodest, and lacking in the "moral sentiment", and I will have nothing to do with you. I may be a sneak, a coward, a brute; but at all events, I am untamed by any law, etc.

Before the picnic above mentioned is over, Warwick and Moor have, unknown to each other, both lost their hearts to Sylvia. Warwick may not declare himself, inasmuch as, to do him justice, he considers himself bound by word to the unfortunate beauty of the Havana. But Moor, who is free to do as he pleases, forthwith offers himself. He is refused, the young girl having a preference for Warwick. But while she is waiting for Warwick's

declaration, his flirtation with Ottila comes to her knowledge. She recalls
Moor, marries him, and goes to spend her honeymoon among the White
Mountains. Here Warwick turns up. He has been absent in Cuba, whether
taking back his rude speeches to Ottila, or following them up with more of
the same sort, we are not informed. He is accordingly ignorant of the
change in his mistress's circumstances. He finds her alone on the mountain-
side, and straightway unburdens his heart. Here ensues a very pretty scene,
prettily told. On learning the sad truth, Warwick takes himself off, over
the crest of the hill, looking very tall and grand against the sun, and leaving
his mistress alone in the shadow. In the shadow she passes the rest of her
brief existence. She might have lived along happily enough, we conceive,
masquerading with her gentle husband in the fashion of old days, if Warwick had not come back, and proffered a visit,—his one natural and his
one naughty act. Of course it is all up with Sylvia. An honest man in
Warwick's position would immediately have withdrawn, on seeing that his
presence only served seriously to alienate his mistress from her husband. A
dishonest man would have remained and made love to his friend's wife.

Miss Alcott tries to persuade us that her hero does neither; but we
maintain that he adopts the latter course, and, what is worse, does it like an
arrant hypocrite. He proceeds to lay down the law of matrimonial duty to
Sylvia in a manner which, in our opinion, would warrant her in calling in
her husband to turn him out of the house. He declares, indeed, that he
designs no "French sentiment nor sin", whatever these may be; but he
exerts the utmost power of his "masterful soul" to bully her into a protest
against her unnatural union. No man with any sense of decency, no man of
the slightest common-sense, would presume to dogmatize in this con-
ceited fashion upon a matter with which he has not the least concern. Miss
Alcott would tell us, we presume, that it is not as a lover, but as a friend,
that Warwick offers the advice here put into his mouth. Family friends,
when they know what they are about, are only too glad to shirk the
responsibility of an opinion in matrimonial differences. When a man beats,
starves, or otherwise misuses his wife, any judicious acquaintance will take
the responsibility of advising the poor woman to seek legal redress; and he
need not, to use Miss Alcott's own preposition, have an affinity "for" her,
to do so. But it is inconceivable that a wise and virtuous gentleman should
deliberately persuade two dear friends—dear equally to himself and to
each other—to pick imperceptible flaws in a relation whose inviolability is
the great interest of their lives, and which, from the picture presented to
us, is certainly one of exceptional comfort and harmony.

In all this matter it strikes us that Sylvia's husband is the only one to be pitied. His wife, while in a somnambulistic state, confesses the secret of her illicit affection. Moor is, of course, bitterly outraged, and his anger is well described. Sylvia pities him intensely, but insists with sweet inflexibility that she cannot continue to be his wife, and dismisses him to Europe, with a most audacious speech about the beautiful eternity and the immortality of love. Moor, who for a moment has evinced a gleam of natural passion, which does something towards redeeming from ludicrous unreality the united efforts of the trio before us, soon recovers himself, and submits to his fate precisely like a morbidly conscientious young girl who is engaged in the formation of her character under the direction of her clergyman. From this point accordingly the story becomes more and more unnatural, although, we cheerfully add, it becomes considerably more dramatic, and is much better told. All this portion is, in fact, very pretty; indeed, if it were not so essentially false, we should call it very fine. As it is, we can only use the expression in its ironical sense. Moor consents to sacrifice himself to the beautiful ethical abstraction which his wife and her lover have concocted between them. He will go to Europe and await the dawning of some new abstraction, under whose starry influence he may return. When he does return, it will not be, we may be sure, to give his wife the thorough rating she deserves.

At the eleventh hour, when the vessel is about to start, Warwick turns up, and thrusts himself, as a travelling companion, upon the man he has outraged. As Warwick was destined to die a violent death, we think Miss Alcott might have here appropriately closed her book by making Moor pitch Adam into the water for his impertinence. But as usual, Warwick has his own way.

During their absence, Sylvia sinks into a rapid decline. After a certain interval they start homeward. But their ship is wrecked; Warwick is lost in trying to save Moor's life; and Moor reaches home alone. Sylvia then proceeds to put him and every one else in the wrong by dying the death of the righteous.

The two most striking facts with regard to "Moods" are the author's ignorance of human nature, and her self-confidence in spite of this ignorance. Miss Alcott doubtless knows men and women well enough to deal successfully with their every-day virtues and temptations, but not well enough to handle great dramatic passions. The consequence is, that her play is not a real play, nor her actors real actors.

But beside these facts are others, less salient perhaps, upon which it is pleasanter to touch. Chief among these is the author's decided cleverness; that quality to which we owe it that, in spite of the absurdities of the action, the last half of her book is replete with beauty and vigor. What shall we call this quality? Imagination does not seem to us too grand a word. For, in the absence of knowledge, our authoress has derived her figures, as the German derived his camel, from the depths of her moral consciousness. If they are on this account the less real, they are also on this account the more unmistakably instinct with a certain beauty and grace. If Miss Alcott's experience of human nature has been small, as we should suppose, her admiration for it is nevertheless great. Putting aside Adam's treatment of Ottila, she sympathizes throughout her book with none but great things. She has the rare merit, accordingly, of being very seldom puerile. For inanimate nature, too, she has a genuine love, together with a very pretty way of describing it. With these qualities there is no reason why Miss Alcott should not write a very good novel, provided she will be satisfied to describe only that which she has seen. When such a novel comes, as we doubt not it eventually will, we shall be among the first to welcome it. With the exception of two or three celebrated names, we know not, indeed, to whom, in this country, unless to Miss Alcott, we are to look for a novel above the average.*

---

*From the *North American* 101 (July 1865).

꽃꽃꽃꽃꽃꽃

PREFACE

WHEN "Moods" was first published, an interval of some years having then elapsed since it was written, it was so altered, to suit the taste and convenience of the publisher, that the original purpose of the story was lost sight of, and marriage appeared to be the theme instead of an attempt to show the mistakes of a moody nature, guided by impulse, not principle. Of the former subject a girl of eighteen could know but little, of the latter most girls know a good deal; and they alone among my readers have divined the real purpose of the book in spite of its many faults, and have thanked me for it.

As the observation and experience of the woman have confirmed much that the instinct and imagination of the girl felt and tried to describe, I wish to give my first novel, with all its imperfections on its head, a place among its more successful sisters; for into it went the love, labor, and enthusiasm that no later book can possess.

Several chapters have been omitted, several of the original ones restored; and those that remain have been pruned of as much fine writing as could be done without destroying the youthful spirit of the little romance. At eighteen death seemed the only solution for Sylvia's perplexities; but thirty years later, having learned the possibility of finding happiness after disappointment, and making love and duty go hand in hand, my heroine meets a wiser if less romantic fate than in the former edition.

Hoping that the young people will accept the amendment, and the elders will sympathize with the maternal instinct which makes unfortunate children the dearest, I reintroduce my first-born to the public which has so kindly welcomed my later offspring.

L. M. ALCOTT

CONCORD, January, 1882.

CONTENTS

CHAPTER I: SYLVIA

A girl was at work near by; a slender creature in a short linen frock, stout boots, and a wide-brimmed hat, drawn low over the forehead. Whistling softly, she dug with active gestures; and, having made the necessary cavity, set a shrub, filled up the hole, trod it down scientifically, and then fell back to survey the success of her labors. But something was amiss, something had been forgotten, for suddenly up came the shrub, and, seizing a wheelbarrow that stood near by, away rattled the girl round the corner out of sight. Moor smiled at this impetuosity, and awaited her return with interest, suspecting who it was.

Presently up the path she came, with head down and steady pace, trundling a barrow full of richer earth, surmounted by a watering-pot. Never stopping for breath, she fell to work again, enlarged the hole, flung in the loam, poured in the water, reset the shrub, and, when the last stamp and pat were given, performed a little dance of triumph about it, at the close of which she pulled off her hat and began to fan her heated face. The action caused the observer to lean and look again, thinking, as he recognized the energetic worker with a smile, "What a changeful thing it is! haunting one's premises unseen, and stealing one's books unsuspected; dreaming one half the day and working hard the other half. What will happen next?" (18–19)

Moor watched her with unusual interest, for he remembered the freakish child he left five years ago better than she remembered him. She was a little creature still, looking hardly fifteen though two years older. A delicate yet beautifully moulded figure, as the fine hands showed, and the curve of the shoulder under the pale violet dress that was both exquisitely simple and becoming. The face was full of contradictions; youthful, maidenly, and intelligent, yet touched with the melancholy of a temperament too mixed to make life happy. The mouth was sweet and tender, the brow touched with that indescribable something which suggests genius, and there was much pride in the spirited carriage of the small head with its hair of wavy gold gathered into a violet snood whence little tendrils kept breaking loose to dance about her forehead or hang upon her neck. But the eyes were by turns eager, absent, or sad, with now and then an upward look that showed how dark and lustrous they were. A most significant but not a beautiful face, because of its want of harmony, for the deep eyes among their fair surroundings disturbed the sight as a discord jars upon the ear; even when they smiled the shadow of black lashes seemed to fill them with a gloom never quite lost. The voice too, which should have been a girlish treble, was full and low as a matured woman's, with a silvery ring to it occasionally, as if another and a blither creature spoke. (20–21)

CHAPTER II: MOOR

MOOR was pacing to and fro along the avenue of overarching elms that led to the old Manse. The May sunshine flickered on his uncovered head, a soft wind sighed among the leaves, and earth and sky were full of the vernal loveliness of spring. But he was very lonely, and this home-coming full of pain, for he had left a grave behind him, and the old house was peopled only with tender memories of parents and sister, whose loss left him a solitary man. The pleasant rooms were so silent, the dear pictured faces so eloquent, the former duties and delights so irksome with none to share them, that he was often drawn to seek forgetfulness in the sympathy and society without which his heart was hungry and life barren.

Nature always comforted him, and to her he turned, sure of welcome, strength, and solace. He was enjoying this wordless, yet grateful communion as he walked along the grass-grown path where he had played as a boy, dreamed as a youth, and now trod as a man, wondering who would come to share and love it with him, since he was free now to live for himself.

For an hour he had lingered there, letting thought, memory, and fancy weave themselves into a little song called "Waiting," and was about to go in and put it upon paper, when, as he paused on the wide door-stone for a last look down the green vista, a figure appeared coming from the sunshine into the shadows that made the leafy arches cool and calm as a cathedral aisle.

He knew it at once, and went to meet it so gladly that his face gave a welcome before he spoke. It was Sylvia with a book in her hand, the end of her mantle full of fresh green things, and her eyes both shy and merry as she said when they met,—

"Prue stopped at the Lodge to see Mrs. Dodd, and I ran on to beg pardon for stealing this, as she bade me; also to ask if I could have the other volumes, which I am longing to read."

"With pleasure, and anything else in my library. What made you choose this?" asked Moor, turning the pages of "Wilhelm Meister" with an inquiring smile as they went on together.

"I heard some people talking about 'Mignon,' and I wanted to know who she was; but when I asked for the book Papa said, 'Tut, child, you are too young for that yet.' It always vexes me to be called young, because I feel very old; I was seventeen in April, though no one will believe it."

Sylvia pushed back her hat as she spoke, and lifted her head with a disdainful little air at the stupidity of her elders, looking very young indeed with her lap full of the pretty weeds and mosses children love.

"I was just wishing for a playfellow, for Tilly is rather too young. If your mature age does not prevent your enjoying what I can offer, we may amuse ourselves till Miss Prue arrives. Will you go in and rummage the library, or shall we roam about and enjoy the fine weather?" asked Moor, finding his guest much to his liking, she was in such harmony with time and place.

"Let us go into the garden; I used to walk there very often, and like it very much, it is so old-fashioned and well kept," answered Sylvia, leading the way to a gate in the hawthorn hedge, beginning to redden in the late May sunshine.

Just beyond lay trim beds of herbs; in a warm corner stood a row of beehives, and before them, watching to see the busy people go in and out, sat a little child, humming in pretty mimicry of the bees, who seemed to take her for a flower, so harmlessly did they buzz about her.

Hearing steps, she turned, and at sight of Sylvia uttered a cry of joy, scrambled up, and came running with outstretched arms, for "Silver" was her dearest playmate.

The girl caught her up to kiss the red cheeks, fondle the curly head, and let the chubby hands pat her face and pull her ribbons.

"Tilly has missed you. Do not let her wait so long again, but feel that the garden is as much yours now as ever," said Moor, enjoying the pretty picture they made together.

"I thought I should be in the way, but I did long to come. I hate calls generally, and Prue was charmed when I proposed to make this one. How nice it looks here now!" And Sylvia glanced about her as if glad to be again in the quiet place which still seemed haunted by the presence of the happy family who had lived and loved there.

"This is the old herb-garden put to rights. My father planted it, my mother kept her bees here, and both used to sit upon this rustic seat, he reading Evelyn, Cowley, or Tusser, while she watched her boy and girl playing here and there. A very dear old place to me, though so solitary now."

The voice was cheerful still, but something in the look that wandered to and fro as if searching for familiar forms touched Sylvia, and with the quick instinct of a sympathetic nature she tried to comfort him by showing interest in the spot he loved.

"Let me sit here and play with Tilly while you tell me something about herbs, if you will. I've read of herb-gardens, but never saw one before, and find it quaint and pleasant."

She had evidently proposed a congenial pastime, for Moor looked gratified, and while she settled Tilly in her lap with a watch and chatelaine to absorb her little wits and fingers, he went to and fro, gathering a leaf here, a twig there, till he had a small but odorous nosegay to offer her. Then he came and sat beside her, glad to tell her something of the origin, fine associations, and grateful properties which should give these comfortable plants a place in every garden.

"Here is basil, an old-fashioned herb no longer cultivated in this country," he began. "I see you have read Keats's poem; that gives it a romantic interest, but it has a useful side also. Zelty tells us that 'the smell thereof is good for the head and heart; its seed cureth infirmities of the brain, taketh away melancholy, and maketh one merrie and glad. Its leaves yield a savory smell, and it is said the touch of a fair lady causeth it to thrive.' The farmers in Elizabeth's time used to keep it to offer their guests, as I do mine." And Moor laughingly laid the green sprig in Sylvia's hand.

She liked the fancy, and stroked the leaves with as sincere wish that they might thrive as any ancient lady who had a firmer faith in the power of her touch. Seeing her interest, Moor selected another specimen and went on with his herbaceous entertainment.

"Here is fennel. The physicians in Pliny's time discovered that, having wounded a fennel stalk, serpents bathed their eyes in the juice; thus they learned that this herb had a beneficial effect upon the sight. This perhaps is the reason why old ladies take it to church, that neither sleep nor dimness of vision may prevent their criticising each other's Sunday best."

Sylvia laughed now, and asked, touching another sprig,—

"Is this lavender?"

"Yes. It takes its name 'à lavendo' from bathing, being much used in baths for its fragrance in old times. In England I saw great fields of it, and when in blossom it was very lovely. It was said that the previous balm called nard was drawn from shrubs which grew only in two places in Judæa, and these spots were kept sacred to the kings."

"I can give you a feminine bit of information in return for your wise one. The blossom gives its name to a pretty color, which with a dash of pink makes violet,—my favorite tint, it is so delicate and expressive."

Moor glanced at her hair for the snood he liked to see her wear; but it was gone, and Tilly's great blue eyes were the only reminder of what Sylvia's should have been to make her face as harmonious as it was attractive. With an imperceptible shake of the head he hastened to finish his list, studying his listener meantime as carefully as she did the herbs which he laid one by one upon her knee.

"Here are several sorts of mint, and rosemary once used at weddings and funerals; sweet marjoram and sage, so full of virtues that the ancients had a saying, 'Why need a man die while sage grows in his garden?' 'There's rue for you, and here's some for me; we may call it herb of grace o' Sundays.' And this is thyme."

"I know a bank whereon the wild thyme grows," hummed Sylvia, as if his lines reminded her of one of her favorite songs.

Tilly looked up and began to hum also; then, being tired of the trinkets, ran away to catch a white miller that flew by. "Do the bees never sting her?" asked Sylvia, as she thanked her host and put the little posy in her belt.

"No; she has been taught not to touch them, and they never hurt her. I suspect they understand one another, for there is a sort of free-masonry among children, birds, bees, and butterflies, you know. Some grown people possess it. I have a friend who can charm the wildest creatures, and attract the shyest people, though he is rather an imposing personage himself. You have the same gift, I think, if I may judge by the pets I saw about you once."

"Perhaps I have, for I can always get on with dumb animals, they are so honest and simple. People tire me, so I fly to the woods when books give out," answered the girl, with a sigh, remembering how many hours these friends had brightened when Prue scolded and Max tormented her.

Thinking she was weary of the herb-garden, Moor was about to propose going on, when Prue's voice was heard, and they went to meet her. Leading them in, their host entertained one sister in the drawing-room, leaving the other to enjoy herself at her own sweet will in the library.

It was a pleasant place, lofty, cool, and quiet. Pines sighed before two deep windows, green draperies and a mossy carpet of the same hue softened the sunshine that came in at a third window, before which stood the writing-table. The ancient furniture seemed at home there, the book-lined walls invited one to sit and read, and a few fine pictures refreshed the eye as it wandered from Correggio's Fates, above the old-fashioned fireplace, to portraits of poets, or the busts of philosophers sitting up aloft, serenely presiding over the wit and wisdom of ages stored on the shelves below.

Sylvia enjoyed herself immensely as she roved to and fro, full of girlish curiosity and more than girlish interest in this studious place. She peeped into the portfolios, tried the ancient chairs, pondered over the faces on the walls, and scrutinized the table where a little vase of early wild-flowers stood among wise books in unknown tongues, and many papers suggested brainwork of some sort. Coming at last to a certain cabinet where favorite authors seemed to be enshrined, she possessed herself of the much-desired volumes, and sat down in a great velvet chair to read on. But the murmur of voices disturbed her, and she fell to musing with her eyes on the weird Sisters hanging just above her.

She was wondering how it would have fared with her if this quiet homelike place had been her home, that sweet-faced woman her mother, the benign old man her father, and she the sister to whom Geoffrey had devoted so many years. Would she have been better, happier than now, if she had grown up in the atmosphere of domestic peace, affection, and refinement that still seemed to pervade the place and make its indefinable but potent charm? Her own home was not harmonious, and she felt the need of cherishing as much as a motherless bird in a chilly nest. She had neither the skill nor power to change anything, she could only suffer and submit, wondering as she did so why fate was not kinder.

The old place had always been wonderfully attractive to her, and now, as she sat in the heart of it, she felt a curious sort of content, and wished to stay, sure that it would be long before she tired of this restful and congenial spot. The soft arms of the old chair embraced her as if she sat in a grandmother's capacious lap; the pines whispered a soothing lullaby, the perfume of herbs recalled that pleasant half-hour in the garden; and the little picture of happy parents and children rose before her again, making the silence and solitude doubly pathetic.

Moor found her sitting so, and thought the musing little figure far more agreeable than prim Prue in her rustling plum-colored silk and best bonnet.

"Your sister has kindly gone to give my housekeeper some directions for my comfort. What can I do for you meantime, Miss Sylvia?" he said, with such a friendly air that she felt no hesitation in freely asking anything caprice suggested.

"I was wondering if there was any way of making those old women spin our threads as we want them. They look very stern and pitiless," she said, pointing to the picture.

"If I believed in fate, I should say No; but as I do not, I think we *can* twist our own threads very much as we will, if we only have the patience and courage to try."

"Don't you think there are some persons born to be dissatisfied, defeated in all ways, and dreadfully unhappy?"

"Many people are born with troubles of mind or body that try them very much, but they can be outlived, subdued, or submitted to so sweetly that the affliction is a blessing in disguise. 'Man is his own star,' you know, and a belief in God is far better than any superstition about fate."

Remembering what his own life had been, Sylvia felt that he practised what he preached, and was ashamed to say more about the moods that tormented her and made a blind belief in fate so easy to her. She was strongly tempted to speak, for confidence seemed natural with Moor, and the few times they had met had already made them friends. She wished she was little Sylvia again, to sit upon his knee and tell her perplexities as she once told her childish troubles, sure of help and sympathy. But young as she was in years, the girl was fast changing to the woman, and learning to hide what lay nearest her heart. So now she smiled and turned to another picture, saying with a cheerier ring in her voice, as if caught from his,—

"I'll try for the patience and the courage then, and let the old sisters spin as they will. Please tell me who that is? It looks like Jove, but has no eagle nor thunderbolts."

Moor laughed as he pushed away the curtain that she might see the fine engraving better as it hung in the recess above the cabinet.

"That is a modern Jove, the writer of the book you like so well, Goethe."

"What a splendid head! I wish he lived now, I would so love to see and know him. I always envied Bettina and longed to be in her place. People nowadays are so unheroic and disappointing, even the famous ones."

"I can show you a man who resembles this magnificent old fellow very much. He is not so great a genius, but sufficiently 'many-sided' to astonish and perplex his friends as much as young Wolfgang did his during the 'storm and stress period.' I hope to see him here before long, and I am sure you will not find him unheroic, though he may be disappointing."

"If he looks like that, and is honest and wise, I don't care how odd he may be. I like original people who speak their minds out and don't worry about trifles," said Sylvia, looking upon the picture with great favor.

"Then he will suit you. I will say no more, but leave you to find him out alone; that always adds to the interest of a new acquaintance." And Moor smiled to himself at the prospect of a meeting between his tempestuous friend and this precocious little girl whom he had already named Ariel in his fancy.

"May I dare to ask about this picture too? It is so beautiful I feel as if I ought to pay my respects to the sweet lady of the house."

Sylvia stood up as she spoke, and made a little gesture of salutation, with her eyes on the face of the portrait in the place of honor above the writing-table.

The color came into Moor's cheek, and he thanked her with a look she long remembered; for this mother had been very dear to him and made him what he was. Gladly he told her many things that made the hour sweet and memorable to both listener and narrator; for the son was eloquent, and Sylvia found the woman he described her ideal of that dearest, loveliest of human creatures, a good mother. Tears were in both their eyes when he paused, but the girl begged him to go on, and he told the pathetic little story of his patient sister, making Sylvia ashamed of her visionary trials, and deepening her newly awakened interest in this man to admiration and respect, though he said nothing of himself.

Prue came bustling in as he ended, and there was no chance for poetry or pathos where she was. Their host went with them to the great gate, and they left him standing bareheaded in the rosy sunset that wrapped Sylvia in a soft haze as she went musing home, while Moor lingered back along the path that was no longer solitary, for a slender figure seemed to walk beside him, with tender, innocent eyes looking into his. (31–42)

CHAPTER IV: WARWICK

A WILD STORM had raged all night, and now, though the rain had ceased, the wind still blew furiously and the sea thundered on the coast. It had been a dull day for Sylvia, and she had wandered about the house like an unquiet spirit in captivity. She had sewed a little while with Prue, stood an hour to Max as Clytemnestra with a dagger in her hand, read till her eyes ached, played till her fingers were weary, and at last fallen asleep in the sofa corner when even day-dreams failed to lighten her ennui.

She was wakened by a watery gleam of sunshine, and, welcoming the good omen, she sprung up, eager as a caged bird for air and liberty.

"The sea will be magnificent after this gale, and I must see it. Prue will say no if I ask her, so I will run away, and beg pardon when I come back," thought Sylvia, as she clasped her blue cloak and caught up the hat she never wore when she could help it.

Off she went, through byways, over walls, under dripping trees, and among tall grass bowed by the rain, straight toward the sea, whose distant music sounded like a voice calling her to come and share its tempestuous mood. The keen wind buffeted her as she ran, but its breath kissed fresh roses into her pale cheeks, filled her lungs with new life, and seemed to sweep her along like a creature born to love and live in such wild hours as this. The lonely cliffs looked like old friends to her, though wearing their grimmest aspect, with torn seaweed clinging to them below and foam flying high up their rough fronts. The tide was coming in, but a strip of sand still lay bare, and, climbing down, sure-footed as a goat, Sylvia reached the rock which usually rose tall and dry from the waves that rolled in and out of the little bay. It was wet now, and the path that led to it rapidly narrowing as the tide rose higher with each billow that hurried to dash and break upon the shore.

"Ah, this is glorious!" sighed the girl, with a long breath of the sweet cold air that came winging its way across the wide Atlantic to refresh her. "Now I shall by happy, and can sing my heart out without disturbing any one."

Wrapping her cloak about her, she leaned in the recess that made her favorite seat, and let her voice rise and ring above the turmoil of the waves, as if she too felt the need of pouring out the restless spirit pent up in that young breast of hers. Sweet and shrill sounded the mingled music, and the wind caught it up to carry it with flecks of foam, sea scents, and flying leaves to the cliffs above, where a solitary figure stood to watch the storm.

A strange medley, for the girl set her songs to the fitful music of wind and wave, finding a sort of ecstasy in the mood that now possessed her, born of the hour and the place. Ariel's dirge mingled with the Lorelei's song, and the moaning of the Harbor Bar died away into a wail for Mary on the sands of Dee.

The narrow strip of beach was dwindling to a thread, and on that thread a life depended; but Sylvia did not see it, and the treacherous tide crept on.

The first exultation over, she let her thoughts voyage away as if carried by the ships whose white wings shone against the dark horizon like sea-birds flying to distant homes. She longed to follow with the vague desire that tempts young hearts to sigh for the unknown, unconscious that the sweetest mysteries of life lie folded up in their own bosoms. She pictured in the fairest colors the new world that lay beyond the dim line where sky and ocean met and melted. What friends should she find, what happiness, what answer to the questions that no on could solve here? Would she ever sail away across this wide sea to reach and rest in that fair country, peopled with all the beautiful, heroic shapes her hungry heart and eager fancy conjured up? She hoped so, and, dreaming of the future, utterly forgot the peril of the present.

An ominous sound was in the air, and each billow broke higher on the rock where she lay wrapped in her own thoughts; but Sylvia never heeded, and the treacherous tide crept on.

From wondering and longing for the unknown of this world she passed to marvelling what the change would be when she landed on the shore of that other world, where every wave that breaks carries a human soul. She longed to know, and felt a strange yearning to find again the mother whose very name was but a memory. The tender tie broken so soon still seemed to thrill with a warmth death could not chill, and the girl often felt irresistibly drawn to seek some clearer knowledge, some nearer hold of this lost love, without which life was lonely and the world never could be home to her.

Tears dropped fast, and, hiding her head, she sobbed like a broken-hearted child grieving for its mother. She never let Prue know the want she felt, never told her father how powerless his indulgent affection was to feed this natural craving, nor found elsewhere the fostering care she pined for. Only in hours like these the longing vented itself in bitter tears, that left the eyes dim, the heart heavy for days afterward.

A voice called her from the cliff above, a step sounded on the rocky path behind, but Sylvia did not hear them, nor see a figure hurrying through the deepening water toward her, till a great wave rolled up and broke over her feet, startling her with its chill.

Then she sprung up and looked about her with a sudden thrill of fear, for the green billows tumbled everywhere, the path was gone, and the treacherous tide was in.

A moment she stood dismayed, then flung away her cloak, and was about to plunge into the sea when a commanding voice called, "Stop, I am coming!" And before she could turn a strong arm caught her up, flung the cloak round her, and she felt herself carried high above the hungry waves that leaped up as if disappointed of their prey.

On the first dry slope of the path she was set down, unmuffled by a quick hand, and found herself face to face with a strange man, who said with a smile that made her forget fear in shame,—

"Next time you play Undine have a boat near, for there may be no Kuhlborn at hand to save you."

"I never was caught before, and could easily have saved myself by swimming. Nevertheless, I thank you, sir, though I am hardly worth a wetting."

Sylvia began petulantly, being nettled by the satiric glimmer in the keen eyes fixed upon her; but she ended courteously, though her own eyes were still wet with sadder tears than any from the sea.

"Shall I drop you back again? Nothing easier, if you prefer to weep your life away down there to making it useful and pleasant up here," said the man, still smiling, but with a sudden softening of the face as he read sorrow, not sentimentality, in the young countenance before him.

It touched Sylvia with its quick sympathy, and simply as a child she said, lifting those lovely eyes of hers full of gratitude and grief,—

"I was crying for my mother, and I think if you had not come I should have been glad to go to her."

"Make her glad and proud to welcome you, and never think yourself ready for death till you have learned to live. Shall we go up higher?"

As he spoke the man led the way, and the girl followed, feeling rebuked and comforted at the same time. Half-way up he paused on a little green plateau that nestled in a sunny crevice of the cliff. A hardy flower or two grew there, a slender birch and a young pine stood side by side, and birds were chirping in the branches as they brooded on their nests. It was a pretty place midway between sea and sky, sheltered and safe yet not solitary, for the ocean sang below, the sun shone warmly above, and every air that blew brought some hint of land or sea.

"Rest a moment here; the path above is a steep one and you are breathless," said the man, looking down at Sylvia much as the tall cliffs looked at the little pimpernel close shut in its pink curtains among the stones at their feet.

"It is the wind that takes my breath away. I like to climb, and can show you an easier path than that," said the girl, gathering up the hair that blew about her face in a golden cloud.

"I always take the shortest way, no matter how rough it is. Never fear, I'll pull you up if you will trust me."

"I will, because I know you now." And Sylvia smiled as she looked at the vigorous frame and fine face before her.

"Who am I?" asked the stranger, amused at her answer.

"Adam Warwick."

"Right. How did you guess?"

"Mr. Moor said you were like a picture in his study, and you are. I thought it was meant for Jupiter, but it was Goethe."

Sylvia got no further, for Warwick laughed out so heartily she could not resist joining him, as she leaned against the little birch-tree, glad to get rid of her sadness and embarrassment so easily.

"He glorifies his friends like a woman, and I thank him for saying a good word in behalf of such a vagabond as I. You are Max Yule's sister? I was sure of it when I saw you singing like a mermaid down there. He used to tell of your pranks. I see he did not exaggerate."

Sylvia was annoyed at the idea of her brother's tales, and wished Moor had told her something of this person, that she might know what manner of man he was and treat him accordingly. She was not afraid of him, though he looked very tall and powerful, standing straight and strong against the cliff, with the dark shadow of the pine upon him. A masterful man, she thought, but a kindly one, and original in speech and manner at least, for the first was very blunt and the latter decided, yet genial at moments.

"Shall we go on?" said the girl, anxious to escape all discussion of herself.

"Yes; it is getting late and we are wet. Now then!" And, taking her hand, Warwick literally did pull her up the face of the cliff in half a dozen vigorous strides and swings, planting her on the top and still holding her, for the wind blew a gale above there.

She liked it, however, and stood a moment laughing and panting, while the blue cloak flapped and the long hair fluttered in spite of her efforts to confine it under her hat. Something fresh and strong seemed to have taken possession of her, and a pleasant excitement made her eyes shine, her cheeks glow, her lips smile, and life look happy in spite of the trials that she had just been bemoaning.

Agreeable as it was to watch that buoyant little figure, and listen to its frank conversation, Warwick, more mindful of her damp feet than his own dripping ones, said presently,—

"This is a fine sight, but we must leave it. I shall come again, and hope to find you here rather than down below."

"I shall not try that again, nor this either," answered Sylvia. "It is sad and dangerous in that cave of mine, it is too rough and high and gusty up here for me, but in Mr. Moor's little nook half-way between it is safe and sunny, and there one gets the best of both sea and sky, with green grass and birds and flowers."

Warwick looked at her keenly as she spoke, reading in her face, her tone, her gesture, a double significance to her simple words.

"You are right; keep to the happy, wholesome places in life, and leave the melancholy sea, the wandering winds, and craggy peaks to those who are made for them."

Sylvia glanced up as if surprised at being so well understood, but before she could speak Warwick moved on, saying in a different tone,—

"Will you come to the Manse and be made comfortable? I arrived unexpectedly and Geoffrey is away, but I shall be glad to play host in his absence."

"Thanks, I will run home at once. No one knows where I am, and Prue will begin to worry if I don't appear. Come and let my father thank you better than I can."

"I will. Good-night." And with a nod and a smile they parted, Warwick to tramp down the avenue without looking back, and Sylvia to hasten home, feeling that if she went out seeking for adventures, she certainly had been gratified.

She said nothing to Prue, and when, later in the evening, Moor brought his friend to see Max and inquire for the half-drowned damsel, she emerged from behind the curtains looking as brilliant and serene as if salt water and gales of wind agreed with her admirably.

As Warwick was formally presented to the sisters, Sylvia put her finger on her lips and with a look besought silence regarding her last prank. Warwick answered with a quick glance, a courteous greeting, and turned away as if they had never met before. Moor smiled, but said nothing, and soon the gentlemen were deep in conversation, while Prue dozed behind a fire-screen and Sylvia sat in the sofa corner studying the faces before her. (50–58)

Here several neighbors came in, and when the little stir was over the girl found Warwick on the sofa, to which she had retired again as the guests were absorbed by other members of the family. She thought he would allude to their first meeting, but he sat silently scrutinizing the faces before him as if quite unconscious of his little neighbor.

"I must say something," thought Sylvia, when the pause had lasted several minutes, and, turning toward him, she asked rather timidly,—

"Don't you care for conversation, Mr. Warwick?"

"I seldom get any."

"Why, what is that going on all about us?"

"Listen a moment and you will hear."

She obeyed, and began to laugh, for her ear received a medley of sounds and subjects so oddly blended and so flippantly discussed that the effect was very ludicrous. On one side she heard, "Mr. Moor, it was the divinest polka I ever danced;" on the other Prue was declaring, "My dear, nothing is so good for an inflamed eye as a delicate alum curd;" behind her Max was tenderly explaining, "You see, Miss Jessie, it is the effect of this shadow which gives the picture its depth and juiciness of tone;" and above all rose Mr. Yule's decided opinion that "We must protect our own interests, sir, or the country is in danger."

"Do you like pictures?" asked Sylvia, changing the subject, as her first venture proved a failure.

"That sort very much," answered Warwick, with a glance at the various faces he had been studying so intently.

"So do I!" cried the girl, feeling that they should get on now, for she loved to study character in that way, and was quick to read it. "I fancy faces are the illustrations to the books which people are. Some titlepages are very plain to read, some very difficult, a few most attractive; but as a general thing I don't care to go farther. Do you?"

"Yes; I find them all interesting and instructive, and am never tired of turning the pages and reading between the lines. Let us see how skilful you are. What do you call Max?" asked Warwick, looking as if he found the small volume just opened to him rather attractive.

"He is a portfolio of good, bad, and indifferent pictures. I hope he will fall to work and finish one at least; the portrait of a happy man and a successful artist." And Sylvia's eyes were full of wistful affection as they rested on her handsome, indolent brother, who never gave her an opportunity to be proud of him.

"I think he will if he does not waste his time studying fashion-plates," said Warwick, regarding the young lady whom Max was evidently wooing, very much as a lion might regard a butterfly.

"There is a heart under the ruffles, and we are all fond of Jessie. Don't you think her pretty, sir?"

"No."

"That's frank," though the girl, adding aloud, "Why not?"

"Because she has no more character in her face than the white rose in her hair."

"But the rose has a very sweet odor, and no thorns for those who handle it gently, as flowers should be handled," said Sylvia, with a reproachful look from her brother's happy face to the rather grim one beside her.

"I am apt to forget that, so I get pricked, and deserve it. Will Max's sister forgive Max's friend, who sincerely wishes him well?"

"With all my heart, and thank you for the wish," cried the girl readily, adding in a moment with womanly tact, "But I did not finish my catalogue. Do you want to hear the rest and tell me if I am right?"

"Yes; who comes next?"

"Prue is a receipt book, Mr. Moor a volume of fine poems, and Papa a ledger with dead flowers and old love-letters hidden away in its dull-looking leaves."

"Very good; and what am I? Come, you have made up your mind, I think, and I shall like to see how correct you are."

Sylvia hesitated an instant, but something in the commanding voice and the challenge of the eye gave her courage to answer with a smile and a blush,—

"You remind me of Sartor Resartus, which I once heard called a fine mixture of truth, satire, wisdom, and oddity."

Warwick looked as if he had got another prick, but laughed his deep laugh, exclaiming in surprise,—

"Bless the child! how came she to read that book?"

"Oh, I found it and liked it, for, though I could not understand all of it, I felt stirred and strengthened by the strong words and large thoughts. Don't you like it?" asked Sylvia, taking a girlish pleasure in his astonishment.

"It is one of my favorite books, and the man who wrote it one of my most honored masters."

"Did you ever see him?" asked the girl eagerly.

He had, and went on to tell her in brief, expressive phrases much that delighted and comforted her, for she was a hero-worshipper and loved to find new gods to look up to and love.

It was a delicious half-hour to Sylvia, for the talk wandered far and wide, led by intelligent questions, eloquent answers, and mutual enthusiasm; though almost a monologue, she felt that this was conversation in the true sense of the word. Moor stole up behind them and listened silently, enjoying both speaker and listener, who welcomed him with a look and felt the charm of his genial presence.

The end came all too soon, and Sylvia was forced to leave the fine society of poets and philosophers and bid her neighbors good-night. She felt as if she had fallen from the clouds, and with a vague hope of continuing the pleasant talk she said to Warwick, as they stood together while Moor made his adieux with the old-fashioned courtesy Mr. Yule liked,—

"Tell me what sort of book I am; and tell me truly as I did you."

"'The Story without an End.' Did you ever read it?" he asked with the look of benignity that sometimes made his face beautiful.

"Yes; I wish I might be as lovely, innocent, and true as that is. Thank you very much." And Sylvia put her small hand into the large one as confidingly as the child in the pretty allegory might have done, feeling better for the cordial grasp that accompanied his good-night.

"How do you like Adam, sir?" asked Max of his father when the family were alone.

"A fine man, but he needs polishing," answered Mr. Yule, who had found his guest interesting, but far too radical for his taste.

"What is your opinion, Prue?"

"He rather affects me like a gale of wind, refreshing, but one never known where one may be carried; and when he looks about with those searching eyes of his, I am painfully conscious of every speck of lint on the carpet, for nothing seems to escape him," answered Prue, setting the disordered furniture to rights, lest the thought of it should keep her from sleeping.

"Well, Sylvia, is he odd enough to suit your taste?"

"I like him very, very much, only I feel unusually young and small and silly beside him, and he makes me dreadfully tired, much as I enjoy him."

She looked so, as she pressed her hands against her flushed cheeks, for her eyes were bright and eager, her whole air unquiet yet weary, and she wore the look of inward excitement which henceforth was to mark her intercourse with Adam Warwick.   (63–68)

CHAPTER V: AFLOAT

A WEEK LATER Sylvia sat sewing in the sunshine one lovely morning, longing to roam away as she used to do, but restrained by a hope stronger than obedience to Prue's commands. She had been left much to herself of late, for Max had been away with Moor and Warwick, enjoying themselves in their own fashion, and the girl had only had brief glimpses of the three friends. Max brought home such tantalizing accounts of their sayings and doings that she felt an ever increasing desire to share the good things which were more to her taste than girlish trifles or the solitary revels she used to like.

"I don't see why I must sit here and hem nightcap strings when the world is full of pleasant places and delightful people, if I could only be allowed to go and find them. Prue is much too particular, and thinks all men alike. I know they would like to have me over there if Max would only take me. I've stood hours for him and he forgets it. Brothers are all self-ish, I'm afraid. I wish I were a boy, or could be contented with what other girls like."

Here voices roused her from her reverie, and looking up she saw Max and his friends approaching. Her first impulse was to throw down her work and run to meet them, her second to remember her dignity and sit still, awaiting them with well-bred composure, quite unconscious that the white figure among the vines added a picturesque finish to the scene.

They came up warm and merry from a brisk row across the bay, and Sylvia greeted them with a face that gave a heartier welcome than her words, as she began to gather up her work when they seated themselves in the bamboo chairs scattered along the wide piazza. (69–70)

Stories were told, comic, weird, and stirring, and when it came to Sylvia's turn Max said,—

"We have worked and you have played; now while we rest amuse us with some of your dramatic pictures and pieces, as you do me when you are tired of posing. Make that rock your dressing-room and come out into the firelight when you are ready. She really has a very pretty talent for that sort of thing, and I've taught her to drape and pose well."

Excited by the day's pleasure and emboldened by the shadows, Sylvia needed little urging, for she was very grateful and ardently desired to make herself agreeable in return for the willing service of her "knights and gentlemen." She vanished, taking with her a red rug, a white shawl, and her blue cloak as wardrobe. The friends sat talking of the great actors they had known, and forgot her for the moment. A sudden start from Moor, who faced the rock, made the others turn to see Ophelia standing on the smooth plat of grass that lay between the fire and the sombre pines that made a most effective background for the white figure with its crown of ferns, wild weeds, and falling hair. One hand held the folds of the shawl that draped her, the other slowly drew from it the flowers Sylvia had gathered that day, to offer them now to imaginary spectators with vacant smiles, wandering eyes, and broken snatches of song the more pathetic for their gayety.

Even Max was surprised by the grace and skill with which she played her part; the others looked in silence too charmed to break the spell, and when the poor girl dropped her last garland on the mimic grave with plaintive music, and then went smiling and courtesying away to her sad end, they sat a moment silent with sympathy, before their applause assured the young actress that her effort was successful.

Quicker than they thought possible she was there again, still wrapped in the same shawl, a white scarf about the head, and a pine cone in her hand to represent a candle, for this was Lady Macbeth walking in her haunted sleep. The sightless eyes were fixed, the brow knit with remorseful pain, the hands wrung together as the light fell, and the lips apart to vent the heavy breathing of a sleeper. She spoke the words in a muffled tone that gave an awful meaning to her ominous confessions, and when she vanished, beckoning her accomplice away, the watchers seemed to see the guilty pair going to their doom.

"That is wonderful! The child has more than talent, Max, or has been trained by a better master than yourself," said Moor, looking charmed yet troubled by his display of unsuspected power.

"She has it in her, and needs no master. It is a perilous gift, but has its uses, for the pent-up emotions can find a safer vent in this way than in melancholy dreams or daring action," answered Warwick, remembering the tragic face he had caught a glimpse of when he saved Sylvia from the sea.

"She is a wonderful little thing in many ways, and I often puzzle my head thinking what will become of her, for I am convinced she will never settle down like other girls without some sort of tribulation or adventure," said Max, much flattered by the commendation of his friends.

"It will be interesting to watch the unfolding of this modern Mignon; I hope I shall be here to see it," answered Moor, little dreaming how hard a part he was to play in the drama of Love's Labor Lost.

"Let her alone, give her plenty of liberty, and I think time and experience will make a noble woman of her," added Warwick, feeling a strong sympathy for this ardent girl, who with all the luxury about her still hungered for a food she could not find.

A blithe laugh recalled them, and Rosalind sauntered from behind

the rock wrapped in the cloak, with a little cap improvised from a blue silk
handkerchief upon her tucked-up curls, and a switch in her hand, saying
aside as she feigned to meet Orlando,—

"I'll speak to him like a saucy lacquey, and under that habit play the
knave with him. I pray you, what is't o'clock?"

Then with quick changes of voice and manner from the half-
indifferent man to the audacious maid, she gave the scene between the two
with a spirit and grace which kept her listeners laughing till she disap-
peared looking over her shoulder with a face full of merry malice as she led
the invisible Orlando away.

"Capital! Bravo! Encore!" cried the audience, eager for more; and
inspired by their hearty pleasure, Sylvia gave them the balcony scene from
Romeo and Juliet leaning over the rock with all her bright hair unbound,
white arms bare, and shawl and scarf disposed as effectively as circumstances would permit against the scarlet rug.

This was the best of all, and a revelation even to her brother; for the
excitement of former efforts, the desire to do her best, and the indescribable charm the part always had for her, made her act the impassioned Juliet
to the life. Place and hour aided her, for the moon had risen and shone into
the little glade, lending to the romantic figure an enchantment no stage
moon ever gave it. Max also helped her, for he had played the part, and,
burning to distinguish himself, sprang forward to make a comely Romeo,
in spite of the high boots, blue flannel shirt, and waterproof mantle. He put
Jessie Hope in Sylvia's place, and wooed her so ardently that she was able
to act with all her heart, rendering the tender speeches with looks and
gestures full of an innocent abandon both delightful and dangerous to the
beholders.

"What a lover she will make when the time comes," thought Moor,
with a thrill, as she leaned to Romeo full of a love and longing which made
the girlish face wonderfully eloquent.

"What power and passion the little creature has! and a voice to lure a
man's heart out of his breast," said Warwick, as Juliet cried, with her arms
about her lover's neck,—

> "Sweet, so would I;
> Yet I should kill thee with much cherishing.
> Good-night! good-night! parting is such sweet sorrow,
> That I shall say good-night till it be to-morrow!"

Then, as if abashed at her forgetfulness of self, Sylvia slipped behind the rock, leaving her Romeo to resume his place, exclaiming complacently,—

"That was not bad, I fancy. Shakespeare forgive me for the liberties I took with him! I haven't acted since I played this part with Fräulein Hoffmann in Munich last year. She had no more idea of the part than that cow looking over the wall at us, but Sylvia really did very well."

"Too well for one of her age, I am afraid. Yet it was very lovely," said Moor, looking as if he still saw the white arms outstretched, and heard the tender words.

"Sentiment is perilous stuff; better let her get rid of her romance in mimic love scenes than in real ones, or leave it fermenting in that precocious head and heart of hers."

Yet Warwick had enjoyed it most of all, and was the first to rise and thank her when she came demurely back to her seat, with no sign of the actress about her but a deeper color in the usually pale cheeks, and eyes that seemed to have lost their shadows and grown young.

She took their praises modestly, rejoicing inwardly over the new sense of power that came to her as she saw not only admiration but wonder and respect in the faces of those she most desired to please. Generally she cared nothing for the regard of men, but these two were different from any she had known, and she felt that whatever they gave her was worth the having.

They sat late, for sleep had been banished by pleasure, and they lingered talking over the immortal characters which will always be full of intense interest to those who love to study human nature as painted by the Master who seemed to have found the key to all the passions, and set them to a music of which we never tire.

A distant clock struck eleven; Max suggested bed, and the proposition was unanimously accepted.   (82–87)

CHAPTER VII: A GOLDEN WEDDING

HITHERTO they had been a most decorous crew, but the next morning something in the air seemed to cause a general overflow of spirits, and they went up the river like a party of children on a merry-making. Sylvia decorated herself with vines and flowers till she looked like a wood-nymph; Max, as skipper, issued his orders with the true nautical twang; Moor kept up a fire of fun-provoking raillery; Warwick sang like a jovial giant; the

Kelpie danced over the water as if inspired by the universal gayety, and the very ripples seemed to laugh as they hurried by.

"This is just the day for adventures; I hope we shall have some," said Sylvia, waving her bulrush wand as if to conjure up fresh delights of some sort.

"I should think you had enough yesterday to satisfy even your adventurous soul," answered Max, remembering her forlorn plight the night before.

"I never have enough! Life was made to enjoy, and each day ought to be different from the last; then one wouldn't get so tired of everything. See how easy it is. Just leave the old behind and find so much that is new and lovely within a few miles of home. I believe in adventures, and mean to go and seek them if they don't come to me," cried Sylvia, looking about her as if her new kingdom had inspired her with new ambitions.

"I think an adventure is about to arrive, and a very stirring one, if I may believe those black clouds piling up yonder." And Warwick pointed to the sky where the frolicsome west-wind seemed to have prepared a surprise for them in the shape of a thundershower.

"I shall like that. I'm fond of storms, and have no fear of lightning, though it always dances round me as if it had designs upon me. Let it come; the heavier the storm the better. We can sit in a barn and watch it rave itself quiet," said Sylvia, looking up with such an air of satisfaction the young men felt reassured, and rowed on, hoping to find shelter before the rain.

It was after lunch, and, refreshed by the cooler wind, the deepening shadows, the rowers pulled lustily, sending the boat through the water with the smooth speed given by strength and skill. Sylvia steered, but often forgot her work to watch the faces rising and falling before her, full of increasing resolution and vigor, for soon the race between the storm and the men grew exciting. No hospitable house or barn appeared, and Max, who knew the river best, thought that this was one of its wildest parts, for marshes lay on one hand, and craggy banks on the other, with here and there a stretch of hemlocks leaning to their fall as the current slowly washed away the soil that held their roots. A curtain of black cloud edged with sullen red swept rapidly across the sky, giving an unearthly look to both land and water. Utter silence reigned as birds flew to covert, and cattle herded together in the fields. Only now and then a long, low sigh went through the air like the pant of the rising storm, or a flash of lightning without thunder seemed like the glare of angry eyes.

"We are in for a drenching, if that suits you," said Max, turning from the bow where he sat, ready to leap out and pull the boat ashore the instant shelter of any sort appeared.

"I shall just wrap my old cloak about me and not mind it. Don't think of me, and if anything does happen, Mr. Warwick is used to saving me, you know."

Sylvia laughed and colored as she spoke, but her eyes shone and a daring spirit looked out at them as if it loved danger as well as his own.

"Hold fast then, for here it comes," answered Adam, dropping his oar to throw the rug about her feet, his own hat into the bottom of the boat, and then to look beyond her at the lurid sky with the air of one who welcomed the approaching strife of elements.

"Lie down and let me cover you with the sail!" cried Moor anxiously, as the first puff of the rising gale swept by.

"No, no; I want to see it all. Row on, or land, I don't care which. It is splendid, and I must have my share of it," answered Sylvia, sending her hat after Warwick's, and sitting erect, eager to prove her courage.

"We are safer here than in those woods, or soaking in that muddy marsh, so pull away, mates, and we shall reach a house before long, I am sure. This girl has had the romance of roughing it, now let us see how the reality suits her." And Max folded his arms to enjoy his sister's dismay, for just then, as if the heavens were suddenly opened, down came a rush of rain that soon drenched them to the skin.

Sylvia laughed, and shook her wet hair out of her eyes, drank the great drops as they fell, and still declared that she liked it. Moor looked anxious, Warwick interested, and Max predicted further ills like a bird of evil omen.

They came, whirlwind and rain; thunder that deafened, lightning that dazzled, and a general turmoil that for a time might have daunted a braver heart than the girl's. It is one thing to watch a storm, safely housed, with feather-beds, non-conductors, and friends to cling to; but quite another thing to be out in the tempest, exposed to all its perils, tossing in a boat on an angry river, far from shelter, with novelty, discomfort, and real danger to contend with.

But Sylvia stood the test well, seeming to find courage from the face nearest her; for that never blenched when the sharpest bolt fell, the most vivid flash blinded, or the gale drove them through hissing water, and air too full of rain to show what rock or quicksand might lie before them. She did enjoy it in spite of her pale cheeks, dilated eyes, and clutching hands;

and sat in her place silent and steady, with the pale glimmer of electricity about her head, while the thunder crashed and tongues of fire tore the black clouds, swept to and fro by blasts that bowed her like a reed.

One bolt struck a tree, but it fell behind them, and just as Moor was saying, "We must land; it is no longer safe here," Max cried out,—

"A house! a house! Pull for your lives, and we will be under cover in ten minutes."

Sylvia never forgot that brief dash round the bend, for the men bent to their oars with a will, and the Kelpie flew like a bird, while with stream- ing hair and smiling lips the girl held fast, enjoying the rapture of swift motion; for the friends had rowed in many waters and were masters of their craft.

Landing in hot haste, they bade Sylvia run on, while they paused to tie the boat and throw the sail over their load, lest it should be blown away as well as drenched.

When they turned to follow, they saw the girl running down the long slope of meadow as if excitement gave her wings. Max raced after her, but the others tramped on together, enjoying the spectacle; for few girls know how to run or dare to try; so this new Atalanta was the more charming for the spirit and speed with which she skimmed along, dropping her cloak and looking back as she ran, bent on outstripping her brother.

"A pretty piece of energy. I didn't know the creature had so much life in her," said Warwick, laughing as Sylvia leaped a brook at a bound and pressed up the slope beyond, like a hunted doe.

"Plenty of it; that is why she likes this wild frolic so heartily. She should have more of such wholesome excitement and less fashionable dissipation. I spoke to her father about it, and persuaded Prue to let her come," answered Moor, eagerly watching the race.

"I thought you had been at work, or that excellent piece of propriety never would have consented. You can persuade the hardest-hearted, Geof- frey. I wish I had your talent."

"That remains to be seen," began Moor; then both forgot what they were saying to give a cheer as Sylvia reached the road and stood leaning on a gate-post panting, flushed, and proud, for Max had pressed her hard in spite of the advantage she had at the start.

They found themselves, a moist and mirthful company, before a red farm-house standing under venerable elms, with a patriarchal air which promised hospitable treatment and good cheer,— (118–23)

CHAPTER VIII: SERMONS

THE SUMMER SHOWER was over long before dawn, and the sun rose, giving promise of a sultry day. It was difficult to get away, for the good people found their humdrum life much enlivened by these pleasant guests. The old lady consoled herself by putting up a sumptuous lunch from the relics of the feast; the grateful wanderers left their more solid thanks in Nat's pocket, and departed with friendliest farewells.

It was Sunday, and the chime of distant church bells tolled them sweetly down the river, till the heat drove them to the refreshing shade of three great oaks in a meadow where a spring bubbled up among the gnarled roots of one tree to overflow its mossy basin, and steal into the brook babbling through the grass.

Here they lunched, and rested, the young men going off to bathe, and Sylvia falling asleep among the ferns that fringed the old oak like elves dancing round a giant. A delicious hour for her, so still, so green, so grateful was all about her, so peaceful her own spirit, so dreamless her tranquil slumber. Nature seemed to have taken her restless little child to her beneficent bosom, and blessed her with the sleep which comforts mind and body.

So Warwick thought, coming upon her unaware as he paused to drink, and a soft gust parted the tall ferns that waved above her. She looked so young, so peaceful, and so happy on her green couch, with the light shadows flickering on her face, her head pillowed on her arms, ease, grace, and the loveliness of youth in every limb and outline, that Warwick could not resist the desire to linger for a moment.

Max would have seen a pretty picture; Moor, the creature whom he loved; Adam seemed to see not only what she was, but what she might be. Some faces are blank masks when asleep, some betray the lower nature painfully, others seem to grow almost transparent and let the soul shine through. This comes oftenest when suffering has refined the flesh, or death touched it with the brief beauty that writes the story of a lifetime on perishable clay before it crumbles into dust. In certain high and happy moods unconsciousness brings out harmonious lines, soft tints, and ennobles a familiar face till we feel that we see the true self, and recognize the soul we love.

It seemed so then; and as he leaned against the oak, listening to the music of the brook and looking down at the winsome figure at his feet, Warwick found himself shaping the life and character of the woman still folded up in the girl, and shaping it to fit an ideal he had made and cherished, yet never met. An heroic creature, strong and sweet, aspiring as a flame, and true as steel. Not an impossible woman, but a rare one; and the charm Sylvia had for him was a suggestion of this possibility when time had taught and discipline tamed the wildness that was akin to his own.

He let his daring fancy paint her as she would be ten years hence, himself her lover, and the life they might lead together, as free as his was now, but happier for the inspiration of such sweet and helpful comradeship.

He had forgotten Sylvia, and was just entering a new world with the noble mate he had evoked from his own ardent and powerful imagination, when Moor's distant voice startled him, and, as if unready to be seen in that soft mood, he swung himself up into the tree, rapidly disappearing in the green wilderness above.

The same sound roused Sylvia, and made her hasten to bathe her face with cool drops caught in her hands, to rebraid her long hair, and retrim her dress with knots of wild-flowers at throat and belt; then, her rustic toilet made, she stepped out of her nest, rosy, fresh, and sunny as a little child just waking from its nap.

Fancying a green band for her head, she strolled away to the river-side where the rushes grew, and took her little Bible with her, remembering the commands pious Prue laid upon her "not to be quite a heathen while she was gone."

She lingered for half an hour, feeling unusually devout in that tranquil spot, with no best clothes to disturb her thoughts, no over-fussy sister to vex her spirit, no neglected duties or broken resolutions to make church-going a penitential period of remorse. When she returned to the oaks she found the three friends discussing religion as young men seldom fail to do in these days of speculation and spiritual discontent. She modestly hovered at a distance till a pause came, then approached, asking meekly,—

"Please, could I come to church if I sit very still?"

"Come on," said Max, from the grass where he was lying.

Moor sprang up to offer her the rug with an air of welcome which she could not doubt, and Warwick nodded with a somewhat belligerent expression, as if suddenly checked in some verbal tournament.

"Prue said if we stayed over Sunday I must go to church, and I have done my best," said Sylvia, glancing at the little book in her hand. "Now, if Mr. Moor or Mr. Warwick would give us a sermon, Max and I can say we obeyed her."

"Come Geoffrey, your memory is full of good and pious poetry; give us something new and true. We needn't sing it, but it may suggest a sermon, and that is more in Adam's line than yours," added Max, ready to while away another hour till the afternoon grew cooler.

Moor thought a moment, and then, as if their conversation suggested it, repeated one of Herbert's quaint old hymns.

> "Lord, with what care hast thou begirt us round!
>   Parents first season us: then schoolmasters
> Deliver us to laws; they send us bound
>   To rules of reason, holy messengers,
>
> "Pulpits and Sundayes, sorrow dogging sinne,
>   Afflications sorted, anguish of all sizes,
> Fine nets and stratagems to catch us in;
>   Bibles laid open, millions of surprises;
>
> "Blessings beforehand, tyes of gratefulness;
>   The sound of glorie ringing in our eares;
> Without, our shame; within, our consciences;
>   Angels and grace, eternall hopes and feares.
>
> "Yet all these fences and their whole array,
> One cunning bosome-sin blows quite away."

"There is your text, Adam, take it and hold forth; you were born for a field preacher and have missed your vocation. I wish you would turn minister and beat the dust out of some of the old pulpit cushions, for we need a livelier theology than most of us get nowadays," said Max, as Moor paused and Sylvia looked as if the hymn pleased her much.

"If I did stray into a pulpit you would get the gospel undiluted, and sins of all sorts would fare hardly, for I would cry aloud and spare not."

"Try it now; it will be immensely amusing to be raked fore and aft while lounging here as if we were getting to heaven 'on flowery beds of ease.' Begin with me. I'm fair game, and furnish material for a dozen sermons on a dozen sins," laughed Max, hoping to draw his friend out and astonish his sister.

"Good! I will." And Warwick looked as if belaboring frail humanity was a task he relished.

"Your bosom sin is indolence of soul and body, heart and mind.

Fortune has been our bane, liberty ill used, life your plaything, not your lesson; for you have not learned how to use either fortune, liberty, or life. Pride is your only energy; patience simple endurance of whatever you have not courage to overcome; ambition a vacillating desire for success which every failure lessens, and the aim of existence is to be carried painlessly through a world waiting for every man to help on its salvation by making his own life a victory, not a defeat. Shall I go on?"

"Fire away; every shot tells. It is rather sharp rifle-practice while it lasts, but the target is the better for it, I dare say."

Max spoke gayly and still lounged on the grass; but Sylvia knew, by the gesture that half averted his face, and the interest with which he punched holes in the turf, that it *was* rather hard upon one more used to praise than blame. Warwick knew it also, and there was a perceptible softening of the ruthless voice as he went on.

"You need a purpose, Max, an object beyond your own satisfaction or success. This would show you what good gifts you now neglect, teach you their uses, and prove to you that the best culture lies in perfecting these tools for the education of yourself and others. Adversity may spur you into action, love may supply a noble motive, or experience make you what you should be,—a man with a work and a will to do it. You owe this to your father, and I believe the debt will be honestly paid."

"It shall be!" And Max sat up with a sudden energy pleasant to behold. Resolution, regret, and affection made his usually listless face manly and serious as well as tender, for that allusion to his father touched him, and the thought of Jessie lightened a task he knew would be a very hard one.

Always quick to spare others embarrassment or pain, Moor said pleasantly, "Now take the next member of your flock, and do not spare him, Adam."

Warwick looked as if he would rather let this sheep go, but, loving justice as well as truth, he hardened his heart and spoke out.

"You are enamored of self-sacrifice, Geoffrey, and if you lived in monkish times would wear a spiked girdle or haircloth shirt, lest you should be too comfortable. Unlike Max, you polish your tools carefully and are skilful in handling them, but you use them entirely for others, forgetting that we owe a good deal to ourselves. You have made a small circle your world, and lived in the affections too much. You need a larger life and more brain-work to keep you from growing narrow or weak. One sacrifice beautifully and faithfully made must have its reward. For years you have lived for others, now learn to live a little for yourself, heartily and happily, else the feminine in you will get the uppermost."

"Thank you, I will as soon as possible." And Moor gave Warwick a look which was both grateful and glad, since the friendly advice confirmed a cherished purpose of his own.

"Lost lamb, come into the fold and be shorn!" called Max, enjoying Sylvia's face, which wore an expression of mingled interest, amusement, and trepidation. With a start she gathered herself up, and went to sit on a little stone before the censor, folding her hands and meekly asking,—

"What must *I* do?"

"Forget yourself."

Sylvia colored to her brow, but answered bravely,—

"Show me how."

"My panacea for most troubles is work. Try it, and I think you will find that it will promote that healthfulness of spirit which is the life of life. Don't let fogs hide your sunshine; don't worry your young wits with metaphysics, or let romantic dreams take the charm from the wholesome, homely realities, without which we cannot live sanely and safely. Get out of yourself a while, and when you go back you will find, I hope, a happy soul in a healthy body, and be what God intended you to be, a brave and noble woman."

Warwick saw the girl's color rise, her eyes fall, and in her face a full acknowledgment of the veracity of both censure and commendation. That satisfied him, and before she could speak he turned on Max, saying with a sudden change from gentle gravity to the satiritcal tone more habitual to him,—

"Now you will say, 'Physician, heal thyself,' and ask for my chief sin. I'll give you a sample of it."

Then, looking very much like a war-horse when trumpets blow, he launched into a half-earnest, half-humorous philippic against falsehood everywhere, giving to his vigorous speech the aids of satire, sense, and an unusually varied experience for one of his age. Max sat up and applauded, Moor listened with delight, and Sylvia felt as if the end of all things was at hand. Such an audacious onslaught upon established customs, creeds, and constitutions, she had never heard before; for, as Warwick charged, down went the stern religion that preaches heaven for the saint and hell for the sinner, the base legislation which decrees liberty to the white and slavery to the black, the false public opinion that grants all suffrages to man and none to woman yet judges both alike,—all knavery in high places, all gilded shams, all dead beliefs,—and up went the white banner of infinite justice, truth, and love. It was a fight well fought but not wholly won; for in spite of sagacity, eloquence, and zeal, Warwick's besetting sin was indomitable, and those who listened, while they owned the sincerity, felt the power, admired the enthusiasm, saw that this valiant St. George rode without a Una, and in executing justice forgot mercy, like many another young crusader who, in his ardor to set up the New Jerusalem, breaks the commandments of the Divine Reformer who immortalized the old.

When at last he reined himself in, looking ready for another breakage of idols at the slightest provocation, Max said with a waggish glance at his sister,—

"You seem to be holding on to that stone as if you thought the foundations of the earth were giving way. How do you like your sermon, Sylvia?"

"Very much, what I understand of it; but I do feel as if there had been an earthquake, and it will take me some time to get settled again. It is a little startling to have all the props one has been taught to lean upon knocked away at once, and be left to walk alone without quite knowing where the road ends."

Max laughed; Moor looked as if she had exactly expressed the feeling most persons felt after one of Adam's "upheavals," as his friend called them; but Warwick said, with his decided nod, as if well pleased,—

"That is just as it should be. I'm a pioneer, and love to plough in any soil, no matter how sandy or rough it may be. The sower comes after me, and if the harvest is a good one, I am satisfied to do the hard work without wages."

He certainly received them this time, for Sylvia looked up at him as he rose, evidently tired of longer repose, and said, with the sweetest confidence and gratitude in her face,—

"Let me thank you for this and many other lessons which will set me thinking, and help me to be what you so kindly hope. I shall not forget them, and trust they have not fallen on a barren soil."

It was not a child's face that Warwick saw then, but a woman's, earnest, humble, and lovely with the awakening of an innocent, aspiring soul. Involuntarily he took his hat off, with a look both reverent and soft.

"A virgin soil is always the richest, and I have no fear that the harvest will fail. Heaven send you sun and rain, and a wise husbandman to help you gather it in."

Then he went away to get the boat ready for the evening sail. Max went off to a farm-house for milk, and Moor and Sylvia were left alone.

Touched to the heart by the blessing that came with redoubled power from lips so lately full of denunciation, the girl still sat upon her little stone, seemingly wrapped in thoughts that both excited and troubled her, for presently she sighed.

Moor, who lay reading in the grass, stealing a glance at his companion now and then, was glad of an opportunity to speak, and, sitting up, asked in his friendly voice,—

"Has all this talk tired you?"

"No, it has stirred me up and made me feel as if I must lay hold of something at once, or drift away I don't know where. Mr. Warwick has pulled my world to pieces, but has given me no other, and I don't know where to look. His philosophy is too large for me, I get lost in it, and though I admire I cannot manage it yet, and so feel bewildered." Sylvia spoke out as if the thoughts in her mind must find a vent at any cost, and to no one could she so freely utter them as to this friend who was always kind and patient with her moods.

"You must not let Adam's thunder and lightning disturb you. We have seen the world through his glass, which, though a powerful one, is not always well regulated, so we get a magnified view of things. He is a self-reliant genius, intent on his own aims, which, fortunately, are high ones, for he would go vigorously wrong if it were not for the native integrity which keeps him vigorously right. He has his work to do, and will do it manfully when he gets through the 'storm and stress period' of which I told you."

"I like it because I think I am in a little period of my own. If I dared, I should like to ask you how best to get out of it."

"You may ask anything of me!"

Sylvia spoke hesitatingly, but Moor's eager answer made it easy to go on, it was so clear that these confidences were acceptable; she little knew how much so.

"Do you believe in sudden conversions?" she asked presently.

"Yes; for often what seems sudden is only the flowering of some secret growth, unsuspected till the heat of pain or passion calls it out. We feel the need of help that nothing human can give us, instinctively ask it of a higher power, and, receiving it in marvellous ways, gratefully and devoutly say, 'I believe.'"

"That time has not come to me." Then, as if a wave of feeling too strong to be repressed rolled up and broke into words, Sylvia rapidly went on: "I know that I need something to lean upon, believe in, and love; for I am not steadfast, and every wind blows me about. I try to find the help I want. I look into people's faces, watch their lives, and endeavor to imitate all that I admire and respect. I read the best and wisest books I can find, and tire my weak wits trying to understand them. I pray prayers, sing hymns, and go to church, hoping to find the piety which makes life good and happy. I ask all whom I dare to help me, yet I am not helped. My father says, 'Keep happy, dear, and no fear but you will get to heaven.' Prue says, 'Read your Bible and talk to the Bishop.' Max laughs, and tells me to fall in love if I desire beatitude. Every one assures me that religion is a blessed thing and salvation impossible without it, yet no one gives me a simple sustaining faith to love, to lean on, and live by. So I stumble to and fro, longing, hoping, looking for the way to go, yet never finding it, for I have no mother to take me in her arms and show me God."

With the last words Sylvia's voice broke, and she spread her hands before her face; not weeping, but overcome by an emotion too deep for tears.

Moor had seen many forms of sorrow, but never one that touched him more than this motherless girl hiding a spiritual sorrow on the bosom of a rock. Sylvia had ceased to seem a child, and this was no childish grief to be comforted with a kind word. She was a woman to him, dearer and deeper-hearted that she knew, yet he would not take advantage of this tender moment and offer her a human love when she asked for the divine. His own religion was that simplest, perhaps truest type, which is lived, not spoken; an inborn love of godliness, a natural faith, unquestioning, unshakable by the trials and temptations of life. But this piety, though all pervading and all sustaining as the air, was as hard to grasp and give to another. It was no easy task for one humble in his own conceit, a young man and a lover, to answer such an appeal, the harder for the unspoken confidence in him which it confessed. A wise book lay upon his knee, a good book had slipped to Sylvia's feet, and, glancing about him for inspiration in that eloquent pause, he found it there. Never had his voice sounded so sweet and comfortable as now.

"Dear Sylvia, I understand your trouble and long to cure it as wisely and tenderly as I ought. I can only tell you where I have found a cure for doubt, despondency, and grief. God and Nature are the true helper and comforter for all of us. Do not tire yourself with books, creeds, and speculations; let them wait, and believe that simply wishing and trying to be good is piety, for faith and endeavor are the wings that carry souls to heaven. Take Nature for your friend and teacher. You love and feel near to her already; you will find her always just and genial, patient and wise. Watch the harmonious laws that rule her, imitate her industry, her sweet sanity; and soon I think you will find that this benignant mother will take you in her arms and show you God."

Without another word Moor rose, laid his hand an instant on the girl's bent head in the first caress he had ever dared to give her, and went away leaving her to the soothing ministrations of the comforter he had suggested.

When they all met at supper Sylvia's face was as serene and lovely as the sky "clear shining after rain," though she said little and seemed shy of her older comrades; both of whom were unusually thoughtful of her, as if they felt some fear that in handling this young soul they might have harmed it, as even the most careful touch destroys the delicate down on the wing of the butterfly, that is its symbol.

They embarked at sunset, as the tide against which they had pulled in coming up would soon sweep them rapidly along and make it easy to retrace in a few hours the way they had loitered over for days.

All night Sylvia lay under the canopy of boughs Moor made to shield her from the dew, listening to the soft sounds about her; the twitter of a restless bird, the bleat of some belated lamb, the ripple of a brook babbling like a baby in its sleep, the fitful murmur of voices mingling with the plash of water as sail or oar drove them on. All night she watched the changing shores, silvery green or dark with slumberous shadow, and followed the moon in its tranquil journey through the sky. When it set, she drew her cloak about her, and, pillowing her head upon the sweet fern Warwick piled for her, exchanged the waking for a sleeping dream as beautiful and happy.

A thick mist encompassed her when she awoke. Above the sun shone dimly, below rose and fell the unquiet tide, before her sounded the city's hum, and far behind lay the green wilderness where she had lived and learned so much. Slowly the fog lifted, the sun came dazzling down upon the sea, and out into the open bay they sailed with the blue pennon streaming in the morning wind. But still with backward gaze the girl watched the misty wall that lay between her and that charmed river, and still with wondering heart confessed how sweet that brief experience had been; for, though she had not yet discovered it, like the fairy Lady of Shalott,

> "She had left the web and left the loom,
> Had seen the water-lilies bloom,

Had seen the helmet and the plume,
    And had looked down to Camelot." (140–55)

"The sweetest woman I ever met," then checked himself and said more quietly, as if to turn the conversation, "This moonlight recalls our voyage up the river and our various adventures."

"Ah, that happy voyage! I wish it had been longer," answered Sylvia in a tone of such intense regret it was plain she had forgotten nothing. "It is too lovely to go in just yet; come and walk, and talk a little of that pleasant time."

She beckoned as she spoke, and he came out of the shadow wearing a look she had never seen before. His face was flushed, his eye unquiet, his manner eager yet restrained. She had seen him intellectually excited, but never emotionally till now. Something wayward yet warm in this new mood attracted her because so like her own. But with a tact as native as her sympathy, she showed no sign of observing this change, and, fancying some memory or care oppressed him, tried to cheer him by speaking of the holiday he had recalled.

"What did you enjoy most in those four days?" she asked, as they paced slowly up the avenue side by side.

He longed to answer "Our walk together," for that little journey hand in hand seemed very precious to him now, and it was with difficulty he refrained from telling her how beautiful it would be to have that slender figure always walking with him on the longer pilgrimage which of late looked lonely and uninviting. But he folded his arms, averted his eyes, and said briefly,—

"All was pleasant; perhaps the Golden Wedding most so."

"Yes, that did me so much good. I never shall forget it. I think that voyage was the happiest time I ever knew. I seemed to learn more in those few days than in years at home, and all my lessons were helpful ones, for which I shall be better and happier, I am sure."

She spoke earnestly, still looking up, and the moonlight showed how grateful, how perilously sweet and candid, the young face was. Warwick saw it with a quick glance, and said within himself, "I too learned a lesson; better I may be, but not happier." Then aloud, and with a laugh that did not ring quite true,—

"I see my sermon was laid to heart, harsh as it seemed when preached. Some of the melancholy moods were left behind, I think, and brighter ones brought home, if we may judge from the metamorphosis of the dripping Undine I first met to the happy girl who now makes sunshine for us all."

"Yes; I feel as if I found my soul there in the woods, and learned how to keep it in better order than when I half longed to have the sea rid of me of the care of such a restless, troublesome guest."

"You found a soul, and I lost a heart," thought Warwick, still carrying on that double conversation; for even love could not subdue the sense of humor which made much sentiment impossible. Aloud he added, more genially,—

"I often make these excursions into the wilderness when civilization tires or troubles me, and always find medicine for my impatient spirit in the quiet, freedom, and good company waiting for me there. Try it again when other things fail, and so keep serene and happy as now."

"I will. Mr. Moor told me the same, and I like the prescription, for the desire of my life is to be as sunshiny, wise, and excellent as he is."

"You could not have a better model or set your life to finer music than he does. Have you ever read his poetry?"

Warwick spoke heartily now, and seemed glad to slip away from a subject too interesting to be quite safe for him.

"No. Max said he wrote, and I hope I shall see it some time when he thinks I am worthy of the honor. Do you make poems also?" asked Sylvia, as if any feat were possible to this new friend of hers.

"Never! An essay now and then, but pen work is not in my line. First live, then write. I have not time to let fancy play, when hard facts keep me busy."

"When you do write, I think it will be very interesting to read what you have lived. Max says you have been visiting prisons all over the world, and trying to make them better. That is a brave, good thing to do. I wish I were old and wise enough to help," said Sylvia, with such respect and admiration in face and voice that Warwick found it impossible to restrain a fervent—

"I wish you were!" adding more calmly, "I love liberty so much myself, that my sympathy naturally turns to those deprived of it. Yet the saddest prisoners I find are not in cells, and they are the hardest to help."

"You mean those bound by sins and sorrows, temperaments and temptations?"

"Yes, and another class tied by prejudices, creeds, and customs. Even duties and principles make slaves of us sometimes, and we find the captivity very hard to bear."

"I cannot imagine you bound by anything. I often envy you your splendid freedom."

"I am bound this moment by honor, and I long to break loose!"

The words broke from Adam against his will, and startled Sylvia by their passionate energy.

"Can I help you? The mouse helped the lion, you remember?"

She spoke without fear, for with Warwick she always felt the sort of freedom one feels with those who are entirely sincere and natural, sure of being understood, and one's sympathy received as frankly as it is offered.

"Dear mouse, you cannot! This net is too strong, and the lion must stay bound till time or a happy fortune sets him free. Let us go in."

The sudden change from the almost tender gratitude of the first words to the stern brevity of the last ones perplexed Sylvia more than any of the varying moods she had seen that night, and with a sudden sense of some dangerous electricity in the mental atmosphere, she hastened up the steps before which Warwick had abruptly halted.

Pausing on the upper stair to gather a day-lily from the urn that stood there, she looked back an instant before she vanished, and he seemed to see again the Juliet he so well remembered leaning to her lover and bathed in the magic moonlight of the wood.

"That did the mischief; till then I thought her a child. The romance of that scene took me unawares, and all that followed helped the sweet poison work. A midsummer night's dream which I shall not soon forget."

With a long breath of the cool air, an impatient sigh at his own weakness, and a half-angry tug at his brown beard, Warwick went to the drawing-room looking very like the captive lion Sylvia had spoken of.

She was not there, and he fell upon the first trifling task he found, as if "in work was salvation, in idleness alone perpetual despair."

Sylvia soon appeared with the basket of Berlin wools she had promised to wind for her sister.   (160–64)

"Now I know why I am happy!"

How long she lay there musing in the moonlight she never knew. Her sister's call broke in upon the first love dream she had ever woven for herself, and she went down to bid the friends good-night. The hall was only lighted by the moon, and in the dimness no one saw traces of that midsummer shower on her cheeks, nor detected the soft trouble in her eyes, but for the first time Moor felt her hand tremble in his own, and welcomed the good omen joyfully.

Hating all forms, Warwick seldom shook hands, but that night he gave a hand to all with his most cordial expression, and Sylvia felt both her own taken in a warm lingering grasp, although he only said, "Good-by!" Then they went; but while the others paused on the steps, held by the beauty of the night, back on the wings of the wind came Warwick's sonorous voice singing the song that Sylvia best loved. All down the avenue and far along the winding road they traced his progress, till the music died in the distance, leaving only the echo of the song to link them to the singer.

When evening came again the girl waited on the lawn to greet the friends, for love made her very shy. But Moor came alone, and his first words were,—

"Console me, Sylvia, Adam is gone. He went as unexpectedly as he came, and when I woke this morning a note was all the farewell I found."

Pride kept her from betraying the sharp pang this disappointment cost her, and all that evening she seemed her gayest self, supported by an unnatural excitement till alone.

Then the reaction came, and Sylvia spent the night struggling with doubt, despair, shame, and bewilderment. She had deceived herself. It was not love she saw in Adam's eyes last night, but pity. He read her secret before that compassionate glance revealed it to herself, and had gone away to spare her further folly. She was not the woman of whom he thought, forgetful of time and place, of whom he spoke with such a kindling face, to whom he had gone so eagerly when absence grew unbearable.

All night she tortured herself with this idea, but in the morning hope came, always the first consoler of the young, whispering that she *had* read that look aright, that some promise bound him which he had gone to be released from, and when free he would write or come to her. To this hope she clung, saying to herself,—

"He is so true, I will trust and wait."

But days grew to weeks, and Warwick neither wrote nor came. (169–70)

CHAPTER X: NO

NOVEMBER, the dreariest month of all the year, had come; leaves lay sear and sodden on the frosty ground, and a chill rain dripped without as if joining in the lamentation of the melancholy wind.

Winter fires were kindled, and basking in the full glow of one of these lay Sylvia, coiled up in a deep chair, solacing her weariness with recollections of the happiest summer of her life.

As books open at pages oftenest read, she had been reliving that memorable voyage, the brightest hours of which were those spent with Warwick, guarding these as tenderly as patient Elaine guarded the shield, waiting for Launcelot to come again.

So vividly did those days return to her, that Sylvia forgot the pain of suspense, the thorn of regret, and war far away; so strong was the power of Adam's influence upon her even in absence, that he seemed to be before her; so intense was her longing to feel again the touch of his hand, that like one in a dream she stretched her own toward the vision, whispering, half aloud,— (171)

CHAPTER XII: WOOING

"Well, I met a friend from England to-day who told me came across old Adam, who was preparing to join one of the Polar expeditions. Isn't that just like him?" And Max went on with a laugh.

As if chilled by a breath from that icy region, Sylvia's last half-unconscious hope died then and she gave herself with entire abandon to the happiness of others.

Moor had written to his friend when his suit failed, but the letter was still following Warwick in his wanderings, and, receiving no reply, Moor waited to hear some tidings of him before he wrote again to tell his happy news; while Adam, finding time and absence fail to lessen his love, seemed to have decided to go to the ends of the earth and cool his passion among the icebergs.

Max went on to consult Prue about his wedding gloves, and Jessie began to display her purchases before eyes that only saw a blur of shapes and colors.

"I should enjoy my pretty things a thousand times more if you would only please us all by being married when we are," sighed Jessie, looking at her veil.

"I will."

"What, really? Sylvia, you are a perfect darling! Max! Prue! she says she will!"

Away flew Jessie to proclaim the glad news, and Sylvia, with a curious expression of relief and resolve, repeated to herself that decided "I will." (195)

CHAPTER XIV: SYLVIA'S HONEYMOON

"How could I till I heard that Geoffrey had failed? He told me he should labor long and wait patiently till he won you, and I could not doubt that he would succeed. I went away singing the farewell I dared not speak, and for a year have kept myself hard at work. If ever labor of mine is blessed it will be that, for into it I put the heartiest endeavor of my life.

"So strong was my impulse to return to you that I put the sea between us, for I could not trust myself, and knew that Geoffrey would write me if he failed. He did; but, as if Providence meant to teach me patience, that one letter went astray and never reached me till two weeks ago."

"My fate!" sighed Sylvia bitterly.

"No, my fault. I should have written, but I feared to betray myself to Geoffrey. It is hard to hide my thoughts behind words. I knew he would discover me, and sacrifice himself. I meant he should be happy at all costs. I did write him before I was to leave on my long voyage; but the lost letter arrived, and, never waiting for his reply to mine, I came as fast as steam could bring me to find you and tell you this."

He bent to give her a tender welcome to eager heart and arms, but Sylvia arrested him.

"Not yet, Adam. Tell me all, and then I will answer you."

He thought it was some maidenly scruple, and though he smiled at it he respected it; for this coyness in the midst of all her whims had always been one of her charms to him.

"Shy thing! I shall tame you yet, and draw you to me as confidingly as I drew the little bird to hop into my hand and eat. You must not fear me, or I shall grow tyrannical; for I hate fear, and love to see people freely and bravely accept what belongs to them, as I do now to you."

"It is not you I fear, it is myself," murmured Sylvia, adding aloud, anxious yet dreading to have the story done, "What led you hear, Adam, hoping so much, knowing so little?"

Warwick laughed as he shook the hair off his broad forehead, and looked down at her with a look she dared not meet.

"Do I not always aim straight at the end I have in view and pursue it by the shortest roads, heedless of obstacles? I often fail and go back to the slower, surer way; but my own is always the one tried first as impetuously as I hurled myself down that path, more as if storming a battery than going to meet my sweetheart. Among the persons I met on landing was a friend of your father's: he was driving away in hot haste with his son; but, catching a glimpse of the familiar face, I bethought me that as it was the season for summer travel, you might be away, he would know, and time be saved. (219–21)

Her husband found her sitting where he left her, but so pale it filled him with anxiety and self-reproach.

"My poor child, you are tired out, and this rarefied air is too much for you. We will go down at once and you shall rest."

"Yes, mountain-tops are too high for me; I am safer in the valley with you, Geoffrey," she answered, clinging to his arm as if quite spent with the fateful hour that waked her from a dream of forgetfulness. (227)

CHAPTER XV: A FIRESIDE FÊTE

"WELCOME to your new home. May it be a happy one to you, little dearest!" said Moor, some days later, as he led her into the old Manse, now wearing its holiday air in honor of the coming of a mistress.

"It does not seem new but very dear and lovely, Geoffrey. I was always happy here, and hope to be so now, if you are," answered Sylvia, with a wistful look in the eyes that wandered to and fro as if seeking the peace she used to find in this tranquil place.

"No fear for me since you are here. Now will you rest a little or run about and view your new kingdom before you take possession?" asked Moor, eager to see her in the place he had so often pictured her as filling.

"Come and show me everything yourself. But, Geoffrey, please let all go on as before while I learn to be a housekeeper. Mrs. Best will like that, and Prue won't worry over my failures as she did at home when she tried to teach me her own thrifty ways. I had rather be with you, if I may, and not let the prose of married life disturb the poetry too soon. Do you mind?"

Charmed with the suggestion and glad to keep her to himself, Moor readily consented, and Sylvia began her new life so quietly that little seemed changed from the old, except the constant presence of the friend who still was more like a lover than a husband, and lived for her alone, knowing nothing of the inner world his young wife hid from him.

Of Warwick's confession she had never spoken, for it came too late to bring happiness to her, too soon to make it possible for her to cloud Moor's joy by telling it. She would be as brave as Adam, and silently live down importunate memories, dangerous thoughts, vain regrets; folding the leaf over the bitter past, trying to make the present what it should be, leaving the future to Heaven's will submissively.

The knowledge that she had not given that first love of hers unsought soothed her pride, comforted her heart, and made compassion for Adam seem a safe sentiment to cherish, since any softer one was now forbidden. She had suffered so much before that now regret had lost its sharpest sting, renunciation grown easier, and a sincere desire to be worthy the regard of both the men who loved her gave her a strength that for a time at least wore the semblance of content, if not happiness.

Max wondered at the quiet life she preferred, Prue thought her wise to leave the reins in Mrs. Best's accomplished hands, and her father hoped she was safely anchored in a peaceful harbor with a very tender pilot to guard her if storms came. It seemed a lovely home, and those who saw its proud master, its little mistress, fancied that their future was without a cloud, blessed as they were with all that makes this world a foretaste of Heaven.

But the high mood which sustained Sylvia's soul at first, as the pure mountain air braced her body, slowly lost its efficacy when the strain of daily life began to wear upon her nerves, and duty passed from willing effort to a constant struggle to forget. It was possible for days, and she would think she had won an enduring calm, when some trifle would bring the old pang, some truant thought would stray from her control, some involuntary wish startle her with a fear of disloyalty, and the battle was all to be fought over again.

Moor felt a subtle change in her, indescribable, yet visible, for she seemed to have left girlhood behind her with her honeymoon, and to be pausing on the threshold of womanhood, half fearing to cross it and assume the weightier duties, more sacred joys, and tenderer hopes that lay waiting for her beyond. He had been a faithful friend and a patient lover, now he was a generous and devoted husband, leaving time and tenderness to make her wholly his. He asked no questions, made no comments, demanded no sacrifices, but bore her moods as if he loved her in any guise she chose to wear, and never doubted that he should one day understand all that perplexed or troubled him now. So three months passed, and then Moor unconsciously marred his own peace by a vain effort to please Sylvia, whose growing ennui could not escape his anxious eyes.

"Just a year to-night since a hard-hearted little girl said she would not even try to love me. I thought she would change her mind, and this proves that I was right. Were you thinking of it also?" he asked, coming into the study one dull November evening to find Sylvia in the great chair gazing at the fire that glowed on the wide hearth.

She looked up and smiled, as she always did when he joined her.

"No; this splendid fire reminded me of another before which I once sat roasting corn and apples, and telling stories."

"Ah, that was our voyage up the river. You enjoyed that very much, I remember."

"Yes, I was a little girl then, and felt so free, so happy, it is impossible to forget it."

Sylvia spoke honestly, for she was always true when it was possible, as if the memory of one secret made her anxious to have no more.

"Dear child, you speak as if you had left youth far behind you and 'age had clawed you in its clutch,'" said Moor, leaning over the high chair-back to smooth the wavy gold of the beloved head that leaned there.

"I do feel very old sometimes. My responsibilities rather weigh upon me, and I want to drop them for an hour and be a little girl again. Just one of my moods; don't mind it, Geoffrey."

"Nothing shall burden you if I can help it. Drop these troublesome responsibilities now, and be a little girl again. I'll show you how."

Moor spoke so cheerfully, looked so well pleased at something, and seemed so ready to grant her wish that Sylvia sat up with an inquiring face, a lighter tone in her quiet voice.

"You are always ready to please me and I'm very grateful dear. What shall we do? You look as if you had some nice little plan or surprise waiting to be told."

"I have; but my surprise comes to-morrow, and you can amuse your-self with guessing what it is till then. My plan now is to sit upon the rug and roast apples, pop corn, tell stories, and be young again. It is so rainy no one will come, unless Max happens in, and he will give us another comrade. I wish Adam were here, then we should have all the actors in that pretty little play of ours."

Sylvia did not echo the wish aloud, but as if the escape from thought by action, she sprang up eagerly, and Moor, fancying the plan pleased her well, threw himself heartily into it for her sake.

"That sweeping dress of yours and the crown of hair with which you try to make yourself look matronly will never do for the little girl. Run away and change yourself into the Sylvia you were that summer, then nothing will break the illusion. I'll put on my garden-jacket and look as much like the old Geoffrey as possible."

"Yes, do; I always like you so because you look like Shelley, with the round jacket, the fine forehead, and poetic eyes," said Sylvia, with the affectionate pride which pleased him, though he vaguely felt its lack of wifely warmth.

"I'll write you a poem in return for that compliment. Now I must set the stage and prepare for a fireside fête which shall prove that all the poetry is not gone from married life." (228–33)

"I know you did not expect us till to-morrow, but Mr. Warwick was impatient, I was a little anxious, and so we came on at once," said Miss Dane, looking about her as if the cheerful scene and faces were the reverse of what she expected to find.

Warwick also looked rather bewildered and very anxious. But Moor seemed quite satisfied with the effect of his surprise, for he had written to both simply saying that he wanted them at once.

"We are playing children to-night, so just put yourselves back a dozen years, and let us all be merry together. Sylvia, this is the cousin of whom I have told you so much. Faith, here is your new kinswoman, not as imposing as she would have been if you had not taken base advantage of us. Little dearest, I invited these friends because I thought they would do us good. I wanted you to know Faith, and could not resist the desire to catch Adam before he set off to the North Pole, if he ever does." (238–39)

CHAPTER XVI: EARLY AND LATE

Sylvia, I want to tell you something which will both amuse and interest you, I hope. Faith wrote me some time ago that she had met Adam, and found him all I had told her. He also sent me a message once, that he had discovered a superior woman, who sympathized in his ideas and purposes. I mentioned it at the time to you, I think? We so seldom hear from this nomadic fellow that news is an event."

"Yes, I remember."

Sylvia's head was bent as if to enjoy the sweetness of the flower she held, and all her husband saw was the bright hair blowing in the wind.

"Now you will laugh, for I confess that, being very happy myself, I took it into my head that these two fine creatures belonged to one another, and only needed a little gentle management to find it out. I wanted to see them together, so invited them here, knowing you would enjoy them, and hoping they would take a hint from us and go and do likewise."

"God forbid!" thought Sylvia. The pathetic unconsciousness of her husband filled her with new remorse, and made it impossible for her to wish Warwick the shadow of happiness which she vainly tried to change into its substance.

"I never thought you would turn match-maker, Geoffrey. Isn't it a dangerous part to play?" she asked, half wishing some insurmountable barrier might rise between her and the man whose presence always dominated her will and excited her heart.

"Not as I shall play it, and you can help. I fancy Adam already feels the hand of the great tamer, and that explains the new gentleness I see in him. I intend to study him and satisfy myself of this. You must say a good word for him to Faith, as you women so well know how to do. You like and believe in him; paint him in your vivid, happy way, and help her to know him. A mate like Faith is what he needs to perfect him, and we can show him this unless I am greatly mistaken."

"Perhaps for all his blindness Geoffrey is right; perhaps in this way I may atone for the pain I have given Adam. Heaven help me to do my duty and forget myself," thought Sylvia, feeling as if a new page in the tragic romance of her life was turned for her by the hand that tried to make it a tender, happy story for them all.

"I had best not meddle, Geoffrey, I am so ignorant, so unlucky. Let me see you play the good genius and not risk spoiling your work."

"I think you will soon be glad to lend a hand; most women find it impossible to abstain. I mean to make the week very pleasant to them both. Adam shall revisit his old haunts, and we will show Faith ours. In the evening we will have Prue, Max, and Jessie over here, or all go and entertain your father; so the days shall be busy and the nights cheerful with the sort of pleasure we all like best. Faith longs to know you, and I am sure she is the friend you need to fill a place I cannot fill."

A touch of regret made the last word a little sad, and Sylvia felt it like a keen reproach; but less now than ever could she tell the secret that would destroy her husband's peace and mar all his happy hopes for others. With an earnest longing to find Faith all he suggested, she answered with a look of satisfaction that gratified Moor more than her words,—

"I know that I shall love her; and if I need any one beside you, dear, she shall help me to be what I ought, to make you as happy as I wish you. Now let us speak of something else, or my telltale face will betray that we have been talking of our guests, when we meet them." (247–49)

CHAPTER XIX: WHAT NEXT?

"I feel that, and am comforted already. Tell me first which of the two who love me I should have married had fate given me a choice in time."

"Neither."

Sylvia paled and trembled, as if the oracle she had invoked was an unanswerable voice pronouncing the truth she must abide by.

"Why, Faith?"

"Because you were too young, too unstable, and guided by impulse, not by principle. You, of all women, should have waited long, chosen carefully, and guarded yourself from every shadow of doubt before it was too late."

"Had I done so, would it have been safe and happy to have loved Adam?"

"No, Sylvia, never."

"Why, Faith?"

"If you were blind, a cripple, or cursed with some incurable infirmity of body, would you not hesitate to bind yourself and your affliction to another?"

"You know I should not only hesitate, but utterly refuse."

"I do know it, therefore I venture to tell you why, according to my belief, you should not marry Adam. There are diseases more subtle and dangerous than any that vex our flesh,—diseases that should be as carefully cured, if curable, as inexorably prevented from increasing, as any malady we dread. A feeble will, a morbid mind, a mad temper, an evil heart, a blind soul, are afflictions to be as much regarded as bodily infirmities; nay, more, inasmuch as souls are of greater value than perishable flesh. (304–05)

"Then it is scarcely necessary for me to tell you that I think this unequal marriage would be but a brief one for you; bright at the beginning, dark at its end. With him you would exhaust yourself in passionate endeavors to follow where he led. He would not see this; you would not confess it, but too late you would both learn that you were too young, too frail in all but the strength of love, to be his wife. It is like a wood bird mating with an eagle; straining its little wings to scale the sky with him, blinding itself with gazing at the sun, vainly striving to fill and warm the wild eyrie, and perishing in the stern solitude the other loves."

"Faith, you frighten me! You seem to see and show me all the dim forebodings I have hidden away from myself because I could not understand or dared not face them. How have you learned so much? How can you read me so well?

"I had an unhappy girlhood in a discordant home, and there was no escape except by a marriage that would be slavery to me. Many cares and losses made me early old, and taught me to observe the failures, mistakes, and burdens of others. Since then solitude has led me to study and reflect upon the question toward which my thoughts inevitably turned."

"But, Faith, why have you never found a home and partner for yourself, as other women do?—you who are so nobly fitted for all the duties, joys, and sorrows of married life?"

"Because I never met the man who could satisfy me. My ideal is a high one, and I believe that whatever we are worthy of we shall find and enjoy hereafter is not here."

"Not even Adam? Surely he is heroic enough for any woman's ideal."

"Not even Adam, for the reasons I have told you. I know his value, and feel the charm of his strength, truth, and courage, but I should not dare to marry him. Sylvia, unhappy marriages are the tragedies of the world, and will be till men and women are taught to make principle not pleasure, love not passion, mutual fitness not reckless impulse, the guides and guards to the most beautiful and sacred relation God gives us for our best training and highest happiness."

"Ah, if some one had told me these things a year ago, how much pain I might have spared myself and others! Prue thinks whatever is is right, and poor Papa cares only to see me happy. All this will break his heart."

Sylvia paused to sigh over his great disappointment; then returned with a still heavier sigh to her own.

"Who told you so much about us? You cannot have divined it all?"

"Concerning yourself Geoffrey told me much, but Adam more."

"Have you seen him? Has he been here? When, Faith, when?"

Light and color flashed back into Sylvia's face, and the eagerness of her voice was a pleasant sound after the despair which had saddened it before. Faith answered fully and with care, while the compassion of her look deepened as she spoke,— (307–09)

"Faith, what must I do?"
"Your duty."
"And that is?"
"To love and live for Geoffrey."
"Can I ever forget? Will he ever forgive? Is there anything before me but one long repentance for the suffering I have given?"

"The young always think that life is ruined by one misfortune, one mistake; but they learn that it is possible to forget, forgive, and live on till they have wrung both strength and happiness out of the hard experience that seemed to crush them. Wait a year, do nothing hastily, lest, when the excitement of this hour is past, you find you have renounced or promised more than you can give up or perform. Geoffrey will pardon freely, wait patiently, and if I know you both, will welcome back in time a wife who will be worthy of his love and confidence."

"Can time work that miracle?" asked Sylvia, ready to learn more, yet incredulous of the possibility of such an utter change in herself.

"You have been the victim of moods, now live by principle, and hold fast by the duty you see and acknowledge. Let nothing turn you from it; shut your ears to the whispers of temptation, keep your thoughts from straying, your heart full of hope, your soul of faith, humility, submission, and leave the rest to God."

"I will! Faith, what comes next?"

"This." And she was gathered close while Faith confessed how hard her task had been by letting tears fall fast upon the head which seemed to have found its proper resting-place, as if, despite her courage and her wisdom, her woman's heart was half broken with its pity. Better than any words was the motherly embrace, the tender tears, the balm of sympathy which soothed the wounds it could not heal.

Leaning on each other, the two hearts talked together in the silence, feeling the beauty of the tie kind Nature weaves between consoler and consoled. Faith often turned her lips to Sylvia's forehead, brushed back her hair with a lingering touch, and drew her closer, as if it was very sweet to see and feel the young creature in her arms. Sylvia lay there, tearless and tranquil, thinking thoughts for which she had no words, trying to prepare herself for the life before her, and to pierce the veil that hid the future. Her eyes rested on the valley where the river flowed, the elms waved their budding boughs in the bland air, and the meadows wore their earliest tinge of green. But she was not conscious of these things till the sight of a solitary figure coming slowly up the hill recalled her to the present and the duties it still held for her.   (312–14)

"Faith has told you what has passed between us, and the advice she gives us in our present strait?"

"I submit, Sylvia; I can still hope and wait."

So humbly he said it, so heartily he meant it, she felt that his love was as indomitable as Warwick's will, and the wish to be worthy of it woke with all its old intensity, since no other was possible to her.

"It is not for one so unstable as I to say, 'I shall not change.' I leave all to time and my earnest longing to do right. Go, and leave me to grow worthy of you; and if death parts us, remember that however I may thwart your life here, there is a beautiful eternity where you may forget me and be happy."

"I will go, I will stay till you recall me, but death will not change me. Love is immortal, dear, and even in the 'beautiful eternity' I shall still hope and wait."

This invincible fidelity, so patient, so persistent, impressed Sylvia like a prophecy, and remained to comfort her in the hard year to come.   (315)

CHAPTER XX: A YEAR

SYLVIA was spared all effort but passive endurance during the first month of trial, for she fell ill. The overwrought mind preyed upon the body, and exhaustion forced both to rest. For a few days there was danger, and she knew it, yet was not glad as she once would have been. Lying in the shadow of death, her life looked such a sorrowful failure she longed for a chance to retrieve it. What had she done worth the doing? Whom had she made happy? Where was the humble satisfaction that should come hand in hand with death? There was a time when she would have answered these self-accusations by saying, "It is my fate," and so drifted on to life or death, ready for neither. Now conscience as well as heart suffered, and a nobler courage than resignation was growing in her. An earnest desire to atone, to rise above all obstacles and turn the seeming defeat into a sweet success, so possessed her that it seemed cowardly to die, and she asked for life, feeling that she had learned to use if not to enjoy it more truly than before. In those quiet weeks of enforced seclusion she grew fast, and when she rose a stronger and more patient soul shone through the frail body like the flame that makes the lamp transparent.   (320)

As if to sever the last tie that bound her to the old home and make the new one her most natural refuge, Mr. Yule died suddenly. So painlessly and peacefully that no memory of suffering, no sad decay of mind, added to the sorrow of those who loved him most. His last words had been for Sylvia, "Good-night, my daughter, and God bless you." His last kiss was given to her, and she was the first to find him in the morning wrapped in the sleep from which there was no awakening here.

Then the tender satisfaction of knowing that her dutiful affection had been all in all to him was a cordial that sustained her, lightened her grief, and for a time made the new loneliness unfelt.

Max was master now, and Jessie took the seat Prue had filled so long. Sylvia wished it so, and thought to slip into her old place again as if nothing had been changed. But it was impossible; the wayward girl was gone, and in her place a thoughtful woman who could not be satisfied with what had fed her once. Youthful pleasures, hopes, and fancies were replaced by earnest aspirations, faithful labor, and quiet joys. She dreamed no more but lived, and in holy living and high thinking found the secret of self-knowledge and self-help.

As spring came on a great longing for a home of her own grew up in her, and where should she so naturally go as to the Manse, still waiting for its mistress? When she spoke of this Max inwardly exulted and Jessie openly rejoiced; both feeling that she would not long remain content there without recalling its master. They were right; for Sylvia's resolve had been strengthening slowly ever since her father died, and to test it she went back to the home she had made so desolate. April saw her there, busy, quiet, but happy, if one might trust the serene face that seemed to brighten the closed rooms even more than the sunshine she let in. Before she left everything to others, now she set her house in order herself with a loving care which plainly betrayed it was for the coming of some dear and welcome guest.

But for the sincerity of her purpose, the warmth of her desire, the fidelity that never wavered from its duty, the memories that haunted the old house would have made it terrible to live there alone. It was sad, and with each day Sylvia longed more ardently for the return of the one companion who had the right to share it with her, the power to make it happy,—not with the former show of peace, but with a sober happiness too genuine to be wrecked again.

Hope painted a future full of content; for the suffering of the past, the hard-won repose of the present, proved that there was compensation for every loss, and that out of bitter sorrow strength and sweetness might be distilled by the Worker of all miracles.

Faith came to help her, as she had come many times that year, confirming each step she made, and cheering her to climb on with a brave heart and eyes fixed on heaven.

When all was ready Sylvia made a little pilgrimage through her Paradise Regained, lingering in many places to relive the sad or happy hours spent there; and when she came again to the study, she stood a moment, looking up at the Fates with something softer than a smile upon her face, as she said aloud,—

"I no longer fear you, pagan sisters. I am learning to spin my own life, trusting to a kinder hand than yours to weave some gold among the gray, and cut the thread when I am ready for a higher lesson."

Faith entered as she spoke, heard what she said, saw the uplifted look, felt that the time she had hoped for and believed in had come, and longed to share it with the other patient waiter.

"Sylvia, I am writing to Geoffrey. Have you any message for him, dear?"

"Yes, this."

Slowly Sylvia drew from her bosom a little note, opened it and held it before Faith, asking as a child might of its mother. "Shall I send it?"

Only three words, but Faith's heart sang for joy as she answered, "Yes!" for the words were,—

"Husband, come home." (332–34)

CHAPTER XXII: AT LAST

NEWS of the wreck reached the Yules some days before Moor could let them know of his safety and Adam's loss. The belief that both were gone was almost too much for Sylvia, and for a week she sat in the shadow of a great despair, feeling that her mistakes and weaknesses had sent them to their death.

"I was not worthy of either, and God denies me the reward I have worked so hard to earn. I could have spared Adam. I have given him up and learned to see that it was best. But Geoffrey, my husband, who had waited so long, who hoped so much, whom I was going to make so happy, never to know how well I loved him after all this pain and separation—oh, it is too hard, too bitter to lose him now!"

This was all her thought, her lamentation; Warwick seemed forgotten, the lesser loss was swallowed up in the greater, and Sylvia mourned for her husband like a woman and a wife, feeling at last the nearness and dearness of the sacred tie that bound them together. Death taught her in the anguish of that hour how impossible it was to love any other with the passion born of that pain, touched with the tender memory of his past loyalty, the fervent desire to atone by future devotion and the sincerest fidelity.

In the midst of this despair came the glad tidings that Moor was safe and on his way to her from the distant port whither the survivors had been carried by the ship that saved them.

Then Sylvia fell on her knees and made a thank-offering of her life, dedicating it with tears and prayers and voiceless hymns of gratitude to this man saved for her by the friend who loved them both better than his own life, and died so gladly for their sake.

Max thought the joy would kill her, but she came out of the room where she had lain in darkness, looking like one risen from the tomb. A peace beyond words to describe transfigured her face, "clear shining after rain," making her silence more eloquent than speech, and every hour seemed to bring new strength, beauty, and serenity to make the wan and weary body a fitter home for a soul just entering into the world of higher thought and feeling to which it had attained after much pain and struggle.

"Go and meet him, Max. I will wait for him at home, and give my welcome there. Come soon, and tell him I have no room for sorrow, my heart is so full of gratitude and joy."

May had come again and the Manse wore its loveliest aspect to greet its master, who came at last and alone. But not to an empty home, for on the threshold stood his wife, not the wayward child he wooed, the melancholy girl he married, but a woman with her soul in her face, her heart upon her lips, and outstretched arms that seemed to hold all that was dearest in the world when they clasped him with the tender cry,—

"Thank God! I have my husband safe."

They had been together for an hour. The first excitement was over, and Sylvia stood beside him pale but calm with intensity of joy, while Moor leaned his weary head against her, trying to forget his great sorrow, and realize the greater happiness that had befallen him. Hitherto all their talk had been of Adam, and as Moor concluded the history of the year so tragically ended, for the first time he ventured to express surprise at the calmness with which his hearer received the sad story.

"How quietly you listen to words it wrings my heart to utter. Have you wept your tears dry, or do you still hope?"

"No, I feel that we shall never see him again; but I have no desire to weep, for tears and lamentations do not belong to him. He died a noble death; the sea is a fitting grave for him, and it is pleasant to think of him quiet at last," answered Sylvia, still tearless and tranquil.

"I cannot feel so; I find it hard to think of him as dead; he was so full of life, so fit to live."

"And therefore fit to die. Imagine him as I do, enjoying the larger life he longed for, and growing to be the nobler man whose foreshadowing we saw and loved so here."

"Sylvia, I have told you of the beautiful change which came over him in those last weeks, and now I see something of the same change in you, as if the weaker part had slipped away and left the spirit visible. Are you, too, about to leave me, just as I have recovered you?"

Moor held her close and searched her face, feeling that he hardly dared believe the beautiful miracle time had wrought.

"I shall stay with you all my life, please God. There will be no shadow of turning now. Let me tell you why I do not mourn for Adam, and why you may trust the love that has cost us all so much."

Drawing his head to its former resting-place, she touched it very tenderly, seeing with a pang how many silver threads had come among the brown; and as her hand went to and fro with an inexpressibly soothing gesture she went on in a tone whose quietude controlled his agitation like a spell.

"Long ago in my great trouble, Faith told me that for every human effort or affliction there were two great helpers, Time and Death. After you left me I fell ill, more ill than you ever knew, dear, and for days believed that death was to end all perplexity and pain for me. I thought I should be glad that the struggle was over, but I was not, and longed to live that I might atone. While lying thus I had a dream which seemed to foreshadow what has come to pass. I did not understand it then, now I do. You have no faith in dreams, I have, and to this one I owe much of the faith that kept me up in those first hard days."

"God bless the dream then, and send another as helpful. Tell it to me, love."

"It was a strange and solemn vision; one to remember for its curious mingling of the familiar and the sublime, one to love for the message it seemed to bring me from lips that will never speak to me again. I dreamed that the last day of the world had come. I stood on the cliffs we know so well, you were beside me, and Adam apart and above us. All around as far as eye could reach thronged myriads of people, till the earth seemed white with human faces. All were mute and motionless, as if fixed in a trance of expectation, for none knew how the end would come. Utter silence filled the world, and across the sky a vast curtain of the blackest cloud was falling, blotting out face after face and leaving the world a blank. In that universal gloom and stillness, high above me in the heavens I saw the pale outlines of a word stretching from horizon to horizon. Letter after letter came out full and clear, till all across the sky, burning with a ruddy glory stronger than the sun, shone the great word Amen. As the last letter reached its bright perfection, a long waft of wind broke over me like a universal sigh of hope from human hearts. For far away on the horizon's edge all saw a line of light that widened as they looked, and through that rift, between the dark earth and the darker sky, rolled in a softly flowing sea. Wave after wave came on, so wide, so cool, so still. None trembled at their approach, none shrunk from their embrace, but all turned toward that ocean with a mighty rush, all faces glowed in its splendor, and million after million vanished with longing eyes fixed on the arch of light through which the ebbing sea would float them when its work was done. I felt no fear, only the deepest awe, for I seemed such an infinitesimal atom of the countless host that I forgot myself. Nearer and nearer came the flood, till its breath blew on my cheeks, and I, too, leaned to meet it, longing to be taken. It broke over us, but you held me fast, and when the bitter waters ebbed away we stood alone, stranded on the green nook where the pine and birch trees grow. I caught my breath and was so glad to live, that when the next billow came in, I clung to you longing to be kept. The great wave rolled up before me, and through its soft glimmer I saw a beautiful, benignant face, regarding us with something brighter than a smile, as the wave broke at our feet and receded carrying the face away to be lost in the sunshine that suddenly turned the sea to gold. Adam was gone, but I knew that I had seen him as he will look in Heaven, and woke wondering what the vision meant. Now I know."

For a moment neither spoke, for Sylvia was pale with the mere memory of that prophetic dream, and Moor absorbed in reading the interpretation of it in her altered face. She helped him by telling what God and Faith had done for her during that long year of probation, effort, and hard-won success. She laid her heart bare, and when the sad story reached its happy end Moor stood up to receive the reward she so gladly yet so meekly gave him, as she laid both hands in his saying with tears now,—

"I love you! Trust me, and let me try again."

No need to record his answer, nor the welcome she received as she was gathered to the home where she no longer felt an alien nor a prisoner.

Standing together in the hush of the pleasant room they both loved best, Sylvia pointed up to the picture which now replaced the weird Sisters, as if she hoped to banish the faces that had looked down relentless on that bitter night a year ago.

It was a lovely painting of the moonlight voyage down the river; Max's last gift and peace-offering to Sylvia. He had effaced himself behind the sail, a shadow in the light that silvered its white wing. But the moon shone full on Warwick at the helm, looking out straight and strong before him, with the vigilant expression native to him touched by the tender magic of the new sentiment for which he had found no name as yet. Moor leaned to look at Sylvia, a quiet figure full of grace and color, crouched under the green arch; not asleep, but just waking, as if conscious of the eyes that watched and waited for an answering look. On either hand the summer woods made vernal gloom, behind the hills rose sharply up against the blue, and all before wound a shining road, along which the boat seemed floating like a white-winged bird between two skies.

"See Geoffrey, how beautiful it is, not only as a souvenir of that happy time, but a symbol of the happier one to come. I am awake now, you see, and you are smiling as you used to smile. He is in the light, parted from us only by the silvery mist that rises from the stream. Could we have a better guide as we set sail again to voyage down the river that ends in the ocean he has already crossed?"

"No. Death makes a saint of him, may life make a hero of me," answered Moor, with no bitter drop to mar the sweetness of that memory now.

"Love and God's help can work all miracles since it has worked this one so well," answered Sylvia, with a look Adam might have owned, so full of courage, hope, and ardor was it as she turned from the painted romance to the more beautiful reality, to live, not dream, a long and happy life, unmarred by the moods that nearly wrecked her youth; for now she had learned to live by principle, not impulse, and this made it both sweet and possible for love and duty to go hand in hand.   (352–59)

EXPLANATORY NOTES

CHAPTER II

1. Chamomilla, the botanical name for chamomile blossoms, a soothing homeopathic remedy commonly administered in the nineteenth century either in pellet form or as tea.

2. Arsenic, mercury, nightshade were three of the more "heroic" remedies used by fashionable ladies in mid-nineteenth century. Arsenic and mercury supposedly brightened eyes and complexions, and nightshade was used as both a stimulant and a cosmetic.

3. Herr Pedalstrum is German for Mr. Pedal Storm, obviously a joke about music masters.

CHAPTER III

1. The holiday trip is based upon Thoreau's account of a week on the Concord and Merrimack rivers and probably also on May Alcott's Clark's Island adventures in August 1863 (*Journals,* Aug. 1863).

2. Elixir or tonic of life.

3. Queen Elizabeth I in her royal barge on the Thames is linked to Adam Warwick. Adam (New World) and Warwick (Castle) may be a gloss on Hawthorne's English notebooks with their fine description of Warwick Castle (Nathaniel Hawthorne, "Warwick Castle," *Atlantic Monthly* [July – Dec. 1862]).

4. Platonics refers to the notion of intense, even passionate friendships that are asexual. See Emerson's essay "Friendship."

5. A tale of diablerie (the French word means devilishness, devilry) is the equivalent of a ghost story.

6. Common brown milk cow, smaller and more gentle than the black and white Holstein dairy cow.

CHAPTER IV

1. Ethiop sweets are blackberries.

2. Casabianca is the ten-year-old hero of Mrs. Felicia Hemans's poem of the same name (1798). Casabianca's father was captain of the ship *Orient* which caught fire and the boy went down with it because he had been ordered by his father never to leave the ship. *Saturday Review,* reviewing the poem in 1874, argued that had the boy been somewhat older he might have used his own judgment and jumped off the ship.

3. Thoreau was famous among his friends for imitating birds and other small animals and thus luring them to him for friendly "visits."

CHAPTER V

1. The War of 1812 went on for three years in an attempt by the American nation to gain territorial sovereignty in the West and neutral rights in the Atlantic. It ended with Andrew Jackson's defeat of British forces at the Battle of New Orleans.

2. Alfred Tennyson, "The Lady of Shalott," pt. 3. Alcott omitted the second line of the stanza, "She made three paces through the room."

CHAPTER IX

1. Circe in Greek mythology, the enchantress daughter of Helios and the nymph Perse. Circe lived on the island of Aeaea, and changed the companions of Odysseus into swine.

2. Lola Montes (or Montez), dancer and adventuress, was born in Ireland in 1818 and spent her childhood in India. After touring Europe as a dancer, she became the mistress of King Ludwig of Bavaria, who built her a castle. She fled during the War of 1848 and toured the US in her own play, "Lola Montez in Bavaria" from 1851 to 1853. Author of "The Art of Beauty" in 1858 she died in Astoria, NY in 1861.

3. Aspasia was the wife of the Athenian orator Pericles. Aspasia was also the heroine in Lydia Maria Child's novel *Pilothea.* Child, a notable antislavery advocate, was a close friend of Abba May Alcott. Louisa May Alcott mentions Aspasia again in *Work: A Story of Experience.*

4. Roland and Corday were Girondist women active in the French Revolution. Madame Jeanne Roland de la Platière established a Girondist salon; arrested

Explanatory Notes

by the radicals, she wrote her memoirs before being led off to the guillotine in 1793. Charlotte Corday, the impoverished descendent of a noble family, was influenced by the Girondists: she went to Paris and murdered Jacobin leader Jean-Paul Marat in his bathtub. Alcott was a great reader of Carlyle and obviously echoed his version of the French Revolution in making these references.

CHAPTER X

1. Clytemnestra, sister of Helen of Troy, married Agamemnon, king of Mycaenae. After his sacrifice of their eldest daughter, Iphigenia, for the Greek expedition against Troy, Clytemnestra took Aegisthus, Agamemnon's cousin, as her lover, and when Agamemnon returned from Troy, they killed him. Alcott is obviously comparing this tragic Greek marriage to the American republic's "golden wedding" couple.

2. Anna Alcott was married in a soft grey silk gown, with a knot of snowdrops as decoration. Meg March dons the same garb for her marriage to John Brooke in *Little Women,* and Christie Devon wears it in *Work.*

CHAPTER XIII

1. Cleopatra, queen of the Nile, is famous as a scheming beauty, while Ariel is best known as the airy spirit who acts as Prosero's messenger in *The Tempest* of Shakespeare. Ariel also appears in Goethe's *Faust,* as leader of the elves in Walpurgis Nacht. The poet Shelley mischievously refers to himself as Ariel. In any case, the comparison of Sylvia to Ariel clearly takes the reader back to Moor's first perception of his wife as a young boy.

CHAPTER XIV

1. Griselda is "patient Griselda," the quintessential obedient wife, best described by Chaucer in *The Canterbury Tales.* Jacob, in the Book of Genesis, worked seven years to win the lovely Rachel but got her plain older sister, Leah, as his wife instead; he then worked for her father, Laban, yet another seven years and got Rachel as his second wife.

CHAPTER XVII

1. Shakespeare, *Macbeth*, II.ii. Macbeth has done the deed and Lady Macbeth warns her husband not to think about his murder of the king lest it make them mad. Macbeth replies, "Methought I heard a voice cry 'sleep no more!' Macbeth does murder sleep . . ."

2. Banquo, along with Macbeth, was a general of Duncan, king of Scotland's army. The three witches warn Macbeth that while he will be Thane of Cawdor and "king hereafter," Banquo "shalt get kings." The ambitious Macbeth then orders the death of Banquo and his son Fleance. The ghost of Banquo enters Macbeth's palace and twice sits in Macbeth's place. Only Macbeth sees him and wishes the ghost would "take any shape but that" (*Macbeth,* III.iv). Warwick, like the ghostly Banquo, stands between guilty Sylvia and her husband, Geoffrey Moor.

CHAPTER XX

1. This treatment of the cause of Italian freedom, which draws Warwick and Moor to Europe, is Alcott's tribute to Margaret Fuller. Fuller met Mazzini, the exiled Italian patriot, in London. Inspired by him, she went to Italy in April 1847, and fell in love with Giovanni Angelo Marchese d'Ossoli, ten years her junior, and, as his lover, joined the liberal cause of Garibaldi. With the proclamation of a Roman republic in February 1849, and the French siege in April, Fuller took over direction of an emergency hospital and carried supplies to Ossoli's post. The two had a son, Nino, and married just before his birth. When the republic was overthrown in July, Fuller and Ossoli, with their son, fled to Florence and eventually to England. They then sailed for America in May 1850. The ship went down off Fire Island (New York) and all three were lost. Only the child's body was recovered and buried in Mount Auburn Cemetery, Cambridge, where a monument to the family was erected by friends. Fuller had served as a teacher in Bronson Alcott's Temple School and had translated Johann Peter Eckermann's *Conversations with Goethe,* one of Louisa Alcott's favorite works. Fuller, indisputably, was the most brilliant intellectual woman and the most ardent feminist in the transcendental circle.